MINERVA SERIES OF STUDENTS' HANDBOOKS

NO. 9

General Editor

BRIAN CHAPMAN

Professor of Government
University of Manchester

MACROECONOMICS

GW00599261

THE MINERVA SERIES OF STUDENTS' HANDBOOKS

MACROECONOMICS

F. S. BROOMAN

Professor of Economics, The Open University

SIXTH EDITION

London

GEORGE ALLEN & UNWIN LTD

Ruskin House Museum Street

First published 1962
Sixth edition 1977

© George Allen & Unwin (Publishers) Ltd, 1962, 1965, 1967, 1970, 1973, 1977

ISBN 0 04 330282 3 Paper

PRINTED IN GREAT BRITAIN
in 10 on 11 point Times Roman
BY BILLING & SONS LIMITED
GUILDFORD, LONDON AND WORCESTER

FOREWORD

This book is primarily intended for the use of students who have already had an introductory course in economics and now require a more detailed exposition of the theory of income-determination, employment and money. The first three chapters, however, can be tackled by complete beginners; they assume no previous knowledge, contain neither diagrams nor algebra, and try to set forth in simple terms the accounting concepts and the basic economics of national income. In later chapters, algebraic symbols and equations are used fairly extensively, but they serve as no more than a space-saving shorthand; the reader whose mathematical learning stopped at an elementary level should find no difficulty in following the arguments expressed in symbolic terms.

The present edition updates all statistical information to 1975. Its general structure remains that of the fourth edition. My grateful thanks are due to Professor Roberto Zaneletti of Genoa, and to Professor Henry D. Jacoby of MIT, who in preparing the Italian and American versions of the book made many invaluable suggestions for improvement; to Professors Miles Fleming, J. K. Whitaker and J. Black; and to B. D. Giles, S. R. Merrett and N. Robertson. Their helpful comments allowed me to correct many mistakes: if I have persisted in error in spite of them, the responsibility is wholly mine.

F. S. B.

FOREWORD TO THE FOURTH EDITION

This book is primarily intended for students who have already received a general introduction to economics and now require a more detailed exposition of the theory of income and employment. The first three chapters, however, can be tackled by complete beginners, since they assume no previous knowledge, contain neither diagrams nor algebra, and try to set forth in simple terms the accounting concepts and the basic economics of National Income. In later chapters, though algebraic symbols are used fairly extensively, they serve only as a space-saving shorthand, and the reader whose mathematical training stopped at an elementary level should find no difficulty in following the arguments expressed in symbolic terms.

The present edition differs from the last mainly in giving much more attention to the subject of money. Instead of a single chapter on this, there are now two, while inflation, originally dealt with very briefly within the monetary chapter, has been given one to itself. Another new chapter introduces the concept of aggregate supply, which did not appear at all in earlier editions. New sections have been added to the chapters on employment and economic growth, and numerous minor changes have been made in response to criticisms of the previous edition.

The revision was carried out simultaneously with the preparation of an American edition of the book in collaboration with Professor Henry D. Jacoby of Harvard University, who has contributed substantially to the improvements made in the present volume; his tireless patience and never-failing ingenuity have placed me very much in his debt. Professor Roberto Zaneletti, of the University of Genoa, provided innumerable excellent suggestions while preparing the Italian version of the book, and I gladly take the opportunity to express my thanks to him. I also gratefully acknowledge the generous advice and assistance given by Professor Miles Fleming, who read the whole work in manuscript; by Professors J. K. Whitaker and J. Black; and by B. D. Giles, S. R. Merrett, and Norman Robertson. Their helpful comments enabled me to correct many mistakes; if I have persisted in error in spite of them, the responsibility is entirely mine.

F. S. B.

CONTENTS

CONTENTS

CHAPTER ONE

The Economics of Aggregates

One of the chief objectives of economic theory is to explain the working of the economy as a whole, by identifying and if possible measuring the forces which cause the nation's total output and level of employment to be what they are. But this is an extremely complex matter: total output includes a vast number of different goods and services, about whose production and utilization millions of individual decisions are being taken every day; if it were necessary to examine each one before attempting conclusions about the whole, the economic analyst would be faced with an impossible task. To reduce the problem to manageable proportions, it is necessary to simplify it by aggregation—that is, by arranging the myriad products and decision-makers into a reasonably small number of categories or 'aggregates'; individual differences between one consumer and another, or between one business firm and another, are ignored; it is assumed that if the categories are well chosen, their members will be behaving in a sufficiently uniform way to make generalization legitimate.

The kind of analysis which proceeds in this way is called *macroeconomics*, 'macro' being the Greek for 'large'. Though the word itself is a relatively recent coinage,[1] the method of approach is by no means new—the eighteenth-century Physiocrats, for example, adopted it when they divided society into three 'classes' to show the 'circulation of wealth'; nevertheless, the most important developments in macroeconomic analysis have occurred only within the last few decades, the point of departure being the appearance of Keynes' *General Theory of Employment, Interest and Money* in 1936. The influence of the *General Theory* has been such that the modern theory of output and employment still bears the label of 'Keynesian economics'. From the title of the book, the term 'Employment Theory' has also been adopted as an alternative name for this branch of economics. But macroeconomic analysis seeks to explain a good deal more

[1] It was originated by Ragnar Frisch in 1933.

9

than the level of employment, important though that is as an indicator of the state of the economy; while the 'Keynesian' label is becoming less appropriate in the light of developments since Keynes' death in 1946.

The obverse of macroeconomics is *microeconomics*, which is the analysis of the economy's constituent elements—'micro', of course, being Greek for 'small'. As the name suggests, it is not aggregative but selective: it seeks to explain the working of markets for individual commodities and the behaviour of the individual buyer and seller. Where macroeconomics is concerned with the level of output as a whole, and for most purposes ignores the numbers of kitchen tables, pairs of shoes and barrels of beer which enter into the output, microeconomics reverses the order; its object is to discover why precisely x million tables and y million shoes are produced, why the price of one is greater than the other's, why shoemakers' wages differ from those of table-makers, and to answer a host of other questions relating to the composition, rather than the magnitude, of the economy's output. In 'microanalysis', it is reasonable to take the level of total output for granted when examining the conditions in which the price of a particular commodity is determined, or when studying the behaviour of the individual business firm. Where macroanalysis simplifies by aggregation, microanalysis does so by assuming 'other things equal'.

Though their aims are different, both make use of the concepts of supply and demand and the equilibrium which may be established between them. In microanalysis, the typical market is that for a single commodity: buyers demand a certain quantity at each possible price; sellers decide, in view of the price obtaining, how much to offer; where the amounts demanded and offered are the same, so that no one has any incentive to upset the position, equilibrium can be said to exist. If the price paid by buyers for a certain quantity of the good is so high that even those suppliers whose costs of production are highest can still make abnormally high profits, competition will attract new firms to the market and the amount offered will increase; to tempt buyers to purchase the increased supply, the price of the commodity has to be reduced; by changes in price and in the quantities demanded and offered, a balance of forces is eventually attained.

In the same way, macroanalysis conceives of equilibrium between demand and supply in the economy as a whole: supply consists of all goods and services being made available in the country, while demand is the aggregate of demands for all commodities. In this case it becomes impossible to work in terms of physical quantities, since there is no way in which numbers of, say, eggs, hats and piston-rings can be added together: so demand and supply have to be expressed in money terms, by saying that buyers wish to spend such-and-such a number of pounds, while sellers are prepared, in the circumstances, to offer so many pounds' worth of goods and services. If the amount of money buyers wish to spend is not the same as the value of the commodities which sellers are offering, there is no equilibrium; the lack of it will bring about changes in production and prices, and perhaps in the level of employment as well, since less labour may be required if, for example, a lower level of production is brought about. What is not so clear, however, is whether these changes will necessarily lead the economy towards a balance of aggregate supply and demand; in this respect, the analogy between the single-commodity market and the economy as a whole tends to break down.

This is because there are underlying relationships between demand and supply which can be neglected in microanalysis but which are very important in the working of the economy as a whole. In any single market, it is quite reasonable to suppose that buyers and sellers are for the most part different people: for example, few of the housewives who buy breakfast cereals are likely to be engaged in producing and selling them in any capacity. So buyers and sellers can be imagined to act quite independently of one another, and the two sides of the market will influence each other's decisions only through the market itself. If the firms producing some commodity were to take on more workers, the fact that they were now paying out more wages would mean that the recipients were in a position to spend more than before; but the consequential effect on the firms' sales would hardly be noticeable unless the industry employed most of the community's workers, and unless those workers spent most of their income on the commodity concerned. Since this is very unlikely, microanalysis can legitimately ignore this kind of behind-the-scenes 'feedback' of purchasing power from the supply side to the demand side. When, however, supply and demand are aggregated for the economy as a whole, the 'feedback' can no longer be left out of account. Buyers and sellers are seen to be largely the same people. The money received in exchange for goods and services on the supply side of the economy passes into the hands of spenders who appear on the demand side. The spenders may be individuals, or business firms, or the government of the country; but for the most part they get the wherewithal to spend by selling something to someone else—the major exception, of course, being the government, though even it can be thought of as in effect selling its services in return for the payment of taxes.

Aggregate supply and demand are thus linked through the intermediary of *income*. If buyers should decide to spend more money than
before, and if this has the effect of increasing the value of goods and
services supplied, then the suppliers will receive higher incomes out
of which they can spend yet more on the demand side. If, in another
case, demand should fall, this will reduce the value of commodities
supplied, cut the incomes of those engaged in producing and selling,
and so cause a further fall in spending. Whereas the market for a
single commodity may be thought to work in terms of the confrontation of the two forces of demand and supply, the operation of
the entire economy is to be viewed in terms of a triangular relationship—the three corners of the triangle being respectively aggregate
supply, aggregate income and aggregate demand. Consequently, the
nature of equilibrium will be different in each case. For the individual
market, the price of the product is the crucial magnitude. For the
economy as a whole, the general price-level has nothing like the same
significance: an increase in prices will not necessarily choke off
demand, since by enhancing the value of supplies it will increase the
money incomes of those concerned in production; with higher
incomes, buyers could then afford to go on taking up exactly the
same quantities of goods and services as before, in spite of the general
price-increase. Here the vital consideration is whether or not they
will go on buying the same quantities: only if they should *not* do so
will the balance of aggregate supply and demand be changed. The
question which needs to be asked, then, is not how the economy
reacts to a change in the level of prices, but how it reacts to a change in
the level of aggregate income. In place of the demand schedule, which
in the market for a single commodity shows what quantities buyers
will wish to have at each possible *price*, macroanalysis requires a
schedule showing the level of aggregate demand at each possible
level of *income*.

But *aggregate* demand is made up of many widely differing
elements—it must include, for example, the demand of individual
consumers for meat, cars and bedroom furniture, that of business
firms for machine-tools and factory buildings, and that of local
authorities for the services of dustmen. There is no obvious reason
to think that all buyers will behave in the same way when their
incomes change: some may respond to a fall in income by reducing
their expenditures considerably, while others may not reduce them
at all. It is necessary to split them into groups, within each of which
a reasonable similarity of behaviour can be supposed to exist;
provided the number of groups is not unmanageably large, a fairly
clear pattern of response to income changes can then be obtained.

The usual classification (which will have to be justified later on) divides buyers into four such groups: consumers, business firms, governmental bodies and the overseas customers who buy the country's exports. There may be times when it is desirable to have a different or more detailed grouping: for example, it might be necessary to subdivide consumers between rich and poor, or between wage-earners and others, if there were marked differences in the behaviour of these sub-groups in face of a change in their incomes. Whatever the nature of the classification, however, it must be such as to elucidate the connection between income and aggregate demand.

On the side of aggregate supply, the relationship with income normally requires only one important distinction to be made: that between the goods and services produced within the country and those imported from overseas. The money paid over in exchange for home-produced supplies goes to provide the incomes of the country's inhabitants; payments for imports, however, accrue to the foreigners who supplied them. It is true that payment for imports puts foreigners in a position to contribute to aggregate demand by buying the country's exports: but the connection is more tenuous than that between production, income and demand at home, since import payments may provide only a small part of foreigners' incomes, and those who buy exported commodities may in fact be quite a different set of individuals and firms from those who supply imports. While a rise in the value of home production will certainly increase the incomes of residents of the country and thus increase their demand, a rise in the value of a country's imports, though it will increase foreigners' incomes, will not necessarily cause their demand for the country's exports to change at all. Another consideration is that the level of *employment* within the country depends not on the volume of aggregate supply but only on that part of it which is produced within the country; so when the purpose of analysis is to explain the existence of a particular level of employment it again becomes important to distinguish between home-produced and imported supplies.

When aggregate demand and supply are split up into the component parts described above, the conditions of equilibrium for the economy can be restated accordingly. The money which consumers, business firms, government bodies and export customers together wish to spend at any time must be equal to the value of the country's output plus imports of goods and services. The purchase of domestic output provides those who produce it with incomes, out of which the spending of consumers, firms and the government is done: so in addition to the balance of demand and supply, there must also be a balance between incomes and demand such that spenders are satisfied that their outlays are neither too high nor too low relatively to their incomes. On the supply side, income must be distributed in such a way that producers are willing to provide precisely the amount of output which is needed to satisfy aggregate demand: the part going to profits must be enough to induce business firms to undertake that level of production, while the part going to wages must be such as to induce workers to provide the necessary labour; similarly, the country's ability to spend overseas (derived from export earnings and loans) must be sufficient, given the prevailing terms of exchange, to induce other countries to supply whatever imports are demanded at the current level of income.

When all these conditions are satisfied, the flow of goods and services will be exactly sufficient, in total, to meet the current demand for them. But—as was pointed out earlier—the output of the whole economy includes a vast range of different commodities, which can be aggregated only in terms of their money values; and those values arise from the fact that, instead of being bartered directly for one another, goods and services are exchanged indirectly through the 'circulating medium' of money. In any economy but the most primitive, the multitude of products is so great that direct barter would create intolerable inconvenience; to avoid it, sellers offer their wares for money in the first instance, and with the proceeds in their turn make purchases of their own; and the use of money as an intermediary makes it customary to express the exchange values of commodities in terms of so many pounds and pence. Given the prices at which things are bought and sold, some particular amount of money will be needed to finance the turnover of goods and services in the economy at a given time, as well as to provide for other activities—for example, borrowing and lending—which involve the exchange of money without a corresponding exchange of commodities; if the economy is to be in full equilibrium, the supply of money must be sufficient to meet all these demands for its services. If the existing stock of money happens to be either inadequate or excessive, the imbalance may lead to changes in the aggregate demand and supply of goods and services, and in the general price-level. The conditions for a complete equilibrium are therefore somewhat complex: not only must the demand and supply of commodities be balanced against one another, but also the demand and supply of money.

Even when such an equilibrium is attained, however, it is unlikely to be of long duration. One of the elements of aggregate demand is the expenditure of business firms on new plant and machinery; some of this merely replaces worn-out equipment, but the remainder represents a net addition to their productive capacity. With a given number of workers, firms will become capable of higher output when the additional equipment is installed; alternatively, they will be able to produce the same output as before with less labour. Either the level of aggregate output must rise, or the level of employment must fall, or some mixture of both effects must ensue; but whatever the outcome, the original equilibrium situation will have passed away. No doubt a new balance of aggregate demand and supply will be possible in the changed circumstances, but it will be different from the original one; and it, too, will pass away as yet more additions are made to productive capacity. The greater the lapse of time, the greater the possible increase in the stock of equipment; the greater, also, the possible change in other factors, such as the size of the population and the state of technology, which are important in determining the levels of output and employment in the longer run.

This suggests two lines of approach in studying the working of the economy. The first is to examine its state at a given moment, assessing the balance of forces as they stand at that point of time. This is the method of *static* analysis; it is like the scrutiny of a still photograph in which all motion is arrested; its object is to discover whether equilibrium exists or not. A somewhat less strict procedure is to consider a short period rather than a single moment; during the period, certain movements are possible—in the quantity of output and aggregate demand, for example—but more slowly-changing magnitudes, such as the stock of capital, can still be assumed frozen into immobility. The immediate consequences of a disequilibrium of demand and supply can then be examined without the complications arising from longer-run changes. To deal with the latter, the method of *comparative statics* may be used: the state of the economy at one moment is compared with its state at another, to show the effects of some change (e.g. in the technique of production) which has occurred between the two moments.

The second approach is that of *dynamic* analysis, which investigates the process by which the economy moves from one state to another over time; its aim is to show how the situation at one moment will influence the situation at another. For example, if firms adjust output to changes in demand only after a four-week time-lag, this month's production depends on the state of the market last month; if consumers decide their expenditures in the light of last week's income, this week's income will determine next week's consumption. A knowledge of all the relationships of this sort (including, of course, the length of the time-lags involved) would make it possible to predict the levels of output and employment in the future—provided the relationships and their lags do not themselves change, and no 'outside' forces act to disturb the sequence. It should be noted that the words *static* and *dynamic* refer to the method of analysis, not to the economy itself: the latter may be 'stationary' in the sense that output and employment are the same at all moments of time, or it may be 'progressive' in that output and employment are rising, but the two methods of analysis may be applied to both conditions.[1]

Whether static or dynamic, macroanalysis necessarily runs in terms of the 'aggregates' mentioned at the beginning of the chapter. Each of its quantities is made up of many smaller ones: consumers' expenditure, for example, is the sum of millions of separate individuals' acts of spending; and it has already been seen that the output of the whole economy cannot be stated in simple physical measures, but must be added up in terms of money values. Before proceeding further, it is necessary to define the various aggregates, and this is the subject of the following chapter.

[1] See W. J. Baumol, *Economic Dynamics* (2nd edition, 1959), Ch. 1.

CHAPTER TWO

National Product, National Income and National Expenditure

(a) What is 'production'?

The first concept to be defined is that of aggregate output. In the previous chapter, this was taken to be all the commodities produced in the economy over some period of time, added together by summing their money values. But what exactly are 'commodities', and what is 'production'? This seems a trivial question as long as one thinks only in terms of steel plates, loaves of bread and other tangible objects which are easily recognized and counted. But there are many parts of the economy whose activity is not so easy to classify: for example, can a bank really be said to 'produce'? If so, what is it producing? What about the railway system, doctors and HM Forces? These are cases where it is obviously difficult to identify and measure 'products', but in which a useful if intangible service is being provided, for which, in one way or another, payment is made. It seems reasonable to regard as productive any paid activity which satisfies the individual or collective wants of the community; whatever the physical quantity of a thing which is made, the amount of 'production' should therefore be measured in terms of the degree of satisfaction afforded rather than the number of tons or bushels involved. In this usage 'production' is not an engineering term, but a purely economic concept.

Unfortunately, it is not possible directly to measure the satisfaction of wants: instead, the prices buyers are willing to pay, and the quantities of commodities they buy at these prices, have to be taken as indicating how much satisfaction they expect to obtain. There are objections to this: for example, it may be thought that the expenditure of £100 by a wealthy man will not represent the same expected satisfaction as £100 spent by a poor man—if indeed it is possible to compare the satisfaction of two different individuals. But for practical purposes of statistical computation, prices have to be used for lack

17

of any better measure; and on the whole it seems that rough justice is done if the 'production' of a commodity is expressed as the number of its physical units multiplied by its price. Where the physical units are hard to identify, as in the case of some services, the total payment made by buyers can then be taken as the value of production.

This procedure, however, assumes the existence of markets in which buyers are free to buy as much or as little as they wish and in which the price is both a condition of supply and a reflection of the intensity of the buyers' desire for the commodity. But there are some commodities which are not provided in this way, the leading case being that of public services such as education, defence and the maintenance of public order, all useful 'commodities' satisfying wants of various kinds. Here, the normal practice is to provide the service without collecting a direct charge from the recipients, and to meet the cost from the revenue of taxes, payment of which is compulsory, and whose amount in the case of each citizen is not necessarily equal to the value of the services rendered to him. This means that the 'production' of public authorities can be measured only in terms of cost. If, for example, £120 millions are spent on the provision of police services, it has to be assumed for lack of other evidence that this sum represents the degree to which the desire for that 'commodity' is satisfied.

Another case is that of owner-occupied houses, which clearly provide a service for which their owners, had they been tenants of houses owned by others, would have been willing to pay the necessary rent. Although no money is in fact paid (it would be merely a transfer from one pocket to another as far as the owner-occupier is concerned), the value of the service can be assessed in money by assuming it to be equal to the rent paid by non-owning tenants who occupy houses of similar size and amenities. The existence of a market for such services allows their value to be 'imputed' in cases where the market is by-passed. Logically, the same procedure should be adopted in the case of all types of durable property which are used by their owners—motor-cars, radio sets, furniture, even clothing and footwear. If someone hires a car on 'self-drive' terms, or rents a television set, the payment can be regarded as representing the value of the services rendered, and will be counted as part of the economy's 'production': why not, then, count on a similar basis the imputed value of services yielded by cars and television sets used by their owners? In fact, this is not done by the official statisticians because of the obvious difficulties of calculation.[1]

[1] See *National Accounts Statistics: Sources and Methods*, ed. Rita Maurice (H.M.S.O., 1968), pp. 8–9.

The services rendered by housewives to their families present a similar problem. By cooking, cleaning and baby-tending, housewives obviously render valuable services; logically, these should be treated as production and included in aggregate output. But it seems impossible to set a proper money value on them, since housewives' services are not sold in a free market for a wage;[1] so for lack of information, this form of production is omitted in calculations of the nation's output.

(b) Which products should be included?

So far, it seems that to calculate the value of aggregate output, it is necessary to multiply by their prices the quantities of commodities produced, where these are sold through markets; to include the services of public authorities at cost, and those of dwelling-houses at their imputed rents; and to neglect cases in which no satisfactory valuation of production can be made. But now another difficulty arises. If the value of *all* goods and services is aggregated, the total will overstate the nation's output because some commodities are currently being used in the making of others. The price of a loaf, for example, must include the value of the flour from which it was baked; the price of the flour must include the value of the wheat which was milled to make it. So to add together the value of wheat grown, flour milled, and bread baked, is to count the value of the flour twice and that of the wheat three times over, unless some of the flour or wheat was left unused instead of being consumed in the next stage of production. The value of cloth output would be counted twice if it were included along with the value of clothing made from it; to lump together motor-cars and the steel used to make them would have a similar effect. Another anomaly would arise in the case of commodities made from imported materials: the price of the finished commodity would obviously include an amount representing its 'import content', yet this would not be part of the country's production at all. Unless this kind of 'multiple counting' of products is somehow eliminated, the value of the nation's output will obviously be greatly exaggerated.

Two methods suggest themselves for eliminating multiple counting. The first is that of counting only products which have not been used for making others—i.e. to exclude those which are 'intermediate' in the process of production, and to include only 'final' products. 'Final', however, does not necessarily mean that the products must

[1] On this, see the interesting suggestion by Colin Clark in the Oxford Institute of Statistics *Bulletin*, May 1958.

have reached a form suitable for consumption. Certainly all 'consumers' goods' would be 'final'; but so would any 'producers' goods' which had not been used up during the period concerned. If, for example, 5% of steel output had been stored instead of being used in the making of other things, it would be a 'final product': to include its value in that of the whole economy's output would involve no multiple counting. In the same way, the value of all machinery, factory buildings, and other durable means of production newly constructed during the period, can be regarded as 'final' production; so also may the 'work-in-progress' which each industry will still be processing at the end of any period—the materials which, like the pig during its journey through the sausage-machine, have ceased to be 'input' but have not yet become 'output'. On the other hand, since only the output occurring during the period is to be measured, the value of work-in-progress at the beginning will have to be subtracted; so will the value of whatever stocks of materials existed at the start of the period and have been used in production in the course of it. These things will already have figured as 'final' goods in the output of the previous period, so that to allow their value to appear as part of that of the 'final' goods which embody them now would be to overstate the current period's production.

The last point raises a practical problem in the case of *durable* 'producers' goods'. During the period under consideration the country's stock of machinery and plant will be working to put forth an output, and will sustain wear and tear in the process. Some of its value will be embodied in the products it helps to make: just as the making of, for example, motor-cars absorbs an input of steel, rubber, chromium and other materials, so also will it 'absorb' the machine-tools and other equipment which fashion the materials into the finished product. The difference between the using-up of machinery and materials is simply that the materials are wholly absorbed, the machinery only partly: nevertheless, the value of the stock of durable equipment will have diminished by a significant amount during the period. If machinery normally lasts, say, ten years before being completely worn out, then in any one year about one-tenth of it can be supposed to be passed on and embodied into the commodities it produces. In the case of materials, it was found necessary to deduct from the value of aggregate output the value of stocks existing at the beginning of the period and used in production during it; on the same principle, the diminution in the value of the economy's durable equipment ought also to be deducted. The logical procedure in the case of 'producers' goods', whether they are stocks of materials, or work-in-progress, or durable equipment, is to subtract from the quantity existing at the end of the period the quantity existing at the beginning: there is no obvious reason of principle to exempt durable equipment from this treatment. This means that the machinery, plant, buildings and so on produced within the period should be regarded as 'final' products and included in aggregate output, but that the wear-and-tear sustained by already existing equipment during the period should be excluded. In practice, however, it is a matter of some difficulty to estimate the necessary deduction for this 'capital consumption' or 'depreciation': for example, if a year's depreciation is to be calculated by dividing the value of a piece of equipment by the number of years of its 'life', how can the equipment's 'life' be ascertained until it is finished? Until then, the number of years can only be guessed, and the guess may be wrong. Again, what if the price of a certain type of machinery were to rise over the years? What if it became technically obsolete, so that it had to be scrapped half-way through its previously expected life? These and other considerations put great obstacles in the way of reliable estimates of depreciation, and it is often preferable not to attempt to deduct it: the value of aggregate output is then said to be 'gross of depreciation'. If a deduction were made, of course, the output figure would then be 'net'.

The first method of eliminating multiple counting, therefore, is to add up the value of 'final' products only, taking first the value of consumers' goods produced in the given period, then adding the value of durable producers' goods (gross or net of depreciation according to choice), and finally adding, in the case of other producers' goods such as stocks of coal and steel, the value of the quantity existing at the end of the period less that of the quantity existing at the beginning. Imported consumers' goods would automatically be excluded by this procedure, since only home production of consumable commodities is taken into account: but imports of producers' goods would have to be deducted in order to remove the 'import content' of home production. 'Goods' must, of course, be understood to include services as well as material objects: though most services are 'intermediate' rather than 'final' commodities (the labour of steel workers, for example, is 'absorbed' into their output of steel), work done directly for consumers, like domestic service or hairdressing, must be counted as 'final' and therefore included in aggregate output. The services of public authorities are all counted as 'final' goods, even though some of them seem to be 'intermediate': for example, the protection of property by the police, and the enforcement of contracts by the courts, could very well be regarded as inputs of other parts of the economy since they are pre-requisites for the undertaking of production rather than ends in themselves; but it is obviously impossible to make a satisfactory separation between public services which afford satisfaction directly to consumers and those which assist other forms of production, and so the entire value (at cost, it will be remembered) of such services is included in aggregate output.

The second method of eliminating multiple counting is to estimate, for each sector of the economy, the increase in value which it imparts in the course of production to the inputs which it receives from other sectors, and then to add these increases over all sectors to give the value of aggregate output. The economy is here likened to an enormous assembly-line. At its starting-point, agriculture and mining at home, and imports from abroad, provide primary materials; as these move down the line, they pass from one industry to another, undergoing successive processes until they emerge at the end in the shape of clothing, bicycles, loaves and so on—in the shape, too, of machine-tools, blast-furnaces and other durable instruments of production. At each stage, the materials increase in value by being brought nearer to some ultimately usable shape. The process need not be such as to change the form of the commodities: transport, for example, by removing them from less to more convenient places, increases their value just as surely as the hewing and hammering which go on at other points on the assembly-line; so do the operations of wholesale and retail distribution, by breaking bulk and holding stocks from which consumers can choose. Banks and other financial institutions, though not handling physical commodities, provide subsidiary services which ease the passing of commodities down the line. The government and other public authorities put forth a stream of services at the end of the line, alongside the flows of other goods which have already been through many antecedent processes further back. At each stage along the line, imports will be joining the stream of commodities emerging from anterior stages, and exports will be leaving the line instead of going on to the next process.

To find the value added by each process to the commodities passing through it during a given period, it is necessary to take the value of the products leaving the process and deduct the value of those[1] entering it. In this way, the part of the product attributable to the process is distinguished from the parts attributable to the earlier processes through which it has already passed. When the 'value added' has

---

[1] These will include some services as well as materials, e.g. the motor industry will not only draw on the steel industry for an input of steel, but will use the services of the transport industry to get the steel delivered.

been ascertained for each stage of production, the figures can then be added up over all stages to give the output of the whole economy, with no risk of counting any part of it more than once. Thus, if the iron industry produces pig-iron worth £10 millions in the course of a year (ten million tons at a selling price of £1 per ton), using as materials £3 millions' worth of iron ore (fifteen million tons at twenty pence a ton) and £3 millions' worth of coke (six million tons at fifty pence a ton), the industry will have turned materials worth £6 millions into output worth £10 millions: the 'value added' will therefore be £4 millions. Where some branch of retail distribution sells for £10 millions commodities which cost £7 millions wholesale, 'value added' will be £3 millions: this is the value of the services rendered by shopkeepers and their assistants to the customers who buy the goods. In cases where the input of materials is negligible, as in certain forms of entertainment and various branches of government, the 'value added' will be almost as great as the total value of the commodities produced, since only a very small 'input' deduction will be required. As long as no industry or activity is left out of account, and as long as there is no overlapping of industries causing some firms to be counted more than once, the addition of 'values added' ought to give a correct figure for aggregate output. By this method, the value of imports cannot enter into that of aggregate output, since the cost of imported materials will automatically be deducted from the value of output of the industries using them. The use and accumulation of stocks will also be allowed for: the value of stocks used in production will have been deducted from that of the products made from them in computing 'value added'; while stocks accumulated during the period will merely be the part of current output which has not been sold by the end of the period—in the 'value added' calculation, it is the value of commodities *produced* which is taken, not commodities *sold*—so that they will automatically be included, as they should be, in aggregate output.

The question of depreciation, however, still remains. The 'value added' computation described above consists in deducting the value of the input of materials from that of the output of commodities at each stage of production. The materials are assumed to be entirely absorbed into the process to which they are submitted. But plant and machinery, though not wholly used up, will be partly worn out in production, and its wear-and-tear should therefore be treated as an input on exactly the same footing as the input of materials and deducted accordingly from the value of output. The difficulties of calculating the proper deduction, however, have already been indicated: they are such that in estimating aggregate output by the 'value added' method it is preferable for many purposes to leave it 'gross of depreciation'.

Such, then, is the second method of eliminating multiple counting when measuring the production of the whole economy. Logically, it should give the same result as the first, or 'final products', method. Whereas the 'value added' method counts the flow of output past each process along the assembly-line, the 'final products' method counts the quantity of commodities which are delivered at the end of the line during a given period, with appropriate adjustments for the goods still in transit at the start and finish of the period, and with a deduction to eliminate inputs of imported goods and services. That the two methods must in principle give the same result, can be seen from a simple example. Suppose a loaf priced at 20p is baked from flour that cost 10p, and that the flour is milled from a quantity of wheat that cost 6p; the wheat has been grown from seed that cost 2p, with the aid of imported fertilizer which also cost 2p. The seed was put into store during the previous period, so that it is not part of the current period's output; nor will the fertilizer count as part of the country's current output, since it is imported. Then as far as this loaf is concerned, the 'final products' method would take the value of the end-product (20p), deduct the value of stocks of materials used up (2p) and deduct the value of imported materials (2p)—giving 16p as the value of current output. The 'value added' method would list the outputs of the successive processes, then add them up; thus, the farmer has added two pence to the value of the seed and fertilizers; the miller four pence to the value of the wheat; the baker ten pence to the value of the flour. The total value of their successive contributions is 16p; the same result as that found by the 'final products' method of counting. The practical choice between the two methods, then, must rest on the relative ease or difficulty of collecting the appropriate information in each case.

In fact, the official statistics make use of the 'value added' method of calculation: it accords with normal business accounting procedures, since every firm must for its own purposes record the value of its output and the value of materials used; also, as will be seen later, it has a close affinity with the method of estimating aggregate incomes. The 'final products' method, on the other hand, presents serious difficulties in that it requires a division of actual output into consumers' goods and producers' goods. Some grades of coal, for example, may be used equally well by domestic consumers or by industry: it is impossible to say what part of coal output is to be classified among consumers' goods until it is actually in the possession of householders. Motor-cars are mostly bought and used by private consumers, but a good number are driven by commercial travellers on business, and would then have to be regarded as producers' goods. So would the eating of meals in restaurants, where the entertainment of business associates is a necessary part of some commercial activity. It is hard to find any commodity whose entire output can confidently be put into one, and only one, of the two classes of goods. It seems that the only way to be certain whether a particular product is a consumers' good or not, is to find out whether it is in fact bought by consumers: but this is a classification of expenditures rather than of products, and since expenditures belong to a different side of the economy they should not be included in an account which purports to estimate output. So the 'final products' method of calculation is not employed by the official statisticians who produce the annual Blue Book on National Income and Expenditure.

(c) The National Product in 1975

The actual figures of 'value added' for 1975, as published in the Blue Book, are shown in Table I below.[1] It will be seen that the total is called 'Gross National Product' ('gross' means that depreciation

TABLE I

Value added by—	£ millions
Agriculture, forestry and fishing	2,959
Mining and quarrying	1,684
Manufacturing	30,129
Construction	6,539
Gas, electricity and water	2,995
Transport and communication	8,581
Distributive trades	10,188
Insurance, banking and finance	7,727
Public administration and defence	7,107
Public health and education	7,154
Ownership of dwellings	5,535
Other services	6,831
Less Stock appreciation	−5,203
Add Residual error	920
Total: Gross Domestic Product at Factor Cost	93,146
Add: Net Income from Abroad	949
Total: Gross National Product	94,095

[1] Table 3.1 in *National Income and Expenditure, 1965–75.*

has not been deducted); this official term, since it is precisely defined along the lines described previously, will henceforth be used in place of the looser 'aggregate output'.

The last lines of the table raise a few points of detail which must be explained. First, it will be noted that £5,203 millions of 'stock appreciation' is deducted from the 'value added' figures preceding it. The latter, on the principles described earlier, show for each industry the difference between output and input during the year: that is, the sum of total sales and stocks held at the end of the year, *minus* purchases from other industries and stocks held at the beginning of it. So the 'value added' figures must include the value of any increase in stocks. But they may do more. In 1975, prices were rising, so that a stock of commodities valued at end-of-the-year prices would have had a greater value than an exactly equal stock valued at the prices ruling at the beginning of the year. Thus the appreciation in value of stocks would enter into 'value added' without representing any physical increase in stocks, and would cause the production of the year to appear greater than it actually was. To eliminate this, an amount is deducted from 'value added' which is equal to the difference between (a) 'closing' stocks at end-year prices *minus* 'opening' stocks at beginning-of-year prices, and (b) 'closing' *minus* 'opening' stocks when both are valued at the average prices of the year. This amount is the 'stock appreciation' figure in the table.[1] It should be noted that no deduction would be required had prices remained unchanged, while in a year of falling prices a 'stock depreciation' figure would have to be *added*.

The second item needing explanation is the 'residual error'. It will be shown later that National Product must logically have the same total value as National Expenditure, which is separately calculated from different data. Consequently, if the component items of the latter add up to a total which is different from that of the former, it has to be assumed that an error has been made somewhere; to offset it, an additional item is inserted in the National Product table, just sufficient to make the total equal to that of National Expenditure. This offsetting item, which may be either positive or negative, is called the 'residual error'.

The third point arising from Table I concerns the 'net property income from abroad'. The 'value added' figures shown higher up in Table I record production within the boundaries of the United Kingdom, the total being Gross Domestic Product. But this is not quite the same as the output of the labour and property of the inhabitants

[1] See *National Accounts Statistics; Sources and Methods*, pp. 16–18 and 391–3.

of the country, to which the term 'Gross National Product' applies: some of the means of production located within the country are in fact owned by foreigners, while some British firms own property overseas and some British residents own shares in foreign companies. To find the output produced by the labour and property of the country's inhabitants, it is necessary to add to the production within the country the returns from property located abroad, and to deduct the amounts accruing to foreigners from *their* property located on British soil. The difference between these two items is 'net income from abroad'.

Finally, it will have been noted that the Gross Domestic Product is given 'at factor cost'. This means that the prices at which output is valued exclude indirect taxes and subsidies. The price the buyer pays for a commodity must, of course, include any indirect taxes, such as petrol tax or tobacco duty, which may be imposed; or it may be the case that the buyer of an article pays *less* than the seller would otherwise have charged, if the article carries a subsidy, which can be thought of as a 'negative tax'; the price the buyer pays is called the 'market price'. If indirect taxes are deducted from market prices, and subsidies added back into them, the result is 'factor cost'—that is, the amount paid to the owners of the factors of production which have produced the commodities. 'Values added' *can* be shown at market prices if necessary—but it would not be a very satisfactory way of recording output, since industries whose products bear heavy indirect taxes would seem to produce relatively more than untaxed ones, while the makers of heavily subsidized products might seem to have relatively little output, or even none at all if the subsidy were equal to the difference between factor cost and the value of inputs used. Also, a change in taxation from one year to another could make the market price of a commodity increase sharply, and by the 'value added' method this would seem to show an increase in the physical quantity of production even though none had in fact occurred: it would obviously be anomalous to adopt a reckoning under which Gross National Product seems to rise when indirect taxes go up. For these reasons, it is usually preferable to show the 'values added', and therefore domestic and national product, at factor cost.

Gross National Product (abbreviated to GNP hereafter) can thus be described summarily as the total output of goods and services produced by the labour and property of the country's inhabitants in a given year, valued at factor cost, and with no part of output counted more than once. If an estimate of depreciation is deducted, it becomes Net National Product (NNP). In 1975, depreciation was calculated to be £10,907 millions;[1] when this is taken from the £94,095 millions of GNP, Net National Product is seen to be £83,188 millions.

(d) The concept of income

The second of the important magnitudes which were referred to in Chapter One and which are now to be more rigorously defined, is that of 'aggregate income'. In the economy as a whole, it will be remembered, incomes provide a link between aggregate supply and demand: the production and sale of goods and services puts money in the hands of those concerned in production, so that they can now appear as spenders on the demand side of the market. The next step, therefore, must be to elucidate the concept of income and its relationship with production.

For an individual person, income can be defined as whatever receipts he can spend or give away over a given period of time without becoming poorer than he was to start with. The receipts may be in money or in kind, as in the case of a miner given free coal in addition to his wage; nor need the income be received from others—it would include, for example, the value of vegetables grown in a man's garden for the family table, and the imputed rent of a house occupied by its owner. 'Without becoming poorer' means that the individual's holding of money, goods and other assets, less his debts, must have a value at the end of the period at least equal to its value at the beginning. He may, of course, change the *form* of his holdings—for example, he may sell his house and buy shares with the proceeds, or he may buy a car on hire purchase and thus acquire both an asset and a liability at the same time. But whatever changes he makes, he must not finish up with a smaller value of *net* assets than that with which he began.[2] He must keep his capital intact, or if he is on balance a debtor, his net debt must not increase. His income, there-

---

[1] See *National Income and Expenditure, 1965–75*, Table 12.3. The Blue Book calls it 'capital consumption', to distinguish it from the 'depreciation allowances' actually used by enterprises: the latter are likely to give an unsatisfactory figure for the 'depreciation' described in the text above. See the Blue Book, p. 128.

[2] This raises the question of how the assets and liabilities ought to be valued: for example, should a house be regarded as being worth whatever the owner paid for it (less depreciation if he has had it long), or as worth whatever price it would fetch if sold now? If house prices are rising, and the owner finds he could sell at the end of the year for 10% more than he would have got at the beginning, should he regard the 10% as part of his income? Would the answer be 'yes' if it is only house prices which are rising, but 'no' if *all* prices are rising? See J. R. Hicks, *Value and Capital*, Chapter XIV, for a discussion of the difficulties of defining income.

fore, must come from sources other than loans and the running-down of assets: it must come from his labour, or from the use of his property, or from 'transfers' (i.e. receipts other than those from goods or services rendered or money lent). Income from his labour may take the form of wages or fees. If his property is in securities, such as government bonds or company shares, the income therefrom will be interest or dividends, while if his property is in physical form (for example, a row of rented houses or an ice-cream barrow) income will accrue as rent or profit. Transfers may be pensions, unemployment benefit and other social security benefits, or private gifts.

For business enterprises, the definition of income follows the same principles: it is the sum which a company may expend without worsening its balance-sheet position by causing its assets to diminish relatively to its liabilities. Firms do not, of course, spend their incomes on consumption as individuals do; they generally hand over part of it to their shareholders in dividends, pay another part to the government in the form of Corporation Tax, and use the remainder to increase their assets (e.g. by buying more machinery or accumulating cash) or to reduce their liabilities (e.g. by repaying a bank loan). Companies' incomes consist for the most part[1] of trading profits, which are the excess of the value of output over the costs of producing and selling it—or more precisely, the sum of receipts from sales and the value of stocks held at the end of the year, *minus* the cost of materials purchased and the value of stocks held at the start, *minus* also wages and salaries paid out, rent and rates on premises, costs of fuel and light, depreciation, and any other expenses incurred in the course of producing and marketing the commodity. In calculating profit, it is thus important to ensure that all expenses are correctly deducted. A particularly difficult case is that of depreciation allowances: if the company deducts a charge which is greater than the actual loss of value sustained by its plant and buildings during the year, it will be understating its profit, while it will overstate profit if the charge is too low: yet (as has been seen earlier) this loss of value can only be estimated. For this reason the official statistics show the total of companies' trading profits 'gross of depreciation.' It will have been noted that trading profit is defined so as to include the value of any increase in stocks during the year, and to exclude any reduction: obviously, if a company were to sell off its stocks and distribute the proceeds in dividends, it would in fact be reducing its assets and so would be treating as profit a set of receipts which are not income at all.

[1] Companies may also receive rent on land and buildings, interest and dividends on securities held, fees for the use of patents, and other minor forms of income.

The income of the government, if defined along the same lines as those of individuals and companies, is whatever the authorities can spend without causing the public debt to increase or reducing the state's assets by, for example, selling off the Royal Ordnance Factories. But whereas the incomes of persons are mostly wages, and those of companies mostly profits, government income consists almost entirely of 'transfers' in the form of tax receipts. It is true that the central government, local authorities and other state agencies[1] (collectively referred to hereafter as 'public authorities') provide many services, such as defence and education, in return for the taxes they collect; but the connection is not so close as to make it possible to treat taxation as though it were receipts from the 'sale' of public services, since the tax liability of a person or company is in no way determined by the benefits he derives from the state, and in any case the authorities are not obliged to collect in taxes the precise sum needed to cover the costs of their activities. Tax receipts account for more than nine-tenths of public authorities' revenue. The remainder accrues from rents on public lands and buildings, from profits on certain trading activities, and from interest on loans; this property income is similar to that received by persons and companies in that it is the residue left after deducting expenses from receipts—in the official statistics, however, depreciation is not deducted, so that public authorities' property income is shown 'gross'.

Individual persons, companies and public authorities account for most of the income received in the country as a whole: however, there remain a few recipients not obviously belonging to any of these groups, such as charitable trusts, churches, trades unions and the nationalized industries. The last-named are not included among 'public authorities' since they are legally and organizationally separate from the state: but their activities are much the same as those of companies, and for many purposes they can be included in the 'company sector'. Their principal difference from companies is that they have no shareholders and therefore pay over no dividends to the 'personal sector' of the economy. When it is thought desirable to separate their incomes from those of companies, they are described in the official statistics as 'public corporations'. Apart from these, other corporate bodies are treated as 'collective persons'[2] and their incomes are lumped in with those of individuals in the 'personal sector'.

With these adjustments, all income recipients are now accounted for. *Persons* (including the corporate bodies mentioned above)

---

[1] But not the nationalized industries or 'public corporations'.
[2] *National Accounts Statistics; Sources and Methods*, pp. 99–100.

receive wages and salaries, fees, rents, interest, dividends, profits and 'transfers'; *Companies* (and public enterprises) receive profits, rents, interest and dividends; and *Public Authorities* receive transfers and a relatively small amount of profits, rent and interest. It would be misleading, however, to take the grand total of all these incomes as giving the income of the nation as a whole, because a number of items have to be cancelled out in the process of consolidation. All transfers must disappear from the picture, since they represent a redistribution of income rather than the accrual of income as such: for example, to count *both* public authorities' income tax receipts *and* the whole of the private incomes from which the taxes are paid would clearly be counting the taxed part of private incomes twice over. Dividends are not transfers in the above sense of 'a payment for which nothing is given in exchange', but they cannot be added into the total along with the profits made by companies, since the distribution of dividends is merely the passing on of income which the companies have already received: the shareholders, as the owners of the companies, are in effect receiving through intermediaries the profits arising from the use of property which they own and operate, as it were, at one remove. So if dividends are included as part of personal incomes, only undistributed profits should be brought in from the company sector: while if it should be found more convenient to take company profits as a whole, dividends should be excluded from personal incomes. By the same token, any dividends received by one company from another (for example, those distributed by subsidiaries to parents) should be cancelled out when incomes are being added up.

(e) National Income in 1975

When all possibilities of double-counting have been thus eliminated, the incomes which remain can be added together to give the *National Income*. The cancelling-out of transfers means that only those incomes which accrue from labour or from the use of property are counted: so National Income may be defined as the sum of incomes received by the owners of factors of production—'factor incomes' for short—over a given period of time. Strictly, National Income should always be given net of depreciation, but because of the difficulties of calculating the appropriate deduction it is often left gross, in which case it is commonly referred to as 'National Income plus Depreciation'. This is an unwieldy phrase, however, and it seems better to use the terms 'Gross National Income', when depreciation is not deducted, and 'Net National Income' when it is—

though it must be admited that they do not have the sanction of official usage.

National Income, as defined for purposes of the official statistics, is not the total of factor incomes arising within the geographical limits of the United Kingdom, but the total factor incomes accruing to United Kingdom residents: for the reasons set forth in connection with National Product, it is therefore necessary to add the item 'net income from abroad'.[1] Also parallel with the treatment of National Product is the deduction of 'stock appreciation', since this is not normally deducted in the accounts of firms when profit is being calculated.[2]

The National Income for 1975 is shown in Table II[3].

TABLE II

	£ millions
Wages, salaries, etc.	68,181
Income from self-employment	8,705
Gross trading profits of companies	10,387
Gross trading surpluses of public corporations	2,898
Public authorities' property income (gross)	114
Rent	7,144
Less Stock appreciation	−5,203
Add Residual error	920
Net income from abroad	949
Total: Gross National Income	94,095
Less Capital consumption (depreciation)	−10,907
Net National Income	83,188

In Table II, 'wages, salaries etc.' include the pay in cash and kind of HM Forces, and the payment of National Insurance contributions by employers, which (since they are paid toward the provision of benefits for employees) are regarded as part of employees' remuneration. 'Self-employment' refers to the activity of shopkeepers, farmers, the owners of unincorporated businesses, and certain professions: their incomes are often called 'mixed incomes' because it is

[1] The difference between the income from property owned abroad by United Kingdom residents, and income from property owned in the United Kingdom by residents of other countries. It does not include international transfers, e.g. gifts to or from the United Kingdom government or individual citizens.

[2] See above, p. 26.

[3] Taken from Table 1, *National Income and Expenditure, 1965–75*.

usually impossible to say how far they are the equivalent of wages for work done and how far they are profit from the ownership of enterprises. If the 'net income from abroad' item were to be deducted, the totals would become Gross and Net Domestic Income respectively. All the individual items are, of course, shown 'before providing for depreciation and stock appreciation'.[1]

(f) The identity of National Income and National Product

When Table II is compared with Table I, it will be seen that the totals are identical: Gross National Income equals Gross National Product, while if depreciation is deducted in both cases, Net National Income equals Net National Product. This equality must always hold good. It has been seen that in the case of an individual his income is the yield of the factors of production he owns—his wages if he is a worker, dividends if he is a shareholder, profits if he is the proprietor of a small business, and so on—plus any transfers he receives from the rest of the community. The National Income can be regarded in almost exactly the same way, since the nation is being treated for this purpose as a single entity, albeit a very complex one: so the nation's income must be the yield of the factors of production which its members own, plus any transfers received from other nations. In practical computations, the transfer element is excluded[2] (and in any case is not very large), so that the officially defined National Income is the sum of the yields of the nation's factors of production—that is to say, the National Product.

This can be demonstrated in another way. The National Product is the sum of the 'values added' over a given period by the various branches of economic activity, and 'value added' is the difference between the total value of the output of processes and the value of their inputs of materials. For an individual firm, it appears as revenue from sales minus expenditure on materials, plus the value of any increase (or minus any decrease) in stocks which occurs during the period. Out of the sum remaining, the firm must pay wages and salaries, rent of land and buildings, interest on borrowed money, and remuneration (such as fees to surveyors) for any other services it receives. What remains, after these payments have been made, is profit. So the whole of the 'value added' by the firm becomes income of one kind or another; and as the same principle must apply to all economic entities, whether firms, individuals or public authorities,

---

[1] Self-employed incomes and company profits are net of payments of Selective Employment Tax.
[2] See *National Accounts Statistics; Sources and Methods*, p. 5.

B

the total of 'values added' in the whole economy—i.e. the National Product—must be equal to the total of incomes paid in return for the services of labour and property—i.e. the National Income.

It should be noted that the two will *not* be equal if the National Product is valued at market prices instead of at factor cost, since the 'value added' will then for many industries include indirect taxes which do not form part of the incomes of the factors of production engaged in making and selling the commodities: as National Income is the sum of factor incomes, it would be smaller than National Product by the amount of indirect taxation. But unless it is specially stated that National Product is being valued at market prices, it is always understood that the factor cost valuation is being used, so that National Product (as the term is normally employed) must be equal to National Income—gross or net, in each case, according to whether depreciation is included or deducted.

A further point to which attention must be drawn, is that profit is defined above so as to include the value of any accumulation of stocks in the hands of businesses. Only when this is done, can the 'value added' be equal to the factor incomes which are generated from it. Entrepreneurs are thought of as paying the owners of other factors in cash, and taking their own payment partly in cash and partly in kind. This may not seem very sensible when a firm is willy-nilly piling up a stock of its own products simply because it cannot sell them: after all, the purpose of enterprise from the entrepreneur's point of view is to make money rather than commodities, and a situation in which all 'profit' took the form of unsold stock would hardly seem very profitable! Also, such a situation implies that the price of the product is probably too high, and that if a lower price were asked the surplus stocks would no doubt be cleared: this in turn suggests that the output of the commodity has been included in the National Product at a price which overstates the contribution it makes towards satisfying the community's wants. However, it is difficult to determine objectively how far stocks are being built up as part of a firm's plans, and how far because firms are unable to sell them: so the only possible course is to treat the value of additions to stocks as part of profits. The same considerations apply in reverse when stocks are being run down. When stocks are treated in this way (which in any case accords with commercial accounting practice), National Product must be equal to National Income.

(g) Other income concepts

In addition to the concept of National Income itself, it is useful to give names to certain other income aggregates which are required for particular purposes. The most important of these is *Personal Income*—the total of incomes received by persons from all sources. It consists of wages and salaries (including HM Forces' pay in cash and kind, and employers' contributions to National Insurance and private superannuation schemes);[1] interest, rent and dividends received by individuals;[2] the 'mixed' incomes of such self-employed persons as farmers, shopkeepers and barristers; and all transfers received from public authorities[3] by persons, such as pensions, sick benefit, unemployment benefit, family allowances, death grants and postwar credits. Personal Income is thus equal to National Income *minus* the undistributed profits of companies and public enterprises, *minus* also the property income of public authorities, but *plus* transfers received by persons.

Personal Income, as defined above, is not the same as the amount of income over which persons have complete command, to spend or save or give away entirely at their own discretion. Income tax and National Insurance contributions represent a use of income over which the recipient of the income has no control—an obligatory rather than a discretionary outlay, so to speak. When income tax, surtax and the National Insurance contributions of both employers and employees are deducted from Personal Income, the result is *Personal Disposable Income*. On this definition, Personal Disposable Income still includes contributions to private pension schemes, which may be a condition of employment and therefore compulsory; also, individuals may have fixed commitments, such as the repayment of building society mortgages and hire-purchase instalments, which further reduce the part of their incomes over which they have complete and immediate discretion as to its disposal. When all possible outlays of this sort have been taken away, the remainder may be called 'discretionary income'—though this is not official usage and no estimate of it is provided in the Blue Book on National Income and Expenditure.

In addition to personal income, it may be useful to have the concept of *Corporate Income*, i.e. the profits and other income of companies and public corporations; when direct tax payments are

[1] See *National Accounts Statistics; Sources and Methods*, pp. 100 *et seq.*, for details of 'income from employment'.

[2] Including the corporate bodies, such as churches and clubs, which are treated as 'collective persons' (see p. 30 above).

[3] Transfers under private pension schemes are not included, because the pension funds are classed as 'collective persons' and counted as part of the 'personal sector': their payments of pensions are thus treated as transfers *within* the personal sector, and cancel out when the aggregate of personal incomes is taken.

deducted, this becomes *Corporate Disposable Income*. If the income of public corporations were taken away, the remainder would be *Company Income*; deducting taxes from this gives *Company Disposable Income*.[1]

TABLE III[2]

	Factor Incomes (£ millions) (1)	Net Receipts (+) and Payments (−) of Taxes and Transfers (£ millions) (2)	Disposable Incomes (Column 1 minus Column 2) (£ millions) (3)
Personal Incomes:			
From employment	68,181	−17,978	50,203
From self-employment	8,705 ⎫	−2,811	14,458
Rent, dividends and interest	8,564 ⎭		
Public current transfers (pensions, etc.)	—	+10,208	10,208
Companies and Public Corporations:			
Undistributed income	13,445	−1,897	11,548
Public Authorities:			
Trading income, rent, interest, etc.	4,229	—	4,229
Interest payments on public debt	−3,957	— ⎫	
Receipts from taxes on incomes	—	+22,993 ⎬	8,521
Less current transfers paid out	—	−10,515 ⎭	
Unallocated items	−789	—	−789
Less Stock appreciation	−5,203	—	−5,203
Add Residual Error	920	—	920
Total: Gross National Income	94,095	—	94,095

[1] All of the forms of income mentioned above will be 'gross' or 'net' according to whether depreciation has or has not been deducted. In the case of Personal Income, depreciation is likely to be a significant item only in the accounts of small businessmen, farmers and other 'self-employed' persons.

[2] Table III is adapted from various tables in *National Income and Expenditure, 1965–75*. It will be noticed that public authorities appear to pay out £307 millions more in current transfers than persons actually receive; the difference is due to tax payments on these incomes. 'Taxes on incomes' include not only Income Tax, Surtax and Corporation Tax, but also National Insurance contributions. The incomes of the self-employed and of public authorities, and the undistributed income of companies, are gross of provisions for depreciation and stock appreciation.

When the disposable incomes of all the sectors are put together, they must add up to the same total as the National Income itself, because the effect of the various taxes and transfers is merely one of redistribution. No new income can be generated in this process: the only income available is that originally accruing to the owners of the factors of production. But the redistribution is nevertheless of great importance when the spending of income comes to be considered: in so far as spenders are influenced by the size of their incomes in deciding on their outlays, they will have regard to disposable income rather than to their factor earnings.

Table III gives a comparison, for 1975, of the incomes arising directly from production in the various sectors (i.e. factor incomes) and the disposable incomes which remained after taxes had been deducted and transfers made.

It will be noted that the arrangement of factor incomes is not the same as in Table II. Both rent and net income from abroad have been distributed among the sectors, instead of being shown separately as in Table II; payments of dividends and interest have been taken from the corporate sector and credited to persons and public authorities— so that the property income of the latter becomes £4,115 millions greater than in Table II. On the other hand, interest payments on public debt have been brought in: they are treated as a transfer from public authorities and included in personal incomes from property. Public debt interest, as a form of income, is hard to classify: to the recipients it seems to be property income rather than a transfer, since they are giving the authorities the use of their money in exchange for the interest payments; on the other hand, the state is not using the borrowed funds to create income through production—most of the money originally borrowed has been expended on the prosecution of wars in the past, and has left no productive capacity behind it. So debt interest has to be regarded as a 'transfer out' by public authorities, offsetting this part of property income received by other sectors.

The second column of the table shows the net amounts lost through income taxation and gained in the form of transfers; since public authorities' tax revenue (net of the transfers they pay out) is shown as a 'transfer in' to their account, the items in this column necessarily add up to zero. The third column shows the disposable incomes which result from this process of redistribution, and which are the relevant magnitudes when the spending behaviour of the various sectors is being examined; in the case of public authorities, however, it should be remembered that their disposable income is augmented by the revenue from indirect taxes, which are not included in the table.

(h) The aggregation of expenditure

National Product and National Income have now been described in some detail: it remains to define National Expenditure.

The first point to be made is that National Expenditure is not the sum of *all* expenditures made in the country during a given period. To count not only the expenditure of consumers on boots and shoes, but also the expenditure of manufacturers on wages, leather and so on, would be 'multiple counting' of exactly the same kind as that which had to be eliminated in the calculation of National Product, and would involve the same risks of misinterpretation: for example, a commodity which changed hands many times along the production 'assembly-line' would register an expenditure at every stage in the course of its evolution towards the finished product, whereas if the same commodity had been produced by a single firm from start to finish it would contribute only its final selling-price to total expenditure. It is necessary, therefore, to exclude all purchases which are 'intermediate' in the sense that they are offset, within the same period, by the re-sale of the commodities bought, either in their original form or after processing and absorption into other commodities. The transactions which remain will then refer to the purchase only of 'final' goods and services, which do not change hands again during the period of time over which expenditure is being measured. Some 'final' commodities will be completely used up in consumption or in public authorities' activities, leaving nothing behind; others may be intermediate goods which happen to have gone no further along the 'assembly-line' of production when the period finishes—they may have been added to stocks of semi-finished materials, or they may take the form of durable plant and machinery which has been bought during the period but has not yet been absorbed into the commodities produced with its aid.

On this basis, National Expenditure must include all purchases made by consumers,[1] and all purchases by the overseas customers of

[1] A few points of definition require to be made here.

(a) consumers' purchases do not include expenditure on new dwelling-houses, which are regarded as part of 'capital formation' as explained later.

(b) hire-purchase sales are included at the full value of the goods involved, even though consumers appear to be spending only the initial deposit at the time of purchase.

(c) where consumers provide *themselves* with goods and services, such as accommodation in owner-occupied houses, the value is reckoned as part of their expenditure.

Consumers' expenditure is not necessarily the same thing as consumption: one may buy food and not eat it. Nevertheless, the two terms are often used synonymously. A more important distinction is that between consumers' expenditure

our export trade—it is true that many of these exported commodities will be used as intermediate goods when they reach their destination, but they will have left the assembly-line as far as the home economy is concerned and can thus be treated as 'final' purchases. All spending done by public authorities on goods and services is included, but a distinction is made between 'current' and 'capital' expenditure: 'current' items are those which do not result in any addition to the community's stock of durable means of production, and which can be said to represent 'government consumption'—examples are the purchase of the services of soldiers and civil servants, the purchase of food for consumption in prisons, and expenditure on bandages and other medicaments in hospitals; 'capital' transactions, on the other hand, are those which represent an exchange of money for assets, for example by expenditure on the building of married quarters for HM Forces or on the acquisition of fire-engines. In the official statistics, public authorities' current expenditure is shown as a separate item, while their capital expenditure is usually merged with that of all other sectors of the economy in the item 'capital formation' (which will be explained presently). One form of public spending which is not included in National Expenditure, is the paying out of transfers to pensioners and other recipients of 'unrequited payments'. To the Chancellor of the Exchequer, the issue of family allowances naturally appears to be just as genuine an item of state expenditure as the provision he makes for the armed forces: but National Expenditure, by definition, includes only payments for goods and services, and all transfers must therefore be excluded from it.

It is the purchases of business firms (here including both companies and unincorporated enterprises) which present most difficulty when the shares of the various sectors in National Expenditure are being measured. Obviously, a very large part of business expenditure must be classed as 'intermediate': firms buy materials, hire labour, rent buildings and so on, and sell the resulting output to some other purchaser, so that the original purchases are wholly or largely offset by subsequent sales within the same period. It is only when purchases are not offset in this way that they can be regarded as 'final' and included in National Expenditure. It must be the case that all *services* bought by businesses (such as labour, the use of land and buildings, and the use of money borrowed at interest) are absorbed into output in the course of production, so that the sale of the output will offset the purchase of services. But *materials* need not be absorbed within a

---

and the value of *output* of 'consumers' goods': these will not necessarily be the same at all.

given period, so that stocks which have been bought but not used within the period will count as 'final' expenditure. This does not mean,.however, that the total value of stocks at the end of the period should be thus counted, if firms began with a stock of materials carried over from the past: in so far as these previously accumulated stocks have been used in current production, the purchase of new materials has been needed to replace them, so that only the excess (if any) of 'closing stocks' over 'opening stocks' of materials will qualify as final expenditure. The purchase of machinery and other durable equipment will count as a final purchase: no doubt a small part of the value of such equipment will be absorbed into output during the period (and should therefore be 'offset' by the deduction of depreciation), but the greater part of the expenditure on new plant will be offset by use only during subsequent periods. So the part of business spending which qualifies for inclusion in National Expenditure is that which creates assets either by adding to stocks of materials or by providing new durable equipment.

This formulation, however, leaves two loose ends. First, there is a question as to the meaning of 'stocks of materials'. Do these consist of goods held at the input end of each process, such as raw cotton in the case of textile firms, or do they also include stocks of finished products which firms have not yet sold? If the latter, then how can the value of the unsold goods enter into National Expenditure? It is clear that purchases of 'input' materials must count, but it is hard to see how the 'output' stocks can be included, since no one has yet bought them and no expenditure can therefore have occurred. Nevertheless they are so counted, under a convention by which the producing firms are regarded as having purchased the finished commodities from themselves. Although this procedure may appear somewhat artificial, it can be made to seem quite reasonable in cases where firms *plan* to increase their stocks of their own products: had they not wished to do so, they could no doubt have sold all of their current output and used the revenue for other puposes; thus, to keep some output in hand is in effect to employ the money it would have realized in improving the firms' ability to meet sudden demands for their products in the future. When, however, firms are 'buying' their own output simply because no one else will, the notional purchase of the stock hardly seems to fit the sense in which the word 'expenditure' is ordinarily used. Yet it is very hard to distinguish in practice between those increases in stocks of finished products which are planned for and those which are involuntary: so they are all regarded as part of firms' 'final' expenditure.

The second loose end concerns depreciation, which has already been mentioned in connection with expenditures on *new* durable equipment during the period. But what about the depreciation of *old* machinery and plant bought in the past? In so far as some of the value of old equipment is being embodied in current output, it will require to be replaced, and the sums spent on replacement can be thought of as 'intermediate' expenditure. Were a firm not to own the machines it uses, but to hire them on the understanding that it should replace them as they wear out, then the sums spent on making good the wear-and-tear of machinery would appear as an intermediate expenditure on all fours with the payment of wages and the purchase of materials. Most firms, of course, do not hire their plant, so that the logic of the situation is in most cases less obvious; but the principle nevertheless applies, that sums spent on making good depreciation should not be treated as a 'final' expenditure. However, because of the usual difficulties of identifying the part of capital expenditure devoted to replacement rather than to expansion of productive capacity, business spending on new equipment is usually given 'gross of depreciation', and when an estimate of National Expenditure includes it on this basis, it is called Gross National Expenditure.

Business spending on new equipment and on increasing stocks is termed '*capital formation*' in the official statistics. For the nation as a whole, capital formation includes that done by companies and public corporations, by unincorporated enterprises such as those of farmers and shopkeepers, by public authorities of all kinds, and also by individuals when they purchase new houses. The common characteristic of all such expenditures is that they have the effect of maintaining and increasing the nation's power to produce goods and services. Economists habitually use the term '*investment*' as a synonym for 'capital formation', but it is liable to misunderstanding since in its everyday use it can mean the purchase of bonds and shares and other assets of a purely financial kind, as well as the purchase of such 'real' assets as machinery and buildings. For the nation as a whole, the exchange of bonds and shares among its members can of itself add nothing to total wealth, nor can dealings at second-hand in plant and buildings which were constructed in the past and form no part of current output, and in land, which of course never had to be produced at all. All that is done by transactions of this sort is to redistribute ownership of the nation's assets. 'Investment', in the sense of capital formation, must therefore exclude all expenditure on previously existing assets, and stand for expenditure on current additions to the nation's durable equipment and stocks of materials and products. Capital formation will be 'gross' or 'net' according to whether depreciation is included or excluded. If purchases only of durable assets are being considered, the terms '*fixed* capital formation' or '*fixed* investment' are used: capital formation in the form of additions to stocks is usually referred to merely as 'increase in stocks' (or, of course, 'decrease in stocks' if they have been run down). Finally, a distinction may be made between capital formation *at home* and investment abroad: the former would include only those increases in assets located within the country, while the latter would refer to changes in assets located abroad, including not only physical equipment and stocks held overseas but also the aquisition of financial claims on other countries, for example by the purchase of foreign governments' bonds.

So far, National Expenditure has been defined so as to include all spending by consumers, except for purchases of dwelling-houses; all current expenditure on goods and services by public authorities; purchases by overseas customers of goods and services; and all spending on capital formation. But the total of these items would not yet give National Expenditure, since it includes payments for imported commodities of all kinds: all the four classes of expenditure distinguished in the previous sentence must have an 'import content' since they include purchases both of imported finished products and of home-produced commodities made from imported materials. Until the value of imports is deducted, the sum of these expenditures is officially termed 'Total Final Expenditure', and records the flow of spending which enters the country's markets to buy *all* the goods and services available there—to buy, that is, National Product *plus* imports of goods and services. But for a good many purposes it is only the purchase of National Product which needs to be taken into consideration, and it is then convenient to eliminate imports from both sides of the market, leaving National Product on the one side and Total Final Expenditure *minus* imports on the other. The quantity which remains on the spending side will then balance against National Product, and is appropriately termed National Expenditure.

The deduction of imports makes it possible to regard National Expenditure as the sum of 'final' purchases by the residents of the country. This is quite clear when the value of imports happens to be exactly equal to that of exports: the two then cancel out, leaving only consumers' expenditure, public authorities' purchases of goods and services, and domestic capital formation—all of these are clearly the spending of residents. But when exports exceed imports, the surplus will be counted as part of National Expenditure, which must then appear to include an element of spending by non-residents. The export surplus can, however, be seen in another light. The sale of goods and services to overseas customers has the effect of bringing foreign currency, and other financial claims on outside countries, into the hands of United Kingdom residents; the purchase of imports, on the other hand, creates counter-claims in the hands of foreigners. If there should be a surplus of exports over imports, that will mean that UK residents' claims on other countries are not all required to offset the counter-claims for imports, so that a residue will remain, which can take the form of holdings of foreign currency or of debts owed by foreigners to the UK, or which can be used to acquire physical assets situated overseas. All of these uses represent an increase in the assets of the nation, so that the export surplus can in fact be regarded as a form of capital formation, or 'net investment abroad'.[1] The inhabitants of the country are thus seen as receiving claims from the sale of exports, using some of them for the purchase of imports, and 'spending' the remainder on increasing the nation's overseas assets. If domestic capital formation is to be regarded (as it must be) as a part of the country's 'final' expenditure, so may overseas investment be thought of as a form of spending. Were imports to exceed exports, investment abroad would be negative, since the nation's wealth would to that extent be reduced; total capital formation would be less than domestic capital formation by the amount of the import surplus. If the difference between exports and imports is regarded as part of capital formation in this way, National Expenditure becomes the total of consumers' spending, public authorities' expenditure, and capital formation at home and overseas—i.e. the sum of 'final' expenditures by residents of the country.

In the preceding paragraphs, imports and exports have not been precisely defined. It should be noted that they include not only trade in merchandise but also payments for services: for example, when a British shipping firm conveys cargoes for foreign merchants, or when a British bank performs financial services for foreigners, this results in the earning of foreign currency: when French hoteliers supply meals and accommodation to British tourists, a service has been sold to UK residents involving the payment of sterling to France; these are 'invisible' exports and imports. Among these 'invisibles' there will also be included all payments of dividends, interest and profits accruing from overseas to United Kingdom residents and paid from the United Kingdom to recipients abroad: the exports and imports in this case are the services of assets owned abroad by British residents and owned in the United Kingdom by individuals, firms and

---

[1] 'Net' means in this case that the acquisition by foreigners of assets in the UK is subtracted from the acquisition by UK residents of assets abroad. No reference to depreciation is intended.

public authorities overseas. When a Briton receives interest on a foreign government bond, for example, this is a payment for the use of his money; when a British firm receives profit from some branch of its organization overseas, it is payment for the services rendered by British capital and enterprise to the foreign country's economy. In the preceding paragraphs, imports and exports have been taken to include all these 'property income' payments in addition to other goods and services. On occasions when it is desired to restrict the meaning of imports and exports to transactions in goods and in services other than those of capital, it is necessary to segregate property incomes into the 'net income from abroad' item which appears in Tables I and II above.

(i) National Expenditure in 1975

Details of Gross National Expenditure in 1975 are shown in Table IV.[1] The left-hand column shows expenditure at market prices: the amounts are those actually paid by spenders for the goods and services they bought. For comparisons with National Income and Product, however, it is necessary to give National Expenditure at factor cost by removing the element of indirect taxation from market prices (and adding back·subsidies, since these are negative taxes).

TABLE IV

	At market prices £ millions	At factor cost £ millions
Consumers' expenditure	63,373	55,818
Public authorities' current expenditure on goods and services	22,907	21,793
Gross domestic fixed capital formation	20,510 ⎫	18,313
Value of physical increase of stocks and work-in-progress	−1,349 ⎭	
Exports of goods and services	26,093	25,470
Less Imports of goods and services	−32,255	−28,248
Add Net income from abroad	949	949
Total: Gross National Expenditure at Market Prices	100,228	
Less 'Net Indirect Taxes'	−6,133	—
Gross National Expenditure	94,095	94,095

[1] From Table 1.8 in National Income and Expenditure, 1965–75.

This is done for each class of expenditure in the right-hand column, whose figures show the amounts actually received by producers. The total of the right-hand column thus gives the factor cost valuation of Gross National Expenditure. To reconcile this with the total of market-price expenditure in the left-hand column, it is necessary to deduct indirect taxes. In 1975, total indirect taxes were £14,046 millions, offset in some part by £3,906 millions of subsidies; however, imports bore £3,020 millions of indirect taxes, and as the import figure appears in the table as a deduction, this part of taxation is already eliminated when the total of Gross National Expenditure at Market Prices is reached. So from this total only the *remainder* of indirect taxes, *minus* subsidies, is deducted (i.e. £14,046 million – £4,007 million–£3,906 million); this is the amount shown in the table as 'net indirect taxes'. As 'net income from abroad' is shown as a separate item, imports and exports must be taken as excluding dividends, interest and profits. The increase in stocks is described as the 'value of physical increase' rather than 'increase in value' because stock appreciation has been deducted. Finally, the total is called *Gross* National Expenditure because it includes provision for depreciation; were this deducted, the result would be *Net* National Expenditure.

When Gross National Expenditure is valued at factor cost (as it is usually assumed to be unless otherwise specified), it is equal to Gross National Product and Gross National Income. The identity of product and expenditure is easily demonstrated. The goods and services produced in any period will either be sold or left in the hands of the producers. If they are sold, then someone must have bought them; the buyers cannot have bought more or less than what has been sold; to this extent, therefore, expenditure and product are merely two aspects of the same flow of transactions on the market. If producers do not sell their output to others, the commodities will be added to their stocks: in that case, the conventions by which National Expenditure is computed regard these additions to stock as having been bought 'internally' by the producers in whose hands they have accumulated. Thus, all products must be 'sold' in one or other of the two senses of the word, and since there can be no sale without a purchase, National Expenditure must be equal to National Product.

(j) Summary of the principal concepts

To conclude this chapter, it may be useful to summarize the definitions of the magnitudes which have been described, and to set forth the relationships between them. It will also be useful, for convenience in later argument, to adopt a set of symbols for them: the symbols are nothing more than a set of conventional abbreviations, as will be seen below.

Gross National Product (GNP) is the sum of 'values added' by the various industries and activities of the economy. It is valued at factor cost, unless explicitly stated to be at market prices.

Gross National Income (GNI) is the sum of incomes earned by the owners of factors of production in any year. The factors need not be located within the country, but the owners must. Factor incomes consist of wages and other income from employment, the trading profits of companies and public corporations, the 'mixed' incomes of the self-employed, rent, and public authorities' property income. The symbol Y is often used to denote National Income (gross or net as indicated in the context). A different income concept is that of *Personal Disposable Income* which is the sum of employment incomes, self-employed incomes, distributed profits, rent and interest received by persons, and transfers, *minus* all forms of income taxation paid by persons.

Gross National Expenditure (GNE) is the sum of all 'final' expenditures in any year by United Kingdom residents, consisting of consumers' expenditure (C), public authorities' current expenditure on goods and services (G), gross capital formation at home (I) and the difference between exports (E) and imports (M). When these expenditures are shown at market prices, it is necessary to deduct indirect taxes *minus* subsidies (T_g).

GNP, GNI and GNE are all identical in value. If depreciation is deducted, they become *Net*, i.e. Net National Product, Net National Income, and Net National Expenditure; and NNP $\equiv$ NNI $\equiv$ NNE. (The symbol '$\equiv$' denotes identity.)

With the aid of the concepts defined above, it is now possible to discuss in more detail, and with greater precision, the nature of macroeconomic equilibrium; and this is the subject of the following chapter.

CHAPTER THREE

The Equilibrium of the Economy as a Whole

(a) Aggregate demand and supply

In Chapter One, the equilibrium of the economy was roughly described in terms of aggregate demand and supply. It was said that when the amount of money everyone wishes to spend is equal to the value of the goods and services currently being made available for purchase, the economy is in equilibrium in the sense that the situation will not of itself cause changes in the general level of prices, in the level of output, or in anything else. But the idea of equilibrium implies the possibility of disequilibrium: aggregate demand *may* be equal to aggregate supply, but it can also happen to be larger or smaller at any particular time. In this, there is a marked contrast with the relationship between National Expenditure and National Product, since these are identical in amount at all times and under all circumstances: they can never be said to be in equilibrium, because they can never differ. None the less, the concepts defined in the previous chapter can be used to throw light on the conditions of equilibrium between aggregate demand and supply.

For the time being, the notion of aggregate supply will be assimilated to that of National Product. This does not mean that the two are to be regarded as identical: National Product is simply a numerical measure of the flow of output, whereas the concept of supply involves the idea of volition—it is the quantity which sellers *wish* to sell, rather than that available from current production. Firms will be content to produce a given level of output only if they believe that they could not improve their profits by either increasing or reducing it. It will be shown in a later chapter[1] that this depends on the current relationship between prices and wages: if labour-costs are low relatively to sales revenue, firms are likely to feel that it would be profitable to expand output, while in the opposite case they will wish to contract it; moreover, the prices/wages relationship itself may alter as the volume of output changes. It follows that a

[1] See Chap. Ten below.

given level of National Product can be identified with aggregate supply only if prices and wages happen to bear the appropriate relationship to one another. In this and the next few chapters, however, it will be convenient to make the simplifying assumption that this condition is satisfied at all levels of National Product: firms will then be willing to provide whatever volume of output is needed to satisfy aggregate demand, and their only concern will be to avoid excesses or shortfalls between production and sales. This assumption will be relaxed at a later stage, but for the time being it means that aggregate supply coincides with the current level of National Product, whatever this happens to be.

The original definition of equilibrium—that aggregate demand should be equal to aggregate supply—can then be restated in three ways. First, aggregate demand (including, of course the demand for additional stocks[1]) will be equal to National Product. Second, aggregate demand will be equal to National Income when equilibrium exists, since National Income is necessarily equal to National Product: all income-recipients must between them be willing to spend on currently-produced goods and services the whole of their combined incomes, no less and no more. It is not necessary, of course, that each individual income-recipient should wish to spend the exact amount of his *own* income: some may spend a good deal less, while others may borrow, or use previously accumulated funds, in order to spend more than the amount of their current incomes—business firms, in particular, are likely to be in the second category; but as long as spending plans are such that the under-spending of the first group exactly offsets the over-spending of the second, the sum of all incomes will be equal to aggregate demand and the economy will be in equilibrium. Thirdly, the equilibrium of aggregate demand and supply can be restated in terms of equality between aggregate demand and National Expenditure: the total amount of money which everyone *wishes* to spend on goods and services must be equal to the amount which actually *is* spent.

From the last statement, it is clear that the concept of aggregate demand will have to be retained when the equilibrium of the economy is under investigation. As has been seen, the concepts of National Product and National Income can be used without modification. It is not possible, however, to put National Expenditure in place of aggregate demand, since they are quite distinct concepts and are equal only when the economy is in equilibrium. The total of National Expenditure is necessarily identical with National Product, because nothing can be sold without being bought; such an identity can

[1] This demand, as has already been observed, may be either positive or negative.

therefore tell us nothing about the conditions of equilibrium. But the total of aggregate demand need not be equal to National Product, just as demand need not equal supply in the market for a single commodity; there is no reason why buyers should always wish to buy exactly the quantity which sellers wish to sell, and indeed the two sides of the market will find that their respective intentions are mutually compatible only when equilibrium exists. For the equilibrium of the whole economy, then, aggregate demand is the significant magnitude, not National Expenditure.

Nevertheless, this does not mean that the attention given to National Expenditure in the previous chapter was wasted. When aggregate demand is submitted to more precise definition, it must fall into the same mould as the details of National Expenditure were found to do. Just as it was found necessary to eliminate 'intermediate' expenditures and to count only 'final' ones, so also in the case of demand must multiple counting be eliminated by the inclusion only of 'final' demands in the total. The demand for fixed capital formation can be taken as 'gross' or 'net', according to whether it is made to include or exclude depreciation, just as *actual* expenditure may be 'gross' or 'net'. The classification of demand into categories— consumers' demand, public authorities' demand for goods and services, and so on—follows logically exactly the same pattern as that adopted for expenditure. If statistics of demand were available, they could be tabulated in a form precisely similar to that of Table IV (p. 44) in which particulars of National Expenditure are given; if the demand figures were then placed beside the expenditure figures, both sets would show the same layout of items, and the details of definition would be exactly the same for each set, except that one column of figures would show *actual* spending while the other would show *intended* expenditures. The parallel is so close that many writers have preferred to retain the word 'expenditure' for both aggregate demand and National Expenditure—the former being referred to as 'intended' or 'planned' expenditure, the latter as 'actual' or 'realized' expenditure. Swedish economists[1] have applied the terms *ex ante* and *ex post* to make a similar distinction: *ex ante* ('as of before it happens') expenditure is what everyone expects to spend when looking forward from the beginning of a period, while *ex post* ('as of afterwards') expenditure is what people find they have spent when they look back on the period after it has ended. The 'before and after' connotation of these terms, however, may be misleading in the present context:[2] intended expenditure, or aggregate demand, is

[1] The terms were first used by Gunnar Myrdal in 1927.
[2] As used by the Swedish writers, *ex ante* and *ex post* have a dynamic signi-

to be thought of as co-existing with actual expenditure—at the same time as spenders are attempting to buy £X millions' worth of commodities they may in fact be succeeding in buying only £Y millions' worth. Indeed, it is when spenders are *simultaneously* wishing to do one thing and in fact doing another that disequilibrium exists in the economy.

If aggregate demand is to be regarded as a more significant magnitude than Nationa Expenditure, it would seem to have a serious disadvantage in ´ .at no comprehensive statistical information is available about it. Wishes are less amenable than actions to observation and measurement, so it is hardly surprising that there are no officially-provided figures of *intended* expenditure comparable to those published for National Expenditure.[1] But this is not a fatal objection to the use of the concept of aggregate demand, any more than it would be when a demand schedule is assumed in the case of a single commodity's market. Very often the objective of economic reasoning is not to make detailed predictions in a particular case but to establish general relationships which can reasonably be expected to hold good whatever the precise details of the situation may be. To say, for example, that X is bigger than Y, or that Q gets bigger whenever R increases, may be quite possible even without a precise knowledge of the magnitudes of X and Y, or Q and R, at any particular time. If the statistical information is available it is useful in verifying such relationships, but the relationships themselves are usually asserted to exist on other than purely statistical grounds. Since the concept of aggregate demand is required for this kind of purpose rather than for detailed factual prediction (in the present context, at any rate), the lack of detailed information about it need not prevent it from being extremely useful.

It can be argued, moreover, that in a good many situations there will be a very close correspondence between the figures of National Expenditure and those which would appear, if they were known, in a detailed statement of aggregate demand. Consumers, for example, can be assumed to spend whatever amounts they wish (given the

---

ficance which is not relevant to the present description of *static* equilibrium. See B. Ohlin, 'The Stockholm Theory of Savings and Investment', in *Readings in Business Cycle Theory*.

[1] This does not mean there are no official figures at all: for example, the Board of Trade collects information from business firms regarding their intended capital formation over the coming year, and various official publications give rough estimates of expected changes in the main categories of demand. But the figures are obviously less 'firm' than the records of past expenditure, and they are much less detailed.

prices of commodities, their own incomes and so on) unless for some reason the available quantities of the commodities they desire are inadequate to meet their demands—in which case some of the spending which consumers wish to do will not in fact get done. If, on the other hand, commodities are in plentiful supply, consumers will buy what they want and leave the rest of the available commodities in the hands of the sellers. In short, consumers' *intended* expenditure may conceivably exceed their *actual* expenditure, but it cannot fall short of it. This will be true also of the expenditure of public authorities, of the purchase of imports and exports, and of expenditure on fixed capital equipment: in all these cases, buyers may have to put up with less than they would have liked to purchase, but they cannot be made to buy more than they want. Therefore, unless demand in all these categories is so high that it causes great difficulties of supply, it can be supposed that the statistics of National Expenditure coincide with those which would have existed for demand had it been possible to obtain them. The single category of expenditure for which this does not hold good is that on increases in stocks: here, it is possible for actual spending to exceed intended expenditure, because of the convention by which firms are regarded as buying from themselves any unsold accumulation of their own products. Firms may produce a certain output, hoping that it will be bought from them by consumers, public authorities and so on, with the exception perhaps of a certain quantity of their products which they themselves wish to retain as an addition to their stocks. If, however, demand is less brisk than was expected, the firms will find that a larger part of their output is left on their hands than the increase in stocks they had originally intended. The firms' *demand* is the originally planned stock increase; their *expenditure*, on the other hand, is the increase in stocks which in fact occurs. If other sectors' demand were unexpectedly strong, firms might find their existing stocks drained away in the effort to keep their customers supplied, and the result in this case would be to cause firms' expenditure on stock increase to be *less* than their demand for additional stocks.[1] Unless the excess of aggregate demand over National Product is so great that the entire stocks held by firms are (when added to current output) inadequate to meet demand in other sectors, it would seem that the difference between demand and output in the whole economy is likely to be concentrated wholly in the 'increase in stocks' item.

[1] It might, of course, happen that firms planned to *decrease* stocks; but if the actual draining away of stocks were still larger than the planned reduction, demand would still exceed expenditure in this respect—though both would be negative.

(b) Symptoms and effects of disequilibrium

Other possible consequences of disequilibrium between aggregate demand and National Product may be seen when the constituent elements are tabulated in detail, as in Table V below. Imaginary

TABLE V

Demand (at Market Prices)	Thousand £ millions	Supply	Thousand £ millions
Consumers' demand	60·0	Gross National Product (at factor cost)	90·0
Public Authorities' demand for current goods and services	20·0	Imports (at factor cost)	30·0
Demand for gross fixed capital formation at home	20·0	Indirect taxes (less subsidies)	10·0
Demand for increases in stocks	4·0		
Demand for exports	30·0		
Total demand	134·0	Total supply	130·0

annual figures are used for purposes of illustration, though it may be observed that the order of magnitude is not very much different from that of the authentic 1975 figures which appear in previous tables. The left-hand column includes all the elements of demand which over the year come forward in search of the various goods and services available in the country; the right-hand column summarizes what is supplied—Gross National Product (which might be called 'internal supply of goods and services' on the argument given on pages 47–8) and imports, which appear here as a flow of commodities into the home market from abroad, rather than a deduction from the left-hand side as in the conventional presentation of Gross National Expenditure displayed in Table IV. Demands are shown at market prices, since these are what spenders must actually take into account when making their plans; but Gross National Product and imports are shown at factor cost on the right-hand side, since this is considered to give better representation of the quantity of goods and services coming on to the market, and it is therefore necessary to bring in indirect taxes[1] to make the 'market-price' demands in the left-hand

[1] The amount is that of indirect taxes payable at current rates on the goods and services included in Gross National Product and imports—not the taxes payable on the quantity of goods the spenders would apparently wish to buy.

column comparable with the total of supplies in the right-hand column. If equilibrium existed, the two totals would be equal: if the symbols introduced at the end of Chapter Two are brought into use,[1] this would mean that

$$C+G+I+E = GNP+M+T_g$$

(where C is consumers' demand, G that of public authorities, I the demand for investment, E that for exports, M the supply of imports and T_g indirect taxes). In the situation imagined in the table, however, total demand exceeds total supply; the left-hand side of the equation is larger than the right-hand side.

It is clear that, as things stand in the table, all spenders cannot be fully satisfied: they wish to spend £134,000 millions, while the value of goods and services available to be purchased is only £130,000 millions. An 'excess demand' of £4,000 million exists. But actual expenditure cannot exceed the value of goods and services purchased: perusal of Table V suggests that there are six ways in which the equality of expenditure and supplies may be established.

(i) Firms may satisfy other sectors' excess demand by throwing into the breach their accumulated stocks, as described on page 51. If their stocks are large enough (i.e. at least £4,000 millions in this case) and if they are prepared to use them in this way, their action will permit all other sectors to satisfy demand to the full—though of course the firms' own demand for increased stocks will be completely frustrated.

(ii) If firms' stocks are too small for this, or if they are not prepared to give them up in the necessary quantities, demand in *all* sectors may be frustrated: the 'excess' £4,000 millions will go a-begging, as it were. Consumers will find themselves faced with shortages; government departments will be unable to procure all the supplies called for by their spending programmes for the year; export customers will be told that their orders are being placed on waiting lists; and so on.

(iii) Instead of a general shortage of supplies arising in all sectors, it may happen that export customers are made to take the strain by the diversion to the home market of commodities originally produced for export. The probability of this outcome depends on many things—for example, if the country's exports normally consist of commodities adapted to the special requirements of foreign customers (such as icebreakers, narrow-gauge railway locomotives, and fezzes) it may not be possible to sell these things at home, and exports will continue as before; if, on the other hand, overseas markets are generally

[1] The symbols are given the sense of 'intended' rather than 'actual' expenditure in the above context: *ex ante*, rather than *ex post* as they were in Chapter Two.

regarded as overspill for products of which the bulk is normally sold domestically, it will be easy to divert the entire supply to customers at home.

The first three possible outcomes of the disequilibrium which is being imagined, are all concerned with the *demand* side of Table V. The remaining three possibilities appear as possible changes on the *supply* side.

(iv) The converse of (iii) is an increase in the quantity of the country's imports. If overseas suppliers can easily increase their consignments to the home country, all of the excess demand may be met in this way; instead of demand being frustrated, the supply of imports will rise to meet it.

(v) It may be, however, that the volume of imports is already at a maximum: this could be the case if foreign producers are working at full capacity to produce the particular commodities which the country imports, and for technical reasons are unable to expand production further. It may be, also, that the government of the country is apprehensive of possible ill consequences from a surplus of imports over exports, and therefore takes steps to prevent such a surplus arising, for example controlling imports by a system of licences. The quantity of commodities supplied can then increase only by a rise in home production—i.e. in Gross National Product. If the economy is in an 'under-employment' condition initially, with many of its workers unemployed and a good part of its plant and equipment lying idle, it will be quite possible to increase output very quickly simply by calling back into use some or all of these unemployed resources. The £4,000 millions of excess demand will quickly be met by a rise in the physical quantity of output of equal value.

(vi) However, there may be no reserve of temporarily idle resources available to expand the quantity of output: the economy may be already in 'full employment'. In that case, the physical quantity of output can be increased only by giving the fully-employed labour force more equipment, or by improving the productivity of resources already available; how feasible this will be must depend on the increase in production required and on the length of time within which it must be provided. If the time is too short for additions to plant and equipment through capital formation to make much difference to the volume of output, the only remaining way in which supply can increase to match demand will be by a general rise in prices. The 'excess' £4,000 millions can all be spent, if the same physical quantities of goods and services are made £4,000 millions dearer. The increase in prices is almost certain to extend to any imported commodities which are being sold alongside similar home-produced goods, if it is not possible for the *quantity* of imports to rise as in (iv); how far the prices of other imports will rise, must depend on the reactions of foreign suppliers. As the original market value of all supplies, both home-produced and imported, was £130,000 millions, an average rise in prices of about 3% will suffice to bring the figure up to one of equality with aggregate demand.

These, then, are the immediate consequences which may result from the 'excess demand' situation imagined in Table V, a situation which might be described as 'inflationary'—though nothing has yet been said on the subject of inflation, so that the word is not here intended in a very precise sense. The six possible outcomes are by no means mutually exclusive: they might all operate simultaneously. For example, an average increase of 1% in prices would raise the value of supplies by £1,300 millions; a rise of 1% in the physical quantity of home production would contribute a further £909 millions;[1] an increase in imports of £100 millions, a decrease in exports of £100 millions, and an increase in stocks of only £3,500 millions instead of the £4,000 millions which had originally been planned, would between them offset all but £91 millions of the £4,000 millions excess demand: this small remainder might then be the degree of 'frustration' experienced by consumers, public authorities and business firms seeking to obtain new plant and machinery. Exactly how much of the impact would be borne in each of the six ways, must depend on the circumstances. Obviously, price-increases are more likely if there is no possibility of quickly increasing the physical quantity of output— if, that is, the economy is already fully employed. But even then, much depends on the attitude of business managements: some boards of directors may feel that taking advantage of buoyant demand to raise their products' prices could damage their goodwill in the long run, and may therefore keep prices unchanged even when it is quite clear that they could be increased without reducing sales; other firms, taking a shorter view, may put up their prices as soon as opportunity offers; the net result for the price-level in general will depend on which of these attitudes is more prevalent among policy-makers in industry and commerce.

Such questions as these will have to be considered in detail later on. At present it is more important to observe that the various possible

---

[1] At the original price-level, it would have been £900 millions, but that figure must be increased by 1% since prices are assumed to rise this much. A further complication is that an increase in supplies and an upward movement of prices will ordinarily cause indirect tax payments to rise—but this is neglected here for the sake of simplicity.

effects of excess demand will not immediately lead to the restoration of equilibrium in the economy. The three possibilities on the demand side—i.e. (i), (ii) and (iii) above—merely leave part of aggregate demand unassuaged: either it is partially frustrated in all sectors, or the frustration is concentrated among business firms seeking to hold a particular level of stocks, or among export customers. This 'blocking off' of demand may be the main consequence in the current period (the figures were assumed to refer to an imaginary year), but it will presumably mean that excess demand will be carried over into next year, so that the disequilibrium situation will be reproduced and further effects brought about when the current year is finished.

Alternatively, the effects on the supply side will cause incomes to increase through the rise in output and/or prices (possibilities (v) and (vi) above)—though not, it should be noted, when the main consequence is an increase in imports (i.e. (iv) above). Where output or prices increase, it must follow that the owners of factors of production are receiving more remuneration in money terms, since National Product is always equal to National Income.[1] Every penny paid over in exchange for goods and services must be received by someone, and these payments, after the elimination of multiple-counting, will constitute factor incomes; whether more is paid because a larger quantity of commodities is being bought, or because the same quantity is being bought at higher prices, makes no difference to the fact that more money is being received as income. Whether the extra income takes the form of higher profits, or of increased wages, or of larger 'mixed' incomes, must depend on a number of circumstances; but whoever actually receives it, it will become available, after the usual processes of taxing and transferring, as disposable income to be used by the recipients as the basis for further demands for goods and services. Even if neither prices nor home output go up, but imports increase to the full extent of the excess demand, this will bring about a rise in incomes for the people overseas who produce the imported commodities; they, in their turn, may increase their demand for the exports of the original country—but this 'feedback' will be less direct than that resulting from increased domestic incomes, and may be much weaker; if it were negligible (for example, because foreigners spend their additional income entirely on their own products) the original country will have 'exported', as it were, the whole of its excess demand.

Unless the excess demand is channelled off through the purchase of extra imports, then, it will pass into home incomes and reappear on the demand side: if *all* of the increase in income were to reappear

[1] See Chapter Two, pp. 33–4.

as additional demand, the situation will now be that both aggregate demand and the value of supplies have been increased by £4,000 millions, leaving demand in excess of supply by just as much as before. If this were to happen, the excess demand will once again pass round the circuit, increasing the value of supplies, augmenting incomes and consequently raising demand yet again by £4,000 millions; which in turn will reproduce itself, leading to an infinite series of further increases in incomes and demand. Equilibrium, it would seem, will never be attained; it is not possible for aggregate demand to come into equality with the value of available supplies, if the *whole* of the original excess of demand circulates at every turn of the circuit. If, however, the adding of £4,000 millions to incomes results in an addition of *less* than that amount to aggregate demand, then the increase in incomes which occurs on the next 'round' will be only (say) £3,600 millions; if less than this is added to demand on the next turn of the circuit, the next but one increase in incomes will be again smaller; further turns of the circuit will be made by successively smaller amounts, until in the end the addition to demand will be negligible and equilibrium will at last be reached.

The relationship between incomes and demand is therefore crucial for the attaining of equilibrium. It is necessary to know how each of the categories of spenders will react to changes in income. Suppose, for example, that in the imaginary situation of Table V, it is known that none of the £4,000 millions of excess demand will have the effect of increasing imports, and that Gross National Product is made to rise by exactly £4,000 millions through rises in prices, or in output, or a mixture of both: then Gross National Income will rise by the full £4,000 millions. Now suppose that four-fifths of this becomes the disposable income of *persons*, and that on the average people try to spend on consumption three-quarters of any rise in disposable income: this will mean an addition to consumers' demand of £2,400 millions at the next stage. Suppose, further, that business firms try to spend on capital formation exactly the amount of their disposable undistributed profits, which happen to be a tenth of the increase in Gross National Income: this means that £400 millions of further demand will arise in this sector. Finally, suppose that public authorities and export customers do not react at all to the change in Gross National Income. Then the income increase of £4,000 millions will cause an increase in demand of £2,800 millions altogether—that is to say, seven-tenths of the rise in income is passed on in increased demand to the next stage. When the £2,800 millions then emerges as a further increase in Gross National Income, and seven-tenths of *that* is added to the demand, only £1,960 millions will be passed on at this further turn round the circuit; this will generate yet more demand equal to seven-tenths of £1,960 millions, and so on. The successive additions to demand can be written as a series (the figures are in millions of pounds)—2,800; 1,960; 1,372; 960; 672;—and so on. Though aggregate demand was in the first instance £4,000 millions higher than the value of supplies, the excess is gradually being whittled away. Both demand and supply increase (in monetary terms) with each tour of the circuit, but demand does not maintain its lead; eventually, the excess demand will be reduced to an amount so insignificant as to be hardly worth counting, and equilibrium will have been achieved.[1]

The possibility of equilibrium existed in the above example, because the relation between incomes and demand was assumed to be such that only seven-tenths of any rise in income was translated into further demand for goods and services. As long as less than the whole of income is passed on in this way, equilibrium is attainable. If, on the other hand, the spending habits of the various sectors are such that a rise in income would lead to attempts to increase spending by *more* than the amount of extra income—if, for example, the £4,000 millions of extra income imagined earlier were to cause consumers to raise their demands by £3,600 millions and business firms to attempt extra capital formation of £600 millions—then not only will equilibrium not be possible, but the original excess of aggregate demand over supply will become steadily greater, and will go on growing without limit. So everything depends upon the way in which the various categories of spenders react to changes in their incomes: it is a matter of such importance that several subsequent chapters will be devoted to exploring the connection between income and demand. Meanwhile, however, some further points must be made regarding the nature of the equilibrium of the economy, as it has so far been outlined.

(c) The saving–investment relationship

The first of these concerns *saving*, which has not so far been mentioned, and which may be defined in a general way as that part of disposable income which is not spent on consumption. In the case of

---

[1] It should be noted that this is 'static' equilibrium, as defined in Chapter One, pp. 15–16. It is assumed that there are no important time-lags in the process of circulation described above: demand causes the value of supply to increase, incomes rise, and demand rises further, all in too short a time for the process itself to produce any important changes in the system. The 'time-path' of the circuit is at this stage deliberately ignored; but the effect of time-lags will be explored in Chapter Six.

individuals, this seems a fairly straightforward concept. Whatever is left of a man's income after he has paid his taxes will be available to him for outlay in various ways. He may spend it on commodities which he consumes—in which case nothing will be left behind as wealth to be carried over into the future—or he may use it in some other way which will leave him better off. He need not accumulate cash, of course: he may buy government bonds or company shares; he may acquire a house; if he is the owner of a small business, he may use part of his income to increase its equipment or its stock-in-trade. Saving is thus not the opposite of spending, but merely the alternative to the spending of income on consumption. Consumption and saving will between them account for the whole of the individual's disposable income.

For the nation as a whole, the definition of saving is slightly more complicated. It would not be correct to subtract consumers' expenditure from National Income and call the remainder saving, because this would make no allowance for the 'collective consumption' represented by public authorities' current expenditure on goods and services. When local authorities, for example, spend money on street lighting and sewage disposal, they are satisfying their citizens' wants in a way which uses up resources without leaving any assets to be carried over into the future; they are doing things which might have been objects of private consumers' expenditure had it not been found more convenient to provide such services publicly. To calculate the saving of the whole nation, then, it is necessary to deduct from National Income both private consumers' expenditure and current expenditure on goods and services by public authorities.[1] When this is done, it will be seen that the nation's saving is exactly equal to capital formation at home (including increases in stocks as well as expenditure on fixed capital equipment) *plus* exports *minus* imports of goods and services. This is because National Expenditure consists of the spending of consumers and public authorities, plus capital formation, plus exports and minus imports; National Income equals consumers' and public authorities' expenditure, plus saving; National Income and National Expenditure are always equal, so that if public and private consumption is subtracted from both, the remainders—capital

---

[1] If consumption and public authorities' expenditure are valued at market prices, it will be necessary to add indirect taxes to the National Income before subtraction takes place: the saving thus calculated will then be on a market price basis of valuation. If consumption and public expenditure are both taken at factor cost, no adjustment of the National Income figure is required, and saving will be given on a factor cost basis. Unless all indirect taxes are borne by consumers' commodities and 'government goods', the figure of 'market price' saving will be larger than that of 'factor cost' saving.

formation *plus* exports *minus* imports in the case of National Expenditure, saving in the case of National Income—must necessarily be equal. This may be restated more compactly with the aid of the conventional symbols (among which S, for saving, is now included):

GNE = C+G+I+E—M (all taken at factor cost, so that indirect taxes may be omitted)

$$GNI = C+G+S$$

$$GNE = GNI$$

$$\therefore C+G+I+E-M = C+G+S$$

Subtract C+G from both sides of the equation; then

$$I+E-M = S$$

Expenditure and income are both shown gross of depreciation, so that saving here includes allowances set aside for replacing assets, and this part of saving must be equal to the actual expenditure on making good depreciation which is included in gross capital formation. If depreciation were to be deducted from both, the result would show the equality of 'net' saving and 'net' domestic capital formation *plus* exports *minus* imports. Since the difference between exports and imports is the amount of the country's overseas investment,[1] capital formation at home *plus* exports *minus* imports can be called simply 'investment': it is the total of capital formation at home and abroad. In this sense, the nation's investment is necessarily equal to its saving at all times. The only way in which the whole nation can carry over current income into the future is by creating new capital equipment, piling up stocks of commodities, and acquiring claims on the rest of the world. Saving and investment, indeed, appear to be the same thing.

From this, it might appear that the concept of saving is an unnecessary one: if it is always the same as investment, why not keep only the latter concept and discard saving? The answer is that the 'saving' defined above is *actual* rather than *intended*: it is the difference between income and whatever expenditure is in fact made on private consumption and public authorities' current goods and services. But, as has been seen, these expenditures may not be the same as the

[1] See above, pp. 42–3. The *form* of overseas investment does not matter in the present context: the export surplus may bring in a holding of foreign currency, or it may be used to buy shares in foreign companies or actual physical equipment situated overseas. All possible uses of the export surplus, however, represent an increase in the country's wealth. If there were a surplus of imports over exports, this would be 'overseas disinvestment'—the country would be reducing its wealth.

spending which consumers and public authorities planned to do; if *intended* consumption (both private and public) is subtracted from income, the result is *intended* saving—and this may not be the same as either actual or intended investment. Saving, in this *ex ante* sense, can be regarded as that part of income which consumers and public authorities are content to leave available for other purposes; National Income equals National Product, so saving is also equivalent to the quantity of goods and services not required for public and private consumption. If the plans of business firms and other bodies for capital formation at home and abroad happen to call for exactly the quantity of goods and services left over from consumption—if, that is, intended investment equals intended saving—then equilibrium will exist; aggregate demand will be in balance with aggregate supply. But it could easily happen that the amount of capital formation which is desired differs from the amount of intended saving: by planning to consume too little, consumers and public authorities may leave for capital formation purposes a larger part of output than is in fact wanted. This excess of saving over investment will result in a failure of producers to sell as much of their products to others as they had expected: stocks will pile up higher than was called for by firms' own plans to increase them. When firms attempt to work off these excess stocks by reducing current output, or by cutting prices, or by a combination of both, the effect will be to reduce the money value of National Product. If the fall in National Product (and in National Income which is always equal to it) causes changes both in the amount of intended saving and the demand for investment at home and abroad, in such a way that saving and investment (in the *ex ante* or 'planned' sense) become equal to one another, equilibrium will be reached and there will be no further fall in National Product. A similar sequence of events could be imagined if intended saving should fall short of intended investment: in that case, the demand for consumption would not leave available a large enough slice of the economy's output to satisfy the demand for new capital equipment, additions to stocks and overseas investment. When firms respond to this situation by attempting to increase the quantity of output, or by putting up prices, or by a mixture of both, the value of the National Product will rise; it will continue to increase until the willingness to save becomes great enough to provide for capital formation purposes a sufficiently large part of output to satisfy the demand. Saving and investment, when taken in the *ex ante* sense, will therefore be equal to one another only in equilibrium: though *actual* saving and investment must always be equal, *intended* saving and investment may very well differ.

That decisions to save should at times be incompatible with plans for capital formation, is hardly surprising when it is observed that these decisions and plans are made by different groups of people. An individual whose income accrues as a wage or salary, or as dividends or interest, may save part of it, but will hardly be likely to put the saving into the form of industrial machinery or stocks of commodities; instead, he will accumulate cash, or lend his savings to someone else by buying bonds, or acquire an interest in some company by buying shares. A business firm, on the other hand, need not rely only on its own undistributed profits when it wishes to expand its productive capacity by installing new machinery, or to increase its stocks of materials; it can borrow from a bank, or from the public at large by issuing new bonds or shares; when the firm sees an opportunity for capital formation which it thinks will be profitable, it may first decide on its programme of plant expansion and then look round for the means of financing it. It is true, of course, that companies' undistributed profits have for many years been a major source of finance for their capital investment, and in some cases the decision as to how much of current profits should be retained in the company instead of given out in dividends to shareholders must have been taken in the light of the company's requirements for new capital equipment and stocks. Here, the link between saving and investment is as close as possible: plans for capital formation are made, in such cases, by the same people who decide how much shall be saved from the companies' profits. In the same way, an individual who is running his own business may plan to save part of his profits in order to buy new machinery, letting his desire for capital formation determine his decisions regarding saving. To this extent, saving and investment plans will be kept in line with one another because the same people are making both types of decision; but as long as only a part of the nation's saving is decided on in this way, and as long as the capital formation planned to be made from firms' own savings is only a part of the whole nation's intended investment, there will be a sufficient degree of dissociation between saving decisions and investment decisions to make it possible for the nation's intended (or *ex ante*) investment to differ from its intended saving—giving the disequilibrium situation, described earlier, which will lead to changes in the value of National Product and Income.

For the economy as a whole, then, the condition of equilibrium is that intended saving must equal intended investment; and this is merely another way of saying that aggregate demand must equal aggregate supply, since investment (in the *ex ante* sense) is aggregate demand *minus* the demands of consumers and public authorities, while saving is the part of income (and therefore of National Product or aggregate supply) not required to meet the demands of public and private consumers. Is there any advantage in restating the equilibrium condition in terms of saving and investment? It must be admitted that it would be quite possible to give a fairly complete account of macroeconomic theory without saying much about saving, because saving is merely the difference between income and consumption, and all the various influences which determine the level of consumption must automatically determine the level of saving also. If, for example, people decide to spend four-fifths of their incomes on consumption, they are *ipso facto* deciding to save one-fifth of their incomes; consequently, it makes no difference whether the causes of these decisions are investigated as influences on consumption or influences on saving. It may even be thought undesirable to eliminate consumption from the picture by discussing equilibrium entirely in terms of saving and investment: the influence of consumers' and public authorities' demands is felt only negatively in such a formulation, and this may give the impression that consumption demand is somehow less important than the demand for capital formation. Such an impression would not, of course, have any logical basis, but it could none the less be influential in causing a misplacement of emphasis in the analysis of particular situations.

On the other hand, the savings–investment approach does focus attention on the aspect of equilibrium which is most important from the point of view of *monetary* theory and policy. Where savers are not the same people as those who take decisions about capital formation, questions of finance must be important. For investment purposes, business firms must somehow or other get control of funds sufficient to allow them to buy the goods and services not wanted for consumption: the simplest and most obvious method is for the firms to borrow the savings of income-recipients, in which case the rate of interest offered on loans, and the dividend rate expected on company shares, become important. It may be that savers are not prepared to part with their money even when offered attractive inducements in the way of interest and dividends; if they prefer to accumulate their savings in cash, it may be necessary for the monetary authorities to increase the quantity of money in circulation so that firms bent on capital formation can still obtain the necessary funds, and the powers and policies of those authorities will then be important. If it is considered (for reasons which need not be detailed at this stage) that the government ought to rely mainly on monetary policy in controlling the economy, its preoccupation will be with such matters as the quantity of money and the level of interest rates;

and the part played by these things in the working of the economy
may be more conveniently studied in terms of the savings–investment
relationship.[1]

(d) Changes in the price-level: the use of index numbers

The second matter which remains to be discussed in connection
with the equilibrium of the economy, is that of the general price-level.
The point was made above[2] that one of the consequences of an excess
of aggregate demand over supply (and therefore, of course, of
intended investment over saving) may be a general increase in prices.
If there exist plenty of unemployed men and machines, additional
demand may induce business firms to set them to work to increase the
physical *quantity* of output; if, on the other hand, there are practically
no reserves of labour and equipment available, an increase in the
quantity of production may be impossible for the time being; and an
increase in demand will then tend to force up prices. But how are
increases in the quantity of output to be distinguished from increases
in the value of output due to price-changes? It was pointed out in
Chapter One that in calculating *aggregate* output it is necessary to
add the money values of all the different goods and services produced
in a period of time. It is not possible to add together physical quantities of different commodities, but the total of aggregate output may
nevertheless be found if the quantity of each commodity's output is
multiplied by its price and all the resulting 'value of output' figures
are then added together. Also, since production is to be thought of as
the satisfaction of wants rather than the fabrication of objects, the
use of prices in aggregating output will have the effect of putting
different commodities into the total in the right proportions—the
'weight' given to a good priced at 10p will be one-tenth of that given
to something priced at £1. But suppose it should be necessary to
compare one year's output with another, when both are calculated in
money terms? If it is important to say what part of the difference

---

[1] This argument has lost some of its force in present conditions. If all new
borrowing were by business firms and public authorities seeking the means of
financing capital formation, the savings-investment approach would obviously
be appropriate. But in 1971, *consumers* contracted £2,001 millions of new hire-
purchase debt (while also making repayments of £1,757 millions), and borrowed
£1,774 millions net for house purchase. The financing of consumption clearly
involves a good deal of borrowing and lending, and there is a risk that its importance may be overlooked if attention is restricted to the finance of capital formation by business and public authorities, as it tends to be by the savings–investment
approach.

[2] See pp. 54–5.

between them is due to increases in the quantities of commodities produced, and what part due to changes in prices, a means must be found of separating the two while still permitting aggregate output to be stated in terms of money. Again, suppose the reactions of income-recipients to an increase in National Income are being investigated; *any* increase in the value of National Product, whether it arises from price-changes or quantity-changes, will bring about a rise in factor incomes, as has been seen above; but will consumers, business firms and others react to an increase in money-income which accrues from higher production in the same way as they will to one which accrues from higher prices? If a consumer, for example, finds that his income has gone up 10% but must be spent on commodities whose prices have also gone up 10%, his 'real' income (that is, his income valued in terms of the quantities of goods it will buy) will be unchanged; unless he is unduly impressed by the fact that he is getting more money, and unduly forgetful of the rise in prices—unless, in other words, he is suffering from what has been called 'money illusion'—he will no doubt go on buying much the same quantities of commodities as he did before, and the amount of his money expenditures will rise 10%. If, on the other hand, he were to enjoy a 10% rise in income while the prices of goods and services remained the same as before, he might very well increase his spending so as to enjoy greater consumption: but there is no reason to think he would increase his spending by exactly 10% in this case also. If, then, consumers' behaviour differs according to the nature of the rise in income, it is important to know whether the increase is in the quantity of goods and services available, or whether it is in terms of money only.

For this purpose, it is necessary to use 'index numbers'. If the general price-level in a given year (say 1975) is taken as 100, the price-levels of other years can be shown as numbers larger or smaller than 100 according to the relation they bear to average prices in 1975; for example, if all prices are one-fifth higher in 1976, that year's index number will be 120; if, by 1980, prices are one-quarter *below* the 1975 level, the index number will have become 75. The year whose number is taken as 100 is called the 'base year', and the rise or fall of the price-level is thus shown as a percentage change from the level in the base year. Given a set of such index numbers, the money value of output over a number of years can be adjusted in such a way as to show only changes in the physical quantity of goods and services produced. For example, if Gross National Product in 1975, 1976 and 1977 were respectively £90,000 millions, £105,550 millions and £115,000 millions, and if the index numbers of prices in the three years were 100, 115, and 125, then all that is necessary is to divide each year's

C

GNP by the year's index number and multiply by 100. This will change 'GNP at current prices' into 'GNP at 1975 prices', and the results are shown in the following table:

| Year | Index of Prices | Gross National Product | |
		At current prices £ millions	At 1975 prices £ millions
1975	100	90,000	90,000
1976	115	105,000	91,304
1977	125	115,000	92,000

In place of a series of GNP figures in which changes in prices are mixed up with changes in the quantities of commodities produced, there is now (in the last column of the table) a series showing how much GNP would have been if prices had remained unchanged— GNP 'at constant prices', in fact. The procedure by which price-changes are eliminated is called 'deflating' in this case, because prices were rising as the years passed; had prices been falling, it would have been necessary to 'inflate for price-changes'.[1]

This, of course, assumes that a suitable set of price-index numbers is already to hand, and that the numbers themselves can be accepted as an authentic representation of movements in the general price-level. Unfortunately, no index of this kind is free of ambiguity. To measure the 'general level' of prices, some sort of averaging is necessary: for example, if there are only three commodities, A, B, and C, whose prices have risen 10%, 20% and 30% respectively since last year, it would be simple to average these percentages and say that the general price-level has risen 20%. Taking last year's prices as 100, this year's index will then be 120. However, this will be clearly unsatisfactory if the commodities are not of equal importance as objects of expenditure; if they happen to be (say) bread, meat and matches, it would be absurd to give the price of matches the same 'weight' as those of meat and bread—but that is what a simple average does. Obviously it is necessary to make an adjustment. If half of total expenditure is on commodity A, two-fifths on B and only one-tenth on C, their price-increases can be 'weighted' according

[1] Table 2.1 in *National Income and Expenditure, 1965–75* shows GNP at 1970 prices for the years 1954–75; Table 2.4 gives index-numbers of costs and prices (with 1970 as the base year) for 1954–75. The fact that consumer goods and services are shown as having risen 79·2% in price between 1970 and 1975, while the prices of capital goods rose 106% and those of imports 109%, suggests the difficulty of indicating changes in the 'general level' of prices.

to the number of tenths of expenditure made on each of them: this means multiplying A's 10% increase by 5, B's 20% by 4, and C's 30% by 1, adding the results together and dividing by 10. The 'average' price-increase now appears to be 16%—a good deal less than the 20% found earlier.

Here, however, a fundamental difficulty may arise: this year's pattern of expenditure may not be the same as last year's. Suppose that this year the fractions of total expenditure allotted to A, B and C are one-fifth, two-fifths and two-fifths respectively: this implies 'weights' of 2, 4, and 4 instead of last year's 5, 4 and 1. Applying this year's weights gives 22% as the rise in the general price-level (i.e. 10%×2, *plus* 20%×4, *plus* 30%×4, the whole divided by 10), giving a price-index of 122 instead of the 116 found in the previous paragraph using last year's weights. If last year's National Product was £20,000 millions and if this year's is £24,000 millions at current prices, deflating by the 'last-year's-weights' price index of 116 will make National Product appear to have risen by £690 millions 'at constant prices'; deflating by the 'this-year's-weights' index of 122 will make it seem to have *fallen* by £330 millions. The two methods of weighting thus lead to very different results: yet there is no reason to prefer either as being more 'correct' or 'valid' than the other; nor is there any logical superiority in a compromise which splits the difference between them.[1]

This 'index-number problem' is not a mere matter of the incompatibility of different statistical methods: an issue of economic significance is involved. The way in which spenders choose to lay out their money is assumed to provide some indication of the satisfaction they obtain (or at least expect) from the commodities they buy: production, it will be remembered, is essentially the satisfying of wants rather than the making of physical objects, and the measurement of National Product involves the assumption that spenders preferred the pattern of outlays they actually made in a given period to any other they could have chosen at that time, given the purchasing-power at their disposal. But as time goes by, tastes are liable to change quite considerably; when this happens, the same collection of commodities will not give the same satisfaction as before—whether less, or more, depends on the way in which preferences have altered. Consequently, a given proportionate change in the quantities of goods and services received cannot be assumed to represent an equivalent change in the satisfaction of wants: the 'base year' quanti-

[1] The above account of the matter is extremely crude; for a full-length explanation of index-numbers, see Croxton and Cowden, *Applied General Statistics*, Chaps. 20 and 21.

ties may now have a different significance in terms of the satisfaction they afford. Because it is not possible to measure and compare degrees of satisfaction, estimates of changes in the 'real' National Product have to be made in terms of commodities, and they inevitably, therefore, involve logical difficulties of this sort.[1] In subsequent chapters the word 'real' will be used to mean that the magnitude to which it is applied has been 'deflated' (or, where necessary, 'inflated') by the use of some appropriate price-index; but it should be borne in mind that such procedures impart a certain haziness and ambiguity to the 'real' quantities involved.

There remains, finally, a third aspect of macroeconomic equilibrium which requires to be investigated before the relations between income and aggregate demand are explored. This is the employment aspect. Whatever the level of National Product, there will be some particular number of man-hours which must be worked in order to produce it; if unemployment exists, it may be because aggregate demand calls for a National Product too low to require the employment of all the workers who would be willing to provide their services, and official policies aimed at reducing or preventing unemployment must seek to do so by influencing the level of aggregate demand. The connection between National Product and employment is thus of great importance, and the following chapter will be devoted to the examination of it.

[1] It was the consideration of these difficulties which led Keynes to work in terms of 'wage-units'; see the *General Theory*, Chap. 4, esp. pp. 40–1.

CHAPTER FOUR

The Level of Employment

(a) *The relationship between output and employment*

To increase the flow of goods and services which make up the National Product, more labour and capital equipment must be brought into use, or else existing resources must be employed more efficiently through improvements in the methods of production. But improved methods are partly the result of chance discoveries, partly of sustained research which takes time to carry out and whose outcome cannot be guaranteed in advance; even when better methods have been devised, time will still be needed for the modification of processes at shop-floor level, for getting workers used to the new methods, and for consulting trades unions about changes in working conditions. If it is necessary to increase output quickly, changes in production techniques cannot be counted on to help very much: over a short period of time, they must be accepted as temporarily fixed.[1] Higher output can then come only as a result of larger inputs of the factors of production—more labour, more capital equipment, or a combination of both.

But to increase the quantity of capital equipment will also take time, when the economy is considered as a whole. An individual firm may be able to obtain plant quickly by buying existing machinery from someone else; but this would merely redistribute equipment between owners—it would not increase the total amount at the nation's disposal. That can be done only by constructing additional plant. Machines must be produced, buildings must be erected to house them, sources of power must be installed, and provision for various ancillary services must be made. A rough estimate suggests that Britain's productive capacity can be increased by three or four

---

[1] In practice, improvements in methods and investment in new equipment tend to go together; the separation made above is a logical distinction only. But if, as often happens, the introduction of new methods must wait upon the installation of a new type of machine, this is another reason for regarding methods as unchangeable in the short run.

per cent a year[1] through fixed capital formation: if it should be necessary to raise output by 10% in three months, very little help could be expected from the additions to capital equipment made in that time. Like the methods of production which are in use, the stock of fixed capital must be assumed to be practically constant over a short period.

This leaves labour as the only input which can be rapidly increased. To raise production quickly, more workers can be employed, or those already in work can be asked to work longer hours, or both. Conversely, if output is to be reduced, the number of man-hours worked can be cut down at very short notice, by dismissing some workers altogether and putting others on short time. Within the short period during which capital equipment and productive techniques are virtually unalterable, changes in output will thus be associated exclusively with changes in the employment of labour. The number of man-hours worked will then determine the quantity of goods and services produced.

The objection may be made, however, that labour and capital are not being treated here in comparable fashion: if the input of labour can be varied by the working of more or fewer man-hours, may not the input of the *services* of capital equipment be similarly altered by the use of more or fewer machine-hours? Fixed capital has been regarded as a stock of productive capacity; if labour were dealt with on the same basis, it would appear as a stock of 'labour-power' rather than a flow of services. Just as the country's total labour-power is employed to an extent measured by the number of man-hours worked, so also the stock of capital could be regarded as being used less or more intensively according to the number of machine-hours involved. Closing down a factory is therefore analogous to the unemployment of labour; working machines harder, for example through the introduction of shift working which permits machinery to be used round the clock, is analogous to the working of overtime by the labour force. On this view, production does not vary uniquely with the input of labour, but with man-hours and machine-hours taken together. A given increase in the employment of labour, without

---

[1] *National Income and Expenditure, 1965–75* gives estimates of the stock of fixed capital. Table 12.11 shows it net of depreciation, at current replacement cost, for the years 1965–75; Tables 12.12 and 12.13 show it gross, at current replacement cost, over the same period. The totals (for 1975, £322·1 billions in Table 12.11, and £215·8 billions in Tables 12.12 and 12.13) include *all* fixed assets, for example roads as well as plant and machinery; the latter accounted for 31% of the total in Table 12.13. Between 1965 and 1975, the average annual increase in the gross capital stock at 1970 replacement cost was 4%; for plant and machinery alone, the average annual increase was 4·9%.

any increase in the quantity of equipment in use, will obviously add less to output than it would if each newly-employed worker could be provided with capital equipment which had previously lain idle.

This argument is not unreasonable; none the less, it need not invalidate the original conclusion that the volume of output depends, in the short run, directly on the input of labour. The enterprises whose managers decide the quantities to be produced are also the owners of the nation's capital equipment; whether they make full use of it or not, their plant remains in their possession and they must meet the various costs involved in its upkeep. They are not, however, the owners of the labour-power they use: they can employ as much or as little as they choose within the limits of what is available; however many man-hours the workers themselves wish to work, it is not they but their employers who decide how much use shall be made of their capacity to produce. Neither the owners of capital equipment nor the owners of labour-power have any reason to want their resources to remain unused; but since it is the owners of the fixed capital who are in control of production, they can be assumed to work their plant as fully as possible even when they have decided on a low level of output, by employing relatively little labour and spreading it thinly over all the available equipment. In such a situation, output per worker may be fairly low, because the amount of labour is too small to take the best advantage of the plant and machinery at its disposal; if more man-hours are worked, output will increase in a greater proportion because equipment is now being used on a scale nearer to that for which it was designed; finally, if still more labour input is employed, the plant will be working above its 'capacity', and output, though still increasing, will not rise in proportion to the increase in man-hours; in the end, there may come a point at which further labour will add nothing to output at all. This sequence exemplifies the 'law of variable proportions', according to which successive additions of one factor of production (in this case labour) to fixed quantities of other factors (capital and natural resources) will bring first increasing, then constant, then diminishing and finally zero marginal returns. A situation in which the technical relationship between labour and equipment is very rigid (for example, where each machine requires exactly one operative) merely presents a special case of the general 'variable proportions' principle: instead of a smooth transition from increasing to diminishing marginal returns, the sequence here shows constant returns falling immediately to zero returns when all machines are in use. Even though it is technically impossible, in such cases, to bring all capital equipment into action when the employment of labour is low, the equipment can still be regarded as a 'fixed' factor of production: it is not necessary to invoke the concept of 'machine-hours' so as to treat the input of capital as variable. The technical restrictions imposed by the nature of the capital equipment influence the relationship between labour input and commodity output, but they do not make it necessary to invoke a second relationship, i.e. between capital and output, alongside the first.

For the economy as a whole, then, employment determines output in the short period within which capital equipment and methods of

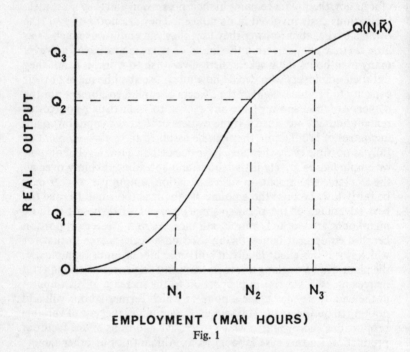

EMPLOYMENT (MAN HOURS)

Fig. 1

production can be assumed not to change to any significant degree; the greater the input of labour, the greater the quantity of goods and services produced. This characteristic of the economy can be summarized in symbolic terms by means of an aggregate 'production function':

$$Q = Q(N, \bar{K}),$$

where the Q on the left-hand side is aggregate output, N is the number of man-hours worked and $\bar{K}$ is the capital stock (with the fact that K is temporarily constant being indicated by a 'bar' above the symbol), while the Q on the right-hand side stands for the relationship between them.[1]

The law of variable proportions suggests that the relationship will be something like that shown by the line $Q(N,\bar{K})$ in Fig. 1. At a fairly low level of employment, such as N_1 man-hours, output is low at Q_1, and output per man-hour is Q_1/N_1; as employment increases to N_2, output rises to Q_2, and the proportionate increase in output is obviously greater than the proportionate increase in employment (i.e. Q_1Q_2/OQ_1 is greater than N_1N_2/ON_1). When N_2 man-hours are worked, output per man-hour is Q_2/N_2, and this clearly exceeds Q_1/N_1. When employment increases still further, to N_3 man-hours, output rises to Q_3, but this represents a *smaller* proportionate increase than that which has occurred in the number of man-hours— Q_2Q_3/OQ_2 is smaller than N_2N_3/ON_2. Meanwhile, output per man-hour has fallen to Q_3/N_3 (which can be seen to be smaller than Q_2/N_2). The levelling-out of the curve $Q(N,\bar{K})$, as it moves to the right-hand side of the graph, suggests that further man-hours will increase output, but by smaller and smaller amounts. Because the amount of capital equipment is fixed, only one level of employment will bring labour and equipment into their most productive relationship (i.e. where output per man-hour is at its maximum): this level is at N_2. Where employment is lower than N_2, the number of man-hours is too small to make the best use of the available plant; where more than N_2 man-hours are worked, the plant becomes inadequate in relation to the labour being used in conjunction with it.

It should be noted that these different employment-output situations are not to be thought of as succeeding one another over a period of time, but rather as a set of alternative possibilities all of which are present at a given moment of time. The economy *could* use N_1 man-hours, and if it did, output would be Q_1; or it could employ N_3 man-hours, and it would then get Q_3 as its output. These alternatives, and all the others shown by the line $Q(N,\bar{K})$, are available only during the short period during which capital and productive methods do not change significantly. The curve $Q(N,\bar{K})$ does not trace out a path of development occurring over time, but merely shows the amount of labour required to produce each possible level of output.

[1] Most readers will have encountered the word 'function' before, but it may be convenient to have a rough definition here. Where a quantity y varies with another quantity x in some definite way, y is said to be a function of x, and the relationship can be represented symbolically as $y = y(x)$. In the production function shown above, N is the 'independent' variable and Q is the 'dependent' variable which is 'determined' by N according to the functional relationship, $Q(\ldots)$.

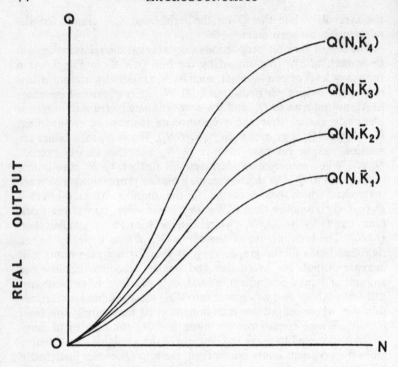

EMPLOYMENT (MAN-HOURS)

Fig. 2

If the time perspective were to be lengthened beyond the short period, it would be necessary to take account of possible changes in the economy's stock of capital equipment and in its methods of production. This would give rise to a whole family of curves, as shown in Fig. 2. Each curve shows the employment–output relationship for a given stock of capital used according to given techniques. As the stock of capital grows and methods of production improve, a given quantity of labour will become capable of producing more and more output; a given level of output will require less and less labour. The greater the amount of equipment, and the better the methods of production, the higher the curve: $Q(N,\bar{K}_2)$ shows output produced by labour which has more plant to work with than is assumed in $Q(N,\bar{K}_1)$; $Q(N,\bar{K}_3)$ implies still more equipment than $Q(N,\bar{K}_2)$, and so on. If the stock of capital were assumed always to grow and never to diminish, and if techniques were assumed always to improve, $Q(N,\bar{K})$ would move up the diagram in consequence of these developments; in this case, the time factor would play an important part, since each curve relates to a different point in time. A capital stock of $\bar{K}_2$ refers to a later date than that of $\bar{K}_1$, $\bar{K}_3$ to a later date than $\bar{K}_2$, and so on. The actual length of time taken to get from one position of the curve to another must depend on the rate at which the nation's capital equipment is being increased, and the speed with which its techniques are being improved. This will be an important consideration when the long-period growth of the economy comes to be investigated.

Meanwhile, the short-period employment–output relationship presents another feature which must be noticed. In Fig. 1, the vertical axis does not measure numbers of physical units of a single commodity, but 'output' in the National Product sense; the man-hours shown on the horizontal axis are assumed to be the labour input of *all* industries, and the output is therefore a mixture of many different goods and services, added together in terms of their money-values and adjusted for changes in the general price-level so that the total is given in 'constant pounds'. This particular mixture, however, is only one of a large number of possible combinations of commodities which could have been produced with the same number of man-hours: if labour had been differently distributed between industries, total output might have contained more bicycles and fewer perambulators, more beef and less wheat, and so on; had some other combination of products been produced, its total value (in constant pounds) would not necessarily have been the same as that of the existing combination. In a given situation it may happen that the strength of demand for certain commodities causes many man-hours to be allocated to their production, even though output per man-hour is not particularly high; if the pattern of demand were to shift so as to encourage the transfer of labour to the production of other commodities for which output per man-hour is higher, the increase in the value of production in the second group of commodities will exceed the reduction in the first group, and aggregate output will then be greater even though exactly the same total number of man-hours is being worked as before. Thus in Fig. 1, OQ_2 is not the only possible level of output which can be produced by ON_2 man-hours, even under the 'static' conditions of unchanging capital and techniques: a different pattern of preferences, giving a different distribution of demand between the various commodities, could cause the output from ON_2 man-hours to be either larger or smaller than OQ_2.

Similar considerations apply to *changes* in the volume of employment within the short period. In Fig. 1, N_3-N_2 extra man-hours give rise to an increase in output of Q_3-Q_2. But Q_3-Q_2 is a conglomeration of many different goods and services, of which the quantities produced depend on the strength of the demand for them; if the commodities most in demand happen to be those whose production has reached the stage of sharply diminishing returns, the rise in aggregate output (Q_3-Q_2) is likely to be less than it would be if the main weight of demand called for further output of commodities whose producers were still operating under increasing or constant returns. The increase in aggregate output, therefore, depends not only on the additional man-hours which are worked, but also on the distribution of demand among the commodities produced by those man-hours. Both the height and the shape of curve $Q(N,\bar{K})$ in Fig. 1 are affected by the pattern of demand; different patterns give different curves. This means that any particular curve, like $Q(N,\bar{K})$, is drawn on the assumption of a given, and for the time being unchanging, distribution of demand between commodities.

The assumption that the pattern of demand does not change within the short period for which the capital stock and methods of production are also fixed, does not seem to be unrealistic; over a longer period, however, it would be unlikely to hold good. This means that the employment–output relationship will change over time, not only as a result of capital formation and improved techniques as shown in Fig. 2, but also because of changes in demand; as Fig. 2's curve $Q(N,\bar{K}_1)$ moves up to become successively $Q(N,\bar{K}_2)$, $Q(N,\bar{K}_3)$ and so on, some part of its movement may be due to alterations in the allocation of demand between commodities—an influence which may cause the curve to move either faster or slower, further or less far, than it would have done had its movement depended only on additions to the stock of capital equipment and on changes in technique. For the moment, however, these dynamic possibilities will be left unexplored and attention directed back to the short period in which, by assumption, only one employment–output curve (such as $Q(N,\bar{K})$ in Fig. 1) can exist.

Given this static relationship, the actual level of employment will be determined by the strength of aggregate demand and the efforts of enterprises to meet that demand. At any particular time, the forces described in the previous chapter will be interacting in such a way as to cause a certain volume of goods and services to be produced: this need not be 'equilibrium output' in the sense that it is of exactly the right dimensions to satisfy demand, but it will tend to approach equilibrium level as enterprises make efforts to adjust their production to meet the desires of their customers. The actual level of employment will then be the number of man-hours required to produce this volume of output. If aggregate demand should fall, so that enterprises find their production is more than enough to meet demand (including, of course, their own demand for increased stocks), they will attempt to reduce output by an appropriate amount, and will therefore employ fewer man-hours. If demand should increase, more employment will be offered so that output can be stepped up.

It may happen, however, that the level of demand is so high that it is not possible to raise production sufficiently to meet it, because of the physical limits on the employment of labour. There must be some number of man-hours which represents the maximum possible effort of the economy's labour-power: when every individual, young or old, male or female, rich or poor, is working every minute not required for eating and sleeping, the limit will have been reached, and the number of man-hours available in such circumstances will be 'maximum employment'. Given the employment–output relationship, there will be some level of output corresponding to maximum employment, and this will be the utmost of which the economy is technically capable in the short run. There is no such obvious physical limit to aggregate demand, on the other hand; spenders may be prepared to buy a much larger quantity of commodities if it were possible to supply them, and if that happened to be the case it would not be possible for the economy to attain an equilibrium of aggregate demand and supply.

Maximum employment, however, merely sets a *technical* upper limit to the input of labour: it is hard to imagine a situation in which the community would be willing to work so hard. The desire for leisure is strong enough to make workers wish to limit the working day and cease work altogether at week-ends and holidays: the community as a whole insists on keeping children out of the labour force until they have completed full-time schooling; elderly people expect—and are expected—to retire from employment after a certain age. In a community where people are free to work as much or as little as they choose, and where most labour is sought and offered for wages in a market, a man who is well paid may feel he can afford more than the usual amount of leisure; a man who is rich may decide to do no work at all; a husband with ample earnings may insist that his wife and daughters shall not take employment even though the housework is not enough to occupy them fully. In almost any conceivable circumstances, even when everyone is working as many hours as he wishes, the amount of work done will fall a long way short of 'maximum employment'. The practical limit to the input of labour, in fact, is determined by people's desire for leisure as well as by their capacity for work: this limit is 'full employment', which may be roughly defined as the number of man-hours which are worked when everyone is enjoying as much leisure as he wishes to have, and no more, given the prevailing cost of leisure in terms of real wages forgone.

(b) Demand and supply in the labour market

If all units of labour were exactly alike, if workers were highly mobile between places and occupations, and if there were perfect competition in the buying and selling of labour, it would be possible to define full employment as the number of man-hours at which equilibrium exists between demand and supply in the labour market. On these assumptions, the supply of labour at any given real wage-rate would depend on its marginal disutility. Work entails fatigue, boredom and the loss of leisure, and the oppressiveness of these things increases more than proportionately to the number of hours worked; a man working a thirty-hour week will find an extra hour less onerous than he would if he were already working sixty hours. To persuade workers to supply a given number of man-hours, the wage-rate (in terms of the goods and services it will buy[1]) must be high enough to compensate for the disadvantages to workers of the 'marginal man-hours'—the additional labour which brings the total hours worked up to the given number. If still more man-hours were required, the wage-rate would have to be raised to offset the greater disutility of the extra labour; if fewer were wanted, the wage could be reduced since marginal disutility would be less for a smaller number of man-hours. Workers' views as to the disadvantages of labour are likely to be modified, however, by the fact that wages are normally their only source of income: a reduction in the hourly wage will cause earnings to fall unless hours are proportionately increased, and the prospect of lower earnings will no doubt diminish the attractions of leisure; workers may therefore respond to a cut in wage-rates by offering *more* labour, not less. Similarly, a rise in the wage-rate gives workers the

[1] This assumes that wage-earners have no 'money illusion', i.e. that they are influenced not by the 'nominal' wage-rate offered them, but by its purchasing-power in terms of commodities. However, changes in the purchasing-power of money, due to movements in the general price-level, are hard to assess (as was shown at the end of the previous chapter in the section on index-numbers), while the nominal wage-rate, by contrast, is a precise and unambiguous quantity; it is natural that workers should pay more attention to the latter than to the former, with the result that they sometimes ignore relatively small movements in the general price-level. This may, at times, suggest that 'money illusion' is present, even though wage-earners are well aware that rising prices may erode their 'real' earnings.

opportunity to enjoy more leisure at the same income, if they reduce their labour exactly in proportion to the wage-increase; even if man-hours worked were reduced by only 5% in response to a wage-rise of 10%, earnings would still be about 5% higher than before, and workers would have more leisure in which to spend their extra income. This 'income-effect', then, may make the supply of labour vary *inversely* with the wage-rate, even though the 'marginal disutility' considerations mentioned earlier would by themselves cause the supply to vary *directly* with the wage-rate. Because of this, it is not possible to attribute any characteristic shape to the supply curve of labour: on balance, the number of man-hours workers are willing to work may either rise or fall when a higher wage-rate is offered.

The demand for labour is usually said to depend on its marginal productivity (though, as will be seen presently, this is subject to an important qualification). If, at a given level of production, the addition to output would be greater than the real wage which would be paid to a unit of additional labour, it will pay firms to increase employment. As more man-hours are used, diminishing returns will cause the successive additions to total output (i.e. the marginal product of labour) to become smaller and smaller, since the additional labour is not accompanied by any increase in the quantities of other factors of production. When the level of employment has risen to the point at which the marginal product no longer exceeds the real wage, firms have no further incentive to increase the input of labour. At a given real wage, then, the most profitable level of employment, from the point of view of the enterprises which are employing the labour, is the number of man-hours at which labour's marginal product equals the wage-rate.[1] Because the marginal product falls as more labour is employed, the quantity of labour demanded will be greater, the lower the wage-rate; where the amount demanded is equal to the amount supplied, the market will be in equilibrium. Since the supply depends on the marginal disutility (conditioned, as has been seen, by the income effect), the equilibrium wage-rate will be equal both to the marginal product of labour and to the marginal disutility of labour.

---

[1] In symbols, the condition for profit maximization is

$$\frac{w}{p} = \frac{dQ}{dN}$$

where w/p is the real wage (W, i.e. the money-wage w divided by the price-level p) and the right-hand term represents the rate at which output is changing in response to the input of labour, i.e. the marginal product of labour. If this condition is maintained, the demand for labour may be stated as a function of the real wage, i.e. $D = N_d(W)$.

The argument is illustrated in Fig. 3. The demand curve for labour, DD, shows the amount of the marginal product at different levels of employment. The supply curve, SS, shows the value set by workers on the marginal disutility of labour at each level of employment. The intersection at Q shows the equilibrium of demand and supply, where N_2 man-hours are worked at an hourly wage-rate of W_2. The demand curve can occupy only the single position DD as long as the short-run assumptions of unchanging capital stock, given techniques and a fixed demand pattern are valid; the marginal product of labour is given by the slope of the curve $Q(N,\bar{K})$ in Fig. 1 (since the working of an extra man-hour will cause a movement along the $Q(N,\bar{K})$ curve by an amount equal to the addition to total output), and as long as $Q(N,\bar{K})$ is fixed in position, the curve DD in Fig. 3 must also be fixed. The supply curve SS will also be fixed in position as long as workers' preferences as between earnings and leisure remain unchanged. If the income-effect were very strong, it would make the supply curve slope downwards from left to right, so that it could conceivably occupy the same position as the demand curve DD: in that case, *every* level of employment would be an equilibrium level. Another possibility is that SS might be parallel with DD: if that were so, no equilibrium would be possible at *any* level of employment. Apart from such extreme cases, however, it appears that there will normally be only one position of equilibrium, which will be that of full employment; at wage-levels lower than W_2, demand will be in excess of supply, while at wage-rates higher than W_2 unemployment will exist in the sense that the supply of labour will exceed the demand for it.

The picture of the labour market presented in Fig. 3 may, however, be misleading in a number of ways. The first problem concerns the interpretation of the DD curve, which has so far been referred to as 'the demand curve for labour'. In the typical market of *micro*analysis, the demand curve normally indicates a straightforward causal relationship between price and quantity demanded; to increase or diminish the amount of a commodity people wish to buy, it is sufficient to lower or raise the price. But Fig. 3's DD curve cannot be read simply in this sense. For the demand for labour to be N_1, it is not enough that the real wage should be W_1; another condition must be fulfilled as well. With a fixed stock of capital equipment, and with given methods of production, there will be a unique relationship between the input of labour and the output of commodities, so that each level of employment is associated with a particular level of production as shown by the $Q(N,\bar{K})$ curve in Fig. 1 above. In deciding whether or not to employ a given number of man-hours,

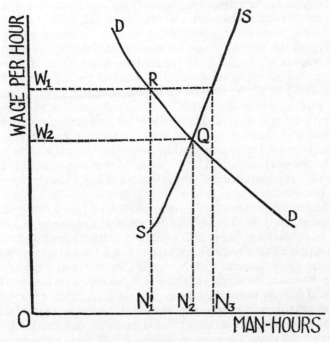

Fig. 3

firms will have to consider whether or not they can *sell* the resulting output. If they produce the exact quantity needed to satisfy demand (that is, if they are not prepared to accumulate unsold stock by producing more than they can sell, nor to run down existing stocks in the opposite case), their labour requirements will depend on what the volume of aggregate demand for their output happens to be: in symbols, $D_n = nD_g$ where D_g is the aggregate demand for commodities, D_n is the demand for labour, and n is the number of man-hours needed to produce a unit of output.[1] It follows that, for N_1 units of labour to be demanded, it is necessary for aggregate demand to be of exactly the right amount to absorb the output they produce, as well as for the hourly real wage to be W_1. If both these conditions are not satisfied simultaneously—for example, if the real wage happens to be W_2 when aggregate demand calls for the output of only N_1 man-hours—the implication is that supply is not matched

---

[1] The value of n (the inverse of the *average* product of labour) will, of course, be likely to vary with the level of output, as explained on pp. 73 above.

by demand in the market for commodities. Aggregate supply is the volume of output which firms would *like* to sell because it is most profitable; since profit is maximized when the marginal product of labour equals the real wage, the most profitable output when the real wage is W_2 is that which requires the employment of N_2 man-hours. But if aggregate demand is satisfied by the commodities produced by only N_1 man-hours, an excess of supply over demand will exist,[1] equal to the output of N_2-N_1. To eliminate this excess supply, the real wage and/or the level of aggregate demand must change until they are consistent with one another. Equilibrium can exist in the market for commodities only when the real wage is equal to the marginal product of labour at the level of employment needed to satisfy aggregate demand: the DD curve of Fig. 3 merely expresses this equilibrium condition.[2]

The second problem in the interpretation of Fig. 3 concerns the *results* of disequilibrium between the demand and supply of labour at a given real wage. Suppose, for example, that the aggregate demand and supply of commodities are balanced at a level of output which requires the employment of N_1 man-hours at a real wage of W_1. Here, however, the supply of labour is N_3, so that there is unemployment of N_3-N_1 man-hours. In the market for a single commodity, such a situation would cause the commodity's price to be forced down to the equilibrium level: sellers would underbid one another in the effort to sell more, the price reductions would elicit more demand, and the process would continue until supply and demand were balanced. It might seem reasonable to expect similar competitive forces to operate in the labour market, reducing the real wage from W_1 to W_2 and bringing about full employment at N_2 man-hours; but this would be a mistake, since it would not take full account of the significance of the DD curve. A fall in the real wage will certainly mean that firms *wish* to employ more labour, and therefore to supply

[1] This does not necessarily mean that firms will actually be producing the output which requires N_2 man-hours: they may, in fact, restrict output to the quantity they can sell, and employ only N_1. But at a real wage of W_2, they will certainly *wish* that the demand for commodities allowed them to produce and sell the output of N_2. To say that supply exceeds demand merely means that sellers *wish* to sell more than buyers are prepared to buy, whatever the *actual* level of production happens to be.

[2] Because the DD curve cannot be interpreted as showing that the demand for labour is determined solely by the level of real wages, some writers have urged that it is inappropriate and misleading to call it 'the demand curve for labour', and prefer to call it merely 'the marginal-product-of-labour curve'. See P. Davidson and E. Smolensky, *Aggregate Supply and Demand Analysis* (1964), pp. 175–7; and E. J. Mishan, 'The Demand for Labour in a Classical and Keynesian Framework', *Journal of Political Economy*, December 1964.

a larger quantity of commodities; however, unless the aggregate demand for commodities increases in step with supply, an expansion of output will merely result in an excess of supply over demand in the market for commodities, as a result of which the real wage is likely to be forced up again.[1] But there is no obvious reason why aggregate demand *should* increase by precisely the amount needed to maintain equilibrium. It is true that if firms expand output and employment to the level consistent with profit-maximization at W_2, incomes will rise by an amount equal to the additional output; but to keep aggregate demand equal to aggregate supply, the community would have to be willing to spend the *whole* of the addition to its income, however large that happened to be. In the previous chapter a hypothetical example was given[2] in which aggregate demand rose by only seven-tenths of any increase in income: if spenders were to behave in a similar way in the present case, it will not be possible to achieve a new equilibrium at the full-employment level of N_2 man-hours, because there would then be excess supply in the market for commodities. Further consideration of this question must be postponed until the relations between income and aggregate demand have been investigated in the next few chapters; for the time being, it must be noted that it is not possible for a disequilibrium in the labour market to be corrected without an appropriate change in the market for commodities.

In what has just been said, it was assumed that the existence of unemployment in a competitive labour market will normally exert downward pressure on the real wage. But it must be remembered that workers and employers bargain in terms of *money*-wages (w), whereas the *real* wage (W) is the money wage divided by the general price level of commodities (i.e. w/p). Excess supply in the labour market will cause w to fall, and if prices remain unchanged there will be an equivalent reduction in W. However, if firms respond to this by expanding output and employment to the point where W once again equals the marginal product of labour, and if the aggregate demand for commodities has not increased sufficiently to absorb this increase in supply, the resulting excess supply of commodities will cause the general price level to fall, thereby offsetting in whole or in part the original fall in money-wages; this will renew the original pressure on money-wages in the labour market, with the result that both commodity prices and money-wages continue to decline. An

---

[1] For example, if firms reduce their selling prices in the attempt to dispose of excess output, this will automatically raise the real wage again, since the latter is the money-wage divided by the average level of prices (w/p).

[2] On pp. 57–8 above.

important consequence of this will be to reduce the amount of money needed to effect the economy's purchases and sales, both in the labour market and in the market for commodities; if the amount of money in existence is not reduced, there will now be an imbalance between the supply of money and the demand for it, and the effects of this may be such as to alter the situation in the market for commodities—for example, by making it easier to borrow money and thereby stimulating aggregate demand. These possibilities, however, cannot be traced in detail until the monetary side of the economy has been examined; they do, however, provide yet another indication that the working of the labour market cannot be considered in isolation from the rest of the economy.

It was assumed earlier that the employment–output relationship was of the kind represented by the curve $Q(N,\bar{K})$ in Fig. 1, which holds true only during the 'short period' within which the stock of capital and the technique of production can be taken as fixed. As time passes, techniques will improve and capital will increase, so that any given level of employment will produce a larger and larger volume of commodities: the employment–output relationship will be changing in the way illustrated by the upward-shifting curves of Fig. 2. If employment is not to fall as productivity increases, aggregate demand must grow at an appropriate rate in order to absorb the increasing output; in addition, the real wage must change, if necessary, so as to remain equal to the marginal product of labour. How far the marginal product of labour will itself change depends on precisely what is happening to the employment–output relationship. The position and shape of Fig. 3's DD curve are determined not by the *height* of $Q(N,\bar{K})$ in Fig. 1, but by its *shape*: the marginal product, which in Fig. 3 is measured by the height of DD at any given level of employment, is indicated in Fig. 1 by the slope of $Q(N,\bar{K})$ above the corresponding point on the employment-axis. If $Q(N,\bar{K})$ shifts upwards in such a way that its slope remains unaltered along a good part of its length, the corresponding section of Fig. 3's DD curve will remain completely unchanged; although the *average* product of labour will have risen, the *marginal* product will be the same as before, so that the employment of (say) N_1 man-hours will still be consistent with a real wage of W_1. On the other hand, if $Q(N,\bar{K})$ rises in such a way that it becomes steeper at every level of employment, the DD curve will also rise and the real wage appropriate to any given number of man-hours will increase.

If the supply curve of labour retains the position and shape of the SS curve in Fig. 3, the upward-shifting DD curve will intersect it further and further to the right; to maintain full employment, the aggregate demand for commodities must grow faster than labour's productivity is increasing, so as to keep the demand for labour equal to the number of man-hours indicated by the rightward-moving intersection of SS and DD. However, it has already been argued that SS might, in fact, slope downwards from left to right because of the 'income effect'; in that case, full employment could be maintained even if the demand for labour were *diminishing* over time. It is also likely, of course, that the SS curve itself will shift as time goes by, due to population growth and to changes in workers' preferences which affect the marginal disutility of labour. The upshot of all these considerations is that the number of man-hours worked at full employment may either rise or fall as time passes, but that it is unlikely to remain constant; if it is public policy to keep employment full, avoiding both shortages and surpluses of labour, the policy-makers will find that they have to aim at a moving target.

(c) *Types of unemployment*

In the labour market described above, full employment appears to be (at any particular time) a precise quantity of labour (N_2) which could be calculated to the nearest man-hour if sufficient information were available regarding demand and supply. This, however, is the result of the assumptions which were made in the first instance; though useful in simplifying and sharpening the analysis, all of them do violence to the facts in greater or lesser degree, and when they are removed the concept of full employment becomes much less clear-cut. The next step, then, must be to see how the preceding argument is modified when the original assumptions are relaxed.

The first consequence is that the concept of a single labour market for the whole economy must be abandoned. In reality, workers are not perfectly mobile between places and between occupations; their labour is not homogeneous in the sense of being universally adaptable to all forms of production; it is therefore not legitimate to regard all types of labour as entering one general market. Instead, there are many separate markets, each with its own demand and supply curves: conditions in any one of them will no doubt be connected with those in others, but they are none the less distinct since each is dealing in a different commodity. Labour in the light engineering industry is clearly not the same thing as labour in coal mining; bricklayers, actors and solicitors' clerks are selling their services in quite separate markets; the man-hours available in Inverness cannot readily be added to the supply of labour at Merthyr Tydfil. Obviously, it goes against the facts to lump all these together by ignoring the differences between their products and the difficulties of moving labour from one industry or locality to another. But if the buying and selling of labour is regarded more realistically as taking place in a large number of separate markets, the earlier definition of full employment becomes ambiguous: it might mean *either* that employment is 'full' only when the demand and supply of labour are equal in each market individually, *or* that full employment exists when the *sum* of demands in all markets equals the sum of supplies, even though there may be an excess of supply over demand, or of demand over supply, in two[1] or more of the separate markets for particular types of labour. The first alternative, however, is impossibly restrictive. In the economy as it exists in real life, changes in production methods and in the demand for products are constantly altering the pattern of demand for labour, and workers are responding by moving from old industries into new ones and from one place to another; but the response naturally takes time, so that in each of the separate labour markets today's demand is faced with yesterday's supply. At any particular moment, the imperfect meshing of supplies and demands will cause some unemployment to exist, so that full employment in the first sense can never obtain; but as long as the margin of unemployment is matched by equivalent labour shortages elsewhere in the economy, employment can be 'full' in the second sense, and this is the meaning which is normally given to the term.

'Full' employment, thus defined, is therefore compatible with the existence of *some* unemployment, which is conventionally called 'frictional' to distinguish it from that which exists when employment is less than full. The latter type has been called[2] 'involuntary' unemployment, on the ground that no possible effort on the part of jobless workers can find employment for all of them when the *overall* demand for labour is less than the supply; since it arises from a failure of aggregate demand to match the output forthcoming when employment is full, it has also been called 'demand-deficiency' unemployment. The obverse of this is 'over-full' employment, which

---

[1] At least two, because the overall balance of supply and demand requires that excess supply in any of the separate markets must be exactly offset by excess demand elsewhere.

[2] Keynes, *General Theory*, pp. 15–16. It should be noted that the 'voluntary' unemployment which seems to be implied as the logical opposite of 'involuntary' is not the same as 'frictional' unemployment. The term has traditionally been applied to situations where some artificial restriction keeps employment lower than the level which would be established by competitive forces—for example, where trade-union action keeps wages so high that employers cannot afford to employ all who would be willing to work at those wages; or where there is an outright restriction on the number of new entrants into a given occupation.

occurs when the demand for labour exceeds the supply over the whole economy, so that the number of frictionally unemployed workers is less than sufficient to fill existing vacancies. The general criterion, then, is a comparison of the number of unemployed workers with the number of vacant jobs which employers are anxious to fill. If the former exceeds the latter, employment is less than full: if the latter is the greater, 'over-full' employment exists; if the two magnitudes are equal to one another, all unemployment is frictional and full employment prevails.

TABLE VI

Year and Quarter	Registered Unemployed (1)	Unfilled Vacancies (2)	'Excess Labour' (Column 1 minus Column 2)
		Thousands	
1966 ii	270·8	295·0	−24·2
1970 i	603·5	181·5	422·0
1972 iii	769·8	154·8	615·0
1973 iv	491·8	358·7	133·1
1974 ii	538·0	319·3	218·7
1975 iv	1,077·8	114·6	963·2

Some illustrative statistics are given in Table VI, which compares the numbers of unemployed with vacancies at various times.[1] The figures on all lines but the first suggest that employment was then less than full, since the filling of all vacancies would still have left a large number of people without jobs. In the first line, on the other hand, vacancies exceeded unemployed by a perceptible margin, so that 'over-full' employment may be supposed to have existed. It must be emphasized, however, that such figures provide only the roughest of guides. Not all vacancies are notified to the Department of Employment and Productivity; those which *are* notified may not always have the correct numbers set on them (e.g. an employer may ask for ten workers when he really wants six); and notifications are not always cancelled as soon as vacancies cease to exist. The

[1] The figures in the table are taken from the *Monthly Digest of Statistics*. Each of the quarterly figures is an average of the component monthly ones. It is to be noted that they refer only to Great Britain: the corresponding statistics for Northern Ireland are provided separately by the Northern Irish Department of Employment. In 1975, unemployment in Ulster averaged 42,000 and vacancies only 2,900; employment was less full in the United Kingdom as a whole than in Great Britain. The difference is not very great, but it represents an important problem for the people of Northern Ireland.

unemployment statistics, too, must be interpreted with caution: for reasons connected with the method of collection, they may sometimes underestimate the number of unemployed,[1] and in any case they refer only to those who have stopped work altogether, and take no account of short-time working; yet two employees putting in only half their normal hours represent as much unemployment as one who has been dismissed outright, and in certain situations widespread short-time working might mean a significant shortfall below the full-employment level.[2]

Another method of estimating whether full employment exists is to calculate the probable amount of frictional unemployment and compare the result with the number of workers actually unemployed at any time. Lord Beveridge adopted this method in 1944 in his *Full Employment in a Free Society*. He estimated that 1 % of the working population would be 'between jobs' at any particular time in the ordinary course of labour turnover;[3] another 1 % would be out of work because of seasonal variations in employment; and a further 1 % would be unemployed because of fluctuations in export industries[4]—giving a total of 3 % as the measure of 'frictional' unemployment in a situation of full employment. It should be noted that Lord Beveridge's percentages relate to the working population as defined for statistical purposes in the 1930s; but the current unemployment percentages published by the government since World War II relate to a working population defined on a wider and more inclusive basis,

[1] For a detailed description of the statistics of unemployment, vacancies and manpower generally, see E. Devons, *An Introduction to British Economic Statistics* (1958), Chap. III.

[2] The Department of Employment publishes monthly statistics of the numbers of operatives working short-time and of the hours they lost out of the 'normal' 40-hour week. But this information relates only to manufacturing industries and to firms with more than ten employees, so that it may well underestimate the full extent of short-time working. In the fourth quarter of 1975 the average number of workers on short-time was two millions, and their average weekly loss was about 13 hours, or just under a third of the 'normal' weekly hours; thus they can be regarded as equivalent to about 691,000 completely unemployed persons. Adding this to the number of unemployed shown in Table VI would have increased it by 64%.

[3] Lord Beveridge himself restricted the term 'frictional' to this category of unemployment—the word is given a wider meaning in the present text. See *Full Employment in a Free Society*, pp. 127–8 and pp. 408–9.

[4] It might be objected that this is a form of 'demand-deficiency' rather than 'frictional' unemployment, since the demand for exports is one of the main categories of aggregate demand. A fall in export demand, unaccompanied by a rise in demand elsewhere, may cause a reduction in the *total* demand for labour, whereas frictional unemployment (as defined in the text) is essentially a matter of mutually offsetting discrepancies between supply and demand, in a number of separate labour markets, within a context of *given* total employment.

so that a given *number* of unemployed represent a smaller percentage than in the pre-1948 period;[1] in terms of present-day statistics the Beveridge 3% should be amended to something in the region of 2½%. Even this figure, however, is higher than the actual percentage unemployed in many post-war years: from 1958 to 1964, for example, the average was 1·9%; in 1961, when vacancies and unemployed were approximately equal in numbers, it was 1·5%. Even in December 1975, when unemployment was 1,200,800 and vacancies 103,000, the unemployment percentage was still only 5·1%; during 1971–5 it has averaged 3·4%. It would seem that Lord Beveridge's percentage was an overestimate,[2] even when some allowance is made for the undoubted existence of over-full employment in some of the post-war years; but any attempt to assess the amount of frictional unemployment directly is likely to run into error, because the degree of friction depends on the structure of the economy and its labour force, and on the rate and direction of changes occurring within it—circumstances which are likely to alter with the passage of time and to vary between countries. If an industry with excess demand for labour can draw in workers lately dismissed from an 'excess supply' industry where their functions have been fairly similar to those they will now be required to perform, the transition should be easy and quick and little unemployment will arise. If, on the other hand, the 'excess demand' industry requires skills quite different from those lately practised by the unemployed, or if it is far removed geographically from the areas where the surplus labour happens to be, there will be a mass of '*structural*'[3] unemployment which will take some time to disappear; if the pace of economic development is such that the pattern of demand and output is constantly changing in fairly radical fashion, fresh numbers of 'structurally' unemployed workers[4] will be continually replacing those who

---

[1] See Devons, *op. cit.* pp. 72–3.

[2] In fairness to Lord Beveridge, it should be said that he regarded his estimate as 'a conservative, rather than an unduly hopeful, one'—implying that it might well turn out to be nearer 2% than 3%.

[3] 'Structural' unemployment is sometimes spoken of as though it were a different thing from frictional unemployment (e.g. Beveridge, *op. cit.*, pp. 409–10). In the text above, it is to be understood as a particular species of frictional unemployment, as defined earlier.

[4] Where workers are displaced through the introduction of labour-saving machinery, or as a result of new methods which raise productivity in other ways, they are sometimes said to be suffering '*technological*' unemployment. But this term must be received with caution, because it has been given several distinct senses in past usage; it has been made to mean

(a) frictional unemployment of the kind discussed above: workers are no

are at last finding work, and the volume of frictional unemployment may then be very considerable.

In some countries, indeed, there is no doubt that it is a more serious problem than demand-deficiency unemployment, because it is continuously fed by strong dynamic forces such as population increase, industrialization and rapid technological advance. A country setting out on the path of economic growth may develop what has been called a 'dual' economy[1] in which an 'advanced' sector, using modern plant and techniques, co-exists with a 'backward' sector where productive methods are still primitive and relatively little capital equipment is employed. To expand the advanced sector and reduce the backward sector may require widespread social as well as economic changes—the transformation of a peasantry into a mass of urban wage-earners, the supplanting of independent crafts by factory production, and so on. If, in addition, capital equipment in the advanced sector happens for technological reasons to have very rigid labour requirements of the 'one man, one machine' sort, it will not be possible to shift surplus labour from the backward sector into the advanced sector at a faster rate than that permitted by current capital formation;[2] unemployment may, as a consequence, be massive and chronic. On the definition given earlier, this may be entirely frictional: but to say that because there is no unemployment of the 'demand-deficiency' type[3] a state of full employment exists,

---

longer needed in the technically revolutionized industry, but there are vacancies elsewhere even though the workers' skills are unsuitable for them.

(b) demand-deficiency unemployment, which arises because aggregate demand fails to keep pace with rising productivity: new inventions cause $Q((N,\overline{K}_1)$ to rise to $Q(N,\overline{K}_4)$ in Fig. 2, demand fails to rise appropriately, and unemployment ensues.

(c) unemployment which results from a 'flattening' of the $Q(N,\overline{K})$ curve. If the new inventions change the shape of the employment-output relation so as to push to the left the point where diminishing returns begin, the demand curve for labour will fall. If *real* wages are 'inflexible' downwards (e.g. because trade unions resist reductions therein) there will then develop some unemployment of the type which pre-Keynesian writers would have called 'voluntary'.

[1] See V. C. Lutz, 'The Growth Process in a "Dual" Economic System', *Quarterly Review of the Banca Nazionale del Lavoro*, Sept. 1958; and in the same journal for Dec. 1959, L. Spaventa, 'Dualism in Economic Growth'.

[2] This was said to be the case in Italy in the 1950s. See Lutz, *op. cit.*

[3] In fact, there will probably be some of this in a 'dual' economy. Its absence would imply a tremendous pressure of excess demand on the advanced sector, which, if only it had the necessary capital equipment, would offer employment to the excess labour in the backward sector. But the lack of equipment prevents the advanced sector taking on more workers, and its output cannot increase quickly in response to demand; the result may be continuous price-increases in the advanced sector, giving an inflationary character to the whole economy in

would seem highly anomalous—so much so, that some writers have preferred to reserve the term 'frictional' for the relatively small margin of unemployment which it usually represents in advanced economies, and to speak of 'non-Keynesian'[1] unemployment in the case just described.

Whatever names are given them, and whatever their relative importance, the distinction between frictional and demand-deficiency unemployment must be kept clearly in mind when remedial measures are being considered. A government may attempt to eliminate the latter by doing what it can to increase aggregate demand. To do this as a cure for the former, however, would produce a situation in which the demand for labour would be in excess of supply in the economy as a whole if there were no demand-deficiency unemployment to start with; the pockets of unemployment in individual industries and localities would certainly be wiped out if the stimulus to aggregate demand were sufficiently large, but it would be at the cost of creating very great shortages of labour elsewhere and thus setting up severe inflationary pressures. Instead of stimulating expenditure, official policy should seek to remove the sources of friction so that the supply of labour adapts itself more quickly and easily to the pattern of demand for it. The action taken must depend on the nature of the blockage which prevents surplus labour in some fields from coming forward to meet shortages prevailing in others. The difficulty may be one of information, in that unemployed workers, though willing to seek jobs in other industries or towns, simply do not know (or take too long to find out) where the opportunities lie; here a system of employment exchanges can perform a useful service in bringing vacancies to the notice of the unemployed. Where it would be necessary for workers to move to another town or to enter another industry, facilities for relocation and retraining can be provided; something may be done, too, to obviate the necessity for relocating workers if the authorities have the power to control the location of industry. If seasonal unemployment is serious, it may be possible to provide off-season work, for example by persuading toy manufacturers to set up factories in seaside towns. In a 'dual' economy of the sort described above, the government may try to stimulate

---

spite of the unemployment in the backward sector. In these circumstances, the authorities might take action to reduce aggregate demand until the advanced sector is in equilibrium; but this would worsen demand-deficiency in the backward sector.

[1] For example, K. Kurihara, *The Keynesian Theory of Economic Development* (1959), Chap. 6. 'Keynesian' unemployment, by implication, is the 'demand-deficiency' unemployment with which the *General Theory* was chiefly concerned.

capital formation in the advanced sector so as to increase the rate at which it can absorb labour; it may also take action to increase the demand for labour in the backward sector, for example by fostering irrigation schemes to improve agricultural productivity.

To decide which kind of policy to adopt in a given situation, however, the authorities must first determine which type of unemployment exists—and, as has been seen, this is not easy. Indeed, there may even be some difficulty in actually identifying unemployment as such. For example, if a country has a large peasant agriculture, workers losing their jobs in the towns may return to their ancestral farms instead of registering themselves as unemployed; their families may accept them and let them share the farm work, even though there was previously no shortage of labour to do it; in extreme cases, they may add nothing at all to total agricultural output. Official statistics will then show a fall in industrial production but no increase in unemployment. The same thing could occur if craftsmen, shopkeepers and small businessmen were to bring unemployed relatives into their enterprises. Among the self-employed themselves, it may happen that lack of demand leaves them with little to do—but unless they actually give up their businesses and register themselves as seeking wage-employment, they will not be included in the statistics of unemployment. The importance of this 'disguised' unemployment depends, of course, on the economic and social structure of the country concerned; in Britain, where the great majority of the occupied population are urban wage- and salary-earners, it will obviously not be as great as in many countries overseas.[1] These considerations may serve to obscure the statistical picture for authorities seeking to discover the level of employment which is 'full' in the sense that aggregate demand for labour equals aggregate supply.

(d) Market imperfections and wage rigidity

Even this theoretical criterion of 'fullness' may, however, be far from clear in a modern economy. Not only will the labour market be

---

[1] Even in a predominantly industrial, wage-earning community, however, it may take the form of a diminution in the intensity of labour: workers may find ways of reducing productivity so as not to work themselves out of their jobs. The amount of 'disguised' unemployment will then equal the difference between the number of workers employed and the number who would have been needed if productivity had not been reduced.

Yet another form of 'disguised' unemployment may occur in conditions of general labour *shortage*: employers may not have work for skilled men to do, yet may be unwilling to discharge them in case they are unable to get them back later when they need their services. This is the phenomenon known as 'labour hoarding'.

divided into many separate ones, cut off from one another by the 'frictions' described above; the markets themselves may contain 'imperfections' which make it impossible to assume that the equilibrium number of man-hours bought and sold in each market must be that for which the marginal disutility of labour equals its marginal product. An individual worker may be ready to put in 50 hours a week at a given hourly wage-rate, but his factory may be open only 45 hours a week. Employers may be obliged, for technical reasons, to take on workers in groups of given size, so that there can be no close adjustment of marginal product to wage-rate. Firms are unlikely to have precise knowledge of the marginal productivity of labour; they will, no doubt, be led by the desire for profit to seek by trial and error the point where wage and marginal product are equal— but trial and error processes take time. Employers may not always be guided solely by the profit motive, but may retain certain workers on grounds of long service even though their productivity is low. Workers may be employed on a contractual basis which prevents their employers discharging them so as to reduce labour input. Even in the same occupation, man-hours are seldom homogeneous, and instead of a simple 'price of labour' in the shape of a uniform wage-rate, a great many trades have complicated provisions for overtime rates, production bonuses and the like. Above all, there is the fact that wages in many industries are determined, not by the interplay of competitive forces in free markets, but by the processes of collective bargaining between trades unions and employers, under which the latter agree not to pay less than an agreed 'standard rate' in the industry to which they belong.

Because such rates are defined in terms of pounds and pence, they appear to be minimum *money* wages, which will fall in real terms if the general price-level rises. But when this happens, unions normally try to negotiate fresh agreements by which standard rates are increased to offset the rise in prices, while in some industries the agreements contain 'escalator clauses' which automatically raise wage-rates in step with an index of prices; the effect is to maintain minimum rates of *real* wages in the industries concerned. Where their bargaining power is strong enough, unions may go further and attempt to raise standard rates in real terms by claiming increases which are more than enough to compensate for current price rises. If, on the other hand, the price level happens to be falling, a successful defence of the existing money wage will be enough to bring about a rise in the real wage. The choice between alternative union policies—i.e. whether to seek higher real wages or merely to maintain the existing real wage— depends on such factors as the size of a union's membership in relation to the whole labour force in its industry, and its estimate of the degree of resistance employers are likely to offer to fresh wage claims.

The implications of all this for the labour market can be seen, in highly simplified terms, in Fig. 3 on p. 81. It is assumed that there are no market imperfections other than those arising from the existence of trades unions, so labour is taken to be homogeneous and perfectly mobile; but workers are assumed to belong to a single large union which negotiates a standard money wage for all of them. Suppose that, at a given price level, this corresponds to the real wage rate W_1; since no labour can be taken on at a rate lower than this, the horizontal broken line at W_1 now replaces the part of the SS curve which lies below it. Firms can employ any number of man-hours they like, up to a maximum of N_3, at a real wage of W_1. If they want to employ more than N_3 man-hours, they will have to pay higher real wages[1] as indicated by the part of the SS curve which lies above W_1. On the other hand, if they want to use fewer man-hours than N_3, they cannot take advantage of the fact (shown by the part of SS below W_1) that there are some workers who, rather than be unemployed, are prepared to work for a real wage lower than W_1; the union will not allow anyone to be paid less than this. The effect of the wage-agreement, then, is to put a 'floor' into the market. Firms will now find that the most profitable level of output is that which is produced with N_1 man-hours, at which the marginal product of labour is equal to the real value of the standard wage; and if this happens to be the output which satisfies the aggregate demand for commodities, the demand for labour will be N_1, with the result that unemployment of $N_3 - N_1$ man-hours will exist. Here, however, it will not be possible for the excess supply of labour to push down the money-wage as it might be expected to do in a competitive market. It was suggested on p. 83–4 above that a fall in money-wages could have repercussions of a kind which might change the level of aggregate demand for commodities; in the present case, none of these consequential changes can occur, since the existence of the standard rate prevents the money-wage from falling in the first instance.

The fact that the standard rate is fixed in money terms means that the real wage will remain at W_1 only so long as prices do not alter. An upward movement of the price level will, of course, bring about a proportionate reduction in the real wage, causing it to fall to (say)

---

[1] This ignores the possibility that employers may have agreed among themselves not to pay *more* than the standard rate, treating the latter as a maximum wage in the same way that the union regards it as a minimum. In that case, employment could not exceed N_3 man-hours.

W_2; it will remain at this level unless the money-wage is automatically adjusted by the operation of an 'escalator clause', or until the union negotiates a new standard rate which is high enough to offset the price increase and restore the real wage to W_1. If the union is always very prompt in presenting the necessary wage claims, and if it continues to be strong enough to get them conceded quickly, the real wage W_1 will persist as the market 'floor' except during temporary lapses while negotiations are in progress.[1] With a more aggressive policy, and the strength to carry it out, the union will go further and push the real wage up to levels even higher than W_1; such levels could, of course, also be reached if prices were to fall and the union were successful in maintaining the existing money-wage.

It will be noticed in Fig. 3 that the real wage-rate W_2 is at the level of the intersection between the DD and SS curves. Here, the labour input which is most profitable to business firms is exactly equal to the amount of labour which workers are willing to supply; if, in addition, the aggregate demand for commodities is satisfied by the output produced by this number of man-hours, the labour market will be in equilibrium at full employment. However, reducing the standard wage in real terms to W_2 will not in itself suffice to bring about full employment, if the level of aggregate commodity demand remains inadequate; in this respect, the union-dominated labour market is exactly like the competitive market described earlier.

In the economy which exists in real life, wages are never so rigidly fixed as the foregoing discussion has assumed. Instead of a single all-inclusive union, there are many; plenty of workers do not belong to unions at all, and the unions which exist differ greatly in size and bargaining power. Though a few of them have a high degree of

---

[1] If the union leaders are under 'money illusion' (see p. 78, footnote 1, above), they will regard any rise in the standard money-wage as bringing an improvement in their members' livelihood, and think them no worse off as long as money-wages are not reduced; thus, a non-aggressive union would be content to leave the real wage at W_2 and would ignore the price increase which had forced it down from the original W_1 level. However, the fact that the real wage may at times fall to W_2 before the union has been able to negotiate a higher money-wage is not evidence of money illusion in the union's leadership. It should be noted that if the workers (as distinct from their leaders) harbour money illusion, the SS curve will be defined with reference to *money*-wages, and in Fig. 3 it will shift downwards when the price-level rises. If the union leaders, but not the individual workers, are under money illusion, the SS curve will stay put and the real value of the standard rate will shift down when prices rise. Keynes, writing in the depressed nineteen-thirties, seemed to suggest that both workers and unions entertained money illusion (though he did not himself use the term: see his *General Theory*, pp. 14–15), but experience in the more inflationary conditions since World War II suggests that few unions, in any country, are under money illusion nowadays.

control over money-wages and other conditions of work in the industries in which they operate, their influence on the average level of wages in the economy as a whole is necessarily diluted. If mass unemployment existed in all the labour markets of the economy, it is unlikely that the unions could prevent a downward movement of the overall level of money-wages, but they would certainly cause the movement to take place more slowly than it would otherwise have done; in this sense, they can be said to make money-wages 'sticky' or 'inflexible' in a downward direction.

For the purposes of the next few chapters, however, it will be convenient to assume that the inflexibility of money-wages is complete—i.e. that trades unions are strong enough to prevent even the slightest reduction in money-wages, no matter how much unemployment exists. It will also be assumed that the marginal product of labour is the same at all levels of employment likely to be reached, so that variations in the level of output will not cause changes in the prices at which firms are willing to sell their products.[1] The price-level will, of course, rise when aggregate demand becomes so great that even full-employment output is insufficient to satisfy it; but short of that, prices will remain constant as supply is adjusted to the level of demand. These are convenient assumptions to make when the determination of aggregate demand is being investigated, but they will be relaxed at a later stage of the analysis.

[1] Since a competitive firm's most profitable level of output is where $w/p = \text{MPL}$ (i.e. where the real wage equals the marginal product of labour), the price which will induce it to supply this output is $p = w/\text{MPL}$. If both w and MPL are constant, p will be constant also. A constant MPL means that the curve $Q(N,\bar{K})$ of Fig. 1 is a straight line through the origin (so that labour input and the output of commodities rise in the same proportion as employment expands); the DD curve of Fig. 3 will then be a horizontal line, implying that firms are ready to produce any output, up to the full-employment level, at the level of real wages (i.e. the ratio of money-wages to prices) indicated by the height of the line.

CHAPTER FIVE

Income and Consumption

(a) The Consumption Function

In Chapter Three, the short-period equilibrium of the economy was presented in terms of a balance between aggregate demand and output. Consumers, public authorities, capital-forming enterprises and export customers wish to spend money on goods and services; if the total amount, less the value of imports, equals the value at current market prices of the National Product, the economy is in equilibrium; if not, changes will occur in the physical quantity of output, or in the price-level, or in both. To explain why the economy is in equilibrium at a given level of National Product, it is necessary to examine the various components of aggregate demand, and to discover what causes them to be what they are. For reasons already indicated in Chapter Three,[1] it will be necessary to pay special attention to the level of income as a possible determinant of demand: in the case of each component, two questions must be answered. First, how important is the influence of income on demand, as compared with the strength of other forces? And if that influence is important, what exactly is its nature?

In the case of consumers' demand, these questions may be restated in terms of the concept of the 'consumption function'. This is simply a name for the general income-consumption relationship.[2] Just as a demand curve shows what quantity of a commodity will be demanded at each possible price, so the consumption function shows what expenditure consumers will wish to make on consumers' goods and services at each possible level of income. In Fig. 4 the function is represented by the curve CC, from which it can be seen that if income is OA, consumers will wish to spend OL; if income is OB, they will wish to spend OM; for all levels of income, the curve shows what consumers' demand will be. As drawn in the diagram, CC shows that

[1] See pp. 56–8 above.
[2] Keynes originally called it 'the propensity to consume' (*General Theory*, p. 90), but subsequent usage has established the term 'consumption function' in its place.

if income is nil, consumers' expenditure is *OC*—instead of starving at zero income, they draw on past savings, borrow, sell property and so on in order to buy consumer goods; also, the fact that *CC* is a straight line implies that as income rises, consumers' demand increases by an amount which always bears the same proportion to the increase in income, whatever the size of the increase and whatever the original income-level. Whether this is a correct representation of consumers' preferences, however, is a question of fact, on which evidence must be sought; there are very many conceivable shapes

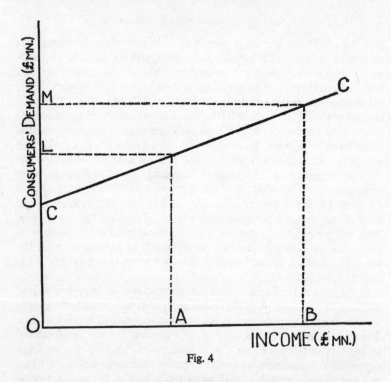

Fig. 4

which the consumption function could take. Two further possibilities are shown in Figs. 5 and 6. In Fig. 5 *OC* is a straight line starting at the origin of the diagram; this implies that consumers spend more as income rises, but always spend the same proportion of income however large or small it may be. The broken line marked '*Y = C*' shows the position *OC* would occupy if consumers' expenditure were always 100% of income; the fact that *OC* slopes less steeply than the broken line implies that the proportion of income consumed is always less than 100%. In Fig. 6 a completely different pattern of behaviour is shown by the curve $C_1C_2C_3$: consumers make a minimum expenditure OC_1, even when income is zero, and this level of consumption remains the same so long as income is not greater than OY_1. At higher income-levels, consumption rises as income rises, but by less than the increase in income; the diminishing slope of the curve between C_2 and C_3 implies that the proportion of income consumed falls progressively as income rises.

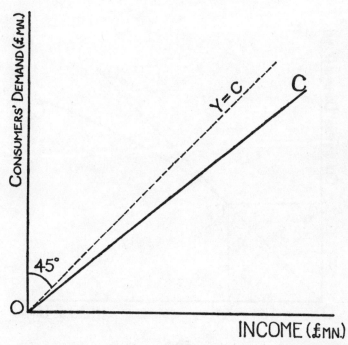

Fig. 5

To ask—as did the second of the questions posed earlier—what is the nature of the relationship between income and consumption, is therefore to ask what is the shape and position of the consumption function. Whatever the answer, however, it would still leave in the air the first of the original questions, i.e. how strong is the influence of income on consumers' demand? Even if the consumption function is correctly evaluated, it does not imply that income is necessarily the main determinant; its influence might be submerged under those of other, stronger forces. Diagrams such as Figs. 4, 5 and 6 are drawn on the assumption of '*ceteris paribus*'; the relationship between income and consumption is the only one considered, and every other possible influence on consumption is held constant. But if, for example, interest rates were known to be much more powerful than income in determining consumers' demand, it would be necessary to show a separate consumption curve for each possible level of interest; instead of a single curve, like *CC* in Fig. 4, there would be a

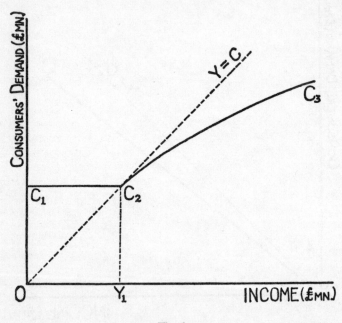

Fig. 6

family of curves. In such a case, the 'other things equal' assumption could not reasonably be made, and the consumption function would have little importance; the direct relationship between interest rates and consumption would take priority as an object of investigation. To justify the use of the consumption function, therefore, it is important to produce evidence to show that income is, if not the sole determinant of consumers' demand, at least the most important of the many factors which can be held to influence it.

(b) *Properties of the Function: the Marginal Propensity to Consume*

So far, then, the consumption function is merely a piece of theoretical apparatus, an 'empty' concept waiting to be filled with a content of fact. Before proceeding, however, it will be useful to note some further aspects of the concept as such.

(i) The relationship is normally presented in terms of *real* income and *real* consumption; the amounts measured along the axes of Figs. 4, 5 and 6 are 'at constant prices'. Consumers may be expected to respond differently to a rise in income, depending on whether or not it is accompanied by a rise in the price-level; if a simultaneous doubling of both income and prices leads consumers to double their spending, while a doubling of income at unchanged prices causes them to raise expenditure by only 75%, it is not possible to describe both reactions by a single curve such as CC in Fig. 4. Unless prices are assumed to remain unchanged, the horizontal axis will be attempting to measure not one independent variable, but two—real income *and* the price-level; to avoid confusion, the latter must be removed to the '*ceteris paribus*' bag. This is not to say that consumers' decisions will remain unaffected by price-changes, but rather that the effects should be investigated separately from those of changes in real income.

(ii) The relationships shown in Figs. 4, 5 and 6 can be expressed as equations, using the notation of Chapter Three; this is sometimes more convenient than diagrammatic representation. The equation of CC in Fig. 4 is $C = a+bY$, where C stands for consumers' demand, Y for income, and a and b are constants. For example, if a were £100 millions and b were 0·8 the equation would mean that consumers wish to spend £100 millions even when income is zero; when they *are* receiving income, they wish to spend four-fifths of it in addition to the basic £100 millions. Thus, if income were £1,000 millions, consumers' demand would be £100 millions *plus* 0·8 × £1,000 millions—i.e. £900 millions. The a of the equation is the amount measured on the consumption-axis at the point where CC cuts the axis, and b is the slope of CC. The equation of OC in Fig. 5 is simpler; because OC starts from the origin of the diagram, there is no a; in this case, $C = bY$, where b is a constant equal to the slope of OC. The curve $C_1C_2C_3$ in Fig. 6 is less easy to put into equation form, because the part between C_1 and C_2 is not a smooth continuation of the part between C_2 and C_3. For the horizontal section where income is equal to, or less than, C_1, consumption is of a fixed amount; in symbols, $C = a$ when $Y \leqslant a$. Where income exceeds a, consumption rises, but at a diminishing rate; because the slope of

C_2C_3 is not constant, the equation cannot be 'linear' (i.e. giving a straight-line relationship) but takes a rather more complicated form, such as

$$C = a + b\sqrt{Y-a} \qquad\qquad (Y>a).$$

Here, if a were 100 and if b were 2, income of 150 would give rise to consumers' demand of about 114; $Y = 200$ gives $C = 120$; $Y = 250$ gives $C = 124$ approximately; and so on.

(iii) Sometimes it is less important to ascertain the general income-consumption relationship than to discover how consumers respond to a given *change* in income; the concept then required is the '*Marginal Propensity to Consume*' (hereafter abbreviated to MPC), which is the ratio between a change in consumers' demand and the change in income which brings it about. In symbols, it is $\frac{\Delta C}{\Delta Y}$, where '$\Delta$' stands for a change in the quantity it precedes.[1] If an increase of £10 millions in income is accompanied by an increase of £8 millions in consumers' expenditure, the MPC is $\frac{8}{10}$ (or 0·8). If the change in income is extremely small, the MPC is the slope of the consumption function at a given point. Where the function is a straight line, as in Figs. 4 and 5, the MPC has the same value along the whole length of the line; in the equations of these curves ($C = a + bY$ and $C = bY$), it is equal to the constant b. Where the function is non-linear, as in the right-hand section of Fig. 6's $C_1C_2C_3$, the MPC varies with the level of income, and its value is different at every point along the curve; in the corresponding equation there is no single term which represents it.

(iv) The consumption function implies a '*saving function*'. Since saving is the part of income not consumed,[2] a decision to consume (say) three-quarters of income is also a decision to save one-quarter. In the diagrams given earlier, a 'saving curve' can be deduced by subtracting from each level of income the consumption indicated by the consumption function. The equations of the curves can be adapted by putting $S = Y - C$; for example, where $C = a + bY$, $S = Y - C = Y - a - bY$ or $S = Y(1-b) - a$. Here, $(1-b)$ is the *Marginal Propensity to Save* (MPS): the MPS always equals 1 − MPC, and is symbolized as $\frac{\Delta S}{\Delta Y}$. When convenient, therefore, all proposi-

---

[1] It is the 'Δ' which makes the MPC *marginal*. $\frac{C}{Y}$ can be called the *average* propensity to consume—the proportion of *all* income which is spent on consumption.

[2] This statement, of course, assumes appropriate definitions of income and consumption. See above, pp. 58–60.

tions about consumption may be translated into propositions about saving.

(c) The logic of consumer behaviour

Is the consumption function, thus defined, a useful concept? As already noted, this depends on whether income is the main determinant of consumers' demand; if it is, it is worth inquiring what the shape of the function is likely to be. On these questions, evidence is needed, and to see what is relevant, it will be convenient to start by considering the individual consumer.

In the ordinary microeconomic theory of consumer behaviour, the individual is endowed with a certain sum of money with which he can buy various commodities at given prices; he decides what quantities to purchase by comparing the satisfactions to be derived from them. The more he has of a particular good, the less will a further £1's worth add to his total satisfaction, and eventually a point will be reached where an extra £1 spent on the good will give less satisfaction than if it were spent on something else. If his expenditure on each commodity stops short at this point, he will be obtaining 'equi-marginal' returns: the last £1 spent on any one good will bring the same satisfaction as the last £1 spent on any other, and he could not switch expenditure from one good to another without a net loss of satisfaction. Such a distribution of resources will maximize the consumer's satisfaction, and this is the pattern of expenditure which he will choose if he is (as he is assumed to be) a rational person trying to satisfy his wants as fully as possible.

On this principle, an individual's decision to leave some resources unconsumed is to be explained in terms of the satisfaction he obtains from so doing. If he could spend £100, but buys only £75 worth of goods for immediate consumption, it is because a 76th £1's worth of consumption would give less satisfaction than the 25th £1 of 'sparing' (as the non-consumption of resources may be called: 'saving' is appropriate only if the consumer has nothing but his current income to spend). The object of sparing may be to postpone consumption to a time when unusual needs are foreseen, or when resources would otherwise be inadequate—next summer's holidays, marriage and old age are obvious examples; or the object may be one which does not necessarily envisage future consumption, as with a man who spares in order to bequeath property to his heirs, or to build up a reserve for emergencies. Achieving these aims by sparing satisfies present wants; in addition, the individual will obtain satisfaction from any income accruing from his unconsumed resources—for example, he will receive interest if he continues to hold bonds instead of selling them to finance consumption. In allocating his resources, then, he must balance the satisfaction from sparing against that derived from consumption in such a way as to get equi-marginal returns.[1] Exactly where the balance will be struck depends partly on the individual's temperament—if he is of a thrifty disposition, he will no doubt spare more than a less provident person; on his family circumstances—a *paterfamilias* must consider his dependents' consumption wants as well as his own; and on his age, since this determines the 'time-horizon' in his plans for future consumption. The balance will also depend on the amount of the individual's resources: the smaller they are, the larger the proportion he will consume; the greater they are, the greater the proportion of sparing.

This follows from the obvious fact that some minimum of consumption is necessary to sustain life. If an individual can afford only this minimum, he would be acting irrationally were he to spare anything at all, unless he is ready to die of starvation in order to bequeath to his heirs; there would be no point in providing for his own future consumption if he could not survive to enjoy it. Up to the level of resources needed for minimum subsistence, there can thus be no question of sparing; but as the level rises, enabling the individual to consume more if he wishes, the satisfaction obtained from consumption will rise more and more slowly relatively to the expenditure on it, until a point is reached where £1 of sparing gives more satisfaction than an additional £1 of consumption; thereafter, additions to the individual's resources will be divided between consumption and sparing in proportion to the additional satisfactions afforded by them.[2] It is conceivable that when the individual's resources reach some very high level, *all* his consumption wants will be completely satisfied, so that further expenditure on consumption would be pointless; additional sparing, on the other hand, will always give *some* satisfaction—a man can provide for still larger bequests to his

---

[1] For a more rigorous account of this logic of choice, see W. J. L. Ryan, *Price Theory*, pp. 180–96.

[2] The individual will still be devoting a larger proportion of his *total* income to consumption than to sparing; if he had to choose between consuming *all* his income and sparing all of it, he would choose consumption because the satisfaction given by the (say) 50th £1 of consumption (when no sparing is done) must be greater than that from the 50th £1 spared (when no consumption is taking place). This is the idea behind Irving Fisher's concept of 'time preference', defined as the proportionate 'excess of the present marginal want for one more unit of *present* goods over the *present* marginal want for one more unit of *future* goods' (*The Theory of Interest* (1930), p. 62). The argument in the text above implies that time preference varies according to the level of the individual's resources.

children, or build up a still larger reserve. At this point, all additional resources will be spared and none consumed; the proportion of *total* resources spared will be high. As the level of resources rises from the minimum-subsistence level, at which no sparing is done, towards the very high level just mentioned, it seems that the proportion spared must increase; obversely, the proportion of resources consumed will fall as resources increase.

This is not to say that the proportions will always change *steadily* with the level of resources. There may be ranges of resource-levels over which the proportions change hardly at all; alternatively, they may change sharply at certain points. Between the two extreme positions of minimum subsistence and the complete saturation of consumption wants, there is for most people an intermediate level of consumption—the 'normal standard of living' to which they are accustomed. It is common experience that cutting consumption a little below the normal standard causes a loss of satisfaction very much greater than the gain from an equal increase above it; so the attractions of consumption, relatively to those of sparing, will be high when resources are only sufficient to procure the normal standard, and will decrease sharply when the level of resources rises above this critical level; the ratio of consumption to resources will be 'kinked' at this point. But standards can be changed: given time, an individual can get used to a lower or higher consumption norm if some change in his circumstances makes it necessary; the influence of this factor will be greater in the short run than in the long.

(d) The consumer's assets and liabilities

An individual's expenditure on consumption, then, will depend on his temperament, his family circumstances, his age and his total resources; there is an *a priori* expectation that his consumption will rise with the level of resources, but in such a way that it takes a smaller proportion of them the larger they are. This relationship, however, is not the consumption function defined earlier, since the latter relates consumption not to resources but to income, and there may be a considerable difference between the two. As well as his income, the individual may have a stock of money on which he can draw; he may have made loans which he can call in; he may possess bonds and shares, or physical assets such as house property, which can be sold to finance consumption.

Where such sales might be necessary, the price the assets would fetch is important: if they would have to be offered much below their original cost to attract buyers, their owner may be disinclined to reckon them among his resources when deciding how much to consume. Other non-money assets may not be realizable at all for the time being: for example, where a loan has been made for a specified period, it will not be possible to 'call' it before the period ends, and in the meantime the lender may not be able to raise money by getting someone else to take his place as creditor; such assets cannot be used to finance consumption until they mature. Because of this, the individual's consumption decisions may be influenced less by his *total* assets than by the part which is 'liquid'—that is, which can be turned into money quickly without loss. However, liquidity is not an 'all-or-nothing' quality, but one which assets may possess in different degrees; and, as will be seen, it is a quality which may vary with circumstances, so that the same assets may have greater liquidity at some times than at others. This makes it difficult to divide an individual's assets neatly into liquid and illiquid parts.

Even if they were so divided, it would be unwise to assume that illiquid assets do not influence consumption decisions at all: for example, the owner of a house may find it hard to sell quickly without loss, and will thus not count its value among his consumable resources—but the fact of possessing a house eliminates the need to save up to buy one, so that he may consume more than he would otherwise have done. If this is true of house ownership, it must also apply to other 'consumer capital': a man who already has a car, a television set and a houseful of furniture will consume more than one whose income and liquid assets are the same but who owns none of these things. However, the inclusion of consumer durables among the individual's assets means that the purchase of new ones must not be counted as part of his consumption expenditure: only the part of their value consumed during the year (i.e. their depreciation) can be regarded as consumed, the remainder being counted as saving—a procedure not followed in the official statistics of consumption.[1]

Against the individual's assets must be set his liabilities. He may have borrowed money by outright loan in the past; he may be buying a car on hire purchase, or a house on mortgage; he may have unpaid bills outstanding. The greater his liabilities the less he can spend on consumption. Just how much less, however, depends on the nature of the liabilities: if a debt need not be repaid for many years, the debtor need not for the moment set aside funds for repaying it, and may devote all his resources to consumption if he so wishes; but if repayment is just falling due, he must divert the whole amount from resources which would otherwise have been available for consumption. The latter kind of debt may be called 'liquid', the former

[1] See above, p. 18.

'illiquid'; the greater the liquidity of an individual's liabilities, the more they will restrict his ability to spend on consumption.

If liabilities are deducted from assets (all appropriately valued, and weighted according to their liquidity) the result is the individual's 'net assets' or 'net worth': this amount, along with his income, is available for consumption if he wishes it. But this need not be the limit of his resources. He may, in addition, be able to count on credit if he should require it: he may know that his bank would lend him up to (say) £500, or that he could buy goods up to a certain value on hire purchase, or that he could run up a bill with his grocer. The ability to borrow allows him to anticipate future income; instead of gradually accumulating funds by saving, he can obtain money now and earmark the future saving for repayment of the loan. Even where the loan must be secured by an existing asset, his power to consume will be increased if he offers an illiquid asset as security: the overall liquidity of his assets will be increased thereby. Anything which increases the individual's borrowing power (such as a general extension of hire-purchase facilities, or a bank's more generous assessment of his credit-worthiness) will thus increase his ability to consume and may lead him to spend more on consumption.

The remainder of the individual's resources is his income. But not all of this can be counted on to finance consumption: income-tax payments, for example, remove some of it out of his reach. For this purpose, it is *disposable*, rather than total, personal income which must be brought into account. If he is paying interest on past borrowings, these payments should also be deducted, leaving 'discretionary' income (as defined above on p. 35); however, if his 'consumer durables', such as his car, are being treated as assets which by their services give him income in kind, and if those durables were originally bought with borrowed money, the interest thereon must not be deducted from income, since it will be, in effect, a pre-committed consumption expenditure which is 'buying' the services of the durable assets.

The consumer's total resources, then, are his net assets *plus* his borrowing power *plus* his disposable income: the greater the total of these, the greater his consumption expenditure, as shown in Fig. 7. Here, total resources are measured along the horizontal axis OR, consumption on the vertical axis OC; the relation between them is given by the line $OC_1C_2C_4$, whose shape implies that consumption increases less than proportionately with resources above subsistence level C_1 (as was argued in the previous section). If the consumer has net assets *plus* borrowing power equal to OA_1, and income A_1Y_1, his consumption will be LY_1. The *consumption function* is that part of

$OC_1C_2C_4$ which lies to the right of A_1, i.e. C_2C_4; if the vertical axis were A_1C' instead of OC, the part of the diagram to the right of A_1C' is the same as Fig. 4 on p. 98. An increase in non-income resources to OA_2 will push the consumption function's axis to the right so that it becomes A_2C''; the consumption function itself is now C_3C_4 instead of C_2C_4; with the same income $(A_2Y_2 = A_1Y_1)$ the individual is now spending more on consumption than before— Y_2M instead of Y_1L. If the new consumption function C_3C_4 were to be plotted against the original vertical axis A_1C', it would appear to

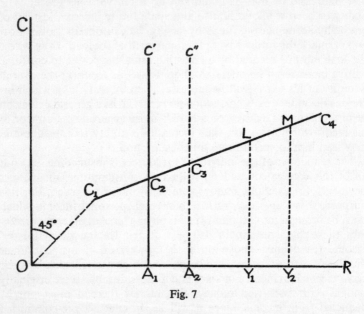

Fig. 7

have shifted upwards because of the rise in the consumer's non-income resources. Similarly, a fall in non-income resources will cause the consumption function to shift downwards. A rise in income itself (e.g. from A_1Y_1 to A_1Y_2) will, of course, merely move the consumer *along* the original consumption function (i.e. from L to M) if no change in other resources has occurred at the same time.

To treat income as the main determinant of consumers' demand, by focusing attention on the consumption function, is to imply that the influence of non-income resources can usually be left out of account, either because they are small relatively to income or because they do not change very much. Some relevant evidence is contained in the Savings Surveys made by the Oxford Institute of Statistics in

1952–5.[1] The 1953 Survey found[2] average net assets per 'income-unit'[3] to be about £800, which was 185% of the average income (£434). But *liquid* assets per income-unit were only £194—a quarter of total assets and 45% of average income; the largest item among assets was owner-occupied houses, averaging two-fifths of the total. Moreover, asset ownership was highly concentrated—a mere 3% of income-units owned almost half the total of net assets, while 35% had either no net assets or had net liabilities. One-third of all income-units had no *liquid* assets at all; almost half of those with incomes below £400 p.a. had none. It would seem that for the majority of consumers in Britain in the early 1950s, the influence of net assets on consumption decisions must have been slight compared with that of income; though it must be remembered that the figures just quoted do not include estimates of the income units' borrowing power, which must undoubtedly have increased later in the 1950s because of the growth of hire purchase facilities.

For the minority of consumers whose net assets are substantial, however, changes in their value and liquidity may be important: the causes and effects of such changes will be examined in later sections. But first another question must be considered.

(e) Lags, expectations and experience

In the foregoing account of the consumer's resources, the 'income' which was included was his *current* income, i.e. that which accrues during the same period in which his consumption spending is done. But most people receive their incomes in arrears—wage-earners at the end of the week, shareholders at the end of the half-year, and so on. Obviously, money cannot be spent until it has been received: if it is last week's wages which the wage-earner is spending this week, should not the consumption function relate the consumption of a given period to the income of the preceding period?

It is true that an individual who cannot borrow, and who cannot realize other assets, cannot spend more than the income received at the end of the last period. But to say that current consumption is *limited* by last period's income is not to say it is *determined* by it; this is a constraint, not a causal relationship. During the period, the

---

[1] For the results of the 1952 Survey, see H. F. Lydall, *British Incomes and Savings*; for subsequent Surveys, see the Oxford University Institute of Statistics *Bulletin*, 1953–8.

[2] K. H. Straw, 'Consumers' Net Worth', OUIS *Bulletin*, February 1956.

[3] An 'income-unit' is a single person over 18 or a married couple considered jointly.

individual's income accrues in the form of debt owed to him by someone else (e.g. his employer in the case of a wage-earner); at the end
of the period the debt is liquidated by a cash payment. If he knows
that his income is accruing at a higher rate than in the previous
period, he may very reasonably decide to spend more on consumption because his resources are increasing; in that event, it will be the
amount of his current, not last-period, income which has determined
his consumption. He may be prevented from consuming as much as
he wants by the fact that his resources include too little cash and too
much credit, but this is a matter of the *composition* of his resources,
not their total amount. If he is, after all, assumed to be able to
borrow, there need be no difficulty: for example, he can run up bills
with his grocer and other suppliers to be settled at the end of the
period when his income is paid to him in cash.

The presence of an income-payment lag, then, does not mean that
consumption decisions are necessarily determined by last-period
income. Nevertheless, past income *may* influence current consumption in another way. The individual may not know what his current
income is (shareholders, for example, must wait for dividend
announcements to know what their shares have earned); he may
therefore proceed on the assumption that it will be the same as in the
previous period, and decide his consumption accordingly. Alternatively, he may take an average of the incomes received in the last five
or six periods; or he may add to last period's income the average
increase over the last few periods; whatever his procedure, he will be
using past experience as a means of estimating present income. Even
if he does know his current income, he may wish to compare it with
those accruing in past periods in order to decide whether it is unusually high or low. Should it seem abnormally high, he may think it
unwise to increase consumption to a level he may not be able to sustain; if it is abnormally low, he will not reduce consumption if he
expects that his income will soon regain its normal level. In this case
the individual will be deciding his consumption in the light not of
current income but of some estimate of 'normal' income based on
past experience.

His consumption may also be influenced by expectations as to
what his income will be in the future. If he has reason to think it will
be larger (for example, because he expects promotion in his job, or
because he is on a 'laddered' salary scale), he may consume more
than if he expected it to continue at its present level. If he takes a
really long view, he will look ahead to prospective income during the
rest of his working life, and try to arrange his consumption so that it
is smoothed out over his life-span in the most satisfactory way. This

is, indeed, the '*Life-cycle Hypothesis*' of F. Modigliani and R. Brumberg,[1] who argue that consumption in any period is 'a facet of a plan which extends over the balance of the individual's life, while the income accruing within the same period is but one element which contributes to the shaping of such a plan'. Milton Friedman[2] proceeds on similar lines in his '*Permanent Income Theory*': actual, or 'measured', income y may differ from normal, or 'permanent', income y_p by what Friedman calls 'transitory income' y_t; consumption also has 'permanent' and 'transitory' components c_p and c_t, the former being the individual's normal expenditure, the latter that arising from unforeseen contingencies; while c_p is causally determined by y_p, there is no such relationship between c_t and y_t (either or both of which may be negative). Thus, a rise in current income will affect permanent consumption only if it causes the individual to revise his estimate of *permanent income*.

The Friedman and Modigliani-Brumberg theories have not so far received full empirical confirmation, nor have they been generally accepted[3]; but they are at least instructive in showing possible ways in which consumer decisions may be affected by expectations as well as by current income.

(f) Changes in the price-level

The consumption function was defined above (p. 101) in terms of *real* income and consumption, not in terms of money values which may alter solely because of price changes. Since National Product is necessarily equal in value to National Income, a rise in prices must increase both in the same proportion; it may seem, therefore, that a 10% rise in the general price-level will give consumers 10% more money income to spend on commodities which are 10% dearer on the average, so that they may be expected to consume the same *proportion* of income as before, leaving the situation unchanged in real

[1] F. Modigliani and R. Brumberg, 'Utility Analysis and the Consumption Function', in *Post Keynesian Economics* (ed. K. Kurihara, 1955).

[2] M. Friedman, *A Theory of the Consumption Function* (1957).

[3] Obviously, the 'permanent' income-consumption relationship cannot be directly tested against statistics of actual income and consumption. Also, both Friedman and 'M–B' assume the relationship to be independent of the level of income, i.e. to be like that shown in Fig. 5 (p. 99): though not an integral part of the theories, this has been much criticized. See Friend and Kravis, 'Consumption Patterns and Permanent Income', in *Papers and Proceedings* of the American Economic Association, May 1957; articles by Friend, Klein and Liviatan, and Tobin and Watts in 'Savings Behaviour: A Symposium', OUIS *Bulletin*, May 1957; and M. J. Farrell, 'The New Theories of the Consumption Function', *Economic Journal*, December 1959.

terms. Nevertheless, price-changes may affect consumers' decisions in a number of ways.

To begin with, a change in the general price-level is unlikely to involve an equal proportionate change in the price of each single commodity: for example, food prices may rise only 5% while clothing prices rise 15%. If consumers react by buying less clothing (because it is relatively, as well as absolutely, dearer) but go on buying the same quantity of food (even though it is relatively cheaper), total consumption will have fallen in real terms.

Secondly, a change in National Income does not necessarily mean an equal change in personal disposable incomes. When prices rise, firms receive more money for the commodities they produce: but they may retain it (for the time being, at any rate) as undistributed profits, so that it does not get into the hands of personal consumers. Even if it all passes into personal incomes, the recipients may find themselves pushed into higher 'tax brackets' under a system of progressive income taxation; disposable income will then rise by a smaller percentage than the rise in National Income. When prices fall, these effects will of course be reversed.

Thirdly, changes in the general price-level will give rise to what has been called[1] the 'Pigou effect' or 'real-balance effect'. Individuals who possess money balances will feel worse off when prices rise, and better off when prices fall, because of the change in the real value of their money. When prices fall, the effect is the same as if their money balances had increased while prices remained the same: with greater real resources, they will now spend a higher proportion of income on consumption. The same considerations apply to individuals holding assets such as bonds, which entitle the holders to interest fixed in money and to a fixed sum on redemption. On the other hand, those who have contracted fixed-interest debts in the past will now find that the real burden of their obligations has increased, and may reduce consumption accordingly; if all the fixed-interest assets owned by consumers were the liabilities of other consumers, the higher consumption of creditors may be offset by the reduced consumption of debtors and the net effect of the fall in prices would be nil. But the most important single debtor in the community is not an individual at all: it is the State. If the government does not alter its behaviour in response to the fall in prices, the increased consumption of its creditors will not be cancelled out by a reduction in anyone else's. Companies, too, are fixed-interest debtors, whose creditors

[1] The terms were coined by D. Patinkin, in 'Price Flexibility and Full Employment', *American Economic Review*, 1948, and *Money, Interest and Prices* (1st edition, 1956) p. 21.

(i.e. the owners of their debentures) may raise their consumption when the price-level falls; but because lower prices will have reduced the money value of firms' turnover and profits, the necessity to pay the same amount of debenture interest as before may induce companies to cut dividends by a greater proportion than that in which prices have fallen, which will lead to a reduction in shareholders' consumption—and this will offset the increased expenditure of debenture-holders. If, however, companies were to maintain the level of dividends unchanged in real terms,[1] there would be no such offset, and the rise in debenture-holders' consumption could be included along with that of the owners of government securities and money balances as a consequence of the fall in prices. If the community's real income is assumed to have remained unchanged, the consumption function will have been shifted upwards.[2] Conversely, a rise in the price-level, by reducing the real value of money balances and of fixed-interest assets, will push the function down. The strength of this 'Pigou effect' will depend on the proportion which such assets bear to the total of consumers' resources; it has been suggested earlier (p. 109) that for most consumers this proportion is probably small, so that for the community as a whole the effect is unlikely to be very important.

Finally, changes in the price-level may set up expectations of further movements in the same direction. A fall in prices, for example, may lead consumers to expect further reductions, and so to postpone some consumption in the hope of getting more for their money later on; the consumption function will be shifted downwards. Conversely, the expectation of rising prices may cause consumption to increase, and the consumption function will be pushed up. These expectational effects of price-changes work in the opposite direction to the 'Pigou effect', and will tend to neutralize it.

(g) The influence of interest rates

A rise in interest rates makes lending more remunerative; if this induces consumers to save a higher proportion of income so as to have more to lend, the consumption function will shift downwards. Conversely, a fall in interest rates will reduce the attractions of saving-and-lending, and the consumption function will move upwards.

---

[1] This would, of course reduce their undistributed profits in real terms, and they might reduce their demand for investment in consequence. But this is by no means certain: they might decide to maintain their original investment plans and to finance them by borrowing.

[2] See above, p. 108 and Fig. 7.

But will consumers necessarily react in this way? If an individual wishes to secure income of a fixed amount in future, a rise in the rate of interest will enable him to do so by lending *less* than before, and the proportion of income he consumes may therefore increase rather than diminish. It is conceivable that the increased consumption of people who behave like this ('Sargant men' as Sir Dennis Robertson has called them[1]) might exactly offset the increased saving of those who respond to higher interest rates in the opposite way; this would leave the community's aggregate consumption function unchanged.

If there are no 'Sargant men', a rise in interest rates will reduce the proportion of income consumed: but this is not to say the reduction need be very great. The prospect of earning interest is, after all, only one of the considerations which induce people to leave resources unconsumed; even if no interest were obtainable, the desire to provide for emergencies, for old age and for bequests to heirs would lead some individuals to save; if these motives were very strong relatively to the desire for interest, a very large change in interest rates might be needed to produce even a small shift in the consumption function.

For people whose resources include a high proportion of interest-bearing assets, however, changes in interest rates may be important in another way. The income from a bond is a fixed percentage of its 'nominal' value: thus, a 4% £100 bond gives £4 per annum. But if the rate at which new loans are being made is 8%, £4 p.a. can be obtained by lending £50, and no one will give more than that for the 4% bond. Because the market value of fixed-interest assets changes inversely with current interest rates, their owners will feel poorer when rates rise; they will also feel less willing to consider selling them, because of the capital loss involved—i.e. the liquidity of such assets will be reduced; the reduction in the value and liquidity of their resources will induce individuals to cut consumption. Conversely, a fall in interest rates, by making resources more valuable and more liquid, will increase consumption. The results here are similar to the 'Pigou effect' described in the preceding section, and are subject to the same limitations: they may be neutralized by expectational effects.

On the whole, the conclusion must be that the influence of interest-rate changes on the consumption function is unlikely to be very marked, except perhaps in the case of people who own many fixed-interest assets.

---

[1] In 'Some Notes on the Theory of Interest', in *Money, Trade and Economic Growth; Essays in Honour of J. H. Williams* (1951), p. 196. Sir Dennis was referring to Marshall, *Principles of Economics*, p. 235.

(h) Emulation: the 'relative income' hypothesis

So far, the individual's consumption has been assumed to depend on preferences formed independently of other people's choices—preferences which may be called (in sociological terms[1]) 'inner-directed'. But observation suggests that much consumption is 'other-directed': people are influenced by what they see of their neighbours' and workmates' spending. Also, consumption standards are often taken to be an indication of income, which in many societies determines status; by keeping up with the Joneses' consumption, the Smiths hope to share their status and the esteem it brings. In view of this, J. S. Duesenberry has suggested[2] that an individual's consumption depends not on the absolute amount of his income, but on its size relatively to other people's, i.e. on his position in the income-scale. His response to a change in income will differ according to whether others' incomes have changed by a like amount: if they have, his consumption will change in the same proportion as his income; if they have not, it will change in a smaller proportion. A rise in aggregate income, if it leaves everyone in the same relative position as before, will therefore be associated with an equal proportionate rise in aggregate consumption; the community's consumption function will be a straight line like OC in Fig. 5 (p. 99), even though each individual's function taken by itself may be like those shown in Figs. 4 and 6. Statistical testing of the 'relative income' hypothesis has not shown it to explain the facts better than the theory that consumption depends on absolute income,[3] but it is instructive in drawing attention to the importance of the distribution of incomes in determining the aggregate consumption function—a matter which must now be considered.

(i) The aggregate Consumption Function and the distribution of incomes

The list of possible influences on the individual's consumption is already long, yet even now it is by no means complete; advertising, for example, may cause him to consume more than he would otherwise have done; moral attitudes about 'the virtue of saving' may restrain his expenditure. But no statistical evidence has so far been presented on these matters: investigations of the 'cross-section' type,

[1] David Riesman, The Lonely Crowd, Chap. 1.
[2] J. S. Duesenberry, Income, Saving and the Theory of Consumer Behavior (1949).
[3] See J. Tobin, 'Relative Income, Absolute Income and Saving', in Money, Trade and Economic Growth, cit.

in which a sample of individuals are asked to give details of income, assets, expenditure and so on, seem to show that current income is the chief determinant of consumption, and asset-holdings the next strongest; age and number of dependents also play a part, though the direction and importance of their influence is not very clear.[1]

The object of investigating individual consumer behaviour, however, is to draw conclusions about the determination of *aggregate* consumption; as was seen in Chapter Three, it is important to know how the community's total consumption will react to a change in National Income. This may seem a mere matter of addition: if, say, three men are each known to consume seven-eighths of income, it is clear that their collective consumption will be seven-eighths of their combined incomes. But this is obvious only because they were assumed to have identical consumption functions. If A consumes three-quarters of his income, B seven-eighths and C nine-tenths, and if their combined incomes are £3,000, it is not possible to say what total consumption will be unless their individual incomes are also known. If, for example, A's income is £1,600, B's £800 and C's £600, their combined consumption will be £2,440; but if C had had £1,600, A £800 and B £600 their combined consumption would have been £2,565. Here, the aggregate consumption function is a weighted average of the individual functions, the weights being the individuals' incomes; the change in income-distribution has shifted the aggregate consumption function by altering the weights.

The effects of redistributing incomes may be shown with the aid of a diagram. In Fig. 8 the consumption functions of two income-groups A and B are shown as CF_A and CF_B and their incomes as OA and OB respectively. If their incomes are now equalized[2] so that each receives OC (B's loss of CB being equal to A's gain of AC) it appears from CF_A that A will consume CQ and save QN; previously A consumed AL and saved nothing, because L lies on the broken line '$Y = C$'. B, on the other hand, formerly saved TM but now saves nothing, since N is where CF_B cuts the '$Y = C$' line. After equalization, *total* income is unchanged, and saving is QN instead of

---

[1] See the references in Note 1, p. 109, to the Oxford Savings Surveys; also M. R. Fisher, 'Exploration in Savings Behaviour', OUIS *Bulletin*, August 1956. Fisher found 'considerable evidence that both current income and liquid asset holdings assist in explaining saving behaviour'; 'liquid assets, *ceteris paribus*, exert a negative influence upon savings and income a positive influence'; also, 'savings are negatively related to age and family size, though the influence of the former is highly uncertain'.

[2] The following argument will still hold good, even if incomes are not completely equalized—e.g. if the B group is taxed to provide transfer incomes for A, but in such a way as to leave A's income less than B's.

TM. If CF_A and CF_B are parallel, the triangles *LNQ* and *NMT* are congruent and $QN = TM$; in this case, saving (and therefore consumption) is unchanged, because the MPC of *A* (the slope of CF_A) equals the *MPC* of *B* (the slope of CF_B) over the range of income between *A* and *B*. The same result would occur if CF_A were identical with CF_B, or if each group's consumption function were the same straight line running through the origin of the diagram (line *OC* in

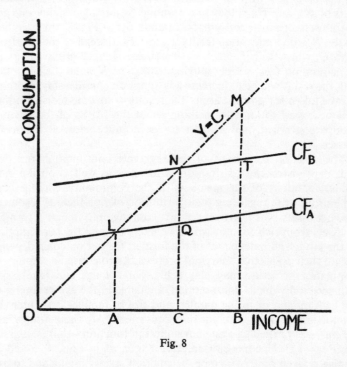

Fig. 8

Fig. 5, p. 99). Redistributing income will change aggregate consumption only if

(i) the groups' functions are straight lines differing in slope; in Fig. 10, *TM* will exceed *QN* if the slope of CF_B is less than that of CF_A;[1] or if

---

[1] If the slope of CF_B were *greater* than that of CF_A, the combined consumption of *A* and *B* would fall when incomes were equalized. The usual assumption is that the higher income-groups have smaller MPCs than the lower groups: but it is not impossible to imagine a community in which the poor are so hidebound by custom that extra income hardly changes their consumption, while the rich are eager to increase their consumption when a rise in income occurs.

(ii) the groups' functions, even if identical or parallel, are curved so that they slope more steeply above point A on the income-scale than above B.

Even these conclusions are subject to both groups staying on their respective consumption functions: but this may not happen. Income tends to be associated with social status, though there is a good deal of overlapping; different social classes have different 'norms' of consumption expenditure. If redistribution gives more income to members of a 'lower' class, they may respond by joining a higher one and thereby change their consumption standards; in Fig. 8, the members of the A-group may jump from CF_A to CF_B, instead of moving from L to Q, when their incomes are increased; if the B-group insists on remaining on CF_B, merely moving from T to N when their incomes fall, the result will be to increase consumption considerably. Nothing can be taken for granted about the results of income-redistribution; it is necessary to know something about the MPCs of the income-groups concerned, and also to assess mobility between the social classes.

The position and shape of the aggregate consumption function thus depends on the distribution of incomes as well as on the individual functions of the members of the community. Similar considerations arise regarding the distribution of non-income resources (i.e. net assets plus borrowing power) among consumers: a transfer of assets from rich to poor would be likely to raise the consumption of the latter and reduce that of the former, the net outcome depending on their respective 'marginal propensities to consume resources'. Population structure may play a like part: if age and family size influence individuals' consumption, a change in the age-grouping of the community, or in the number and size of families, will alter the proportion of aggregate income consumed. All these things are *parameters*[1] of the aggregate consumption function—that is, a given position of the income-consumption curve, as in Figs. 4, 5 and 6, implies a given state of income-distribution, age-grouping and so on; should any of them change, the effect is to move the entire curve bodily up or down.

Finally, it must be noted that the aggregate consumption function has so far been defined so as to relate consumers' demand to the total of personal disposable incomes, not to National Income. It will be recalled that personal disposable incomes are equal to National Income *minus* undistributed profits, *minus* also public authorities' property income, *minus* also taxes on personal incomes, *plus* transfer

[1] For a precise definition of this term, see R. G. D. Allen, *Mathematical Analysis for Economists*, p. 44.

incomes received by persons. If the relationship between National Income and consumption were under consideration, it would be necessary to observe whether any of these items tends to show a systematic variation with the level of National Income. An obvious example is progressive income taxation, under which the proportion of income taken in tax rises with the level of income: if this were the only variable item among those just mentioned, the difference between National Income and personal disposable incomes would be greater, the higher the level of National Income. If consumers' expenditure were now to be plotted against each level of National Income in a diagram, the resulting consumption function would lie below that plotted against personal disposable income; it would slope less steeply, and its slope would tend to diminish (i.e. it would be curved like C_2C_3 in Fig. 6, p. 100) even if the 'personal disposable income' consumption function happened to be a straight line.

(j) Statistical measurements: the long-run Consumption Function

If income *is* the chief determinant of consumption, outweighing all the other influences mentioned in the last few pages, it is reasonable to expect a close correlation between their recorded values. In Fig. 9, these have been plotted[1] for the years 1967–73: each cross shows, for the year indicated by its accompanying number, the amount of personal disposable income per head and of consumption expenditure per head, measured in £ of constant (1970) purchasing power.[2]

[1] Quarterly figures of consumers' expenditure and personal disposable income per head during 1967–73, measured at 1970 prices and seasonally adjusted, are taken from pp. 37–9 in the 1976 Annual Supplement to *Economic Trends*. To keep the diagram simple, only eight pairs of annual values are actually shown in Fig. 9, but all twenty-eight pairs of quarterly values have been used in calculating the equation given overleaf. The 'per head' figures of income and spending may seem unrealistically small, even allowing for inflation since 1970: this is because they were obtained by dividing the national totals by the whole of the nation's population, which is a good deal larger than the number of individual income-recipients and spenders.

[2] Prices rose about 55% between 1967 and 1973. This would have caused the current-price values of income and consumption to rise in step with one another, even if both had remained unchanged in real terms; a systematic relationship would have appeared to exist, but would have been due not to the influence of income on consumption but to the fact that both variables were equally affected by a third factor. To avoid 'spurious correlation' of this sort, it is necessary to express both variables in constant-price terms. Population growth (2·63% between 1967 and 1973) could produce a similar effect, by causing *real* income and consumption to increase together; it is to eliminate this that 'per head' figures have been used.

The line *CC* shows the average relationship between income and consumption implied by the distribution of the crosses; its equation is of the '$C = a+bY$' type described on p. 101, and is calculated to be

$$C = 31 \cdot 4 + 0 \cdot 86\, Y.$$

The fact that the crosses all lie close to the line suggests a very strong association between income and consumption. To assess the strength of such relationships, statisticians use a 'correlation coefficient' denoted by the symbol *r*, whose square (which they call the 'coefficient of determination') measures the extent to which changes in one

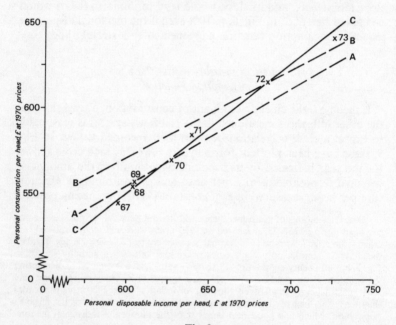

Fig. 9

variable can be attributed to changes in the other. If, in Fig. 9, all the crosses lay precisely on the line *CC*, r^2 would have a value of 1·0, and this would be consistent with the hypothesis that consumption is determined entirely by the level of income and nothing else. If, on the other hand, the crosses were scattered higgledy-piggledy over the diagram, the value of r^2 would be close to zero, implying that the influence of income on consumption is almost negligible.[1] In the present case, the arrangement of the crosses suggests that the value of r^2 is much closer to $1\cdot0$ than to zero; when calculated, it turns out to be $0\cdot87$. However, the fact that consumption and income were both rising throughout the 1967–73 period (the former rose 18%, the latter 22%, over the seven years) would of itself produce a certain degree of correlation even if there were no causal connection at all between the two variables.[2] Consequently, the very high value of r^2 is not conclusive evidence of the strength of the income-consumption relationship, and it is necessary to find a way of estimating it which will eliminate the effect of the rising trend. One such method is to compare quarterly *changes* in income and consumption instead of their absolute values. When this is done, the value of r^2 is found to be almost negligible at $0\cdot07$; that is, hardly any of the variation in consumption can be explained as being due to variations in current income—a result which hardly seems to permit much reliance to be placed on the consumption function in further analysis.[3]

[1] For a full explanation of the concepts and methods of calculation, see Croxton and Cowden, *Applied General Statistics*, Chaps. XXII and XXV.

[2] This is by no means the only possible pitfall in the interpretation of r^2; another consideration, for example, is whether the number of observations, from which the r^2's have been calculated, provides too small a sample to justify accepting conclusions drawn from it. See Croxton and Cowden, *op. cit.*, p. 768 ff.

[3] 'Consumption' is, of course, a very broad category, made up of expenditures on many separate commodities; for each of these, demand will be related to income in a different way. For example, spending on 'consumers' durables' (C_D), such as cars, furniture and TV sets, shows the following relationship with personal disposable income in 1967–73:

$$C_D = 0\cdot27\,Y - 126\cdot5$$

—all quantities being £ per head at 1970 prices. This means that the demand for durables would have been zero whenever income was less than about £460 p.a., while when income exceeded that figure, C_D would have been about a quarter of the difference. If a line were drawn in Fig. 9 to show this relationship, it would start from the horizontal axis to the right of the origin, and its slope would be less than those of CC, AA and BB. A rather different case is that of expenditure on food: the equation is

$$C_{food} = 21\cdot5 + 0\cdot16\,Y$$

(in £ per head, 1970 prices), implying that people will always buy food whatever their incomes, but that only a small part of any rise in income will be spent on additional food. In fact, food expenditure per head, at 1970 prices, rose less than 4% between 1967 and 1973, even though income per head rose 22%. When it is necessary to 'disaggregate' the income-consumption relationship in this way, breaking it up into separate equations for different branches of consumption, it is important to bear in mind that the various relationships may be strongly influenced by relative prices; thus, the demand for durables may rise not only because income increases but also because durables have become cheaper relative to other kinds of consumer goods.

However, it must be remembered that the relationship given in the equation was deduced from statistics of income and consumption extending over a period of some years. The consumption function presented at the beginning of this chapter is not a concept which describes consumers' behaviour over a considerable length of time. It indicates a set of simultaneously existing possibilities which arise from the state of preferences at a particular moment: given incomes of £20 billions, consumers will wish to spend (say) £17 billions, but if incomes are £12 billions instead of £20 billions, they will spend £10 billions; incomes of £15 billions will give rise to consumption of £13·5 billions—and so on. To accept the line CC in Fig. 9 as an estimate of 'the consumption function' in this sense, is to assume that the function remained unchanged in shape and position for a whole decade: but this is a very dubious assumption. It is not unreasonable, for example, to assume that consumers' assets remain unchanged during a period as short as six months, or even twelve: over several years, however, saving may cause personal wealth to grow sufficiently to make consumers feel they can afford to consume a larger proportion of income, and the function will then have shifted bodily upwards. Thus, the broken line AA shown in Fig. 9 might represent the consumption function which existed in 1969–70, while the line BB shows the function as it might have been in 1972, the upward shift being due to increasing wealth, to consumers' becoming accustomed to higher living standards, and to similar long-run influences; other lines, more or less parallel to AA and BB, might be supposed to run through each of the crosses representing the consumption and income of other years, and the resulting family of curves would show how the short-run function had moved throughout the whole period. The line CC cuts through this set of curves, since it is derived from a series of *successive* observations, each of which may have referred to a point on a different short-run consumption function; its equation is merely a summary statement of the way in which amounts actually spent on consumption were associated with the amounts of income received during 1967–73. It may be thought that the association is sufficiently systematic to justify calling CC a 'long-period consumption function', but it will obviously differ from any short-run function in being affected by influences (such as the growth of assets already mentioned) which remain practically constant in the short run but change considerably over a number of years. It is hardly surprising, therefore, that the value of r^2 deduced earlier for changes in income and consumption should have been found to be fairly low: the logical presumption is that the influence of current income on consumers' demand was much stronger in the short run.

When the short-period function is distinguished from the long-period one, it has to be admitted that it is not easy to discover the characteristic shape of the former. The statistical material cited above provides, for any single year, only four pairs of quarterly values of Y and C from which to deduce curves of the type of AA in Fig. 9; to use two or three years' quarterly values would violate the short-run assumptions on which such curves are drawn. It might be thought that this difficulty could be overcome by the use of cross-section data of the sort provided by the Oxford Savings Surveys referred to on p. 109 above; such surveys show the incomes and the consumption expenditures of a large number of different individuals within the same short period, so that a curve fitted to these observations[1] might appear to be an approximation to the short-run consumption function. However, this would hold good only if all the individuals covered by the survey could be assumed to occupy points on the same short-run function. If the situation were similar to that depicted in Fig. 8, with each income-group on a separate function of its own, the survey would merely have revealed a number of points like Q on CF_A and T on CF_B; to draw a line between Q and T and call it 'the consumption function' would clearly be illegitimate. Because of this possibility, estimates derived from cross-section data may be misleading. None the less, it should be noted that they do at any rate provide evidence of a reasonably strong correlation between income and consumption, and agree with time-series analysis in showing consumption to be an increasing function of income—which, indeed is often all that needs to be assumed for many purposes of short-run theoretical analysis, as will be seen in the next chapter. In so far as the necessity does arise to estimate the short-period function more precisely, it may be possible—paradoxical as it may seem—to do so by means of a somewhat different (and, unfortunately, less simple) approach to the long-period relationship.

When the statistical evidence was considered earlier, it was presented in terms of a straightforward confrontation between income and consumption, by using simple equations of the $C = a+bY$ type; but this failed to give a complete explanation of changes in consumption, since influences other than current income were left out of the reckoning. It should be possible to improve on this by bringing these other influences explicitly into the relationship; for example, if there are reasons for thinking that consumers' decisions are affected not

[1] For some examples of cross-section 'savings functions', see Erritt and Nicholson, 'The 1955 Savings Survey', OUIS *Bulletin*, May 1958, p. 142; see also L. R. Klein, 'The British Propensity to Save', *Journal of the Royal Statistical Society*, Series A, 1958, Part I.

only by their present incomes but also by those received in the recent past,[1] the earlier equation could be amended to

$$C_t = bY_t + cY_{t-1}$$

where the subscript t refers to any given short period and $t-1$ to that immediately preceding it; thus, if b were 0·5 and c were 0·25, and if Y_{t-1} were £400 and Y_t £440 (per head of population, and at constant prices), C_t would be £320. Here, cY_{t-1} replaces the constant a of the original equation. If income is regularly rising from one period to the next, the effect will be that of a continuous increase in the value of a; if drawn in a diagram, the function will appear as a set of curves, each higher than the preceding one, instead of a single line like CC in Fig. 9. Each of the curves will be associated with a particular income-period, and its slope, b, will measure the short-run MPC; but the equation will also trace the growth of consumption over time, and a curve relating the successive values C_t, C_{t+1}, C_{t+2}, etc., to those of income in successive periods will have a slope steeper than b, and will thus overestimate the short-run MPC.

In the same way, if the amount of consumers' assets is an important influence on their spending, the relationship can be made explicit in the form

$$C_t = bY_t + dA_t$$

where A_t is the amount of personal assets (per head, at constant prices) at the beginning of period t. Assets are accumulated through saving; if consumption has been less than income during previous periods, A_t will be larger than A_{t-1} (assets at the beginning of period $t-1$) which will, in turn, have been larger than A_{t-2}, and so on; this growth of assets will give a rising trend to consumption, causing it to go on increasing even at times when income remains unchanged. Since one period's assets are those of the previous period plus the

[1] This may happen because people regard past income as 'normal', and suspect that current changes in income may not be lasting—a 'Friedman' approach. It may also arise from inertia: having become accustomed to their previous level of income, consumers take time to respond fully to a new one. In this case, it may be last period's consumption, rather than the income itself, to which they have become habituated; next period, they will repeat that consumption plus or minus a proportion of any change in income, so that

$$C_t = C_{t-1} + b(Y_t - Y_{t-1}).$$

If the proportion between C_{t-1} and Y_{t-1} is d, and if $(d-b)$ is equal to the c of the expression in the text above, the two equations are merely different ways of saying the same thing; but it may be useful to distinguish in this way between 'consumption inertia' and 'income habituation'.

saving done in that period (i.e. $A_t = A_{t-1} + Y_{t-1} - C_{t-1}$), and, since $C_{t-1} = bY_{t-1} + dA_{t-1}$, the earlier equation can be rewritten

$$C_t = bY_t + d(1-b)Y_{t-1} + d(1-d)A_{t-1}$$

—so that the influence of assets on consumption is seen to imply a relationship between current consumption and past income,[1] similar in form to that discussed in the previous paragraph. The connection with past income would be less simple if (for reasons indicated on p. 106 above) consumers were influenced by the amount of their *liquid*, rather than their total, assets: the last equation would then have to include a term representing the proportion borne by liquid assets to consumers' total wealth, and there is no obvious reason to suppose that this proportion will either remain fixed or change at some regular rate over time.[2] In spite of this, liquid assets have often been used as a 'proxy variable' to represent total assets, simply because of the extreme difficulty of obtaining statistical information about the latter.[3]

As well as past income and consumers' wealth, the consumption equation can be made to include terms for the distribution of incomes, the age-structure of the population, the cost and availability of credit, the amount of advertising expenditures, and anything else which may be thought to exert a significant influence on consumers' behaviour, with appropriate subscripts to indicate any time-lags which may be involved. So far, all the lags which have been mentioned have been of fixed length. Some writers, notably J. S. Duesenberry, have suggested a different type of lag in the case of past in-

---

[1] 'Past income' refers not only to the Y_{t-1} which appears explicitly in the equation, but also to Y_{t-2}, Y_{t-3} and so on. This is because
$$A_{t-1} = A_{t-2} + Y_{t-2} - C_{t-2} = A_{t-2} + Y_{t-2} - bY_{t-2} - dA_{t-2}$$
$$= Y_{t-2}(1-b) + A_{t-2}(1-d);$$
when this is substituted for A_{t-1} in the equation in the text, it becomes
$$C_t = bY_t + d(1-b)Y_{t-1} + d(1-d)(1-b)Y_{t-2} + d(1-d)^2 A_{t-2}$$
—and A_{t-2} could in turn be expressed in terms of Y_{t-3} and A_{t-3}. The original A_t, in fact, implies a series of terms involving income during *many* previous periods.

[2] Changes in the proportion could occur in a number of ways: for example, the distribution of assets between the various 'sectors' of the economy (personal, corporate and public) may alter so that the personal sector holds more cash and fewer long-term bonds; or there might be an increase in the total amount of money and other liquid assets relatively to total assets in the economy as a whole, with the personal sector getting a proportionate share.

[3] In 'The Short-run Consumption Function', *Econometrica*, October 1957, A. Zellner used U.S. quarterly data for 1947–55 to estimate ten different consumption functions, of which five included L_{t-1} (liquid asset holdings in the previous quarter) as a variable. The coefficients of L_{t-1} varied from 0·219 to 0·396 suggesting that liquid assets exert a strong influence on consumption.

come: instead of consumption depending on income received (say) two periods previously, it may be affected by the highest level of income attained at *any* time in the past. Consumers (it is supposed) have adjusted their spending to the last 'peak' of income, and are loth to reduce it when income falls again; thus,

$$C_t = bY_t + cY_0$$

where Y_0 represents the last highest level of income. As long as income is increasing from one period to the next, Y_0 will equal Y_{t-1}; if, on the other hand, it were to fall for several periods in succession, Y_0 will denote the income of the period before the recession began, and will continue to do so until it is replaced by a new peak when income rises again. When income falls, the fact that cY_0 retains a constant value means that the equation is then equivalent to $C = a + bY$, instead of the form $C_t = bY_t + cY_{t-1}$ which it assumes when income is rising. In diagrammatic terms, this means that the function can be represented by a series of curves like AA and BB in Fig. 9, but with the special condition that only upward shifts are possible; that is, successive increases in income will move the short-period function from AA to BB and so on up the diagram, but a subsequent fall in income will not shift it back again—the presence of Y_0 in the equation acts as a ratchet, holding the curve at the highest position so far attained. Thus, a point relating consumption and income will travel up Fig. 9's line CC as long as income is rising, but when income falls it will move to the left along whichever curve of the AA—BB family happens to intersect CC at the 'peak' level of income. A function of this sort was shown by Duesenberry to be consistent with United States experience in the years 1929–40.[1]

It seems, then, that by ringing the changes on the number of variables to be included and on the time-lags to be inserted, a large number of different consumption functions can be devised. Which of them best explains consumers' behaviour must depend on circumstances: the function most appropriate[2] to the United States, for

---

[1] Duesenberry's function was

$$S_t/Y_t = 0 \cdot 25 \, (Y_t/Y_0) - 0 \cdot 196 \qquad (r^2 = 0 \cdot 81)$$

—in dollars of constant purchasing power, per head of population. This is equivalent to

$$C_t = 1 \cdot 196 \, Y_t - 0 \cdot 25 \, Y_t(Y_t/Y_0)$$

—which is somewhat more complicated than the expression in the text above. See his *Income, Saving, and the Theory of Consumer Behavior* (1949), pp. 89–92.

[2] In the sense of meeting certain criteria, such as the ability to predict consumers' expenditure within a certain margin of error; it may be found that *no* function meets all the criteria. See Zellner, *op. cit.*

example, may be very different from those which give the 'best fit' in Britain and France; even within the same country, the development of the economy may make it necessary to bring in new variables which had not previously been of importance, so that no particular function can be expected to retain its relevance from one decade to the next; in any case, statistical information is lacking, in most countries, about many variables which have a good claim to be included on a *priori* grounds. Certainly, there is no function which is generally accepted as *the* Consumption Function in Britain in the nineteen-sixties. What *is* generally agreed, however, is that the dependence of consumption on current income is sufficiently great in the short run as to justify the use of such a relationship in theoretical analysis; if this can be taken for granted, certain results follow with regard to the equilibrium of the economy as a whole, and the next chapter will be devoted to a consideration of them.

CHAPTER SIX

The Multiplier

(a) The Consumption Function and equilibrium

If consumers' demand is related to income through a consumption function of some kind, certain consequences follow for the equilibrium of the economy. The condition of equilibrium—that aggregate demand shall equal aggregate supply—was amplified in Chapter Three[1] into

$$C+I+G+E-M = GNP+T_g$$

where all the symbols on the left-hand side of the equation stand for *ex ante* quantities. This may be simplified, for the time being, by assuming an economy which has no government expenditure, no foreign trade, and no indirect taxes; if Gross National Income (Y) is substituted for Gross National Product (since the two are identical), the equilibrium condition becomes

$$Y = C+I.$$

If, further, it is assumed that there are no income or profits taxes, no transfer incomes, no undistributed profits and no public authorities' property income, Y will be identical with the total of personal disposable incomes. If the consumption function is $C = cY$, where c is some fraction which does not change with the level of income, this can be substituted in the last equation, giving

$$Y = cY+I$$

$$Y(1-c) = I, \text{ or } Y = \frac{I}{1-c}$$

For equilibrium to exist, therefore, Y must take whatever value is required to make the excess of income over consumers' demand equal to the demand for investment. If (as is assumed at present) I is

[1] See above, p. 53.

128

not influenced at all by the level of income, this means that it is investment demand which determines income. Thus, if c is 0·75 and investment demand is £100 millions,

$$Y = \frac{100}{1-0·75} = 400 \text{ millions.}$$

If I were £150 millions, $Y = £600$ millions; and so on.

This can also be stated in terms of saving. Saving has been defined as income minus consumption; the latter is defined by the consumption function $C = cY$, so

$$S = Y-C = Y-cY = Y(1-c):$$

this is the 'savings function', which could also be written

$$S = sY \text{ (where } s = 1-c).$$

The equilibrium condition is that

$$I = sY, \text{ i.e. } Y = \frac{I}{s}.$$

Investment demand must equal the amount the community wishes to save: but because the latter is dependent on income and the former is not, income must adjust itself to the level of investment if equilibrium is to exist.

If the consumption function were $C = a+bY$ instead of $C = cY$, the equilibrium condition

$$Y = C+I$$

becomes

$$Y = a+bY+I$$

so that

$$Y = \frac{a+I}{1-b};$$

if $a = £50$ millions, $b = 0·8$ and $I = £100$ millions, the value of Y must be £750 millions in equilibrium. Here, income is determined not only by I and b but also by a, which is the part of consumers' demand independent of the level of income. Similarly, any element of aggregate demand which is '*autonomous*', in the sense that it does not depend on the level of income, will play a part analogous to that of a and I: if government expenditure (G) and foreign trade ($E-M$) are

E

assumed to be autonomous and are brought back into the equilibrium
condition, this becomes

$$Y = \frac{a+I+G+E-M}{1-b};$$

equilibrium income equals the sum of autonomous demands divided
by $(1-b)$, where b is the marginal propensity to consume.

This is illustrated in Fig. 10, which resembles Fig. 4 (p. 198) in
showing the consumption function, CC, as a straight line starting

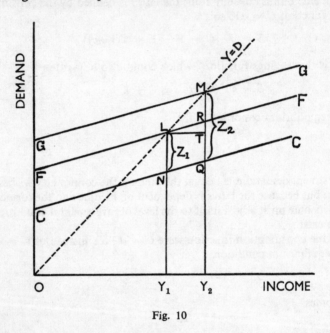

Fig. 10

from a point on the vertical axis. The latter, however, measures not
only consumers' demand but aggregate demand in general. Income is
measured on the horizontal axis; the broken line '$Y = D$', passing
through the origin O at 45°, indicates all the possible positions of
equilibrium where aggregate demand is exactly equal to income. If
the non-consumption elements of demand (I, G etc.) are Z_1, and are
assumed autonomous, they can be added to consumers' demand at all
levels of income to give an 'aggregate demand function' FF parallel
to CC; FF's vertical distance FC above CC equals Z_1. FF cuts the
broken line '$Y = D$' at L, where income is OY_1; here, aggregate

demand LY_1 equals income OY_1 and the equilibrium condition is fulfilled. If autonomous non-consumption demand were Z_2, the 'aggregate demand function' would be GG (where $GC = Z_2$) which cuts the '$Y = D$' line at M, giving equilibrium income of OY_2. In fact, income is in equilibrium wherever the vertical distance between CC and the '$Y = D$' line is exactly filled up by Z, the sum of non-consumption demands.

The same principle applies where the consumption function is not linear—i.e. where instead of being a straight line it is a curve with diminishing slope, as it would be if its equation were (say) $C = a+bY-cY^2$. It also applies even when non-consumption demands are not wholly autonomous: if, for example, investment were responsive to the level of income, getting larger at higher income-levels, the 'aggregate demand function' (FF or GG) would not be parallel to CC, but would diverge from it towards the right-hand side of the diagram, opening up an ever-increasing gap between itself and CC; nevertheless, equilibrium would still require that the gap between CC and the 'aggregate demand function' should equal that between CC and the '$Y = D$' line. These more complicated situations, however, will be set aside for the moment.

(b) The static Multiplier

In Fig. 10, two equilibrium levels of income were shown: OY_1 when non-consumption demand is Z_1 and OY_2 when it is Z_2. If these positions are compared, it is clear that OY_2 exceeds OY_1 by an amount greater than the difference between Z_2 and Z_1. The horizontal line LT equals the difference in incomes Y_1Y_2; since the '$Y = D$' line slopes at $45°$, LT also equals the vertical length MT, so that $MT = Y_1Y_2$; but Z_2 exceeds Z_1 by only MR, which is less than MT. Obviously, the difference (RT) will be greater, the steeper the slope of the consumption function CC.

In economic terms, this means that a given autonomous change in investment (or in any other form of demand) will be associated with a change in income larger than itself; how much larger, depends on the Marginal Propensity to Consume. In the numerical example given on p. 129 above, income was £400 millions when investment was £100 millions; with investment at £150 millions, income was £600 millions—i.e. a difference of £50 millions in investment was associated with a difference of £200 millions in income, the MPC being 0·75 throughout.

If the consumption function is $C = a+bY$, a given level of investment I_1 will be associated with a certain level of income Y_1; a higher level of investment I_2, with higher income Y_2. The two equilibria are

$$Y_1 = a + b Y_1 + I_1$$

and

$$Y_2 = a + b Y_2 + I_2.$$

The difference between the two situations is found by subtracting the first equation from the second, giving

$$(Y_2 - Y_1) = b(Y_2 - Y_1) + (I_2 - I_1)$$

from which

$$(Y_2 - Y_1) = \frac{(I_2 - I_1)}{1 - b}.$$

The difference between the income levels (which for brevity may be written ΔY) is equal to the difference between the levels of investment (ΔI) multiplied by $\frac{1}{1-b}$. The ratio between ΔY and ΔI is thus

$$\frac{\Delta Y}{\Delta I} = \frac{1}{1-b} = \frac{1}{s}$$

—where b is the MPC and $(1-b)$ is the Marginal Propensity to Save, s. This ratio is called '*the Multiplier*' and is conventionally represented by the symbol k. Its value is automatically defined when the MPC is known: e.g. if the MPC is $\frac{3}{4}$, the MPS is $\frac{1}{4}$, and k (which is the reciprocal of the MPS) is 4. The higher the MPC, the higher the value of k; a MPC of $1 \cdot 0$ would give k equal to 'infinity'—that is, there would be no possible equilibrium of income if a change in investment were to disturb the original equilibrium. Conversely, a MPC of 0 gives $k = 1$: the change in income would be equal to the 'multiplicand', ΔI, itself. The lower the value of the multiplier, the less will a given ΔI alter the level of income.

The multiplicand has so far been assumed to be a change in investment. But it could just as well be a change in government spending, or in the demand for exports, or in any other element of aggregate demand—provided the change is autonomous, i.e. not induced by a change in income itself. It could even be a change in the autonomous part of consumption, i.e. the a in $C = a + b Y$, since a does not vary with the level of income. If the consumption function was initially $C = 40 + 0 \cdot 75 Y$, and if it now changes to $C = 50 + 0 \cdot 75 Y$ (i.e. the value of a rises from 40 to 50), income will rise by 40, i.e. $(50 - 40) \times \frac{1}{1 - 0 \cdot 75}$. It may sometimes be convenient to speak of a 'consumption multiplier' or an 'investment multiplier' according to the nature of the multiplicand in a particular case; but the numerical value of the multiplier will be the same whatever the multiplicand may be.

It is possible that not only consumption but also other elements of demand may be responsive to the level of income: for example, investment may consist of an autonomous part (h) and a part which rises as income rises (iY), so that $I = h + iY$ where i is the 'marginal propensity to invest'. Equilibrium is then

$$Y = C + I = a + bY + h + iY;$$

if autonomous investment rises by Δh, income rises by

$$\Delta Y = b\Delta Y + i\Delta Y + \Delta h \quad \text{(there being no change in } a\text{)}$$

and the multiplier is

$$k = \frac{\Delta Y}{\Delta h} = \frac{1}{(1 - b - i)}.$$

This has been called the 'compound' Multiplier to distinguish it from the 'simple' Multiplier $\frac{1}{1-b}$. If b and i are added together in an inclusive 'marginal propensity to spend' (which could also include marginal propensities in other elements of demand), the multiplier principle can be generalized into the proposition that any autonomous rise in demand (ΔZ) will be associated with a rise in income (ΔY) whose size will depend on the marginal propensity to spend (σ) in such a way that

$$\frac{\Delta Y}{\Delta Z} = \frac{1}{1 - \sigma}.$$

So far, income and all other magnitudes have been assumed to be at constant prices; for example, the difference between Y_1 and Y_2 in Fig. 10 represents a physical quantity of goods and services, not a change in money income only. The Multiplier has, in fact, been defined in real terms: a change in the volume of goods and services demanded necessitates a multiple rise in the physical quantity produced. This may seem to raise a difficulty, since there is an obvious limit to increases in *real* income: whatever the size of the Multiplier, income and output cannot exceed the physical quantity the economy is capable of producing at full employment. A rise in autonomous demand, when full employment prevails, may very well cause *money* income to rise through effects on the general price-level, but it could not bring about a rise in *real* income: it might seem, therefore, that the Multiplier should have a value of zero at full employment: if

$\Delta Y = 0$, $\dfrac{\Delta Y}{\Delta I}$ must also be 0. This is false reasoning, however: the Multiplier does not show what level of income will *actually* be reached, but the level it would have to reach to attain equilibrium. It shows the overall change in aggregate demand which results from an autonomous change in a particular element of demand: it could be symbolized as $\dfrac{\Delta D}{\Delta Z}$ where D is aggregate demand and ΔZ is the multiplicand. Putting ΔY in place of ΔD tacitly implies that the equilibrium condition is satisfied. If this is physically impossible, the Multiplier will simply indicate the extent of the disequilibrium resulting from a change in demand.

The Multiplier so far described is a *static* concept. It gives little insight into the process by which the economy tries to achieve a new equilibrium. The process by which output adjusts itself to a new level of demand is assumed to take place instantaneously, or at least so quickly that none of the parameters of the system has time to change—consumers' preferences remain unchanged, the distribution of incomes stays as before, and so on. In real life, it is very unlikely that this would hold good. But if lapses of time are introduced into the working of the Multiplier, it ceases to be a comparison between two different positions of equilibrium: attention must be directed to the sequence of events by which the economy moves from the one to the other, and this inevitably brings in the time factor.

(c) *The dynamic Multiplier*

The 'multiplier process' was crudely sketched in Chapter Three.[1] An initial rise in (say) investment demand gives rise to expenditure on new plant; the incomes of those concerned in supplying it are increased and, they in turn increase their expenditure according to their 'marginal propensities to spend'. If investment does not rise any further, and if other kinds of demand remain unchanged, subsequent 'rounds' of spending will be on consumption only, and each 'round' will bring less spending than the last if the MPC is less than $1 \cdot 0$. To satisfy the increase in demand at each stage, production must be increased. If, for example, retailers meet a rise in consumers' demand from stock, they are assumed to order replacements, since willingness to hold lower stocks would amount to a reduction in investment demand—and this has been assumed not to change after its initial rise; the rise in production will then take

[1] See above, pp. 56–8.

the form of replacement of retailers' stocks. Rising demand may also be met by increases in prices: but this will merely increase the money incomes of those who charge higher prices, and will cause the next stage of the process to be transacted in higher values: the physical quantities involved will be the same, unless the change in prices has affected the consumption function to a significant extent.[1]

If the MPC remains (say) 0·8 throughout, an increase of £10 millions in investment demand will first raise income and output by £10 millions as the initial increase in demand is satisfied; the recipients of the £10 millions will wish to spend eight-tenths of it on consumption, and satisfying *this* demand will raise income and output by £8 millions; at the next stage, £6·4 millions of income and output will be added, causing consumers' demand to rise by a further £5·1 millions—and so on. At the tenth 'round', the increase in income will be only £1·07 millions; at the twentieth, £0·115 millions; at the thirtieth, £0·01 millions; eventually, the repercussions will become virtually imperceptible. In symbols, the initial rise in income, ΔY_1, equals the rise in investment ΔI; in the next period, the increase in income[2] ΔY_2 is equal to c (the MPC) times ΔY_1, i.e. $c\Delta I$; in the third period, ΔY_3 is $c^2\Delta I$; similarly, $\Delta Y_4 = c\Delta Y_3 = c^3\Delta I$, and so on up to the nth period, when $\Delta Y_n = c\Delta Y_{n-1} = c^{n-1}\Delta I$ (n being some large number). The whole series of increases in income over all the n periods, i.e.

$$\Delta Y_1 + \Delta Y_2 + \Delta Y_3 + \Delta Y_4 + \ldots + \Delta Y_n$$

—or $Y_n - Y_0$, where Y_0 is the income of the period before that in which the initial investment took place—is therefore equal to

$$\Delta I + c\Delta I + c^2\Delta I + c^3\Delta I + \ldots + c^{n-1}\Delta I$$

which can be reduced[3] to

$$\Delta I\left(\frac{1}{1-c}\right);$$

[1] See above, pp. 111–3.

[2] In this and the following paragraphs, ΔY stands for the difference between current income and the income of the previous period, *not* between current income and the income of the original period before the multiplier process began; for example, $\Delta Y_4 = Y_4 - Y_3$, not $Y_4 - Y_0$ (where the subscripts stand for periods equal in length to the 'rounds' referred to earlier).

[3] The series can be written $\Delta I(1 + c + c^2 + \ldots + c^{n-1})$. Let the sum of the terms inside the brackets be denoted S, i.e.

$$S = 1 + c + c^2 + \ldots + c^{n-1}$$

Now multiply both sides of this equation by c, giving

$$Sc = c + c^2 + c^3 + \ldots + c^n$$

and subtract the second equation from the first; on the right-hand side, all terms

consequently,

$$\frac{Y_n - Y_0}{\Delta I} = \frac{1}{1-c}$$

which appears to be the same as the 'static' multiplier described in the previous section, except that n periods are required for the full effect to be experienced.

The resemblance is due to the fact that the rise in investment-demand is assumed to be permanent: having risen by ΔI in the first period, investment remains at its new level throughout the rest of the process. But this is by no means the only possibility. It might happen that investment increases only during the first period, falling back to its original level in the second and remaining unchanged thereafter. In this 'single-injection' multiplier process, the initial increase in income, ΔY_1, is ΔI as before; but in the next period the consequential rise in consumption, $c\Delta I$, will be accompanied by a reduction in investment offsetting the initial increase, so that $\Delta Y_2 = c\Delta I - \Delta I$. In the third period, the second 'round' of consumption spending due to the original rise in investment will take place, but there will also be a *fall* in consumption resulting from the reduction in investment which occurred in the previous period: thus, $\Delta Y_3 = c^2\Delta I - c\Delta I$. If c is less than 1, ΔI will be greater than $c\Delta I$, and $c\Delta I$ will be greater than $c^2\Delta I$; so ΔY_2 and ΔY_3 will both be negative if ΔY_1 was positive. Income has risen during the first period by the amount of additional investment, but in the second and third periods it has been falling; the decline will continue until, in the nth period, $\Delta Y_n = c^{n-1}\Delta I - c^{n-2}\Delta I$. Since n is assumed to be a large number, both c^{n-1} and c^{n-2} will be so small as to be negligible, and the difference between them will be smaller still; for practical purposes, $\Delta Y_n = 0$. Income will now have returned to its original level. The sum of the income-changes which have occurred is

$$\Delta I + c\Delta I - \Delta I + c^2\Delta I - c\Delta I + \ldots + c^{n-1}\Delta I - c^{n-2}\Delta I$$

in which all the terms cancel out except $c^{n-1}\Delta I$, which is assumed to

---

cancel out except 1 and c^n, so that
$$S(1-c) = 1-c^n.$$

Because c is a fraction, c^n will be very small if n is very large; it can therefore be omitted without making any serious difference to the solution of the equation, so that
$$S = \frac{1}{1-c}.$$

Thus, $$\Delta I(1 + c + c^2 + \ldots + c^{n-1}) = \Delta I\left(\frac{1}{1-c}\right).$$

be so small that it can be neglected; so $Y_n - Y_o = 0$. The original stimulus ΔI has at last been completely offset by subsequent reductions in income.[1]

Whether the rise in investment is sustained or not, the whole multiplier process is likely to take a considerable time to work itself out, even if each of the n periods is itself fairly short. Strictly speaking, the process will *never* finish; though ΔY_n will be very small if n is very large, it will never quite reach zero value,[2] and how small it must be before it can be regarded as negligible is obviously a matter of judgement. It may happen, however, that only the first few periods are really of interest: well before the nth has been reached (and consequently, well before the value of ΔY has become negligible) it may be necessary to see how far the process has gone, and to compare the current level of income with that existing before the initial stimulus was given. If the series ΔI, $c\Delta I$, $c^2\Delta I$ ... (which occurs when investment rises to a new level and remains there) is carried only as far as the jth period, where j is a good deal smaller than n, the sum of the increases in income will now[3] be

$$\Delta I\left(\frac{1-c^j}{1-c}\right)$$

—so that if, for example, ΔI is £10 millions, $c = 0.8$ and $j = 6$, the level of income will have risen by £36·89 millions altogether since the process began, and the value of the multiplier—i.e. $(Y_j - Y_o)/\Delta I$—will be approximately 3·7. This incomplete, or 'truncated', multiplier is obviously less than the 'full' multiplier, which in this case is 5·0 since the total increase in Y over all n periods will be £50 millions; but it may be more useful to know the value of the former than of the latter.[4] If the whole n-period process would take two or three years

[1] The 'single-injection' multiplier might well be regarded as a combination of two processes of the 'repeated-injection' type described earlier. Thus, Multiplier A starts off in period 1 with ΔI, and continues $c\Delta I$, $c^2\Delta I$, etc.; in period 2, Multiplier B starts with $-\Delta I$ (so as to reduce investment to its original level) and continues $-c\Delta I$, $-c^2\Delta I$, and so on, but always one period behind A; the process described in the text results from the addition of A and B in each period. On this approach, the 'repeated-injection' sequence may be considered the *basic* multiplier process, all other multipliers being merely variations caused by the introduction of fresh sequences.

[2] In mathematical terms, ΔY_n approaches zero as n approaches infinity.

[3] The derivation is the same as in footnote 3, p. 135, except that c^j now appears in place of c^n. Because j is not large enough to make c^j negligible, the latter term cannot be discarded from $S(1-c) = 1-c^j$, and must therefore be retained in the expression given in the text above.

[4] See F. Machlup, 'Period Analysis and Multiplier Theory', *Quarterly Journal of Economics*, 1939; reprinted in the American Economic Association's *Readings in Business Cycle Theory* (1944).

to work itself out, the more distant repercussions will be irrelevant to analysis which seeks to forecast developments during the coming six months; moreover, the longer the time taken by the n periods, the greater the likelihood that the later 'rounds' will be distorted and even overwhelmed by the consequences of changes in consumers' preferences, in the distribution of incomes, and in other parameters of the system.

The one-period 'consumption lag' in the above sequences (often called the 'Robertsonian' lag[1]) implies a consumption function of the form $C_t = c(Y_{t-1})$ or $C_t = a + c(Y_{t-1})$. But, as was seen in the previous chapter, the function may be more complicated than this. If consumers' demand depends partly on their 'net worth', and if this is growing from period to period, an additional element will enter into aggregate demand in each period; changes in income-distribution, caused by the change in aggregate income, may affect consumers' demand in subsequent periods; rising income may alter the expectations on which consumers' decisions are based. If c (the MPC) changes from period to period, it may be impossible to reduce ΔY_n to a simple multiple of ΔI as was done in the last two sequences worked out above. As time goes by the chances of further autonomous changes in demand will become greater, so that the sequence may be disturbed by the injection of a fresh change in (say) investment demand, which will set up subsequent reactions of its own concurrently with those persisting from the original sequence.

In the examples given above, it is assumed that the level of output adjusts itself immediately to changes in aggregate demand: this was shown by setting the change in income ΔY (which is identical with the value of output) equal to the change in demand for consumption and investment occurring in each period. If output lags behind the change in demand, this will have effects of its own which are investigated in the next section.

(d) The effects of an 'output lag'

When demand rises, producers may need to train additional workers and replan processes before they can increase output to meet it. When demand falls, it may be cheaper to finish off work in hand than to abandon it. Producers may be unwilling to alter output until convinced that the new level of demand is going to last. In the meantime, they may use their stocks as a buffer, drawing on them if sales are rising or adding to them if sales fall; if the rise in demand

[1] After Sir Dennis Robertson: see his *Banking Policy and the Price Level* (1926) p. 59.

finds their stocks low, they may simply let buyers wait, so that demand is frustrated; or they may allow prices to alter appropriately. Whatever the ultimate consequences of the change in demand, output will remain the same for the time being.

Suppose it takes one period for output to catch up with demand: $Q_t = D_{t-1}$ where D is demand, Q is output, t is any given period and $t-1$ is the preceding period. Excess demand $(D_t - Q_t$, i.e. $D_t - D_{t-1})$ is met from stock, excess output is put into it, and firms try to readjust their stock to normal in the following period. Their demand for stock replacements is a form of investment demand (which may, of course, be negative if excess output occurred in the previous period); total investment demand in period t, then, will be $A_t + (D_{t-1} - D_{t-2})$, where A_t is autonomous investment. Consumption is assumed to depend on current income, i.e. $C_t = c Y_t$; here 'Y_t' is actual income generated by, and identical with, current output Q_t; because $Q_t = D_{t-1}$, $C_t = c Y_t$ implies $C_t = c D_{t-1}$. Aggregate demand D_t consists of consumption and investment, so

$$D_t = c D_{t-1} + A_t + D_{t-1} - D_{t-2}$$
$$= D_{t-1}(1+c) - D_{t-2} + A_t.$$

If D_{t-1} and D_{t-2} are both 100, and if $A_t = 20$ and $c = 0.8$, D_t will be $100(1.8) - 100 + 20$, i.e. 100. Now let autonomous investment rise by 10, giving $A_{t+1} = 30$, and then return to its original level so that A_{t+2}, A_{t+3} etc. are all 20. Then

$$D_{t+1} = D_t(1+c) - D_{t-1} + A_{t+1}$$
$$= 100(1.8) - 100 + 30 = 110;$$
$$D_{t+2} = D_{t+1}(1+c) - D_t + A_{t+2}$$
$$= 110(1.8) - 100 + 20 = 118.$$

By a similar calculation, $D_{t+3} = 122.4$. Now, however, demand falls again: $D_{t+4} = 122.3$ and $D_{t+5} = 117.8$; the decline continues until period $t+10$, when $D_{t+10} = 77.6$, after which demand begins to rise once more.[1]

The presence of the output lag (or 'Lundbergian lag' as it is sometimes called[2]) has thus enabled the rise in autonomous investment to

---

[1] The reader may carry on the calculation, if he wishes, by inserting numerical values; unfortunately, this is a laborious procedure. A short cut is to find a 'general solution' for such a series of equations (which are known as *difference equations*); for methods, see W. J. Baumol, *Economic Dynamics*, Chaps. 9, 10 and 11; W. T. Dowsett, *Elementary Mathematics in Economics*, Chaps. 21, 22 and 23.

[2] After E. Lundberg, *Studies in the Theory of Economic Expansion* (1937).

set up a *cyclical* movement in aggregate demand. From one period to another, demand increases not only through the simple multiplier effect of the rise in investment, but also because of the carrying over of a backlog of demand for stocks. As output approaches the level at which the backlog of demand begins to be satisfied, the very act of catching up on the backlog will eliminate it from next period's demand, so that eventually demand will fall again. But a fall in demand must mean the accumulation of surplus stocks, if output is not immediately reduced; the effort to work these off will cause demand to fall further—and so on through the cycle.

Where firms merely leave excess demand unsatisfied, instead of meeting it from stock, the effects should be exactly the same; the backlog of demand is accumulated by 'final buyers' instead of by producers whose stocks are depleted. If, however, the excess of demand over supply in the opening periods causes prices to be driven upwards, this may change the pattern of demand through the expectational and 'Pigou' effects described in the previous chapter,[1] thus complicating the cycle.

So far, it has been assumed that the output lag is of fixed length; but in real life this would hardly be true. A pronounced upward or downward trend in demand may induce firms to alter output quickly, perhaps even to anticipate the trend; small changes may leave them in a 'wait and see' frame of mind, so that the lag will increase as the multiplier effects taper off. If a rise in demand calls for output at or near the full employment level, the physical difficulties of increasing output will be much greater than those met when there are plenty of idle resources available: the lag will therefore increase as output rises. No such difficulty will arise when it is a question of reducing output to match falling demand, and since the embarrassment of piling up stocks of unsold goods is greater than that of not being able to satisfy demand fully, firms may be expected to cut output more quickly than they increase it; in general, then, the output lag is likely to be shorter when demand is falling than when it is rising.

The practical measurement of output lags is difficult. If differences between demand and output were always met from (or put into) stock, and if stocks never changed for any other reason, then a rise or fall of stock would signalize a lag of output behind demand. But firms may buy more stock when they think the prices of materials will rise in future, or run down stock if they think price-reductions will allow cheaper replacement later. A rise in demand may sometimes be directed mainly upon industries (e.g. transport) which cannot store their output, sometimes upon industries which can. Firms

[1] See above, pp. 112–13.

whose stocks run down may be spurred into finding ways of econo-
mizing them, so that their customers' demand will be partly offset by
a permanent fall in firms' own demand. Nevertheless, L. A. Metzler
was able to conclude, on the basis of American data for 1921–38, that
'the lag in consumers' expenditure is short, relatively to the lag in
output,'[1] and this is very likely to be true of present-day Britain also.

(e) Corporate saving and the Multiplier

As well as investigating lags in consumption and output, Metzler
sought evidence of an 'earnings lag', i.e. an interval between the actual
generation of income in production and its receipt by the owners of
factors of production. To the extent that higher output is achieved by
increasing employment, wages will rise a week (and salaries a month)
later. To the extent that higher output entails a rise in profits, these will
remain in the hands of firms for the time being: companies distribute
dividends half-yearly, so a rise in production in January may not raise
shareholders' income until July, even if dividends are increased at the
earliest opportunity—and they may not be increased even then, if
directors wait to see whether the higher profits will be sustained.
Thus, a rise in output may cause shareholders' incomes to increase only
after a lag of many months. This will extend whatever consumption
lag already operates, so far as shareholders are concerned.

There is, in fact, little statistical evidence of a shareholders' earnings
lag in Britain in recent years, nor did Metzler find one in pre-war
America: whatever lag exists is presumably no longer than the half-
yearly accounting period itself. However, reference to the statistics
of profits and dividends brings to light another phenomenon about
which there can be no doubt at all: that is, the large proportion of
profits which are retained by companies instead of being distributed
in dividends. From their gross income (which includes certain non-
trading receipts as well as gross trading profits) companies must pay
taxes, provide for depreciation and stock appreciation, and service
fixed-interest debt; whatever remains after these payments have been
made (the 'distributable income' of companies) is used partly for
distribution in dividends and partly for retention within the company. In 1975, companies' total 'distributable' income was £2,479
millions, of which £1,483 millions, i.e. 60%, were distributed to
shareholders; over the whole period 1968–75 the average percentage

---

[1] L. A. Metzler, 'Three Lags in the Circular Flow of Income', in *Income,
Employment and Public Policy* (Essays in Honour of Alvin H. Hansen) (1948),
p. 30.

was 52·6%, while the proportion of any *change* in income distributed[1] was roughly 17%. Thus, companies had a 'marginal propensity to save' of more than four-fifths of distributable income and an 'average propensity to save' of rather less than a half. By retaining profits, companies are saving on behalf of their shareholders; the question is, however, whether the latter would have saved the same amount if the *whole* of the companies' discretionary income had been distributed in dividends. If they normally treat an increase in dividends as a rise in their personal incomes, to be divided between consumption and saving in the usual way, it is evident that total saving would have been reduced, and it becomes necessary to modify the earlier formulation of the Multiplier.

Instead of the consumption function $C = cY$ (where Y is National Income, i.e. the sum of factor incomes), the function $C = cY_d$ (where Y_d is the sum of personal disposable incomes) will be used. The equilibrium condition $Y = C+I$ then becomes $Y = cY_d+I$. If taxes and transfers are neglected, Y_d is National Income *minus* undistributed profits (U). The 'corporate propensity to save' relates U to total profits P; if one-half of profits are normally left undistributed, $U = \frac{1}{2}P$; then, if total profits are normally one-sixth of National Income, $U = \frac{1}{2}(\frac{1}{6}Y) = \frac{1}{12}Y$. Let the symbol j stand for the 'corporate propensity to save' multiplied by the share of profits in National Income, so that $U = jY$; then

$$Y_d = Y-U = Y-jY = Y(1-j).$$

The equilibrium condition $Y = cY_d+I$ now becomes

$$Y = cY(1-j)+I.$$

If the average propensities c and j are the same as the marginal propensities, a change in income will be

$$\Delta Y = c\Delta Y(1-j)+\Delta I$$

and the static Multiplier will be

$$k = \frac{\Delta Y}{\Delta I} = \frac{1}{1-c+cj}.$$

The value of the Multiplier will thus be smaller, the greater the

---

[1] The relationship between dividends (D) and companies' distributable income (P) during 1968–75 was approximately $D = 1,021+0·17\ P$ (£ millions, at current prices).

corporate marginal propensity to save and the greater the share of company profits in National Income.[1]

Similar modification of the dynamic Multiplier, with a one-period 'Robertsonian' consumption lag and no output lag, will give the following series of income-changes in response to an initial rise in investment which is not repeated after period 1:

$$\Delta Y_1 = \Delta I_1$$

$$\Delta Y_2 = c\Delta I_1(1-j) - \Delta I_1$$

$$\Delta Y_3 = c^2\Delta I_1(1-j)^2 - c\Delta I_1(1-j)$$

leading in the nth period to

$$\Delta Y_n = c^{n-1}\Delta I_1(1-j)^{n-1} - c^{n-2}\Delta I_1(1-j)^{n-2}.$$

Here, the 'corporate marginal propensity to save' (if positive) reduces the proportion of income handed on from each period to the next, causing total income to rise less at first, and taper off more sharply and quickly, than if all profit had been distributed in dividends.

Bringing companies' behaviour into the Multiplier sequence naturally increases its realism: it is obviously very unlikely that an increase in autonomous expenditure will bring about an immediate increase of the same magnitude in personal disposable incomes. It would indeed do so if the 'multiplicand' were expenditure on a project involving only an increase in labour employed, for example the digging of a ditch with spades drawn from stores. But most investment projects involve the purchase of machinery and the placing of contracts, for which payments are made to companies in the first instance: they in turn[2] pay out wages, buy materials from other firms, pay dividends out of whatever profit they make and retain the rest undistributed. If the distribution of dividends comes some time after

---

[1] It must be emphasized that the above reasoning assumes that companies allocate income between dividends and retentions in fixed proportions. But this may not, in fact, be in accordance with their usual behaviour: see p. 162 below for some statistical evidence on this. If companies' policy were to distribute a fixed *amount* in dividends, rather than a constant proportion of their income, their 'marginal propensity to save' would be equal to 1, and the j of the formula would be the share of profit in national income. Other policies would make the Multiplier much more complicated.

[2] The actual order of payments may very well be the other way round: contractors may not receive payment until the job is finished, and in the meantime will pay for labour and materials as the work proceeds by borrowing, or using funds of their own. But this means that they *behave* as though payment had been made when the order was first placed, and the sequence of income-generation then proceeds in normal multiplier fashion.

the payment of wages, the subsequent effects of a rise in investment will be complicated by an earnings lag: for example

$$\Delta C_t = c_1 w \Delta Y_{t-1} + c_2 z \Delta Y_{t-2}$$

(where w is the share of wages, and z the share of dividends, in any increase in income) describes a situation in which dividends lag one period behind wage-payments. In this equation, the MPCs of wage-earners and shareholders are c_1 and c_2 respectively; if they happen to differ from each other, this will add a further complication to the sequence.

(f) The 'multi-sector' Multiplier

The more 'realistic' the account of the Multiplier, unfortunately, the more complicated it becomes: this, if nothing else, should be clear from the last two sections. The original version given on p. 132 owed its apparent simplicity to the fact that income, consumption and investment were treated as large aggregates, within each of which no distinction was made between component elements. But in fact, consumption may change much or little in response to a rise in income, depending on how the latter is distributed between groups of consumers: if Scotsmen have a lower MPC than Englishmen, a rise in investment north of the Tweed will produce a different effect from that of one south of it. When demand increases, the response of output may be quick or slow according to which industries are called upon to produce more: if consumers want more clothing, labour and materials will be required to meet the demand, whereas if they wish to go to the cinema more often, it may be possible to accommodate them merely by filling empty seats. Some industries may carry large stocks from which to meet a rise in demand, others may not. To increase the output of industry A, it will be necessary to employ more labour, but relatively little extra capital equipment will be needed; in industry B it may be the other way about, so that a good deal will depend on whether a rise in demand is directed towards A's product or B's. Obviously, there will be a considerable gain in realism if the aggregates are 'disaggregated' so as to allow for such differences between industries and between groups of consumers.

For this purpose, transactions between the various sectors of the economy can be set out in a 'matrix', of which Table VII is a simple example. Each entry (except for the totals) shows the amount paid by the sector named on the left of the row to the sector named at the head of the column. All transactions are for goods and services: 'capital transfers', such as the purchase of stocks and shares, are

TABLE VII

Paid By ↓ \ Received By→	Industries A	B	C	Consumers £ millions	Totals
Industries A	—	40	60	100	200
B	50	—	50	150	250
C	50	100	—	250	400
Consumers	80	100	220	—	400
Totals	180	240	330	500	1,250

excluded. Thus, payments by consumers to the various industries represent purchases of the industries' products; payments *by* industries to consumers are wages, dividends and interest. Transactions between industries represent the purchase of materials: for example, the £50 millions in the second row of the first column is Industry *B*'s purchase from *A* of goods to be processed into the output *B* sells to other sectors. Transactions *within* sectors are cancelled out. Because consumers' total receipts are £500 millions and their total payments £400 millions, personal saving is £100 millions. Industry *A* pays out £20 millions more than its receipts, Industry *B* £10 millions and Industry *C* £70 millions; this represents the purchase of plant and buildings and the accumulation of stocks—i.e. the investment undertaken by the three industries; total investment, of course, equals total saving. If saving (a capital payment) and investment (a capital receipt) were explicitly shown in an extra column and row, each sector's total payments would equal its total receipts.

Such matrices (often called 'input-output tables' or 'Leontief systems'[1]) can be made more detailed, with extra rows and columns for imports, exports and government transactions, and with a larger number of industries.[2] Ideally, there should be a separate row and column for each 'sector' within which spenders' behaviour is much the same; for example, if rich consumers have a different consumption function from poor ones, they should be divided accordingly. However numerous the rows and columns, however, the principle is the same as in Table VII, which has been restricted to four sectors for the sake of simplicity.

Altering any one of the figures (or 'elements') in the table will

[1] After W. W. Leontief, who pioneered this approach: see his *The Structure of the American Economy, 1919–39*, 1941.

[2] Cf. the April 1976 issue of *Economic Trends*, which gives a matrix of 37 rows and 35 columns relating to transactions in 1972.

obviously change the relevant column total, the row total, and the grand total in the bottom right-hand corner. But it will do more than that. The proportions in which an industry's payments are divided between the other sectors are determined by the nature of its product and by its technique of production. Just as the manufacture of a given quantity of steel requires certain definite quantities of pig-iron, fuel and labour, so Industry A could not be producing its output without buying inputs from B and C, and from consumers (who contribute labour and the use of their property), in the proportions 40:60:100 respectively. The distribution of consumers' payments to A, B and C is determined by their preferences, and the consumption function relates the total of consumers' payments to their total receipts. The proportions between the individual elements and the grand total (the so-called 'technical coefficients') thus form a pattern which gives a set of equilibrium conditions for the system: if the coefficients are simple percentages, an autonomous change in any single element must cause equal proportionate changes in all of the others.

However, the coefficients may not be simple percentages. Because consumers spend four-fifths of their receipts when the latter are £500 millions, it does not follow that an addition of £100 millions to their receipts will cause their spending to rise by £80 millions—this is a matter of the marginal, rather than the average, propensity to consume. Similarly, the proportions between the *extra* inputs needed for a given increase in an industry's output may not be the same as those between the *total* inputs shown in Table VII; the distinction here is that between marginal and average costs of production. Thus, when an autonomous change in expenditure occurs, the results will depend on the *marginal* values of the technical coefficients, some of which may even be zero; when the system is completely adjusted and a new equilibrium has been established, the multiplier effect will be disclosed by a comparison of the figures appearing in the table before and after the disturbance occurred. This version of the Multiplier, working through the transactions relationships of the various sectors, may be called the '*Multi-sector*' or '*Matrix*' *Multiplier*. Introducing time-lags (which need not, of course, be the same for all sectors) will make it dynamic, and raises the possibility of oscillations as it did in the Lundbergian case. Further analysis, however, would require the use of matrix algebra, with which the reader is not assumed to be familiar; in the present text, therefore, the matter will be left at this point.[1]

[1] See R. M. Goodwin, 'The Multiplier as Matrix', *Economic Journal*, December 1949. In 'Some Notes on Multiplier Theory', *American Economic Review*, 1953, R. Turvey works with a matrix simplified to two sectors, one for goods and

(g) The 'employment Multiplier'

So far, the Multiplier concept has been presented in terms of *output*: an autonomous change in demand induces further changes, leading to a multiple rise in the equilibrium level of National Product. It should be noted, however, that the Multiplier was first introduced (by R. F. Kahn in 1931[1]) as a ratio between levels of *employment*: an initial rise in investment creates 'primary' employment for workers engaged directly on new capital projects, and their spending then gives rise to 'secondary' employment in the industries producing consumer goods: the ratio between the overall rise in employment and the primary employment is the 'employment Multiplier'.

If the proportion between output and employment—i.e. the productivity of labour—were the same for all levels of output, there would be no difference between the value of the Employment Multiplier (k^*) and the ordinary Multiplier (k). But (as was argued in Chapter Four, on p. 73) output per unit of labour may be expected to fall as output increases toward the Full Employment level; if this happens, k^* should be larger than k when the Multiplier is working to increase output and employment, but smaller when it works in the opposite direction. Any level Y of income and output must be equal to N, the number of man-hours worked, multiplied by output per man-hour, M. The ratio between two levels of output, Y_2/Y_1, therefore, equals $N_2 M_2/N_1 M_1$; so $N_2/N_1 = (Y_2 \div M_2) \div (Y_1 \div M_1) = Y_2 M_1/Y_1 M_2$. If $Y_1 = 100$ and $Y_2 = 110$, while $M_1 = 100$ and $M_2 = 90$, $N_2/N_1 = (110 \times 100) \div (100 \times 90) = 1 \cdot 22$; that is, a rise of 10% in the level of production, accompanied by a 10% fall in output per man-hour, requires an increase of 22% in the level of employment. In this case, k^* is twice as large as k.

If time-lags are introduced into the employment Multiplier, its value may be reduced by improvements in labour productivity *over time*. If the economy's capital equipment is being improved and increased through investment, output per man-hour will be rising, between one period and another, for *all* levels of output: the employment-output curve of Fig. 2 (p. 74) will have moved upwards from $Q(N,\bar{K}_1)$ to $Q(N,\bar{K}_2)$. The fall in productivity due to diminishing returns will then be offset by the rise due to investment, and the *dynamic* Employment Multiplier will be a good deal smaller than the static one.

With these adjustments for changes in labour productivity, the

services, one for factors of production. For matrix algebra as such, see W. T. Dowsett, *op. cit.*, Chaps. 11–14; and R. G. D. Allen, *Mathematical Economics*, Chaps. 11–14.

[1] R. F. Kahn, 'The Relation of Home Investment to Unemployment', *Economic Journal*, June 1931.

employment Multiplier is completely analogous to the 'output' Multiplier, and everything which has been said of the latter applies to the former also. In all Multipliers, the basic principle is that changes in the level of activity (whether in terms of output or employment) are initiated by changes in the autonomous elements of demand, of which investment has traditionally been regarded as the chief. The next chapter, therefore, will be devoted to the subject of investment and its determinants.

CHAPTER SEVEN

The Determinants of Investment

(a) The categories of investment

The first thing to notice about investment is its multifarious character. Of the £20,510 millions expenditure in Britain during 1975 on gross fixed capital formation, 24% was done by the central government and local authorities, 19% by public corporations, 42% by companies and the remaining 16% by 'persons' (e.g. unincorporated businesses and house-purchasers). About 33% of the total represented purchases of plant and machinery, while 20% was spent on dwelling-houses, 38% on other construction, and 9% on vehicles, ships and aircraft. 'Capital consumption' was £10,907 millions: that is, more than half of all fixed investment merely offset the year's wear-and-tear.[1] Investment also includes increases in stocks, but in 1975 stocks were actually run down by £1,349 millions. This disinvestment, however, was exceptional: normally, stockbuilding is a positive item of investment. In 1974 it had been £1,144 millions.

With such a variety of spenders and objects of spending, it seems unlikely that a single, simple theory will explain what determines investment. The motives of a company buying new machinery obviously differ from those of a local authority ordering the building of a school; considerations relevant to the company's decision may have no bearing on the local authority's. Building up stocks serves one set of purposes, constructing new factories serves another; firms' decisions to replace equipment may involve different criteria from decisions to expand it. In general, no doubt, each kind of investment expenditure can be assumed to envisage a future yield of some sort, which the spenders wish to maximize: school-builders aim to increase 'educational output' in the most economical manner, just as businesses aim to raise future profits; but general resemblances may

---

[1] *National Income and Expenditure, 1965–75*, Tables 11.3 and 12.3 The statistics do not include expenditure on research and development, though this should be noted as yet another category of investment—and one which is of increasing importance.

be overwhelmed by particular differences, and the present chapter will therefore separate the categories of investment demand in trying to discover their determinants.

As earlier with consumption, so now with investment, special attention must be paid to its relationship with income. If changes in investment demand typically arise from causes other than changes in income, multiplier effects will follow on the lines described in the previous chapter, and the level of investment will determine the equilibrium level of income. It is, therefore, particularly important to decide how far each category of investment demand is 'autonomous' and how far it is responsive to income and to changes therein.

(b) The Marginal Efficiency of Investment

The category most frequently discussed in the literature of the subject is the net fixed investment of profit-maximizing firms—i.e. companies and unincorporated businesses; nationalized industries may be included in so far as they are seeking to make profits, though they may have other aims as well. Suppose a firm has the opportunity to buy a new machine costing, say, £10,000. How is it to decide whether or not to do so?

Installing the machine will give a physical output whose sale will provide the firm with a revenue, the amount of which will depend on the price of the product. If that product is something quite new, the firm will have to estimate the price at which it can be sold when it comes on to the market. If the product is already on sale, some estimate must be made as to what the price is likely to be during the period over which the machine will be operating. It may not be easy, indeed, to foresee how long that period will be: no doubt the machine's makers can forecast its 'life' from an engineering point of view, but there is always the possibility of sudden obsolescence through the introduction of technological advances. Obviously, the assessment of prospective revenue from the machine will be subject to a large margin of uncertainty.

Against the revenue must be set the various expenses of operating the machine. It will use materials, fuel and lubricants: it may require the employment of additional labour, and it will occupy floor-space. The physical quantities of these inputs will be known to the firm, just as the quantity of its 'capacity' output will be; but the firm cannot be sure what the costs of the inputs will be during the life of the machine, since these will depend on the future course of prices and wages. However, the firm must 'take a view'; having decided on the most probable level of input cost, it can subtract it from its estimate of revenue to obtain estimates of the net yield to be expected from the machine during its life; the annual yield can then be expressed as a percentage of the current price, giving a *rate* of yield.

This is analogous to compound interest on a loan of money. If a principal sum P is lent for n years at compound interest, it will accumulate to a sum A such that $A = P(1+r)^n$, where r is the interest rate. Given P, r and N, A can be calculated; alternatively, if A, r and n are known, the value of P is given as

$$P = \frac{A}{(1+r)^n};$$

here, future receipts A are 'discounted' by r to give a 'present value' P; r appears as a rate of interest when the reckoning is forward from the present to the future, and as a 'rate of discount' when reckoning is backward from the future to the present.

If a firm buys a machine for £10,000, expecting a lump-sum net yield of £15,000 five years hence, the annual rate of yield r can be deduced from the formula

$$£10,000 = \frac{£15,000}{(1+r)^5}$$

i.e.

$$r = \sqrt[5]{\frac{£15,000}{£10,000}} - 1 = 0{\cdot}084 = 8{\cdot}4\%.$$

More typically, yields accrue continuously over the life of the machine, rather than all at once; the series of annual net yields is $A_1 + A_2 + A_3 + \ldots + A_n$, where the subscripts stand for years and n is the number of years for which the machine is expected to last. This is as though a number of loans had been made simultaneously, each accumulating at compound interest over a different number of years: P_1 for one year, P_2 for two years and so on, so that

$$P_1 = \frac{A_1}{(1+r)}, \qquad P_2 = \frac{A_2}{(1+r)^2}, \qquad P_3 = \frac{A_3}{(1+r)^3}, \text{ etc.}$$

Adding these gives P, the total sum laid out; and

$$P = \frac{A_1}{(1+r)} + \frac{A_2}{(1+r)^2} + \frac{A_3}{(1+r)^3} + \ldots + \frac{A_n}{(1+r)^n}.$$

If the machine costs £10,000, if each year's net yield is expected to be £3,000, and if $n = 5$, the value of r which satisfies the equation is approximately 0·15 or 15%. The annual net yield need not be the same in each year—the series may run £2,000, £2,600, £2,900 and so on; but whatever the values of A_1, A_2 etc., some value of r will satisfy the equation,[1] and this will be the rate of yield. It should be noted that the analogy with compound-interest lending requires that the depreciation of the machine shall not be counted as an expense of production; just as a lender of money receives back his principal at the end of n years as part of the accumulated sum A, so the investing firm will recover the original outlay on the machine as part of the series of yields received during its life.

The rate of yield r is conventionally called the *Marginal Efficiency of Investment* (MEI). The word 'marginal' must be emphasized: the MEI is the r of an *additional* machine, and may be quite different from the rate of yield expected from others already ordered. Keynes originally[2] called it the 'Marginal Efficiency of Capital', but it is preferable to use a term which refers explicitly to investment. The MEI must also be distinguished from the 'marginal product of capital', which is the increase in *current* output arising from the addition of one more unit of capital to the currently employed factors of production; obviously, this is a physical quantity analogous to the marginal product of any other factor (whereas the MEI is a percentage rate), and it does not involve expectations about the yield from the unit of capital during the remainder of its life as the MEI does.

A firm considering the purchase of a new machine may be supposed to compare the MEI with the cost of the funds required to buy it. If the firm does not itself possess the necessary funds, it must acquire them by borrowing,[3] in which case the 'cost of funds' is the rate of interest on the loan. If the firm already has the money in hand, the cost is the return which could have been obtained by making some other use of the money; here the choice is between employing it within the business to get an 'internal rate of return' and lending it out to get an 'external' rate. If the MEI is greater than the rate of interest to be paid or forgone, the machine is worth buying.

This may be put in another way. If money can be borrowed or lent at an interest rate i, the series of expected yields A_1, A_2 etc., can be

---

[1] This burkes a mathematical point. If any of the A's are negative, as they might be where a firm was prepared to face losses in the earlier stages of an operation, the equation may give *several* values for r: see Pitchford and Hagger, 'A Note on the Marginal Efficiency of Capital', *Economic Journal*, September 1958. In the text, this possibility is ignored for the sake of simplicity.

[2] J. M. Keynes, *The General Theory of Employment, Interest and Money*, pp. 135–6.

[3] The possibility of issuing shares is for the moment neglected, but is considered later (pp. 159–61).

discounted by i to give their 'present value', i.e. the sum of money which, if lent at interest i, would produce the given yields. The 'present value' V is

$$V = \frac{A_1}{(1+i)} + \frac{A_2}{(1+i)^2} + \frac{A_3}{(1+i)^3} + \cdots + \frac{A_n}{(1+i)^n}.$$

If V is greater than the price of the machine, P, it is obviously profitable to make the investment; in buying the machine, a firm is giving up a sum of money smaller than the present value of the yields obtainable from the use of the machine.[1]

If *one* machine is worth buying, why not two, or three, or still more? If the firm can borrow any amount at the prevailing rate of interest i, it will be profitable to buy new machines as long as the MEI exceeds i; this will cease to be the case only if the MEI falls as more machines are bought. Such a fall may occur because the firm expects the price of the product to be depressed as output rises in consequence of the installation of new equipment; rising input prices may be foreseen in response to the increasing pressure of demand for labour and materials; between falling product price and rising input prices, the MEI will be reduced. A small firm, of course, may not fear such an outcome—if its output is small relatively to the market as a whole, it may be confident that even a sizeable rise in its own sales would not disturb the market price; and it may feel sure of obtaining all the inputs it expects to need, without creating price-raising shortages in the markets for labour and materials. Nevertheless, such a firm would still be obliged to limit its investment for another reason. The interest it must pay is certain because fixed by contract, whereas the rate of yield from the machine is a matter of estimation and could turn out to be less than expected; the greater the investment, then, the greater the loss the firm stands to make if things should turn out badly. A small loss might be met from the original resources of the firm, but a large one might ruin it. On M. Kalecki's[2] 'principle of increasing risk', therefore, the firm should make a greater allowance for risk, the greater the investment it undertakes: set against the firm's original yield calculations, this will cause the MEI to fall with each additional machine bought.

The MEI, then, falls as investment increases, and the limit to the demand for new machines will be reached when the MEI is reduced

---

[1] See A. H. Hansen, *Business Cycles and National Income* (1951), p. 125.

[2] M. Kalecki, *Essays in the Theory of Economic Fluctuations* (1939), Chap. 4. Kalecki prefers to include an allowance for risk in the cost of finance, by adding it to the rate of interest; but since risk is here a matter of subjective calculation, it seems better to bring it into the MEI.

to equality with the rate of interest. The inverse relationship between the MEI and the level of investment is illustrated in Fig. 11. Point A refers to a level of investment demand (I_1) and to the value of the MEI (r_1) which is consistent with it. Point B, similarly, associates I_2 with r_2. A line passing through all such points associating values of I with values of the MEI may be called the 'MEI schedule' or 'MEI curve'. For any rate of interest measured on the vertical scale, the MEI schedule shows the level of investment demand at which the

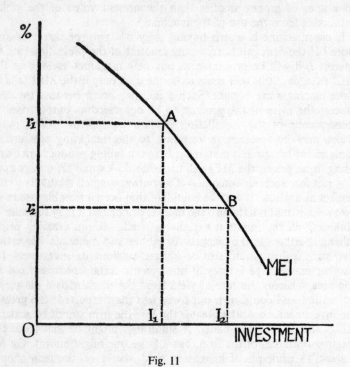

Fig. 11

MEI will be brought into equality with that rate of interest; the schedule is thus a demand curve for investment. Summing the MEI schedules of all firms gives the demand for investment in the economy as a whole.

(c) Investment and interest rates

The foregoing account of the MEI concept seems to imply that investment demand depends on the level of interest rates: e.g. in

Fig. 13 it appears that a reduction in interest from r_1 to r_2 would raise demand from I_1 to I_2. But the available evidence suggests that business firms pay relatively little attention to interest rates when making plans to increase their fixed capital. Replying to a Federation of British Industries questionnaire[1] in 1957, only 37% of the 1,595 respondent firms answered 'Yes' to the question, 'Does your judgement of the profitability of new investment vary from time to time according to the prevailing rate of interest?' Out of 610 firms completing the Birmingham Chamber of Commerce questionnaire[2] in 1957, 185 had postponed or cancelled fixed investment plans in the previous two years, but only 72 had done so because of higher interest rates. The Chairman of Shell, asked by the Radcliffe Committee in 1958 whether a doubling of interest rates would not modify his firm's investment decisions, replied 'I should say not'.[3] The Chairman of Unilever told the Committee: 'changes in interest rates have not affected the volume, pattern or timing of our fixed investment programme directly'.[4]

The conclusion which emerges from inquiries into firms' investment policy is that the interest-cost of fixed investment is often a minor consideration.[5] It seems that the MEI schedule of Fig. 11 is likely to be fairly inelastic with respect to the rate of interest, and that the level of investment demand depends to a considerable extent on other influences which, when they change, shift the whole curve.

Among these, the most obvious is the state of expectations. Earlier, firms were assumed to take definite views about the most probable levels of revenue and costs, and to make precise assessments of the life of equipment. But expectations may be much vaguer than this. A firm may feel fairly sure that the rate of yield will be within certain limits—say between 5% and 30%—but may find it impossible to decide which rate within these extremes is most likely to be realized.

[1] Committee on the Working of the Monetary System (the 'Radcliffe Committee'), *Memoranda of Evidence*, Vol. 2, Part VII, 8.

[2] *Ibid.*, Vol. 2, Part VII, 1.

[3] *Minutes of Evidence*, Question 11543.

[4] *Ibid.*, Question 11478. It is interesting that although the heads of large companies testified that interest costs were of little importance to their own firms, they seemed to believe that smaller firms were sensitive to changes in interest rates.

[5] For a summary of the results of surveys, see J. R. Meyer and E. Kuh, *The Investment Decision* (1957), Appendix to Chap. II, and also p. 189 for the authors' findings from their own survey. On the best-known British investigation, see *Oxford Studies in the Price Mechanism* (ed. Wilson and Andrews, 1951), Chap. I, (iii) and (v). See also Brockie and Grey, 'The Marginal Efficiency of Capital and Investment Programming', *Economic Journal*, December, 1956 and J. C. R. Dow, Radcliffe *Memoranda*, Vol. 3, XIII, 9.

In such a case, only really large changes in interest would alter a decision to go ahead with investment. As well as being uncertain, expectations may also be very volatile: they may change quickly and drastically in response to the general mood of the business community; rumours, news of technical developments, political events, even directors' ulcers may cause a sudden rise or fall of the expected rate of yield.

A particular source of uncertainty is the possibility that plant may become technologically obsolete sooner than had been expected and well before it is worn out physically. This is one reason why firms often work in terms of a 'pay-out period' for new plant: instead of the rate of yield over its whole life, they calculate the rate which must be obtained if the plant is to cover its original cost, in, say, four years; in the fifth year and subsequently, all yields will be net gain. Thus, a four-year pay-out period implies a rate of yield of 25% of the cost of the plant; if a firm thinks it cannot obtain this, it will not undertake the investment, even though the necessary funds could be obtained at 5%. If it turns out that the plant goes on yielding 25% per annum for ten years, it will *then* appear to have been worth buying even with money borrowed at much more than 5%; the essence of the investment decision, however, is that the firm may have no notion of how long the yield will continue when the plant is first bought.

Some machines, it is true, have a fairly short expectation of life: where it is a question of forecasting yield not over ten years but only over two or three, uncertainty will be less, and it might seem that such investment ought to be more interest-elastic than that in longer-living equipment. But here another consideration arises. It was seen above (p. 153) that the prospective yields of a machine may be discounted by the interest rate i to give a present value V; if this exceeds P, the price of the machine, it is profitable to buy it. A rise in i means that yields are being discounted more heavily, so that V will fall; when V falls below P, the machine is no longer worth buying. But the nearer the yield in time, the less will a change in i alter its present value. For example, £100 receivable two years hence, discounted[1] at 5%, has present value of £90·7; at 6%, £89; at 7%, £87·3. The same £100 receivable ten years hence, discounted at 5%, has present value of £61·4; at 6%, £55·9; at 7%, £50·8. Thus, a given machine's

---

[1] Present value $V = \dfrac{A_2}{(1+i)^2} = \dfrac{100}{(1\cdot05)^2} = 90\cdot7$. The other calculations involve increasing i to 0·06 and 0·07, and for the more distant yield A_{10}, discounting by $(1+i)^{10}$ instead of $(1+i)^2$. For a mathematical demonstration of the general relationship between present value, rate of yield and length of yield series, see G. L. S. Shackle, *Uncertainty in Economics*, Chap. XI.

V will be altered relatively little in response to changes in interest if the yields extend only over the next two or three years; for maximum sensitivity, V must include many distant yields—i.e. the machine must be long-lasting.

Insensitivity to current interest rates may also arise from long 'gestation periods' for new projects. If a new plant will take some years to build, the whole of the necessary funds need not be available when the decision to build is first taken: if financing is to be spread out over a long period and the firm expects interest rates to be lower during that time than they are at present, a high *current* interest rate will not affect its decision.[1] It can, indeed, wait for the moment when a long-term loan can be obtained on favourable terms, borrowing on short term in the meantime and repaying short loans out of its long-term borrowing later. In this case, the expectational factor will involve not only the prospective yield from the investment but also the rate of interest itself.

Even if individual projects can be completed fairly quickly, it may not be at all easy to cancel or postpone them. Large firms tend to formulate expansion programmes extending several years ahead, in which the project undertaken in any particular year is merely one link in a chain of developments; to give up any of the current year's investment might disorganize the whole programme, from which the prospective losses might be greater than the saving in interest payments.[2] Cutting current investment may also prevent the realization of expected yields from past investment, if that represented a previous stage of an integrated programme. It appears that long-term planning has come to be practised more and more since the war; to the extent that decisions are less spontaneous—less 'hair-trigger', as Lord Chandos put it in his Radcliffe evidence[3]—investment will be less sensitive to changes in interest rates.

Another reason why large firms may pay relatively little attention to the cost of finance, is that they may have a considerable degree of control over their markets. If a firm is a leading supplier of a commodity, it is not obliged to accept the price which would be settled in a competitive market by supply and demand. It may, therefore, be able to meet higher costs of borrowing by simply increasing the price of its product. Where an entirely new commodity is to be made, the firm will treat interest charges as just another item among its over-

---

[1] Cf. Lord Chandos' evidence to the Radcliffe Committee, *Minutes of Evidence*, Questions 11437–40.

[2] On this, see the Radcliffe evidence given by the chairman of Vickers, *Minutes of Evidence*, Questions 11306–8.

[3] *Minutes of Evidence*, Question 11437.

head costs: the margin of error, in its estimate of what consumers will pay for the new product, may be so great that the level of interest makes little difference. The interest-elasticity of the MEI schedule may therefore depend on the nature of markets in the economy: the less competitive they are, the lower the interest-elasticity.

For all these reasons—uncertainty of expectations, long gestation periods, long-range planning and market imperfection—investment decisions may be insensitive to the cost of borrowing. Insensitivity may appear greater than it really is, however, because of the difficulty of identifying the borrowing cost which is relevant to the calculations of firms. To relate investment spending to 'the rate of interest' is too drastic a simplification: there are many rates of interest, differing according to the duration and conditions of loans, the degree of risk and so on. As J. S. G. Wilson has written, 'no two entrepreneurs will have access to financial resources on exactly the same terms, and . . . even the same entrepreneur will generally find that these costs will be conditioned by the *purpose* for which he borrows'.[1] Whatever the average terms of borrowing may be, potential lenders will assess the prospects and risks of a particular loan in the light of what they believe to be the borrower's present circumstances and past record, and these considerations may cause the 'relevant rate' of a given firm to depart from the average. The average could conceivably change without altering a particular firm's 'relevant rate', so that the firm would have no reason to alter its investment; it would then appear insensitive to borrowing costs, if these were measured by the average rate, even though such costs were an important factor in its investment decisions.

Whatever the rate a firm is prepared to pay, there will be a limit to its power to borrow. Large firms may to some extent succeed in obtaining more finance by offering better terms; small ones, however, may find that they can borrow at a given rate up to some maximum amount, but cannot exceed that maximum whatever they are ready to pay. Banks, for example, decide advances according to the 'credit-worthiness' of borrowers; having assessed, in the light of a firm's turnover, assets and so on, the amount which can be safely lent to it, a bank charges an almost standardized interest rate on borrowings up to that limit, but will lend nothing beyond it. A firm might therefore be obliged to limit investment not because the rate of yield from a further unit would not meet the cost of borrowing, but because its credit limit had been reached; its decisions about investment would

[1] J. S. G. Wilson, 'Credit Rationing and the Relevant Rate of Interest', *Economica*, February 1954.

then depend on the availability rather than the cost of finance, and a rise in interest rates would not necessarily affect those decisions.

For firms proposing to finance investment from internal funds accumulated in the past from undistributed profits, the 'relevant rate' is not that at which it can borrow but the highest rate at which it can lend. If it is prepared to buy other firms' shares it may get a high return: but this means a sacrifice of liquidity, since the shares may fall in price in the future, and most firms are unwilling to take this risk except when they are acquiring 'trade investments', i.e. shares giving control over other firms engaged in similar lines of business. Trade investments, in any case, are usually a means of acquiring control of additional plant, i.e. a roundabout method of buying equipment; the expected return from them is itself a MEI rather than a measure of the cost of finance. If the firm wishes to retain reasonable liquidity when it lends out its funds, it may acquire Treasury Bills, Tax Reserve Certificates, or short-dated government bonds, on which the yield is normally less than that on company shares and debentures. When these 'lenders' rates' are low, the firm will forgo so little revenue by using its funds internally that it can virtually ignore the cost of financing capital expansion; even though 'borrowers' rates' may be relatively high, they will not be relevant to the firm's investment decisions. Thus a firm, which might pay careful attention to interest rates if it were obliged to contract external debt, may appear insensitive to them.

So far, the terms 'cost of borrowing' and 'interest rates' have been used as though they were synonymous. But firms may obtain funds by issuing shares, on which the holders are not entitled to regular fixed-interest payments. Dividends can be made large or small according to the company's profit earnings, and can be 'passed' altogether if earnings are low. Shareholders are part-owners rather than creditors of the firm, and as such they share the risks as well as the gains; by recruiting more shareholders, a firm avoids the dangers associated with fixed-interest borrowing. What, then, is the 'cost' of financing a new project if no fixed-interest charge is incurred?

If the firm is taken to be the original body of 'old' shareholders, the cost of finance is the part of the new project's yield which accrues to the new ones. Conceivably, this could be the whole of that yield. Suppose a company owns equipment and other assets worth £1 millions, earns annual profit of £100,000 and distributes all of this to the owners of its 1 million £1 ordinary shares: the dividend rate is 10%. If it issues 200,000 new £1 ordinaries for £1 each, buys machinery worth £200,000 with the proceeds,[1] and earns an extra £20,000

___

[1] The expense of issuing the shares is ignored.

which is distributed in dividends, the dividend rate remains 10% and the original shareholders have gained nothing.

If the latter are to benefit, the extra machinery must increase the firm's earnings by more than £20,000, or else the new shares must be sold for more than their nominal value of £1 each. On the second alternative, suppose the 200,000 new shares are sold at £2·50 each. The £500,000 thus raised buys equipment yielding additional earnings of £50,000; distributing this raises the dividend to $12\frac{1}{2}$%; the dividend rate is a percentage of the nominal value of the shares (£1), so each share now receives $12\frac{1}{2}$p instead of 10p as previously—a gain of $2\frac{1}{2}$p for the owner of each 'old' share. But $12\frac{1}{2}$p is a return of only 5% on the £2·50 paid over for each newly issued share. Here, then, the 'rate of yield' is 10% (£50,000 earned on £500,000 worth of new equipment) and the 'cost of finance' is 5%. Earnings and dividends may, of course, change in future; if next year the dividend rate is 20%, each new share will obtain 8% on the £2·50 subscribed for it, and the gain accruing to the 'old' shareholders will be less than if the additional £500,000 had been raised by the issue of fixed-interest bonds at 5%. The possibility of such 'earnings dilution' thus makes share issues a potentially costly method of financing investment.

In the first place, however, the company must induce prospective shareholders to pay £2·50 for its shares. Its chances will be small if spending £2·50 on other companies' shares or debentures, or on government bonds, would return much more than $12\frac{1}{2}$p per annum. If buyers see prospects of higher dividends in future, they may pay more than they would for fixed-interest bonds paying $12\frac{1}{2}$p per annum, or for the shares of companies with dimmer prospects; on the other hand, they will not pay as much, if they think the returns are riskier than those obtainable elsewhere. The firm will thus get a price which the buyers think will give them the average rate of return on loanable funds (the 'market rate of interest'), *plus* or *minus* some 'risk and prospects' margin. Subject to this margin, the market rate of interest thus sets the terms on which firms obtain funds by issuing shares, just as it does in the more obvious case of fixed-interest bond issues.

For 'old' shareholders, 'earnings dilution' is a reason for avoiding finance by share issues. But firms are in practice controlled by directors who may not themselves have large shareholdings. For them, the main disadvantage is the threat of 'control dilution': the votes of the new shareholders may be used to impair the directors' command, perhaps even to unseat them. Bond issues, on the other hand, have been seen to entail the 'principle of increasing risk': the more bonds issued, the greater the risk that the firm may be unable to meet the interest charge, in which event the bondholders could insist on a reorganization of the company, including perhaps the dismissal of the directors. If 'lenders' rates' happen to be low, it would seem that directors have strong incentives to avoid the use of 'outside' funds, and to rely as far as possible on using the firm's own resources, i.e. its holdings of liquid assets. It may therefore be the amount of the latter, rather than the level of interest rates, which determines a decision to undertake investment.

Nevertheless, the rate of interest may exert an indirect influence here: in so far as the firm holds interest-bearing securities, a rise in interest rates will depress capital values[1] so that a loss is sustained if the securities are sold; the liquid assets will have become less liquid than before. The firm may hesitate to incur the loss by selling the securities; even if it does, it will have less money than it could count on before interest rates rose; its power to buy new equipment will be diminished. But on the whole, companies tend to hold more cash than securities, and in any case not to hold large quantities of either,[2] so this indirect effect of interest-rate changes cannot be strong.

The main source of internal finance, however, is not the liquid assets held at a given time,[3] but the inflow of profit earnings throughout the year. Some of these earnings must be distributed in dividends to shareholders; though there is no legal obligation to distribute any particular amount, directors may create unmanageable dissatisfaction among shareholders if dividends are exceptionally low. Also, low dividends often mean a low Stock Exchange price for a company's shares, creating the possibility of a 'take-over bid' by which other interests could obtain control of the company.[4] But as long as directors recommend a dividend rate no lower than shareholders will tolerate, they will be able, when earnings are high, to dispose of a mass of undistributed profits for investment purposes. Statistics of profits and dividends in recent years show much smaller fluctuations

---

[1] See above, p. 114.

[2] For example, the accounts of 1,692 companies engaged in manufacturing and distribution show that in 1967 their aggregate holding of cash was £987 millions (3·7% of total assets) as against £314 millions of marketable securities (1·2% of total assets). (*Statistics on Incomes, Prices, Employment and Production*, No. 27, Dec. 1968, Table C.3).

[3] Cf. Lord Chandos: 'No industry should or could be liquid. It is not doing business if it is.' (Radcliffe *Minutes of Evidence*, Question 11447.)

[4] The price in this case is that of 'old' shares, not newly-issued ones; 'old' shareholders are selling their holdings without changing the original number of shares in the company. If the market price of 'old' shares were, say, £1 while the net assets of the company divided by the number of shares were £3, it would pay someone to bid £2 per share to acquire a controlling interest in the company.

F

in dividends than in earnings: in bad years, dividends were maintained at the expense of retained profits, while in good years most of the increased earnings were withheld from distribution. In Table VIII, annual changes in 'distributable' profits (i.e. total company income *minus* tax payments, interest charges, depreciation and stock appreciation) are compared with annual changes in dividends paid during the years 1968–75.[1] It can be seen that when profits rose, dividends increased by a good deal less, while reductions in profits were

TABLE VIII

Change over previous year in	1968	1969	1970	1971	1972	1973	1974	1975
'Distributable' company profits	−116	−169	+28	+693	+583	+395	−806	−546
Dividends paid	−29	+120	−176	+152	−6	+114	−121	−34

usually accompanied by much smaller reduction in dividends; in 1969, dividends were actually increased in spite of the fact that a substantial fall in profits was recorded. The proportion of total profits paid out in dividends was highest in 1969, when it was 73%, and lowest in 1973 when it was only 43%; it has already been noted (on p. 142 above) that companies' 'average propensity to save' was somewhat larger than two-fifths over all eight years. For the company sector as a whole, retained profits were sufficient to finance the greater part of the companies' capital formation during the 1968–75 period.[2]

In these circumstances, it may be the amount of retained earnings, rather than interest rates, which determines how much investment is undertaken: this, indeed, is the essence of the 'Residual Funds' theory of investment put forward by Meyer and Kuh.[3] If firms try to pursue a policy of keeping dividends stable, retained earnings will fluctuate with the level of total profits earned in the recent past. Thus, while the expectation of *future* profits creates the motive for

[1] Figures from *National Income and Expenditure, 1965–75*, Table 5.4, with capital consumption from Table 12.9 for industrial and commercial companies.
[2] *National Income and Expenditure 1965–75* shows in Table 1.7 ('Summary capital account: alternative presentation') the amount of companies' saving (i.e. undistributed profits) net of depreciation and stock appreciation; their net domestic fixed capital formation; and the value of the physical increase in their stocks year by year. Over the 1968–75 period, their saving was equal to 68% of their total expenditure on net fixed investment and stockbuilding.
[3] Meyer and Kuh, *op. cit.*, pp. 204–5.

investment, it may be the level of *past* profits which, by providing the means, determines the extent to which that motive can be indulged.

(d) *Autonomous and induced investment*

From the last section, it appears that the relation between interest and investment is neither clear nor very strong. The MEI schedule in Fig. 11 is probably fairly inelastic to the rate of interest, and a number of other investment-determining factors shift the entire curve to right or left as they vary. To what extent do changes in National Income do this? In the previous chapter, it was suggested that part of aggregate demand is *autonomous* of the level of income, while part is *induced* by it. If the demand for investment is largely income-induced, this will cause the MEI schedule to change its position every time National Income changes, so that investment could vary considerably at a constant rate of interest.

Many of the influences mentioned in the last section have the effect of making investment autonomous. Long-range planning, for example, implies that firms have formed a view of the market demand for their products some years ahead, and are readying themselves to meet it. A firm may invest in order to keep up with its competitors ('We tend', said the Chairman of Unilever to the Radcliffe Committee, 'to set as a minimum the maintenance of our existing share of the developing market'[1]); its policy will then depend on what other firms are doing, rather than on the level of National Income. Firms producing for export markets may invest so as to meet higher demand overseas; this may be due to other countries' incomes growing, but not to changes in the level of income at home. The 'philosophy that some growth is necessary to maintain efficiency',[2] e.g. because the spur of promotion prospects will be greater in a growing company, is another factor which may lead firms to invest without regard to the level of income. Technological progress is yet another; a firm may equip itself to market an entirely new product, confident that its attractions will cause sales to justify the venture, whatever the state of the economy may be when the product is offered for sale; new methods of making existing products may require investment in new plant, which firms may feel obliged to install for fear their competitors

---

[1] *Minutes of Evidence*, Question 11475. This is also a reason for insensitivity to interest rates. 'If we feel that we must "keep up with the Joneses", whether we have to pay 8 per cent or 6 per cent does not make much difference' (Question 11479).

[2] The Chairman of Unilever, *ibid.*, Question 11475.

may do it first. Increasing 'business concentration' (large firms swallowing small ones, and groups of small ones merging), by making the average firm larger, may increase investment if greater resources and easier access to finance make firms more able and willing to face the risks of capital development.

There are many reasons, then, why a good deal of investment should be autonomous of income. But there are also reasons for thinking that another part may be strongly influenced by it. A situation of high output and full employment diffuses a sense of prosperity, causing firms to assess future returns more optimistically than if the economy were suffering from underemployment of labour and equipment. The 'Residual Funds Theory' suggests that when income is high and companies are earning large profits, they will spend a good part of them on investment; at depression levels of income, most if not all profits will be required to maintain dividend-distributions, and investment plans will be held up by the resulting lack of internal finance. When demand is so high that a shortage of labour exists, firms in despair of obtaining additional workers may attempt to expand output by installing labour-saving processes, and this usually means ordering more equipment. The effect of all these considerations will be to shift the MEI curve of Fig. 11 (p. 154 above) upwards and to the right when income is high, downwards and to the left when income is low; at a given interest-rate, this will cause investment to rise and fall with the level of income.

This will mean that there is a positive 'Marginal Propensity to Invest' of the sort mentioned on p. 133. The curve which relates investment-demand to income will no longer be horizontal like AA in Fig. 12 (as it would be if all investment were autonomous), but will slope upwards from left to right after the manner of the line II. This curve is analogous to the consumption function CC in Fig. 4 (p. 98) and may be called the *Investment Function*. The vertical distance OI measures autonomous investment, and the slope of II is the Marginal Propensity to Invest (MPI). The condition of equilibrium is that investment demand shall be equal to intended saving, as shown by the *Saving Function SS*: this occurs where SS intersects II, giving Y_1 as the equilibrium level of income. A rise in autonomous investment will shift II upwards so that it intersects SS to the right of Y_1, and the level of income will then be higher: there will be a multiplier effect whose size will depend not only on the slope of SS (which is, of course, the MPS) but also on the slope of II—it will be, in fact, the 'Compound Multiplier' given on p. 133 above.

A steeply-sloping II-curve, however, could give *unstable* equilibrium. In Fig. 12, income is in stable equilibrium at Y_1; if a momentary disturbance pushed the level of income to the right, saving would exceed investment, implying a deficiency of aggregate demand which would reduce income back to the Y_1 level; similarly, at any income to the left of Y_1 there would be an excess of investment over saving, which would force the income-level back towards equilibrium. If, however, the II-curve slopes more steeply than the SS-curve, all these conditions are reversed; if income were dislodged from Y_1

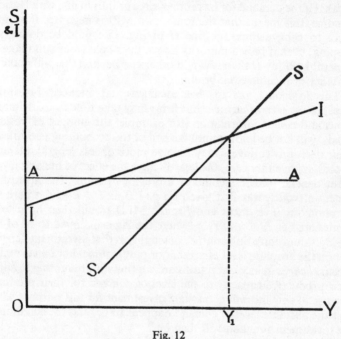

Fig. 12

towards the right, investment would exceed saving and income would increase further instead of returning to Y_1; if it were dislodged to the left saving would exceed investment and income would decline further.[1]

[1] In this case, the 'compound Multiplier' of p. 133 will be negative. The formula $k = \dfrac{1}{1-b-i}$, where b is the MPC and i is the MPI, may be rewritten $k = \dfrac{1}{\text{MPS}-\text{MPI}}$, since the marginal propensity to save is 1 *minus* the MPC. If the value of the MPS were 0·1 and that of the MPI 0·2, the value of k would be $\dfrac{1}{-0\cdot1}$ or -10; a rise in autonomous investment would cause the equilibrium level of income to be *lower* than before—but because the additional investment is pushing income up, the economy will move *away* from this equilibrium instead of towards it.

If the slope of the SS-curve is slight (implying a small Marginal Propensity to Save and a high MPC), even a fairly small MPI gives instability of this sort. On the other hand, it is not completely inconceivable that the MPI could be negative: for example, if a firm would have to suspend or reduce normal output while reconstructing its plant to take additional machinery, it may carry out plant extensions during lulls in demand and may postpone them when demand is brisk;[1] if the demand for its product rises or falls in line with National Income, this means that the firm's own MPI is negative. If all firms were to behave thus, the line II in Fig. 12 would be downward-sloping; even if only a minority do so, their behaviour will make the general MPI lower than it would otherwise be, and this will make for stability of income-equilibrium.

The foregoing analysis has assumed that induced investment depends on *current* income. But firms may take time to form impressions and collect information (for example, the amount of 'residual funds' will not be known until the end of the accounting period), and their decisions to invest may involve more or less lengthy planning processes; in either case, the lag will have the effect of making investment depend on the income of a previous period. The investment function (which was first given on p. 133 as $I = h+iY$, where h is autonomous investment and i is the MPI) would then have to be represented as $I_t = h+iY_{t-1}$ (where the lag is assumed to be of one period's duration). Still another possibility is that investment depends not on the absolute level of present or past income, but on current or recent *changes* in income: if firms are continually attempting to adjust their productive capacity to the level of demand for their products, any rise in demand will necessitate investment for this purpose whatever the absolute level of demand happens to be, and the equation of the investment function will then be

$$I_t = h+i(Y_{t-1}-Y_{t-2})$$

where it is assumed that a one-period lag elapses before firms become aware of, and respond to, the change in income. The lag may, of course, be longer than this, and it may be a more complicated one: some firms, for example, may have regard to the average change in demand over *several* past periods when they are deciding how far to adjust their capacity. Moreover there is no obvious reason why all firms should behave in precisely the same fashion in this respect, so that induced investment in the economy as a whole may very well be determined in all of the ways just mentioned, with one part depending

[1] Cf. the Radcliffe evidence of the Chairman of Tube Investments, *Minutes of Evidence*, Questions 11658–63.

on current income, another on past income, and yet another part on past changes in income. Because of this possibility, it is hardly to be expected that a clear pattern of response will emerge from a statistical comparison of investment and GNP; nevertheless, some relevant figures are presented in Table IX[1] below. Those in column (2), it will be noticed, refer only to the private sector, and exclude expenditure on new dwelling-houses; they therefore represent the 'business

TABLE IX

	(1) Gross National Product	(2) Private Net Fixed Capital Formation at Home, excluding Dwellings	(3) Change from previous year in GNP	(4) Private NFCF
		£ millions at 1970 prices		
1968	42,267	1,869	+1,391	+293
1969	43,133	2,113	+866	+244
1970	44,045	2,163	+912	+50
1971	44,969	2,109	+924	-52
1972	45,766	2,098	+797	-11
1973	48,965	2,270	+3,199	+172
1974	48,842	2,067	-123	-203
1975	47,907	1,806	-835	-259

capital formation' (both by companies and by unincorporated enterprises, though not that done by public corporations) which may be supposed to be influenced by the level of income. When the figures in Columns (3) and (4) are examined, it certainly appears that there is *some* degree of association between changes in GNP and changes in private net capital formation. The three largest increases in GNP—those recorded in 1968, 1969 and 1973—were accompanied by the largest increases in investment; and when GNP fell in 1974 and 1975, investment also fell. On the other hand, there were two years—1971 and 1972—when reductions in private investment occurred even when GNP was increasing; while in other years,

[1] The figures of GNP (at 1970 factor cost) are from Table 2.1 in *National Income and Expenditure, 1965-75*. Those of private NFCF were found by taking the net fixed capital formation figures for companies and the personal sector shown in Table 12.10, subtracting private investment in dwellings from them, and then expressing the results in terms of 1970 prices by applying the index numbers for capital formation given in Table 2.4. It should be noted that the capital formation figures refer to actual, not planned, expenditure; if, for any reason, firms' outlays fell short of what they intended, the figures understate the response of investment-demand to income and income-change.

although both magnitudes were changing in the same direction, there was a considerable degree of variation in the quantitative relationship between them—for example, the increase in GNP in 1973 was more than twice as large as that in 1968, and yet the rise in private investment during 1973 was only about three-fifths of the 1968 figure. Nor is there any indication of a lagged relationship of the kind suggested on p. 166.

These results may appear to be rather disappointing, but it would indeed be surprising if a series of annual statistics of the kind given in Table IX were to give precise confirmation of any theory of induced investment. Apart from the fact, noted earlier, that behaviour may differ considerably between firms and between industries, it must also be remembered that variations occurred in the cost and availability of finance during these years, that there were changes in taxation which probably affected investment-decisions, and that technological innovation was going on throughout the period. Whatever may have been the underlying connection between income and investment, it must have been considerably complicated by these additional factors. However, the proposition that current investment depends on the *absolute* amount of current or past income is less plausible, on *a priori* grounds, than the hypothesis that it depends on past *changes* in income; and this theory—which is known as the *Acceleration Principle*—will now be examined at length.

(e) The 'principle of acceleration'

Suppose a firm produces a commodity X, for which the annual demand has been 1,000 units over the past few years. The firm uses machines which produce 100 units each per year, and which last for ten years. To satisfy demand, the firm thus needs ten machines, of which (it is assumed) one becomes due for replacement each year. This is the initial situation in Year 1. But in Year 2, let the demand for X rise by 100 units; to satisfy it, an extra machine must be installed, so that the firm will now buy two new machines (one additional *plus* one replacement) instead of the customary single one. Next year (Year 3) let demand rise again by 100 X; the firm must install yet another machine, so that it will again buy two instead of the usual single replacement. In Year 4, let demand stay unchanged at 1,200 X; the firm will now need only its customary replacement, so that its order for new machines will be halved. In Year 5, let demand for X fall by 100 units; this time, the firm's requirements for machines having fallen from 12 to 11, it need not even replace the machine which ends its 'life' during the year, so that it will now order no new machines at all.

In this sequence, the initial rise of X-demand creates a proportionately much larger demand for machinery; thereafter, a steady rise in X-demand is required to maintain machine-demand at a constant level; even a levelling-off of X-demand causes machine-demand to fall, while a reduction in X-demand wipes it out altogether. To give a steady annual rise in machine-demand (say 1, 2, 3, 4 . . .), the demand for X would have to increase at an *accelerating* rate— from 1,000 in Year 1 to 1,100 in Year 2, 1,300 in Year 3, 1,600 in Year 4 and so on. This can be expressed in the formula $M_t = m(X_t - X_{t-1}) + R$, where M_t is the number of new machines ordered in Year t, X_t and X_{t-1} are the demand for X in years t and $t-1$ respectively, R is replacements, and m is the number of machines needed per unit of X.

If *all* firms behave in this way, aggregate investment will depend on changes in aggregate demand.[1] These aggregates are, of course, in terms of money, so all the Ms, Rs and Xs must be multiplied by their prices; the total money value of the Xs will be aggregate demand, which will be equal to National Income (Y) if the economy is in equilibrium throughout: thus investment I in year t is

$$I_t = v(Y_t - Y_{t-1}) + R.$$

Here, the physical machine/product relationship m is replaced by v, which is the number of £'s worth of machinery needed to produce £1 worth of output per year; for example, if m were 1/100 as in the example above, and the price of machines were £200 and of X £1, v would be £200÷£100 or 2. The ratio v is a 'capital-output ratio' or 'capital coefficient' expressed in terms of money; in this context it is conventionally called 'the Accelerator'.

It should be noted that the size of v depends not only on the capacity of the machines but also on the period of time over which output is measured. A machine worth £200, which can produce £100 worth of output in a year, will produce £50 worth in six months and £25 worth in a quarter; so if v is measured on a half-yearly basis, it will be £200÷£50, or 4, while if quarterly output is taken, it will be £200÷£25, or 8; similarly, a two-year period would give a v of 1, while a five-year span would make it 0·4. Which, then, is the appropriate time-dimension? This must depend on how quickly firms wish

---

[1] Some accounts of the Acceleration Principle have made investment depend on changes only in *consumers'* demand. But an autonomous rise in demand for new machinery will mean that the firms which produce it require more equipment themselves—machines are needed to make machines. Thus the Principle will operate whatever the nature of the rise in demand.

to equip themselves to meet the increased demand for their products. Suppose the typical firm, having decided to expand its capacity, plans to complete the process within three months. Its investment-demand will then be concentrated into that period, and if all other firms behave in the same way, the I_t of the equation in the last paragraph will represent a single quarter's investment in the economy as a whole; Y_t and Y_{t-1} will be the values of output in successive quarters, and v will be 8. If, on the other hand, firms plan to adjust capacity over a twelve-month period, the subscripts t and $t-1$ will refer to successive years and I_t will represent the amount of *annual* investment-demand. The length of time over which firms plan to carry out their investment-decisions may be called the '*investment period*': the longer it is, the lower the value of v. It will be convenient to assume for the time being that it is always exactly twelve months, so that all measurements—output, investment, and the rate of replacement—are on an annual basis; but it must be borne in mind that this is an arbitrary assumption which might have to be altered.[1]

In the above equation, I is *gross* investment; to show *net* investment, R must be deducted from both sides. If Y_{t-1} exceeds Y_t (i.e. if income is falling), net investment will be negative; but disinvestment cannot exceed R unless firms dismantle equipment which is not yet worn out. Replacement demand appeared to be constant in the example discussed above—the firm always replaced one machine per year; however, an extension of the sequence would have changed this. Machines were assumed to last ten years, so the additional machines added in Years 2 and 3 become due for replacement ten years later; because no machines at all were bought in Year 5, no replacement will be needed in Year 15. The original sequence, in fact, will produce an 'echo-effect' distorting the replacement pattern in the next decade. This gives replacement-demand, for the economy as a whole, as $R_t = v\,(Y_{t-10} - Y_{t-11}) + R_{t-10}$. In turn, R_{t-10} will 'echo' the gross investment of ten years previously, and so on back into the past. For the moment, however, replacement will be ignored, leaving I_t as *net* investment; dropping R_t from the earlier equation gives $I_t = v(Y_t - Y_{t-1})$, *plus* whatever autonomous investment exists. If

[1] The capital-output coefficient v is an example of a 'stock-flow' ratio. Where two 'flows' are being compared—for example, annual consumption and annual income—the ratio between them is independent of the time-span over which both are measured; similarly, the ratio between two 'stocks'—for example, the figure of 'capital per worker' found by dividing the number of workers at a given moment of time into the volume of capital existing at that moment—will also be a pure number. In a 'stock-flow' ratio, however, where one quantity has a time-dimension and the other does not, it is essential to specify the length of time over which the flow quantity is being measured.

firms take time to react to the changing pressure of demand for their output, so that their decisions to adjust capacity are not taken until the end of the year in which demand has altered, there will be a lag[1] such that induced net investment is $I_t = v(Y_{t-1} - Y_{t-2})$. But lagged or unlagged, the theory of investment embodied in these equations is valid only if firms behave as the original X-producing firm was supposed to do at the beginning of this section; and this is very much open to question.

It would certainly appear that the firm *need* not have ordered more machines when faced with higher demand. Had it expected demand to relapse in Year 3 to its original level, it could have met Year 2's increase by working existing equipment more intensively; overtime working, or the introduction of a shift system, would have increased output for the time being. Though machines were assumed to last ten years, it is unlikely that they would be completely useless at the end of that time; last year's superannuated equipment could have been kept in operation, perhaps even the previous year's if it were the firm's practice to keep old machines as a reserve of 'standby' capacity. It would not have been necessary to increase output at all, if the firm had had a stock of X large enough to meet the extra demand; had demand risen not by 100 units but by only 40, it would clearly have been preferable to run down stocks rather than buy an extra machine producing 100. Lacking a stock, a cautious firm might even let the additional demand go a-begging rather than buy an extra machine.

On the other hand, the firm might well have installed *more* than one extra machine in Year 2; the initial rise in demand might have appeared to signalize the beginning of a considerable expansion, for which the firm might have tried to equip itself in advance. To order precisely the number of machines needed to produce the increased output currently demanded implies a gross lack of imagination on the part of businessmen, who will in fact, in view of the risks of investment, consider very carefully whether a current rise in demand augurs further expansion or not. The response of investment to demand-changes thus depends on expectations as well as on the value of the Accelerator v.

---

[1] This lag must not be confused with the 'investment period' defined in the previous paragraph. Given a change in demand for its product, a firm will take time to become aware of the change and decide what action to take; having decided whether or not to adjust its stock of capital, the firm must then decide on the date by which the adjustment is to be completed. The 'investment period' is the length of time involved in the second decision; the lag referred to in the text is that involved in the first decision.

Before ordering extra equipment, cautious firms may wait to see whether demand-increases are sustained; if they do, a time-lag will operate. They may look back over the last few periods to discern what trend, if any, is shown by demand, and decide investment accordingly; in this case, a 'distributed lag' will be present.[1] The gestation period of new plant may also complicate the picture; if a factory takes three years to build, investment demand in the first year will be only one-third of that induced by annual changes in demand for the firm's product—that is, the value of v will be reduced by the existence of a three-year 'investment period'. When new equipment is installed, it may not be the same type as the old; it may be technologically more advanced, perhaps of different size, and giving a greater output per £100 worth of machinery; here, the Accelerator v will itself be changing.

There are, then, many reasons why the Acceleration Principle should not work with the mechanical precision implied in the original sequence.[2] Nevertheless, it contains a strong element of truth. If a firm tries to expand output with an inadequate volume of equipment, the strain on its capacity will put costs up; overtime working, for example, costs more than 'normal time'. Adjusting capacity to the new level of production will thus reduce costs; a sequence of net yields A_1, A_2, A_3 etc., which was earlier (p. 151) described as resulting from the introduction of a new machine, will here arise from cost-reductions, and if the MEI implied by the yields is greater than the interest-cost of the machine it will pay the firm to install it: buying a new machine will be cheaper than incurring extra costs in other directions in the effort to produce more finished goods. Much depends on how the firm's costs change with the level of output: if any attempt to produce above capacity would sharply increase the per-unit cost of labour and materials, the cost-reduction from new machinery will be great; if 'capacity' is a *range* of possible levels of output, at each of which the per-unit cost is the same, the incentive to install new equipment will be nil as long as demand-changes stay within the range. But for sizeable changes in demand which are expected to persist in future, it will almost certainly profit a firm to enlarge its capacity. Obversely, when income falls, costs will rise because output is *below* capacity; the firm will cut its costs if it reduces its stock of equipment by disinvesting.

---

[1] E.g. instead of $I_t = v \Delta D_t$, suppose investment depends on the average change in demand during the last three periods, giving $I_t = v\frac{1}{3}(\Delta D_{t-1} + \Delta D_{t-2} + \Delta D_{t-3})$; the time-lag is 'distributed' over periods $t-1$, $t-2$ and $t-3$.

[2] Cf. A. D. Knox, 'The Acceleration Principle and the Theory of Investment: A Survey', *Economica*, August 1952.

Thus, changes in income can be expected to induce some investment, though in less rigid proportions than the original statement of the Acceleration Principle implied. The latter, indeed, can be regarded as a special case of what R. C. O. Matthews has called '*the Capital Stock Adjustment Principle*'; this asserts that investment will vary positively with the level of income and negatively with the quantity of capital in existence, i.e.

$$I_t = aY_t - bK_t$$

or, if the response to income is lagged one period,

$$I_t = aY_{t-1} - bK_t$$

where K_t is the capital stock at the beginning of period t, and a and b are constants.[1] This is equivalent to the Acceleration Principle if a is replaced by v and b is equal to 1; the capital-output ratio v, multiplied by Y_t, gives the amount of capital required to produce the current level of output, and if this differs from existing capital K_t, firms try to make up the difference by new investment (or, of course, by *disinvesting* when K_t exceeds vY_t). In so far as expectational and other factors are incompatible with this, they can be 'put into' the values of a and b, which will then differ from v and 1.

(f) Investment in stocks

The investment-determining forces described in previous sections —profit expectations, the level of National Income and changes in that level, the cost and availability of internal and external finance, and the stock of capital—were considered in the light of their effects on the *fixed* investment of the private sector of the economy. But, as was noted at the beginning of the chapter, this is only one of the categories of investment: it remains to see what determines other forms of investment-demand. In this section, the demand for increases in stocks of materials and finished products is examined.

On the whole, it appears that interest-rates affect the demand for stocks very little. The reverse has often been argued in the past. By holding stocks, firms are 'locking up' funds which could be realized if the stocks were sold off. If firms use their own money for this, they lose the interest it could have earned; if they use borrowed funds, they pay interest; either way, they must weigh the interest-cost against the advantages of holding the existing quantities of stock. Having a reserve of finished products allows them to meet unexpected demands; with a stock of materials, they are in a position to step up

[1] R. C. O. Matthews, *The Trade Cycle* (1959), pp. 40-3.

output at short notice; but these facilities will become relatively less attractive if their cost rises, and more so if their cost falls. However, this does not mean that firms will actually vary their stockholding when holding-costs change. They may have found by experience that some minimum amount is essential, and see no point in exceeding that minimum; their demand for stocks will be inelastic with respect to holding-costs. ('Our only consideration', the Chairman of Unilever told the Radcliffe Committee, 'is that we must have the minimum necessary for efficiency.'[1]) Even if stock-demand *is* elastic, it is so with respect to *total* holding-cost; if a firm maintains warehouses, insures them and their contents, and employs storemen, these expenses may be so much greater than the interest-cost of the stocks that a small change in interest-rates will make almost no difference. A substantial rise might be a different matter, spurring firms to find more efficient ways of utilizing stocks so as to hold less: but this would be a once-for-all effect—when interest fell again, firms would obviously not resume the less efficient arrangements they had before.

For many firms, the 'relevant rate of interest' affecting stockholding decisions is not that on bank loans but the charge (if any) for *trade credit*: the latter commonly takes the form of a discount on bills for goods supplied, if the bills are paid within a certain period. If trade discounts are left unchanged when other short-term interest rates rise, firms may not experience any rise at all in the cost of holding stocks, and erstwhile bank borrowers may turn to trade credit as a cheaper form of finance unless their suppliers enforce strict limits.

The most important influence on the demand for stocks is almost certainly the level of output and sales: if the demand for a firm's products is liable to rise at short notice by 5% of the normal level of sales, a rise in the latter will automatically raise the stock requirement to cover the 5% margin. This brings in the Acceleration Principle again. If firms raise output in response to increased demand, they will sooner or later wish to raise their stocks to the level appropriate to their increased sales, and this will itself add to aggregate demand; but the satisfying of stock-demand will eliminate it from aggregate demand, which will now be less than the level of output which has been reached, and this will start a contraction of output. Thus, an original change in autonomous demand could set in motion a 'stock cycle' (or 'inventory cycle' as Americans call it) even if output is keeping pace with demand all along; if, in addition, there is an output lag, the 'Lundbergian cycle'[2] will be superimposed on the acceleration-type stock cycle.

[1] *Minutes of Evidence*, Question 11504.
[2] See above, p. 139.

A financial consequence of stock fluctuations may be noted here. If firms rely mainly on retained profits to finance fixed investment, and if the availability of outside finance is limited, increasing stocks will tie up funds which could otherwise be used for fixed investment; the more of the latter they plan to do, the greater the necessity to economize on stocks.[1] Yet the fixed investment may be associated with an upward trend in sales which calls for increased stock holding; the necessity for this may therefore restrain firms from ordering as much new plant as they might otherwise do. When sales fall, on the other hand, the liquidation of stocks will replenish their internal finance, permitting them to go ahead with whatever fixed investment they plan under these less promising conditions.

(g) Replacement investment

In the example given at the beginning of Section (e) to illustrate the Acceleration Principle, the firm was assumed to be using machines each lasting ten years, at the end of which they were replaced. With year-to-year variations in investment the subsequent replacement pattern became distorted, giving an 'echo-effect'. But the assumption of a precise 'life' was seen to be questionable: a machine does not normally crumble into rust all at once, but may continue to be usable for a considerable time after its customary retirement age. If the firm *could* work its machines longer than ten years, why should it normally replace them at that age? Why, indeed, should it not sometimes replace them sooner?

In section (b), the rate of net yield from a new machine was defined as the rate of discount which equates prospective yields with the machine's price—i.e. the r of the equation

$$P = \frac{A_1}{(1+r)} + \frac{A_2}{(1+r)^2} + \cdots + \frac{A_n}{(1+r)^n}$$

where P is the price, n the 'life', and $A_1, A_2 \ldots$ etc. the series of net yields expected from the machine. If r exceeds the rate of interest i, the machine is worth buying. The alternative formulation is

$$V = \frac{A_1}{(1+i)} + \frac{A_2}{(1+i)^2} + \cdots + \frac{A_n}{(1+i)^n}$$

where V is the sum which, if lent out at the interest rate i over n years, would give the series of yields $A_1, A_2 \ldots$ etc. Here, V is the

---

[1] The Finance Director of Boots told the Radcliffe Committee that 'there was a very keen realization throughout the business that the amount of money we could afford to spend on our capital development was very closely associated with the amount of money we could afford to keep in our stocks'. *Minutes of Evidence*, Question 11629.

'present value' of the prospective yields when they are discounted by i. If r exceeds i, then V exceeds P; by spending the amount P, the firm can expect to get a series of yields worth more than P.

This calculation can be made at any stage of a machine's 'life'. After, say, three years, there will be a shorter series of yields to look forward to, so that V will be less than it was. But P, which is now the sum the firm could get by selling the machine, will also have fallen: three years' wear will have reduced its second-hand value—indeed, it may now be worth only what it will fetch as scrap metal. So V, though reduced, may still exceed P by a good margin. But P cannot go below the rock-bottom represented by its scrap value, whereas when the series of yields is at an end, $V = 0$. At some point, therefore, the difference between V and P will fall below the amount by which the V of a new machine exceeds its P; and this is the point at which replacement should occur if the firm wishes to maximize profit.

If the present value of prospective yields is V_1 for the new machine and V_2 for the old, and if the prices of new and old machines are P_1 and P_2 respectively, the gain from replacement will be $(V_1-P_1)-(V_2-P_2)$. This is subject to the condition that V_1 must exceed P_1. The firm is not obliged to buy a new machine even if it scraps the old one, and there would be no point in buying a new one if its expected returns (V_1) were less than its price (P_1); it would pay the firm to go on using the old machine until the passage of time reduces expected returns (V_2) below scrap value (P_2) and then to sell it without buying a new one. The sale might not realize much money, but if lent at interest this would earn more than if it continued to be 'locked up' in the old machine.

A gain from replacement is a loss from *not* replacing: to avoid this, the firm must replace when $(V_1-P_1)-(V_2-P_2) = 0$. If the old machine's prospective yields have declined by a given fraction q per year, $V_2 = V_0-nqV_0$, where V_0 is the erstwhile 'present value' of the yields expected when the machine was new and n is the number of years since it was installed. If P_2 has reached its minimum scrap-metal value before replacement is due, and if this is a fraction s of the original price P_0, it follows that $P_2 = sP_0$ from then onwards: so $V_2-P_2 = V_0-nqV_0-sP_0$. If the price of a new machine is the same as the original price of the old (i.e. $P_1 = P_0$) and if its prospective yields are the same as those the old machine had to start with (i.e. $V_1 = V_0$), the replacement condition becomes

$$(V_1-P_1)-(V_1-nqV_1-sP_1) = 0$$

or

$$nqV_1-P_1(1-s) = 0;$$

if q and s are constants, the value of n which satisfies this equation will be the number of years after which the machine should be replaced, i.e. its profitable 'life'.

But firms do not normally replace machines with identical new ones; since the old one was bought, technical improvements should have provided something better, so that prospective yields will have increased relatively to the price of the machine (i.e. $V_1-P_1>V_0-P_0$); this will hasten replacement. If the *product* of the new machinery is in some way superior to that of the old, this will also cause a sharp decline in V_2; the old machine may still be physically capable of turning out its product, but if this cannot compete with its up-to-date counterpart (or can compete only at a much lower price), prospective earnings will decline sharply and may vanish altogether. This, too, will make for earlier replacement.

Technical advances, however, will not be decisive if the 'state of expectations' deteriorates. Because old machines have a shorter series of yields in prospect, firms may feel more certain of these than of a new machine's longer series—particularly if the latter involves the sale of a new product; so if pessimism causes firms to make a large allowance for risk in assessing yields, this will depress V_1 more than V_2. In general, gloom about market prospects will depress V_1 more than V_2, simply because V_2 represents a shorter future than V_1. A low level of National Income, downward trends in that level, even the failure of the level to rise as fast as is thought normal—all these things may depress V_1 and thus delay replacement as well as discouraging net investment. Improved expectations, on the other hand, will augment the effect of technical progress in stimulating both net investment and replacement.

Because different firms will take different views of the future, their assessments of V_1 and V_2 will differ, so that even the same sort of equipment will be replaced sooner by one firm than by another. Thus, the 'echo-effect' will vary not only with general conditions but also from firm to firm: for a given industry, the bunching of new investment in a given year will thus not result in a similar concentration of replacement n years later. In any case, the existence of many different kinds of equipment, varying considerably in physical longevity, will cause replacements in the economy as a whole to be spread out over many years, even though *all* industries originally installed equipment in the same year. This leaves very little of the 'echo-effect' mentioned above on p. 170. The considerations now put forward suggest, rather, that equipment installed during one surge of investment demand will tend to be replaced whenever the next surge comes along, rather than after some fixed and predictable time-lag.

(h) Changes in the price-level

Decisions about replacement may be complicated by changes in the general level of prices during the life of the equipment. An increase in the price of capital-goods relatively to that of their products will tend to discourage investment. But even if all prices have been rising together, current equipment prices will now be greater than those paid for similar machines some years ago; if, over those years, a firm allocated part of a machine's yield to a depreciation fund in such a way as to accumulate the amount originally spent on the machine, the fund will now be too small to buy an identical replacement, and this may discourage replacement if the firm cannot command other internal or external sources of finance.

More important, perhaps, is the effect of rising prices on firms' policy in future. If they expect the upward trend to continue, they may change their depreciation allowances from an 'original cost' to a 'replacement cost' basis—that is, they will plan to accumulate a fund sufficient to buy new equipment however much its price may have risen, rather than merely to replace the money originally spent. This will incline the firm to distribute less dividends that it might otherwise have done. On the other hand, rising prices make it undesirable to accumulate money balances or to retain holdings of fixed-interest securities, since these will lose value as prices rise; firms thus have an incentive to use their depreciation allowances as quickly as possible for purchasing new equipment. The combined effect of these considerations may be to stimulate investment in general.

Rising prices benefit firms with fixed-interest debt in the form of debentures or loan stock; the higher prices of their products bring them increased money revenue, but the interest charge does not rise; the burden of debt will become steadily lighter in real terms. This is a variation of the 'Pigou effect' noted in Chapter Five,[1] and it may lead firms to increase investment. As against this, firms may possess money balances and fixed-interest securities whose real value decreases as prices rise; here the 'Pigou effect' will cut the other way.

Higher product prices will, of course, be offset by higher input costs: if all prices are rising at the same pace, materials and fuels will be proportionately more expensive and wage-increases will be keeping labour costs in step. If a firm is also charging depreciation on the 'replacement cost' basis, its profits will be rising at exactly the same rate as the general price-level, so that they remain the same in real terms (except for the 'Pigou effect' noted in the previous paragraph). But the assumption that output and input prices change in exactly

[1] See p. 112 above.

the same proportions is a very questionable one. Output prices may be rising because of the pressure of consumers' demand; in the effort to meet this demand, firms may try to obtain more materials, plant and labour and so force up input prices—but these would rise *after* output prices; sales revenue would thus keep ahead of rising costs, to the benefit of profits. On the other hand, the rise in output prices might be the result of higher costs: if material prices and/or wages are rising, firms may be passing on these cost-increases to the consumer by putting up product prices. Here, however, input prices would be in the lead, and profits would suffer. In so far as investment depends on the level of retained profits, it would be stimulated or retarded according to the phasing of the change in prices. For reductions in prices, of course, all these considerations apply in reverse.

When the price-level changes, expectations of further movements are likely to be set up. The prospects of continued price-increases may make firms wish to buy as much equipment as possible while prices are still relatively low: there will be some incentive to introduce labour-saving machinery in view of higher wages expected in future, and firms will buy in stocks as promptly as possible. A rise in prices which is thought to be temporary will have the opposite effect: to buy machinery now, when it is expected to be down in price again soon, would appear bad business. Here, then, it is not the change in prices as such, but the state of expectations it brings about, which determines the outcome.

(i) Investment in housing

The investment so far examined is that of privately-owned enterprises: they hope, by acquiring extra plant and stocks, to be in a better position to supply commodities to the markets where they earn their profits. There remain two further categories of investment: that of public authorities, and the construction of dwelling-houses.

The demand for new dwellings is treated as a separate category for a number of reasons. Houses are 'consumers' durables', and the demand for their services is a part of consumption demand; changes in population, in size of families and other aspects of population structure have obvious effects on the demand for housing; the finance of private house-purchase by building society mortgages makes this the leading type of consumer credit; in the housing field, public authorities play a very great part—in 1975, more than 46% of all new housing was built for local authorities: because houses are long-lived, the existing stock is much greater than the annual output of new ones, so that the market is dominated by 'second-hand' sales and purchases. These peculiarities have been signalized by the occurrence in the past of 'building cycles' whose duration (20-25 years) and phasing has been different from that of the pre-war 8-9 year cycle in general economic activity.

Because of the durability of houses, investment therein is thought to be more sensitive to changes in interest-rates than are other forms of investment. It was shown above (p. 156) that the effect of interest-changes on the 'present value' of future yields is greater, the longer the life of the capital asset, though for most kinds of long-term investment this is offset by the uncertainty of the more distant yields. With housing, uncertainty is much less. A firm constructing houses for rental can be fairly sure of future demand; obsolescence is less important; houses, once built, produce their 'output' of accommodation-service without requiring much in the way of operating cost, so that uncertainty about future wages and material prices need not seriously affect estimates of future net yield.

To the owner-occupier who borrows to buy his house, the annual charge is made up partly of interest and partly of repayments of principal. The longer the period of the loan, the greater the interest element relatively to the repayment element: for example, on £2,000 borrowed at 6% and repayable in annual instalments over 20 years, the housebuyer pays £3,260 altogether, of which £1,260 (i.e. 39%) is interest;[1] on a ten-year loan, interest would have been £660 (i.e. 25%) out of total payments of £2,660. The greater the interest element, the greater the effect of a change in the rate of interest on the monthly payment the householder has to make.

Private investment in housing should therefore be fairly interest-elastic. But in the 1960s, it rose considerably even when interest rates were rising: from £224 millions in 1959, the personal sector's net capital formation in dwellings increased to £318 millions in 1971 (at 1963 prices), whereas building societies' mortgage rates, having been 5½% in 1959, rose to 8% by 1971. This suggests that interest-effects were overborne by the increasing availability of finance as building societies and insurance companies extended their business, as well as by the rise in personal disposable income during these years.

These considerations, of course, apply to private expenditure. But local authorities, as has been seen, are responsible for a good part of

---

[1] Interest is not 6% of the full £2,000 over all twenty years, because the borrower is reducing the amount outstanding each year. The above calculation is very crude: it does not allow for a possible 'smoothing' of repayments to allow the borrower to pay the same amount each year or month; nor does it take account of tax considerations.

housing investment. Their programmes are based on slum-clearance and reconstruction needs; their housing is regarded as a social service rather than a commercial enterprise, and central government subsidies and grants play an important part. If interest charges rise, the extra expense can be met by increasing local rates or by reducing other expenditures: only to the extent that local authorities are unwilling to do this, will higher interest rates cause them to cut investment. Lower interest rates, on the other hand, may have no effect on their investment, since the central government's power to limit local expenditure may be used to prevent any increase.

(j) Public investment

Local authorities' house-building was in 1975 approximately 18% of total public investment, which includes all capital expenditure by central and local government and by public corporations. This, it may be thought, is a category of demand whose amount can be fixed entirely at the discretion of the government, and which can be varied if necessary to offset an excess or deficiency of demand in the private sector. While it is true that some adjustments can be made at fairly short notice, they are not as great as might at first appear.

More than two-fifths of all public investment is done by public corporations, whose problems are akin to those of private industry in that they use inputs of labour and materials to produce commodities, like coal and electric current, which are sold to consumers at prices which are intended to cover costs. In framing development programmes, they must be guided by prospects of future yield. Because of their size, these programmes are generally of an integrated and long-range character which makes it difficult to accelerate or postpone them; to a large extent they are keyed to the growth of the private sector, since a rise in, say, engineering output will require greater inputs of coal for steel-making, more electric current, more railway transport and so on; to check the public corporations' investment may upset the working of the economy later. The semi-independent status of the boards makes government control less immediate than if they were departments; ministers can issue 'directions', but it may take some time to arrange for the corporations' investment to be altered.

Some of these considerations apply to the government's own investment. Road-building, for example, must keep up with the needs of a growing economy if awkward transport bottlenecks are to be avoided. Other forms of investment, such as hospital building, serve social aims which a government may not wish to modify. Defence requirements may make certain projects essential. Educational building by local authorities may be difficult to alter, given the government's aims in this field. Every form of public investment, in fact, is intended to achieve some particular object, which may seem too important in itself to be sacrificed even when general economic policy calls for a reduction in aggregate demand. Because of the difficulty of such decisions, because of the multiplicity of authorities involved, and because of the long-range character of many projects for which contracts are placed some time in advance, the public investment programme is difficult to reduce at short notice. It may be easier to increase it, when economic policy requires expansion: but even then, a good deal of preliminary planning will be necessary, and it would be unreasonable to expect public corporations to invest in projects which do not offer prospects of adequate future returns. To say that the volume of public investment is the result of government decisions is not to say that it can be quickly changed.

CHAPTER EIGHT

Foreign Trade and the National Income

(a) The Import Function

The demand for a country's exports is an element of aggregate demand; it competes with consumption, investment and government expenditure for the country's output, and incomes are generated in producing exported commodities in exactly the same way as in meeting other demands. The country's own demand for imports, on the other hand, is a *negative* element of aggregate demand; it diverts the expenditure of consumers, business firms and public authorities away from home-produced commodities and relieves the pressure on domestic supplies; the incomes generated in meeting it are those of foreign suppliers. If government expenditure and indirect taxes are neglected, the condition of equilibrium is

$$Y = C + I + E - M$$

where E is export demand and M is the demand for imports. If E exceeds M, the equilibrium level of income and output will be higher than it would otherwise have been; if M exceeds E, it will be lower.

Autonomous changes in E and M will set up multiplier effects. Because E is a positive element of aggregate demand, an increase in its value will raise equilibrium income; however, higher import demand will reduce income, since M is negative. In Chapter Five, the working of the Multiplier was seen to depend on the response of consumption (and possibly investment also) to income-changes initiated by any autonomous change in demand; if import and export demand are also sensitive to changes in income, this will affect the Multiplier. There seems no obvious reason to expect the demand for exports to be directly affected by changes in the exporting country's income: the buyers of exports, by definition, are residents of other countries. But it would be reasonable to suppose some connection between income and the level of imports. When output rises, the input of materials must increase, and some of these are likely to be imported; the personal incomes generated by higher

183

output may be partly spent on imported consumer goods; increased investment demand may call for imports of capital equipment and stocks; it may be necessary to employ more foreign shipping to bring in the additional goods, and this too will be a rise in imports, since the latter are here taken to include purchases of services as well as merchandise from abroad.[1]

The general relationship between the level of National Income and the demand for imports is called the *Import Function*. It is a concept analogous to the Consumption and Investment Functions introduced in previous chapters, and it can be represented diagrammatically in similar fashion; if the vertical scale in Fig. 4 (p. 98) were made to measure imports instead of consumption, the curve *CC* (which could be renamed *MM* in this context) would show the import demand associated with each income-level. The slope of the Import Function at any point shows how the nation's demand for imports changes relatively to a given change in income—in symbols, $\frac{\Delta M}{\Delta Y}$: this is the *Marginal Propensity to Import* (MPM).[2] The proportion between total import demand and total income, for a given level of income, is the *Average Propensity to Import* (APM).

In 1975 Britain's imports of goods and services, valued at current market prices, were 34·3% of Gross National Income. The average ratio for the period 1965–75 was 31·6%, and deviations from the average in individual years were seldom large: 1974 had the highest ratio with 40·5%, and 1966 the lowest with 28·0%.[3] So it seems reasonable to suppose that the APM was in the region of three-tenths. The MPM, on the other hand, is not so easily estimated by merely comparing recorded annual changes in imports with annual changes in income. The 'ΔM' of the MPM is the change in demand for imports which is exclusively attributable to the concomitant

---

[1] See p. 43 above.

[2] The MPM should not be confused with the 'income-elasticity of demand for imports', which is the ratio between the *proportionate* change in imports and the *proportionate* change in income, i.e. $\frac{\Delta M}{M} \div \frac{\Delta Y}{Y}$; whereas the MPM is the ratio between *absolute* changes, i.e. $\frac{\Delta M}{\Delta Y}$.

[3] *National Income and Expenditure, 1965–75*, gives imports at factor cost; taxes on imports are shown on p. 106. If imports are valued at factor cost, the 1975 ratio is 30·0%; but market-price valuation is more appropriate here, since market prices are what the buyers of imports actually have to pay. Gross, rather than net, income is used in the calculation because expenditure on making good capital consumption may take the form of purchases of imported equipment.

change in real income ΔY; but at any particular time, the actual change in expenditure on imports will be a response, not only to the rise or fall of income, but also to fluctuations in import prices (relatively to those of home-produced goods), to changes in the cost and availability of finance, to alterations in import duties and quantitative restrictions, and to many other influences. It is therefore hardly surprising that the ratio of annual import-change to income-change, which in 1971 was 22·1%, should have been very different in other years—as low as 14·4% in 1962, as high as 81·4% in 1968, and even negative in 1961, when imports actually fell slightly (by 0·3%) though real income rose 3·6%. The average proportion of import-change to income-change during the period was about two-fifths, but this figure should evidently be treated as only the merest approximation to an estimate of the MPM.

Britain's two 'propensities to import' both appear high compared with those of most other countries: for example, the APM and MPM of the United States seem to be in the region of 5% and 7% respectively, while those of Italy are approximately 13% and 28%. Differences between countries' propensities arise from structural differences in their economies: for example, a country with large agricultural and mining sectors may be fairly self-sufficient in raw materials and food, and thus have a much smaller APM than a country like Britain. Such a country might well, however, have a high MPM: at high levels of output, domestic supplies of materials may become inadequate and have to be supplemented by imports; high personal incomes may induce consumers to demand foreign luxuries which they would not have thought of buying when less affluent; the demand for imports might then rise relatively faster than income, even though total imports were still quite a small proportion of income. But it is not possible to lay down any general rules about the value of the MPM: though it will usually be positive (i.e. greater than zero), even this cannot be taken for granted. A country exporting high-quality products may be consuming cheap imported substitutes; a rise in income might make its people feel rich enough to consume their own produce, and they would then import less, not more; the MPM would be negative, even though the APM were still positive and even high. But such cases can be regarded as exceptional.

Like the Consumption Function, the Import Function can be expressed as an equation, e.g. $M = q + mY$; here q is 'autonomous imports'—the quantity the country would import even if income were nil; m is the MPM. Inserting this, along with a Consumption Function $C = a + cY$, into the equilibrium condition $(Y = C + I + E - M)$ gives

$$Y = a + cY + I + E - q - mY.$$

If an autonomous change in demand occurs, income will move to a new equilibrium; the difference will be

$$Y_2 - Y_1 = a + cY_2 + I_2 + E_2 - q - mY_2 - a - cY_1 - I_1 - E_1 + q + mY_1.$$

If the autonomous change was in investment (ΔI), and if the income-change induces no further alteration in investment nor any change in exports, the change in equilibrium income will be

$$\Delta Y = c\Delta Y + \Delta I - m\Delta Y$$

(where ΔY is put in place of $Y_2 - Y_1$ throughout) from which

$$\Delta Y(1 - c + m) = \Delta I$$

and

$$\frac{\Delta Y}{\Delta I} = \frac{1}{1 - c + m};$$

this is a static Multiplier, similar to that deduced on p. 132 above, but allowing for the effects of foreign trade by the inclusion of the MPM. It could also, of course, be written

$$\frac{\Delta Y}{\Delta I} = \frac{1}{s + m}$$

if s (the Marginal Propensity to Save) is inserted in place of $1 - c$.

If the MPM is positive (as is normally assumed) it will reduce the value of the Multiplier (k). If c (the MPC) is $0 \cdot 8$ in a 'closed' economy (i.e. where there is no foreign trade), k will be $\dfrac{1}{1 - 0 \cdot 8}$, i.e. 5. In an 'open' economy with $c = 0 \cdot 8$ and $m = 0 \cdot 3$, k is $\dfrac{1}{1 - 0 \cdot 8 + 0 \cdot 3}$, i.e. 2.

To the extent that rising demand is being channelled off into the purchase of imports, it is not feeding back into income to generate fresh demand; it represents a 'leakage' of demand out of the process. To buy imports is to refrain from buying home output; in this, the demand for imports is exactly similar to saving, the other 'leakage' by which demand-steam escapes from the multiplier-engine.

(b) The foreign trade Multiplier

In the preceding argument, it was assumed that the demand for exports remained unaffected by changes in National Income. But this may not be true. One country's imports are other countries' exports; the 'leakage' of demand through the MPM will set up a multiplier process abroad, and the consequent change in other countries' incomes may alter their demand for the home country's exports. Indirectly, then, changes in income may induce changes in exports; how much, depends on the MPMs of the countries whose incomes are affected by the original multiplier-leakage, and on the size of their own Mutipliers.

Suppose there are two countries, A and B. The equilibrium condition requires that any rise in aggregate demand shall be met by an equal rise in income and output: i.e.

$$\Delta Y_a = c_a\Delta Y_a+\Delta I_a+\Delta E_a-m_a\Delta Y_a$$

for country A, and

$$\Delta Y_b = c_b\Delta Y_b+\Delta I_b+\Delta E_b-m_b\Delta Y_b$$

for country B. Suppose an autonomous change in investment of £X millions occurs in country A; there is no induced investment in either A or B, so $\Delta I_a = X$ and $\Delta I_b = 0$. If A and B trade only with each other, the demand for A's exports is the same thing as B's demand for imports, so that $\Delta E_a = m_b\Delta Y_b$, and conversely $\Delta E_b = m_a\Delta Y_a$. The above equations may therefore be amended to read

$$\Delta Y_a = c_a\Delta Y_a+X+m_b\Delta Y_b-m_a\Delta Y_a \tag{1}$$

and

$$\Delta Y_b = c_b\Delta Y_b+m_a\Delta Y_a-m_b\Delta Y_b. \tag{2}$$

From the last equation,

$$\Delta Y_b(1-c_b+m_b) = m_a\Delta Y_a,$$

i.e.

$$\Delta Y_b = \frac{m_a\Delta Y_a}{1-c_b+m_b};$$

if this is substituted for ΔY_b in equation (1) above,

$$\Delta Y_a = c_a\Delta Y_a+X+\frac{m_am_b\Delta Y_a}{1-c_b+m_b}-m_a\Delta Y_a$$

and

$$\Delta Y_a\left(1-c_a+m_a-\frac{m_am_b}{1-c_b+m_b}\right) = X$$

This expression becomes less unwieldy if s_a (A's Marginal Propensity to Save) is substituted for $1-c_a$, and s_b for $1-c_b$; so amended, it is now rearranged as

$$\frac{\Delta Y_a}{X} = \frac{1}{s_a + m_a - \dfrac{m_a m_b}{s_b + m_b}} \tag{3}$$

which is a Multiplier similar to that given on p. 186, except that it includes an extra term $\dfrac{m_a m_b}{s_b + m_b}$, which may be called u_a for short. Because u_a has a negative sign, it has the effect of making the Multiplier larger than it would otherwise be: for example, if $s_a = 0.2$, $m_a = 0.3$, $s_b = 0.1$ and $m_b = 0.2$, the Multiplier would be

$$\frac{\Delta Y_a}{X} = \frac{1}{0.2 + 0.3 - \dfrac{0.3 \times 0.2}{0.1 + 0.2}} = \frac{1}{0.3} = 3.3$$

whereas the omission of the u_a term would have made it only $\dfrac{1}{0.2 + 0.3}$, i.e. 2.

In this *Foreign Trade Multiplier*, u_a represents the 'feedback' of demand from other countries which results from the rise in A's investment. The process involved is like the bouncing of a ball: first a rise in investment in A raises A's income and A imports more from B; this rise in B's exports increases B's income so that she imports more from A; A's income is now raised, so that she buys more from B; B now sends back the ball as her imports from A rise again; and so on. The collection of propensities given in Equation (3) above shows the final outcome which will be reached when the ball has stopped bouncing. Obviously, the to-and-fro motion will take time; if any significant lags occur, so that the process cannot be completed in a single period, the Multiplier will work dynamically as described in Chapter Six. Also, the ball will be bouncing between more than two countries in real life; A's increased imports from B may lead B to import more from C, which in turn steps up imports from D; if D now responds by importing more from A, the repercussions of A's original income-increase will have taken some time to come back to her, and the size of the effect may depend on the route it has taken—for example, if country C's MPM is zero, the ball will never get back to A at all.

If A is a small country and B is the rest of the world, m_b will be small. A rise in income may increase world demand for imports considerably, but A's share of the increased trade will not be great—and m_b is not the world's MPM in general but its marginal propensity to import from A. The smaller m_b, the smaller u_a and the smaller A's Multiplier; for example, if $m_b = 0.01$, and s_a, s_b and m_a have the numerical values given in the example earlier, $u_a = 0.027$ and the Multiplier is 2.11—not much more than the value of 2.0 which it would have had with $m_b = 0$.

As long as m_b exceeds 0, however, it will pull more weight in the Multiplier, the smaller is the value of s_b. If s_b were 0, the u_a term $\dfrac{m_a m_b}{s_b+m_b}$ would become simply m_a, which would make the Multiplier $\dfrac{1}{s_a+m_a-m_a}$ or $\dfrac{1}{s_a}$, i.e. the same as it would be in a 'closed' economy; the 'overseas feedback' would exactly compensate for the leakage of demand through the MPM. The greater s_b, the smaller the degree of compensation and the smaller the Multiplier.

Equation (3) on p. 188 gave the Multiplier which operates in response to an autonomous change in country A's investment. It will apply equally well where the multiplicand is a change in consumption or in government expenditure; but where an autonomous change in *exports* starts the process, the results will be different. Country A's exports are B's imports; if A's income is increased through a rise in her exports, B's income must *ipso facto* fall because her imports have increased. While A's experience can still be described by Equation (1) on p. 187, B's Equation (2) must be amended to include a term $-X$, representing the autonomous rise in B's imports which is the obverse of A's rise in exports; this gives

$$\Delta Y_b = c_b \Delta Y_b + m_a \Delta Y_a - m_b \Delta Y_b - X$$

from which

$$\Delta Y_b(1-c_b+m_b) = m_a \Delta Y_a - X$$

so that (with s_b substituted for $1-c_b$)

$$\Delta Y_b = \frac{m_a \Delta Y_a}{s_b+m_b} - \frac{X}{s_b+m_b}$$

Substituting this in Equation (1), and proceeding as before, gives

$$\frac{\Delta Y_a}{X} = \frac{1 - \dfrac{m_b}{s_b+m_b}}{s_a+m_a - \dfrac{m_a m_b}{s_b+m_b}} \tag{4}$$

—a Multiplier which differs from that in Equation (3) by the term $\dfrac{m_b}{s_b+m_b}$ (which may be called z_a for short) appearing in the numerator of the fraction, and which, having a negative sign, reduces the value of the Multiplier as a whole. The value of z_a is greater, the larger

m_b and the smaller s_b—exactly as with the u_a term; but whereas a high value of m_b increases the Multiplier by making u_a large, it reduces the Multiplier by aggrandizing z_a; and $s_b = 0$ actually makes the Multiplier $= 0$, whatever the value of m_b. If numerical values $s_a = 0\cdot2$, $s_b = 0\cdot1$, $m_a = 0\cdot3$ and $m_b = 0\cdot1$ are inserted in Equation (4), the value of the Multiplier is $1\cdot43$; Equation (3) would have given a value of $2\cdot86$. So a good deal may depend on the nature of the multiplicand which sets the Multiplier to work.

(c) The terms of trade, the balance of trade and the exchange rate

So far, changes in the price-level have been ignored: the income-changes induced by the Multiplier have been assumed to be in real terms. But an autonomous rise in A's investment, inducing a multiple rise in aggregate demand, may push up prices as well as 'real' output; A's products will now be more expensive relatively to those of other countries. Her imports will in any case be increasing because her income is rising; they will increase still more because of their price advantage, unless A's price-elasticity of demand for imported goods is zero. Her export customers, on the other hand, may buy less because A's prices are higher; the volume of exports will fall below what it would otherwise have been. The reduction in volume may, however, be offset by the rise in prices; if the quantity demanded falls 5% in response to a 10% price-increase, the *value* of exports will actually rise by $4\frac{1}{2}\%$.

If it is desired to show only 'real' changes in A's income and aggregate demand, values must be deflated in proportion to the rise in A's price-level; the change in exports will then be measured simply by the change in their physical quantity. Imports, however, can no longer be measured at their original price-level, even though this has not risen; when all other values in the equilibrium equation $Y = C+I+E-M$ are being price-deflated, M must be deflated also. If A's price-level has risen 10%, it will be necessary to multiply everything by $\dfrac{100}{110}$; this will restore the basis of valuation of C, I and E to that of A's original price-level, but it will mean that imports are now being valued as though their prices had fallen about 10%. The overall effect on the value of imports will then depend on whether the increase in quantity has been greater or less than this; if it was, in fact, only 5%, the value of M will now be *less* than before.

To the extent that the volume of exports falls, and that of imports rises, A's income will tend to fall; but to the extent that she can now obtain her imports more cheaply—more cheaply, that is, relatively to her domestic price-level—her income will tend to rise. These effects ensue, not from the rise in A's prices as such, but from the fact that they have risen relatively to those of the rest of the world: if world prices had risen 10% and A's by 20%, or if world prices had gone down by 10%, while A's had remained unchanged, the effects would have been much the same. The ratio between world prices and those prevailing in A is called the *terms of trade*: changes therein may be assessed by comparing an index of world prices with an index of A's; if both indices are 100 in a given year, and then change so that world prices are 105 and A's 115 in the following year, the 'terms-of-trade ratio' will stand at $\frac{105}{115}$, i.e. 0·913 as compared with 1·00 previously. For A, imports will now be 8·7% cheaper than before—the terms of trade have moved in her favour.

A change in the terms of trade will therefore have a threefold effect. The *volume* of export demand will change according to its elasticity with respect to the terms of trade: i.e. $\Delta E = +E\varepsilon\tau$, where ε measures elasticity and τ the proportionate terms-of-trade change. The *volume* of import demand will change in similar fashion, but in the opposite direction, i.e. by $-M\eta\tau$, where η is the terms-of-trade elasticity of demand for imports. Finally, the *value* of imports will change in proportion to τ, i.e. by $+(M-M\eta\tau)\tau$. The combined effect on aggregate demand, i.e. $\Delta E - \Delta M$, will be $E\varepsilon\tau - [-M\eta\tau + (M-M\eta\tau)\tau]$; e.g. if E and M are each 100, if $\varepsilon = 2$ and if $\eta = 1$, a 5% fall in the terms of trade ($\tau = -0·05$) will cause aggregate demand to change by $-10 - [+5 - (100+5)0·05]$, or $-9·75$. Had ε been only 0·5, the change in aggregate demand would have been $-2·25$; if ε and η were each 0·5, and if τ were very small, the change would be negligible.[1]

Whatever may be the change in A's aggregate demand when the terms of trade alter, it will set up multiplier effects of its own, on the lines of Equation (4) (p. 189). If, as was assumed at the beginning of this section, the change in the terms of trade was an incidental consequence of the multiplier effects of a rise in A's investment, there will now be *two* multipliers working simultaneously—against one another if the terms-of-trade effect operates to reduce A's aggregate demand, with one another if it increases demand; in either

---

[1] This is a particular case of the general rule that τ will not change the balance of $(E-M)$ if $\varepsilon+\eta = 1$. See J. Robinson, *Essays in the Theory of Employment*, p. 143, note 2. In the text above, nothing is said about elasticities of *supply*, though these may play an important part if they are small: on this, see Robinson, *op. cit.*, pp. 138–46.

case, this will modify the outcome of the original rise in investment. Even if A's income and price-level are not themselves changing, the terms of trade may rise or fall because of a change in prices in the rest of the world and this will set up a 'primary' multiplier effect in A of the Equation (4) type.

If, before these developments occurred, A's exports and imports were equal to one another, they are likely to finish up out of balance. In the simplest case, in which there is no 'feedback' of demand from overseas (e.g. if $m_b = 0$ in Equation (1), p. 187), and where the terms of trade do not change, there is no change in exports, and imports alter by $m_a \Delta Y_a$. Thus, a country whose income is rising is likely to develop a surplus of imports over exports, or to increase the surplus if one existed to start with; there will be a 'worsening' of the balance of trade. Only if the 'overseas feedback' through $m_b \Delta Y_b$, and the terms-of-trade effects, are together of such a nature as to offset $m_a \Delta Y_a$, will the balance of trade fail to deteriorate. Obversely, a fall in income will eliminate a balance-of-trade deficit, and even create a surplus of exports over imports if it goes far enough. On the whole, the balance of trade (in the sense of $E-M$) may be expected to vary inversely with the level of National Income.

Suppose, then, that a rise in National Income causes country A's balance of trade to show a deficit. The amount of foreign currency needed to buy imports will now exceed the amount foreigners are prepared to pay for A's exports; A's demand for other currencies will exceed the supply of them to her. (Alternatively, it could be said that the supply of A's currency exceeds the demand for it, since her demand for foreign currency implies readiness to supply her own in exchange, and the supply of foreign currency implies a demand for A's.) It may be that A's excess demand for foreign currency is being met from foreign loans, which provide a supply additional to that from A's export earnings; the overall supply will meet A's demand, and her *balance of payments* (in the sense of *ex ante* receipts minus *ex ante* payments) will be in equilibrium. But if this is not the case, the consequences of disequilibrium will depend on the policy of A's monetary authorities with regard to the exchange rate.

In the foreign exchange market where currencies are traded against each other, the 'price' at which a given currency changes hands is its exchange rate; e.g. in the case of sterling, the rate is the number of dollars (or of any other currency units) which is given for £1. If, then, there is an excess supply of, say, sterling (implying excess demand by Britain for foreign currency) the price will be forced down, just as it would be in any other market in which supply happened to be in excess of demand; in the absence of official intervention, the rate of exchange will fall. But this is tantamount to a change in the terms of trade: it means that foreign-currency prices of exports are reduced, import prices remaining the same; or in terms of home currency, import prices rise while export prices stay as before. The terms of trade have moved against the home country; the value of τ, in the formula of page 191, is positive; given suitable values of ε and η, the 'terms-of-trade effect' will improve the balance of trade and eliminate the excess supply of the home currency.

Unfortunately, there is no guarantee that ε and η will be of the right size to bring about this result—or at least, to bring it about before the exchange rate has fallen very considerably. So the monetary authorities may prefer to keep the rate fixed, by meeting excess demand for foreign currency out of a reserve kept for the purpose. The reserve may consist of gold, dollars or any other suitable currency: the authorities will be prepared to trade foreign for home currency to any extent at the fixed 'official' exchange rate. The success of such a policy naturally depends on the size of the reserve relatively to the demands on it; if disequilibrium is persistent, it may eventually be drained away. Fearing this, the authorities may impose *exchange control* under which the home currency cannot be exchanged for foreign currency without their permission; by refusing a suitable number of applications, they may be able to frustrate enough of the demand for foreign currency to minimize the drain on reserves. They may also try to limit the supply of the home currency by *import controls*; if all imports must be licensed, the issue of licences can be arranged so as to keep imports lower than they would otherwise have been. Imposing or increasing import duties is another method by which the same object can be sought.

Finally, the authorities may try to influence the internal economy in such a way as to reduce aggregate demand and the price-level, so that the demand for imports falls and the prices of exports become more competitive in world markets. How this is to be done, however, will not be considered at this stage, since the following chapter is devoted to this and other aspects of the government's role in the economy. Meanwhile, another external influence on the home country's income-equilibrium remains to be noted.

(d) An international Accelerator

It was seen in Chapter Seven (section (e)) pp. 168-73) that changes in the level of aggregate demand may induce investment through the 'Acceleration Principle'. Demand-changes arising from foreign trade play the same part as changes in investment or in consumption;

G

in the response of internal investment to, say, a rise in exports, there is no difference of principle from its response to a rise in consumption; a single country's Accelerator will be no different whether the economy is open or closed. Nevertheless, the principle may give some additional insights, if it is translated from national to world level, by relating the demand for investment in the world as a whole to changes in the level of world income; if such changes are the chief determinant of world investment, a country whose exports are mainly capital equipment will be able to sustain a given level of exports only if world income is rising at an appropriate rate.

The position of such a country is like that of the capital goods industry within the national economy. In the example set forth on pp. 168–9, it was necessary for the demand for commodity X to rise at the rate of 100 units per year, if the demand for new machines was to be stabilized at t_1 o per year. In the same way, a stable level of *world* demand for new equipment may require a steady rise in the world's aggregate demand; even a slackening of the rate of growth would lead to a fall in demand for capital goods—and for countries producing such goods, this would mean a reduction in the demand for their exports.

For Britain, this may be an important consideration: in 1967, machinery alone accounted for more than a quarter of her merchandise exports, while other capital goods (locomotives, ships, tractors and so on) made up a further substantial proportion. Obviously, a check to the growth of world income could have serious consequences for this part of her trade. But it was seen in Chapter Seven that the Acceleration Principle is unlikely to operate with mechanical precision and regularity within one country; *a fortiori*, its working in the world as a whole will be even more blurred, so that it would be unwise to attempt detailed predictions from it on a world scale even if the necessary statistical information were available.

CHAPTER NINE

The State and the National Income

(a) Compensatory finance and income taxation

Public authorities, by their expenditure on goods and services, contribute substantially to aggregate demand; they also augment it indirectly through transfers, such as pensions, which give the recipients the power to spend. Taxes, on the other hand, reduce demand by removing funds from the private sector which could otherwise have been used to buy goods and services. By arranging taxes and public spending in an appropriate way, the government can add more to demand than it takes away, or take away more than it adds, or leave aggregate demand unchanged; the aim of 'compensatory finance' is to adjust aggregate demand to the level needed to give full employment without inflation.

This would be a simple matter if each £1 of tax revenue were sure to diminish private demand by exactly £1, and if each £1 of public spending made a net addition to aggregate demand of the same amount. If the government estimated demand to be, say, £100 millions above the full-employment level, it could then arrange for a budget surplus of exactly that amount; a deficiency of demand could be offset by an exactly equal budget deficit, and a balanced budget could be provided if the level of demand happened to be at full-employment level to begin with. But the effects of taxes and expenditures are more complicated and less certain than this. Taxpayers may respond to a rise in tax-rates by reducing their saving as well as their expenditure, so that each increase of £1 in tax revenue may bring about a fall of only 75p in aggregate demand: also, different taxes may have different effects, tax A causing demand to fall 80p per £1 of revenue, tax B reducing it by only 60p. Public expenditure, too, may to some extent act as a substitute for private spending— for example, the existence of a free health service removes the necessity for private expenditure on medical treatment: additional government spending, therefore, may sometimes be offset by a reduction in private demand. A change in the balance of taxation and expendi-

195

ture, by causing an autonomous change in demand, will induce consequential changes in private spending on consumption, investment and imports—i.e. it will have multiplier effects; among these effects, indeed, may be the inducement of further changes in the amounts of revenue and public spending themselves. Thus, though the general principle of compensatory finance is simple, its practical application is likely to be much less so.

With revenue derived from income taxation (T_y) and indirect taxes (T_g), and with expenditures on goods and services (G) and on transfers (Tr), the government's budget is $(T_y+T_g)-(G+Tr)$. It can alter any single item, leaving the others unchanged, or it can alter two, three or all of them simultaneously; each of the possible alternatives is likely to affect the economy in a different way, as well as to produce a different effect on the budget itself. The first possibility, now to be examined, is that of a change only in income taxation, T_y; for the moment, it will be assumed that there are no indirect taxes or transfers, and that goods-and-services expenditure, G, is kept fixed by the government and is not affected by changes in the level of income. Suppose, then, that the current National Income is £100 millions below what the government estimates the full-employment level to be. What change in T_y will close this 'deflationary gap'?

If there are no undistributed profits, and no transfers, personal incomes are the sum of factor incomes—i.e. National Income, Y. Income taxation removes part of this, leaving individuals with disposable income of $Y-T_y$. If consumption depends on disposable income, i.e. $C = a+c(Y-T_y)$, the equilibrium income of the economy (which for simplicity is assumed closed) will be

$$Y = C+I+G = a+c(Y-T_y)+I+G.$$

If a, c, I and G remain the same when income changes, an alteration in tax revenue, ΔT_y, will lead to a change in income

$$\Delta Y = c(\Delta Y-\Delta T_y)$$

so that

$$\Delta Y(1-c) = -c\Delta T_y$$

and

$$\frac{\Delta Y}{\Delta T_y} = \frac{-c}{1-c}$$

—which is an 'income-tax multiplier' whose size depends upon the MPC; for example, if $c = 0.8$ the multiplier is -4, so that the required increase of £100 millions in the level of income can be brought about by a reduction of £25 millions in tax revenue.

The income-tax multiplier is negative for the obvious reason that a fall in taxation leaves more income in the hands of individuals, so that they feel able to spend more on consumption; the less the tax bill, the more they spend. But it also differs from the 'simple' Multiplier $\frac{1}{1-c}$ in having c as the numerator of the fraction, so that (apart from its negative sign) it is smaller; this is because only a part of the additional disposable incomes is used for consumption, the remainder being saved; the autonomous rise in demand is not $-\Delta T_y$ but $-c\Delta T_y$. The fact that tax revenue has been reduced, while public expenditure has been assumed to remain unchanged, means that if the budget was balanced to start with there will now be a deficit of £25 millions.

The calculations above were in terms of total revenue, not of the *rates* of taxation. If incomes are taxed at a uniform proportional rate t (e.g. 10p in the £ gives $t = 0.1$), the revenue T_y will be tY. Let the original rate of tax be denoted as t_1 and the original level of income as Y_1; a change in tax to t_2 and in income to Y_2 will cause revenue to change from t_1Y_1 to t_2Y_2, i.e. $\Delta T_y = t_2Y_2 - t_1Y_1$; thus

$$\Delta Y = \frac{-c\Delta T_y}{1-c} = \frac{-c(t_2Y_2 - t_1Y_1)}{1-c}$$

If Y_2 is written $Y_1 + \Delta Y$, this becomes

$$\Delta Y = \frac{-cY_1(t_2 - t_1)}{1-c} - \frac{ct_2\Delta Y}{1-c}$$

so that

$$\frac{\Delta Y(1-c+ct_2)}{1-c} = \frac{-cY_1(t_2 - t_1)}{1-c}$$

from which

$$\Delta Y = \frac{-cY_1(t_2 - t_1)}{1-c+ct_2}$$

Here the 'multiplicand' is the additional consumption expenditure which taxpayers wish to make when the cut in the rate of tax raises their disposable incomes; for example, if $Y_1 = $ £600 millions and the tax rate is reduced from 10p to 5p in the £, tax revenue will fall by £30 millions, and if the MPC is 0.8 there will be a rise of £24 millions in consumers' demand, which will be multiplied by $\frac{1}{1-c+ct_2}$ (whose value in this case is 4.17) to give an eventual rise in income of £100 millions.

This 'rate-of-tax multiplier' applies to *any* autonomous change in demand, not merely to that caused by a change in tax rates. If income rises in response to an increase in investment, for example, the consequential rise in consumption will be $\Delta C = c(\Delta Y - \Delta T_y)$; at a given tax rate t, $\Delta T_y = t \Delta Y$ so that $\Delta C = c \Delta Y(1 - t)$. The change in income will then be

$$\Delta Y = \Delta C + \Delta I = c \Delta Y(1 - t) + \Delta I$$

so that

$$\Delta Y(1 - c(1 - t)) = \Delta I$$

and

$$\frac{\Delta Y}{\Delta I} = \frac{1}{1 - c(1 - t)} = \frac{1}{1 - c + ct}.$$

In this case, the government is assumed to remain quite passive, in the sense that it does not itself initiate any change in demand; the existence of tax at rate t, however, means that part of the additional factor income is diverted to the public revenue instead of being available for consumption, so that the Multiplier is smaller than it would otherwise have been. Tax revenue will have risen by $t \Delta Y$, so that there will now be a budget surplus if there had been an exact balance to begin with; had income fallen instead of risen, the consequent reduction in tax revenue would have entailed a budget deficit.

The assumption so far made, that the tax rate t is a fixed proportion of income, is of course an unrealistic simplification; in fact, income taxation is *progressive*—the larger an individual's income, the higher the proportion of it paid in tax. A rise in National Income will push taxpayers into higher 'tax brackets' so that the average tax rate t increases; a fall in income, similarly, will reduce t. Exactly how much it will change, depends not only on the amount of rise or fall in National Income but also on how this is distributed between individuals; also, because tax rates apply to the money value of income, t will rise or fall when changes in the price-level bring about changes in money income even though *real* income may have remained the same.

Under a system of progressive taxation, increasing factor incomes will be accompanied by a rise in t, so that a smaller and smaller proportion will be left as disposable income in private hands; the rise in consumption will fall further and further behind the rise in National Income. Should factor incomes fall, on the other hand, t will also fall; as tax lightens, disposable income will fall less than proportionately with the decline in National Income, and consumption, though falling, will be reduced by less than if a *proportional* tax—or no tax at all—had been in operation. As already noted, these effects will ensue in response to changes in money income, whether these are due to changes in the volume of output at constant prices, or to changes in prices at a constant level of physical output. Thus, the existence of a system of progressive taxation will tend to reduce fluctuations in aggregate demand, and thereby make the level of income more stable than it would otherwise be: it will act as a *'built-in stabilizer'* of the economy.

A complication arises from 'partial' income taxation. Companies pay a special Corporation Tax on their undistributed profits. Wage and salary-earners, in addition to income tax, pay a National Insurance contribution whose amount is fixed in money terms and varies only slightly with the contributor's earnings; it is thus a *regressive* tax, in the sense that it takes a higher proportion of the contributor's income, the smaller his earnings. These taxes, superimposed on income-tax and surtax, modify the progression of the system of income taxation as a whole.

Altering the distribution of tax liability between income-groups (e.g. by increasing surtax rates while reducing the National Insurance contribution) will change consumers' demand even though total tax revenue remains the same, if the MPCs of the income-groups are different. Though the distribution of factor incomes remains the same (at least initially) the reallocation of tax implies a redistribution of *disposable* incomes; leaving less in the hands of a group whose MPC is low, and leaving more with a high-MPC group, will lead to greater consumption (as described in Chapter Five, pp. 115–18).

(b) Changes in indirect taxation

Changes in income taxation are only one of the possible methods of compensatory finance open to the government. A second alternative is to alter indirect taxes such as purchase tax, local rates, and the duties on beer and tobacco. To isolate the effects of such changes, it will be assumed that there are no income taxes or transfers, and that goods-and-services spending remains fixed in amount.

Indirect taxes absorb expenditure without generating factor income. When the economy is in equilibrium with indirect taxes yielding a revenue T_g,

$$Y_f + T_g = C_m + I_m + G_m, \text{ or } Y_f = C_m + I_m + G_m - T_g$$

—where Y_f is the sum of factor incomes (i.e. National Income) and spending $(C_m + I_m + G_m)$ is at market prices. A rise in T_g will have the initial effect of increasing prices while leaving money incomes unchanged; but this means real incomes have been reduced, and there will be a fall in the quantities of goods and services demanded. This autonomous decrease in real demand will have a multiplier effect, causing a further fall in the equilibrium level of real income. A *cut* in indirect taxation will, of course, have the opposite effect, causing an autonomous increase in real demand which gives rise to a multiple expansion in real income.

Suppose, as a simplification, that all indirect taxation falls on consumption, so that for I and G market price and factor cost are identical; suppose, also, that I and G are unaffected by changes in the level of income. When indirect taxation is altered, the change in National Income will then be $\Delta Y_f = \Delta C_m - \Delta T_g$. If consumption at market prices is a fixed proportion of factor incomes (there being no income taxes or transfers, and no undistributed profits), $C_m = c Y_f$ and $\Delta C_m = c \Delta Y_f$; so the eventual change in income will be

$$\Delta Y_f = c\Delta Y_f - \Delta T_g$$

from which

$$\frac{\Delta Y_f}{\Delta T_g} = \frac{-1}{1-c}.$$

This 'indirect tax multiplier' is larger than the income taxation multiplier $\left(\dfrac{-c}{1-c}\right)$ given on p. 196, and suggests that the authorities can exert more control over the economy by altering indirect taxes than by changing direct taxation. If it is desired to raise income by £100 millions, and the MPC is 0·8, a cut in indirect taxes of £20 millions will be sufficient, whereas it would be necessary to reduce income taxation by £25 millions to achieve the same result.

This will not hold good, however, if the consumption function is of the form $C_m = a + c Y_f$ and the autonomous element a is at market prices, implying that consumers wish to obtain a given quantity of commodities *plus* whatever a proportion c of their money incomes will buy. When market prices go up because of higher indirect taxation, the value of a will rise proportionately; even though factor incomes Y_f have not changed, the amount of money being spent on consumption will rise.[1] The change in consumers' demand at market prices will thus be $\Delta C_m = ap + c\Delta Y_f$ (where p is the proportionate change in prices), so that the multiplier is

$$\frac{\Delta Y_f}{\Delta T_g} = \frac{-1}{1-c}\left(1 - \frac{ap}{\Delta T_g}\right);$$

[1] It is as though the consumption function CC in Fig. 4 (p. 98) had been shifted vertically upwards.

this is smaller than the previous multiplier, the precise difference depending on the size of a. If factor costs have not changed, the rise in market prices will be wholly attributable to increases in indirect taxation, and p will then be equal to $\dfrac{\Delta T_g}{Y_f + T_g}$; when this is substituted for p in the last equation, the multiplier becomes

$$\frac{\Delta Y_f}{\Delta T_g} = \frac{-1}{1-c} \left(1 - \frac{a}{Y_f + T_g}\right)$$

which means that if autonomous consumption a is (for example) one-tenth of the market-price value of National Income, the indirect-tax multiplier will be only nine-tenths as large as it would have been if a were zero.

It may be that consumers are not sensitive to price-increases, i.e. are under 'money illusion'; they continue to spend on autonomous consumption the same amount of *money* as before, instead of spending more in order to obtain the same physical quantity at higher prices. In that case, there will be no rise in the value of a and the indirect tax multiplier will be simply $\dfrac{-1}{1-c}$ as before. The likelihood of this depends on the proportion in which prices are increased by higher taxes; the greater this is, the more it will obtrude itself on consumers' attention and destroy their money illusion. On the other hand, if the tax increase is not distributed evenly over all commodities (as with a general sales tax) but is concentrated on a few only (as with a rise in the duties on tobacco and beer), consumers may feel that the general level of prices is about the same as before, and may retain their money illusion; here, however, consumers may be induced to switch demand away from the taxed products to those whose prices are still the same, and this will complicate the outcome.

Indirect taxes will modify the response of the economy to autonomous changes in demand other than those resulting from tax changes. Suppose, for example, that a rise in investment occurs: through the Multiplier, aggregate demand will increase, but indirect taxes will divert a proportion of the additional expenditure into the hands of public authorities so that it fails to generate further income. If taxation takes the form of a general sales tax, applied at a uniform rate t to all commodities, $Y_f + T_g = Y_f(1+t)$—i.e. the market value of aggregate output is its factor cost (Y_f) plus 10% (if $t = 0 \cdot 1$). The income-equilibrium equation then is

$$Y_f(1+t) = cY_f + I + G;$$

if G remains fixed, and I changes only by the increase in autonomous investment ΔI, the rise in income caused by the latter will be

$$\Delta Y_f(1+t) = c\Delta Y_f + \Delta I$$

from which

$$\Delta Y_f(1-c+t) = \Delta I$$

so that

$$\frac{\Delta Y_f}{\Delta I} = \frac{1}{1-c+t}$$

—a multiplier which is less than the simple multiplier $\frac{1}{1-c}$, and also smaller than the 'rate-of-income-tax' multiplier $\frac{1}{1-c+ct}$ given on p. 198: indirect taxation is thus more stabilizing than proportional[1] income taxation, when tax rates are kept unchanged.

Attempts to reduce aggregate demand by increasing the rate of tax, however, may be less successful than preceding arguments may have seemed to suggest. When higher indirect taxes raise market prices, the owners of factors of production may be able to neutralize the effect by procuring higher money incomes for themselves. Trade unions may submit wage-claims on the ground that the cost of living has risen, and may be strong enough to ensure the claims are conceded; firms may adjust profit margins appropriately, hoping thereby to keep the real value of profits from falling. If the purpose of increasing indirect taxes is to reduce real incomes and so diminish the inflationary pressure of excessive aggregate demand, the fact that such a policy works by raising prices may create repercussions tending to neutralize it; indeed, the eventual result may even be to stimulate inflation instead of checking it.

(c) Effects on investment

So far, changes in taxation have been assumed to affect only consumption, leaving investment unchanged. If investment demand is sensitive to the level of income (i.e. if there is a marginal propensity to invest) the various tax multipliers will have to be amended to allow for this—for example, the simple income-tax multiplier will become $\frac{-c}{1-c-i}$ instead of $\frac{-c}{1-c}$; changes in the level of aggregate demand may also set up acceleration effects. Finally, tax changes may

---

[1] But not necessarily more so than *progressive* income taxation.

cause autonomous shifts in the investment schedule which will themselves exert multiplier effects.

If investment depends on profit expectations, taxes will diminish
the incentive to invest. Given the prospect of a stream of returns
A_1, A_2, A_3 etc., direct taxation at a rate t (40p in the £, for example,
gives $t = 0.4$) will reduce the disposable yields to $A_1(1-t)$, $A_2(1-t)$
and so on. Higher indirect taxation, by raising market prices, will
reduce the real value of A_1, A_2, A_3 etc.; it may also affect estimates of
the revenue to be expected from the sale of the product—if sales are
likely to fall because of consumers' reactions to indirect taxes, the
amount of prospective yields may be reduced. For maximum effect,
tax increases must be expected to be fairly permanent: if a rise in
Corporation Tax, for example, is thought likely to be reversed next
year, it will affect only the first of the series of yields A_1, A_2, A_3 ...
—and investment decisions must have regard to yields over the *whole*
of an asset's prospective life. Though estimates of the more distant
yields may be very uncertain, a rise in tax has the effect of altering
the odds against the investing firm; for example, if it expects that the
profit earned in the sixth year from now may be anything between
£1,000 and nothing at all, a tax of 40p in the £ will reduce the upper
limit of £600 while leaving the lower limit still at zero; the average
of possible disposable yields will then be lower for this and every
other year in which the capital equipment is to operate. Thus, the
MEI schedule of Fig. 11 (p. 154) will be shifted downwards; if the
schedule is at all elastic with respect to the costs of funds, the level of
investment demand will be reduced. If (as under the 'Residual
Funds' theory described in Chapter Seven, p. 162) the amount of
undistributed profits is an important factor in investment decisions,
a rise in the rate of tax which falls on them will check investment by
reducing the disposable residue of profit.

This general conclusion may need modification in the light of the
detailed operation of the tax system. For example, if a rise in taxation falls only on personal incomes, leaving the rate of tax on undistributed profits unchanged, the effect may be to increase the retention of
profits, and thereby furnish the means for increased investment. The
ploughing-back of profits increases the assets of companies and tends
to raise the market value of their shares; if capital gains are taxable
at a lower rate than personal income, it will benefit wealthy shareholders to have profits retained and reinvested in their companies
rather than distributed in dividends. A rise in employers' National
Insurance contributions (which are an indirect tax on the employment of labour) will raise labour costs, and may give firms an incentive to substitute machinery for labour. If indirect taxes are changed

in such a way as to switch demand towards commodities whose production requires relatively more capital equipment, there may be a net stimulus to investment. Since tax changes tend to be made piecemeal rather than in the form of equal proportional changes in all taxes, their effects on investment may be much less clear-cut than the preceding general arguments have suggested.

(d) Changes in public expenditure

Instead of using changes in taxation as a means of adjusting the level of income, the authorities may adopt the policy of altering their own expenditure on goods and services, i.e. raising or lowering the value of G in the equilibrium equation

$$Y+T_g = c(Y-T_y)+I+G$$

In this equation, both income taxation (T_y) and indirect taxes (T_g) have been included; however, if the revenue from both kinds of tax is assumed to remain unchanged when income alters, and if investment is also unaffected by changes in income, the result of a change in G will be

$$\Delta Y = c\Delta Y+\Delta G$$

so that

$$\frac{\Delta Y}{\Delta G} = \frac{1}{1-c}$$

—which is the simple Multiplier of Chapter Six (p. 132); the effect of a rise in government goods-and-services spending is just the same as that of an autonomous rise in investment or exports. If the MPC is 0·8, the Multiplier is 5: to raise National Income by £100 millions, a rise in G of £20 millions is required.

The outcome will be different, however, if the government keeps the *rates* of taxation unchanged. The assumption made earlier, that tax *revenue* stays the same, implies either that the authorities reduce tax rates as income rises (and raise them when income falls) or that the revenue arises from a poll-tax or other lump-sum imposts. If all revenue is from a proportional income tax at rate t_y, and if this rate is not altered when government expenditure changes, revenue will automatically rise with the level of income and the multiplier will be

$$\frac{\Delta Y}{\Delta G} = \frac{1}{1-c+ct_y}$$

for the reasons given above on p. 198. If it is indirect taxation which provides the revenue, this too will alter when G is changed, so that if the rate of tax remains fixed at t_g,

$$\frac{\Delta Y}{\Delta G} = \frac{1}{1-c+t_g}$$

—this being the 'rate-of-indirect-tax' multiplier given on p. 202 above. With both types of tax in force, the two multipliers combine to give

$$\frac{\Delta Y}{\Delta G} = \frac{1}{1-c+t_g+ct_y}$$

If the MPC is 0·8, and if tax rates are $t_g = 0\cdot1$ and $t_y = 0\cdot2$, it will be necessary to raise G by £46 millions to produce an increase of £100 millions in National Income. Thus, the Multiplier is only 2·17 when tax *rates* are kept fixed, as against 5·0 when *revenue* is maintained unchanged.

As well as altering goods-and-services expenditure, the government may also change the amount of income-transfers, for example by raising retirement pensions or increasing family allowances. The effect will be to increase disposable incomes and thus to stimulate consumers' demand. Transfers may, indeed, be regarded as a form of income taxation in reverse; a rise in transfers has the same effect as a fall in income-tax revenue,[1] so that the Multiplier which applies to the latter applies also to the former, except that it works in the opposite direction, i.e. its sign is positive instead of negative. If consumption depends on disposable incomes Y_d, which are equal to factor incomes *minus* income taxation *plus* transfers, i.e. $C = c(Y-T_y+Tr)$, a change in the amount of Tr (everything else remaining the same) gives

$$\Delta Y = c(\Delta Y + \Delta Tr) = c\Delta Y + c\Delta Tr$$

so that

$$\frac{\Delta Y}{\Delta Tr} = \frac{c}{1-c}$$

which implies that if the MPC = 0·8, an increase of £25 millions in transfers will raise National Income by £100 millions.

Income-transfers take the form of money payments to individuals, to be spent at their discretion. Another kind of transfer is the *subsidy*, paid by the authorities to the sellers of commodities so that they can set market prices below factor cost: instead of receiving cash, consumers obtain the benefit of being able to buy goods more cheaply.

[1] Except where the recipients of transfers have MPCs which differ from those of income-tax payers, as discussed on pp. 210–11 below.

Just as income transfers are income taxes in reverse, so subsidies are negative indirect taxes: an increase in subsidies, therefore, is equivalent to a reduction in indirect taxation, and may be expected to have similar multiplier effects.

With given *rates* of subsidy, the government's total outlay depends on the quantity of subsidized commodities bought, and this will rise and fall along with the level of National Income (though not necessarily in the same proportion). Most kinds of income transfers, on the other hand, will be unaffected when National Income changes: the amount of family allowances paid out depends on the number of families with two or more children, the amount of sick benefit on the number of cases of illness, and so on. An important exception is unemployment benefit: a reduction in the level of income and output, accompanied by an increase in unemployment, will automatically increase the total amount paid out if the rate of benefit per person is not reduced. This will prevent disposable incomes from falling as much as factor incomes, and will sustain consumers' expenditure at a level above what it would otherwise have been, thus tending to stabilize the economy. Like progressive income taxation,[1] a system of unemployment assistance[2] will act as a 'built-in stabilizer': even if the government takes no special action to combat recession, the automatic operation of the stabilizers will tend to check the fall in aggregate demand. Unlike income taxes, however, a system of transfers to the unemployed is a stabilizer in one direction only: it helps to defend the economy against recessions, but cannot do anything to check inflationary pressures when full employment has been attained.

(e) Alternative policies and the budget balance

Various methods have now been examined by which the government can cause the equilibrium level of income to rise or fall. If the level is £100 millions below that required for full employment, and the MPC is 0·8, a reduction of £25 millions in income tax revenue, or of £20 millions in indirect tax revenue, will be required; or if tax revenue is kept unchanged, the same effect may be achieved by a rise of £20 millions in government goods-and-services expenditure, or by a rise of £25 millions in income transfers, or by a rise of £20 millions

---

[1] See p. 199 above.

[2] Where, as in Britain, this is an 'insurance' scheme under which workers pay contributions while they are in work, there will be a double effect: in addition to receiving benefit, the unemployed will cease to pay contributions, so that there will be a reduction in direct taxation as well as an increase in income transfers.

in subsidies. If the government's budget happened to be balanced to start with (i.e. $T_y + T_g = G + Tr$) any of these measures will create a budget deficit: revenue will fall short of expenditure, and the government will finance excess expenditure by borrowing. If it is a question of reducing the level of aggregate demand so as to eliminate inflationary pressures, things will be the other way round: the government will arrange to have a budget surplus, and the excess of revenue over expenditure will be used to repay debt. Balancing the economy may mean unbalancing the budget.

To argue that a budget deficit may sometimes be desirable conflicts with the traditional principle, regarded until the 1930s as virtually self-evident, that the government must at all costs avoid a budget deficit. It used to be taken for granted that if the state spends more than it obtains by taxation, inflation must inevitably ensue. An individual who over-spends his income risks bankruptcy; similarly, it was argued, a government which finances deficits by borrowing may become insolvent; even if it does not, the increase of the National Debt adds to the burden on the community and on posterity which the Debt represents. Indeed, a wise government should make efforts to repay it: the budget, so one nineteenth-century Chancellor said, is 'an animal that needs a surplus'. The superstitious horror in which deficits were held was pathetically exemplified in the Emergency Budget of 1931; though more than a fifth of the working population were unemployed, the government nevertheless insisted on balancing the budget.[1]

These traditional arguments are not logically valid if unemployment exists. A budget deficit, by adding to aggregate demand, will expand employment and output; inflationary price-increases can only occur if the economy is already in equilibrium at full employment, since it will then be impossible to expand output rapidly to meet a rise in demand. The 'inflation' argument against deficits, therefore, assumes the prior existence of the full employment which deficits are intended to achieve. The objection to increasing debt similarly loses force when the economy is depressed: even if the interest on the debt were a net burden on the community, it would be worth incurring if output could thereby be made to rise by more than the interest charge; in any case, internally-held public debt represents a transfer between members of the same community, so that the payment of interest is in effect a transfer from taxpayers to bondholders. The traditional analogy between the State and the spendthrift indivi-

---

[1] See Chapter LXXIX of *An Autobiography*, by Philip Viscount Snowden, in which the 1931 Chancellor describes his efforts to prevent an 'appalling' deficit of £170 millions.

dual[1] is less reasonable than one between the State and a business firm which may quite rationally incur debts in order to increase its output.

Whatever the logic of the matter, however, the authorities may still be constrained to avoid a deficit: if legislators and the public are inexorably convinced of the traditional case for budget-balancing, a deficit will not be practical politics; there may be external considerations—for example, it may be feared that a deficit will alarm foreign creditors, whose efforts to withdraw their loans may then make it hard to maintain the exchange rate; the authorities may fear that an increase of debt may be inconsistent with their current policies of 'debt management'. In these circumstances, the budget may have to be balanced. But this need not leave the government powerless to combat unemployment: even without a deficit, the State can still exert an expansionary influence on aggregate demand.

This possibility arises because of differences between the multiplier effects of taxes and transfers on the one hand and goods-and-services expenditure on the other. Suppose the government (whose budget is assumed to be balanced initially) increases expenditure by ΔG, while simultaneously increasing its revenue from income taxation by ΔT_y. If indirect tax revenue and transfer expenditure do not change, and no induced investment occurs, there will be a change in income

$$\Delta Y = c(\Delta Y - \Delta T_y) + \Delta G$$

so that

$$\Delta Y(1-c) = \Delta G - c\Delta T_y.$$

If the budget is to remain balanced, the increase in tax revenue must be equal to the rise in government spending, i.e. $\Delta G = \Delta T_y$, so the equation could be written

$$\Delta Y(1-c) = \Delta G(1-c)$$

giving

$$\Delta Y = \Delta G.$$

The rise in income is exactly equal to the increase in government expenditure.

Here, two multipliers have been set to work in opposite directions. Had tax revenue been unchanged, ΔG would have increased income by $\frac{\Delta G}{1-c}$; if $\Delta G = 100$ and $c = 0.8$, the rise in income would have

---

[1] This analogy has been well named the 'anthropomorphic fallacy' by S. S. Alexander, in 'Opposition to Deficit Spending for the Prevention of Unemployment', *Income, Employment and Public Policy* (Essays in Honour of Alvin H. Hansen, 1948).

been 500. The rise in tax revenue, if left to work on its own, would have reduced income by $-\dfrac{c\Delta T_y}{1-c}$; with ΔT_y equal to 100, this would have meant a fall in income of -400. Put together, the two multipliers give a change in income of $500-400$, i.e. 100. This result is independent of the value of the MPC;[1] it does not matter whether c is 0·9 or 0·2—the change in income must be

$$\frac{\Delta G}{1-c} - \frac{c\Delta T_y}{1-c},$$

or, since $\Delta G = \Delta T_y$

$$\Delta G \frac{1-c}{1-c}, \qquad \text{i.e. } \Delta G.$$

This is the simplest case of the so-called 'balanced-budget theorem'.[2]

A budget which includes only goods-and-services expenditure and income-tax revenue will always, if balanced, impart a stimulus to the economy; it means the authorities are collecting in taxes income which would otherwise have been partly saved, and are using it all to finance expenditure. If the authorities wish to exert no *net* effect on aggregate demand, i.e. to contribute to it no more than the amount of demand eliminated by taxation, they should budget for a surplus. Thus, given the nineteenth-century view that the state should be as self-effacing as possible in its role as the 'night-watchman' of the economy, the traditional preoccupation with debt repayment makes *political* sense, even though it is not *economically* rational unless a state of continuous full employment is assumed to exist.

However, the budget may include transfers and subsidies on the expenditure side, and the revenue may come from indirect taxes as well as from income taxation. If it is these items which change, the results may be very different from the simple case examined above. For example, if an increase in goods-and-services spending, ΔG, is financed by an increase in indirect taxation ΔT_g, the effect on income will be nil; the additional expenditure will raise income by $\dfrac{\Delta G}{1-c}$, and the additional indirect taxation will reduce it by $-\dfrac{\Delta T_g}{1-c}$; since the budget balance requires the additional indirect taxation to be equal to

[1] In the extreme case in which the MPC $= 1$, the change in income is said to be 'undefined'.

[2] T. Haavelmo, 'Multiplier Effects of a Balanced Budget', *Econometrica*, October 1945. See also R. A. Musgrave, *The Theory of Public Finance* (1959), Chap. 18, for this and other budgetary multipliers, and for further references.

the additional expenditure ($\Delta G = \Delta T_g$) the two multiplier effects cancel out exactly, leaving income the same as before.

Similarly, an increase in transfer expenditures, financed by extra income taxation, may fail to change the level of income. It was seen on p. 205 that a rise in transfers will increase income by $\frac{c\Delta Tr}{1-c}$; additional taxation will reduce it by $-\frac{c\Delta T_y}{1-c}$; if $\Delta Tr = \Delta T_y$, the two effects will exactly neutralize one another, leaving income unchanged. If a rise in transfers were combined with additional *indirect* taxation, the net effect could even be a fall in the level of income.

It may be, however, that the recipients of transfers have a different MPC from that of the taxpayers from whom additional revenue is raised: for example, if the taxes are collected from the incomes of rich people who continue their consumption almost unchanged, while the transfers are small pensions given to old people with no other resources, the net effect will obviously be to increase aggregate demand. Thus, if the rich taxpayers' MPC is denoted by c_1, pensioners' MPC by c_2, and the MPC of the rest of the community[1] by c_3, the effect of an equal increase X in taxes and transfers will be

$$\Delta Y = \frac{c_2 \Delta Tr}{1-c_3} - \frac{c_1 \Delta T_y}{1-c_3} = \frac{X(c_2 - c_1)}{1-c_3};$$

if $c_1 = 0.6$, $c_2 = 0.9$ and $c_3 = 0.8$, an X of £67 millions will raise income by £100 millions, even though the budget is still balanced and no additional public goods-and-services spending is being done.

Transfers were described earlier as an income-tax in reverse; a reduction in tax liability, therefore, is akin to a transfer payment, and the argument of the previous paragraph may be applied to a redistribution of tax incidence between income-groups. If, without any change in the level of government spending or in total tax revenue, tax liability is reshuffled so that people whose MPC is high are left

---

[1] The assumption here is that though taxpayers and pensioners have different MPCs, their expenditure travels through the same 'circuit' of income-recipients each of whom has the same MPC, i.e. c_3. The expenditure by pensioners of $c_2 X$ gives rise to a series of further payments such that the final effect on aggregate demand and income is

$$c_2 X + c_3 c_2 X + c_3{}^2 c_2 X + c_3{}^3 c_2 X + \ldots + c_3{}^n c_2 X$$
$$= c_2 X (1 + c_3 + c_3{}^2 + c_3{}^3 + \ldots + c_3{}^n)$$
$$= c_2 X \frac{1}{1-c_3}$$

Similarly, the taxpayers' reduction of expenditure by $-c_1 X$ will give rise to $-c_1 X \frac{1}{1-c_3}$ as the change in income.

with more disposable income and those with a low MPC with correspondingly less, there will be a net increase in aggregate consumption which through the Multiplier will increase the equilibrium level of income. In the equation above, the substitution for ΔTr of the amount of tax reduction enjoyed by lower-MPC groups is all that is necessary to show the results of such redistribution.

By these methods, then, it may be possible to expand income and employment without incurring a budget deficit. The same logic applies, of course, where it is necessary to *reduce* aggregate demand without a budget *surplus*: public goods-and-services spending may be diminished and tax reliefs of an equal amount given; transfers to high-MPC groups may be cut and taxes on low-MPC groups reduced; or tax liability may be redistributed from high- to low-MPC groups. But it should be observed that the degree of disturbance to the budget will be greater if it has to be kept balanced than if a surplus or deficit is allowed. To raise income by £100 millions by increasing both taxes and goods-and-services spending equally, the latter must rise £100 millions; but in the example on p. 204, where taxes were not increased, only £20 millions' extra expenditure was required. In the 'tax and transfers' example above, £67 millions of additional transfers were needed to raise income £100 millions; had taxes been left unchanged, only £22 millions would have been necessary. If a deficit were to be incurred by reducing taxes without changing expenditure, and if the MPC were 0·8, a £25 millions income-tax cut would achieve the same result as a £100 millions increase in goods-and-services expenditure financed by an equal *increase* in income-tax revenue under a balanced budget.

This last difference may be the best reason for preferring deficit finance. When the economy is depressed, tax reductions are likely to improve the 'atmosphere' of enterprise in the private sector, while increases (even though accompanied by higher government spending) may do further damage to the state of expectations which was seen in Chapter Seven to be important in the determination of investment. The authorities' choice here must depend on which they think will damage business confidence more—higher taxes, or the mystic dread inspired by the spectacle of a deficit.

(f) Limitations and alternatives

To budget for a deficit is unlikely to be very difficult. The real obstacles to compensatory finance may in fact be met when it is necessary to arrange for a surplus to check inflationary pressures. Here, the government's room for manoeuvre may be much less than the foregoing equations have seemed to suggest. Reductions in goods-and-services spending may be impracticable—the scale of defence expenditure, for example, is presumably the minimum needed in view of the political situation, and could not be diminished without endangering the nation; cuts in certain public services, such as police and justice, could impair the working of the economy; reductions in some other forms of public spending, for example on health services, would be offset by higher private expenditures. Attempts to reduce transfers, such as retirement pensions, might be so unpopular that a democratically-elected government could not be expected to make them. In short, the level of government spending, though high, may be the minimum needed for national security, economic efficiency, and the satisfaction of public opinion.[1]

If expenditures are incompressible, the government must turn to tax-increases as a means of disinflationary policy. Yet if taxes are already high, it may fear to raise them further. Apart from the electoral disadvantages of such action, higher income taxation may be expected to damage incentives and to stimulate tax evasion; putting up indirect taxes may merely lead to claims for higher money incomes.

Finally, the time factor must be considered. The authorities need time to analyse the situation and to assess the prospects, time to devise appropriate policies, and time to carry them out. Even when Parliamentary sanction has been obtained for the necessary changes in taxation and expenditure, there will be a lag before these measures begin to exert their effects on the economy.[2] By that time, however, conditions may have worsened so much that the remedies are no longer adequate; alternatively, a cyclical movement may have already begun to reverse itself and the government's measures may turn out to be the opposite of what is required by the time they come into force. A strong argument for having 'built-in' stabilizers, such as progressive taxation and a scheme of unemployment compensation,

[1] An important additional consideration is that 'chopping and changing in government expenditure policy is frustrating to efficiency and economy in the running of the public services. It impairs cost-consciousness and financial discipline at all levels. Short-term "economy campaigns" and "stop-and-go" are damaging to the real effectiveness of control of public expenditure'. These words are from the Plowden Committee's Report on *The Control of Public Expenditure* (Cmnd. 1432), 1961).

[2] These 'policy' lags will be additional to those already present in the working of the economy, i.e. the various lags discussed in Chapter Six. The multipliers given in the present chapter have all been set out in static form; realism would require them to be dynamized by the inclusion of time-lags, and the task of stabilization policy would then appear even more difficult. See the two articles in the *Economic Journal* by A. W. Phillips, 'Stabilization Policy in a Closed Economy' (1954) and 'Stabilization Policy and the Time-Form of Lagged Responses' (1957).

is that they will work to correct an imbalance with less delay. The government's *ad hoc* policy decisions, on the other hand, ought to be framed in such a way as to allow for time-lags, and this is likely to make the problem perplexingly difficult.

If it is thought to be impossible to reduce expenditure, if it would be disadvantageous to increase taxation, and if the time factor would in any case cause such policies to take much too long to ameliorate the situation, the government may prefer to resort to direct intervention in the economy through direct controls. A system of consumer rationing; the licensing of building works and other forms of capital expenditure; quantitative restrictions on imports; government purchase and allocation of raw materials; limitation of hire-purchase terms by specifying minimum percentage deposits and maximum repayment periods—these and other devices may be used to frustrate excessive demand. But these, too, are unpopular measures; regulations may be evaded and black markets may be called into being; the enforcement of really stringent controls may require great expense and effort. In the 1950s, British governments abandoned most of the direct controls set up in war-time, and preferred to rely on *monetary policy*—that is, the attempt to influence the working of the economy through the adjustment of interest rates and the availability of credit. To appreciate the possibilities of monetary policy, it is necessary to examine the part played by money in the economy: and this will be done in Chapters Eleven and Twelve.

CHAPTER TEN

Prices, Wages and Aggregate Supply

(a) The aggregate supply curve

In the last five chapters the various components of aggregate demand —consumption, investment, government spending, exports and (negatively) imports—have been examined in detail, especially with regard to their relationship with current real income. It was found that consumption depends partly on income and partly on such other factors as consumers' assets and liabilities; that investment may be influenced by current income to some small extent, but is much more dependent on firms' expectations of future profit, on past changes in income, and on the cost of financing new projects; that government spending, being largely determined by political decisions on such matters as the necessary scale of defence expenditure, is essentially autonomous of current income; and that, while imports can be expected to vary with income in some degree, exports are affected only indirectly through the 'feedback' described in Chapter Eight. In the light of all these findings, the original 'equilibrium equation'

$$Y = C+I+G+E-M$$

has been amplified and extended in various ways, so as to bring in the marginal propensities to consume, import and invest, to allow for the effects of taxation, to introduce additional variables such as previous periods' income, and so on.

It would obviously be possible to expand and elaborate the equation still further along these lines. However, this would not alter the fact that as it stands the 'equilibrium condition' is subject to a serious limitation—namely, that because all quantities are stated in real terms, it throws no light on the determination of the general price-level. Yet the behaviour of prices is of great interest and importance to individuals, business firms and governments. Large and sudden changes can be highly disruptive, impoverishing or enriching people according to whether they happen to be debtors or creditors, upsetting normal economic calculations, and creating uncertainties which inhibit the rational use of resources. Even where governments aim at minimum interference with the working of the economy, they usually attempt to maintain reasonable price-stability through monetary policy. No theory of the working of the economy as a whole can be complete, therefore, unless it explains the determination of the general price-level as well as the volume of 'real' output. A full explanation will not be possible until *money* has been introduced into the analysis: but first it is necessary to relax certain assumptions on which the argument has been based up to this point.

The assumptions in question are those made at the end of Chapter Four. The first was that, because of the strength of trade unions, money-wages can be regarded as 'inflexible downwards' in the face of unemployment—that is, they will not be forced down by the existence of excess supply in the market for labour. The second was that the employment–output relationship is not such as to give diminishing returns to labour over the range of outputs the economy is likely to be required to produce. The combined effect of these two assumptions has been to ensure that the price-level remained constant at all levels of employment and output, except when aggregate demand became so high that it could not be satisfied by the volume of full-employment output; on this basis, it has been possible to analyse the determination of real income and output without having to deal at the same time with the effects of variations in prices. It can be claimed that neither assumption is wholly unrealistic: unemployment (in the sense of an excess of the number of registered unemployed over the number of unfilled vacancies) has not, in fact, been accompanied by reductions in money-wages in recent years; and the marginal product of labour could for practical purposes be regarded as constant over a certain range of levels of output, if much capital equipment is designed to rigid labour requirements of the 'one man, one machine' variety.[1] But conditions may change over time, and assumptions which are reasonably realistic in one decade may cease to be so in the next; it may happen, too, that both of these particular assumptions do not hold good simultaneously over a wide range of outputs.[2]

[1] Provided, too, that there are 'constant returns to scale' whereby a given proportionate increase in all productive factors always yields the same proportionate increase in output. Then the employment of an additional man, using a machine which would otherwise have stood idle, will always raise output by the same amount, up to the point at which all available machines are in operation.

[2] When employment is high, the fact that labour input is large relatively to the capital stock makes it probable that labour's marginal product will be diminishing markedly—yet in this situation, trade unions will have no difficulty in preventing reductions in money-wages, even though employment is still short of the 'full' level. At low levels of employment, things may be just the other way round, with

To increase the generality of the analysis, it is necessary to consider the effects of relaxing them. To begin with, only the assumption of constant returns to labour will be dropped; for the time being, it will be convenient to go on treating the level of money-wages as being constant at all levels of employment and output.

From now on, then, the marginal product of labour will be assumed to diminish as the level of employment increases. The employment–output relationship is once more of the kind exemplified by the $Q(N,\bar{K})$ curve of Fig. 1 on p. 72 above, whose slope becomes less and less steep as the number of man-hours employed rises beyond N_2. It will be remembered from Chapter Four[1] that firms will not wish to hire more than the number of man-hours at which the marginal product of labour (MPL) equals the real wage (W, or alternatively w/p—the money-wage divided by the price-level), since any additional labour would then cost more to employ than its contribution to output. This condition, $MPL = w/p$, can easily be rearranged as $p = w/MPL$: in this form, it defines the minimum price at which firms will be prepared to sell the output of a given quantity of labour. Thus, if the money-wage w happens to be 50p an hour, and at the current level of employment the MPL is 10 units of output, the lowest price at which firms will be willing to supply their output must be 5p per unit: this is just enough to cover the wage-cost of the marginal unit of output. Firms will not, of course, be loth to receive prices higher than this, but if p were to rise to (say) 10p it would pay them to expand output and employment until the MPL had fallen to 5 units—as long as the money-wage continues to be 50p per man-hour. Since it has already been assumed that w is constant, this means that price will vary inversely with the MPL, which itself varies inversely with employment and output. The greater the volume of output, the higher the price-level at which firms will find it just worth their while to produce it.[2]

It must be emphasized that these calculations take no account of the demand side of the market. The value of p given by w/MPL at any given level of output is a '*supply-price*' which indicates the terms

---

the marginal product of labour virtually constant but with money-wages falling under the pressure of mass unemployment in spite of the unions' efforts. The two assumptions will then be valid only in the middle ground between these extremes —yet the middle ground may not be very wide.

[1] See p. 79 above.

[2] The simple numerical examples in this paragraph would be literally applicable only in an economy which produced a single homogeneous commodity under competitive conditions. In the multi-product economy of real life, p must be taken as an *average* of the prices at which the $p = w/MPL$ condition would be satisfied in the markets for all the separate commodities.

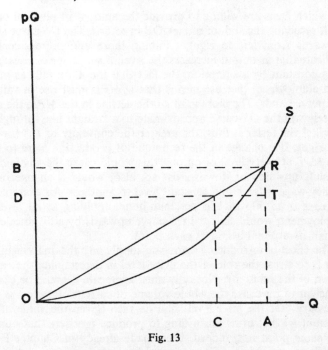

Fig. 13

on which firms would be willing to produce and sell that particular quantity of commodities, whether or not it also happens to be the quantity which buyers are currently demanding. When each level of physical output (Q) is multiplied by its supply-price p, the resulting amount pQ is the total revenue which firms must receive (or at any rate expect to receive) if they are to be induced to supply that output. The relationship between Q and pQ is shown by the '*aggregate supply curve*' OS in Fig. 13 above.[1] At any point along *OS*, the supply-price is shown by the slope of the straight line joining that point to the origin of the diagram; thus, the slope of *OR* (i.e. *OB/OA*) is the price

[1] This should not be confused with the 'aggregate supply function' developed by Keynes (*General Theory*, p. 25) and used by some later writers, notably Professor Sidney Weintraub (e.g. in his *An Approach to the Theory of Income Distribution*, Philadelphia, 1958). Keynes relates 'the expectation of proceeds which will just make it worth the while of the entrepreneurs to give (a particular level of) employment' directly to the level of employment itself; i.e. instead of pQ and Q, his function relates pQ and N. However, this has the disadvantage of not explicitly indicating the price-level implied in any given value of pQ; for the purposes of the argument of the present text, therefore, the aggregate supply curve of Fig. 13 is more convenient.

at which firms are willing to provide the amount of physical output *OA*, receiving the sum of money OB in return. The *OS*-curve slopes upwards from left to right, climbing more and more steeply to indicate that as output increases the level of supply-price rises; since *w* is constant by assumption, the fact that the *MPL* falls as output and employment increase means that *w/MPL* must rise in value as output expands. The more gradual the decline in the *MPL*, the more closely will the *OS*-curve approximate to a straight line through the origin;[1] the faster it falls, the greater the convexity of *OS* towards the right. If a change in the technique of production were to alter the *MPL* at every level of output, this would cause the whole curve to shift upwards or downwards; so, also, would a change in the money-wage *w* from one constant level to another—for example, an increase from 50p to 75p per man-hour, applying at all levels of employment, would shift the *OS*-curve upwards by a distance equal to half its original height at each point.

The effect of introducing aggregate supply into the analysis in this way is to stress the role of the price-level in determining the equilibrium of the economy. Not only must aggregate demand be exactly sufficient to purchase the whole volume of current output: it is also necessary that the price-level shall be such (given the value of the constant *w*) that firms are willing to produce precisely that output. The same point has, indeed, been made already in Chapter Four, though in somewhat different terms. In the labour market depicted in Fig. 3 on p. 81, the *DD*-curve indicates, for any given level of real wages, the number of man-hours which profit-maximizing competitive firms will wish to employ; the volume of output produced by this number of man-hours is the physical quantity of aggregate supply forthcoming at the given real wage, though it may not of course be the quantity required to satisfy the current level of aggregate demand. Since the real wage measured on Fig. 3's vertical axis is the money-wage divided by the price-level (i.e. *w/p*), a movement along the *DD*-curve can be caused either by a change in *w* or a change in *p*. In the context of the labour market, it is natural to focus attention on changes in *w* rather than *p*, and for certain purposes to assume *p* fixed; in the present analysis the emphasis is reversed—it is *w* which is assumed constant, leaving variations in *p* as the cause of changes in the volume of aggregate supply. So far, however, nothing

---

[1] Thus, the original assumption of a constant *MPL* would make the *OS*-curve *perfectly* straight; given $p = 1$, so that the axes of Fig. 13 are graduated in identical units, the *OS*-curve would then be equivalent to the '$Y = D$' line of Fig. 10 on p. 130.

has been said which was not already implicit in the argument of Chapter Four; but it will be recalled that further developments had to be postponed at that stage for lack of information about the behaviour of aggregate demand.[1] The lack having been made good in the last five chapters, it is now possible to carry the analysis further by bringing demand into the picture.

(b) *Aggregate demand and the price-level*

To find the equilibrium level of output and the price-level consistent with it, it is necessary to introduce an aggregate demand curve into Fig. 13. However, the 'aggregate demand function' defined at the beginning of Chapter Six on p. 130, and drawn as the GG-curve in Fig. 10, is not appropriate here, because both income and demand were specified in real terms. To bring aggregate demand into Fig. 13, it is necessary to know not only the physical quantities which buyers wish to purchase at each level of real income, but also the prices at which their purchases are being made. When these physical quantities are multiplied by the appropriate prices, the amounts of money which result can be measured along Fig. 13's vertical pQ-axis to show how much buyers wish to spend at each level of real income—the latter, of course, being measured on the horizontal Q-axis, since real income and output are identical for the economy as a whole. The prices required for this purpose are those already indicated by the aggregate supply curve, if it can be assumed that sellers always offer their products at the supply prices given by the value of w/MPL; the possibilities which arise if they were to do otherwise will be examined later, but for the time being this is a useful simplifying assumption. It will also be assumed, as a way of keeping the analysis clear of needless complication, that the economy has neither foreign trade nor a government, so that aggregate demand is merely the sum of consumption and investment expenditures.

Suppose, then, that firms are producing the volume of output OA and are offering it for sale at prices whose average equals the slope of OR. Suppose, also, that at this level of real income the quantity of commodities needed to satisfy aggregate demand happens to be OC; at the price-level indicated by the slope of OR, this physical quantity can be bought with a money expenditure of OD. The physical output OA is thus associated with aggregate demand, in money terms, of OD, and a curve showing the general relationship between output and desired money expenditure must pass through the point T, which lies vertically above A and is at the same height as D. Here, the

[1] See p. 83 above.

money value of aggregate supply, AB, exceeds that of aggregate demand by BD; firms are unable to sell a part of their output, and are failing to obtain the revenue needed to induce them to produce the output OA. Accordingly, they will now reduce production: as they do so, output becomes less than OA, the point R moves to the left down the aggregate supply curve OS, and the price-level falls as the slope of OR diminishes. Meanwhile, the money value of aggregate demand will also be reduced, partly because of the fall in real income which is occurring as output shrinks: the point T will be moving both leftwards and downwards. The process will continue as long as any excess supply exists—that is, as long as there is a vertical gap between R and T; the volume of output will continue to decrease, and the level of prices to fall, until R and T coincide and aggregate demand and supply are equal. As T moves in response to these changes in output, it will trace out the 'aggregate demand curve' appropriate to Fig. 13, showing the amount of money buyers wish to spend at each possible level of physical output.

It will have been noticed, however, that such a curve has not in fact been drawn in the diagram. This is because it is not yet possible to say what its general shape is likely to be, apart from the fact that it can be expected to slope upwards from left to right. The difficulty is to know how far the *physical* quantities demanded are likely to be affected by changes in the price-level as well as by alterations in real income. It may be, of course, that they are not affected at all: a 1 % rise in prices will then raise both income and demand by exactly 1 % in money terms, leaving the underlying 'real' relationship unchanged. The aggregate demand curve could then be drawn by the simple procedure of (a) ascertaining the 'real' demand associated with each level of real income, and (b) multiplying it by the price-level indicated by the aggregate supply curve for each level of real income. If the 'real' aggregate demand function happens to be an upward-sloping straight line similar to the GG-curve of Fig. 10 on p. 130, this procedure will result in a curve with the general shape of OD in Fig. 14 below. Over most of its length, OD has a curvature similar to that of the aggregate supply curve OS; to the right of the intersection of the two curves at K, OD lies below OS, while to the left of the intersection it lies above it, indicating that K is a point of stable equilibrium with respect both to real output and the price-level. It corresponds to the point M in Fig. 10, where income and aggregate demand are equal; just as aggregate demand in real terms exceeds output to the left of M and falls short of it to the right, so, in Fig. 14, the amount of money which buyers wish to spend is greater than the value of aggregate supply to the left of K and smaller to the right of it.

A numerical example may help to clarify the derivation of the *OD*-curve. Suppose consumers always wish to consume four-fifths of income, and that firms plan a fixed amount of investment, in real

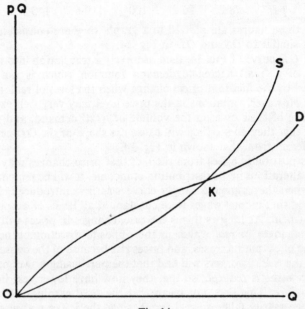

Fig. 14

terms, equal to 20 units of output. At a price-level of £1 per unit of output, the aggregate demand function is $D = 0.8 (Q) + 20$. If the price-level were the same at all levels of output, aggregate demand at selected levels of Q would be as follows:

Q (units)	90	95	100	105	110
D (£)	92	96	100	104	108

This is a 'straight-line' relationship between real income and demand of the kind illustrated in Fig. 10. Now suppose that supply-prices at the various levels of Q are as follows:

Q	90	95	100	105	110
Price (£ per unit of Q)	0.85	0.9	1	1.15	1.35

When both Q and D are multiplied by these prices, the resulting series of pQs are the values of aggregate supply for the different values of Q, and the pDs are aggregate demand in money terms (all figures in £):

Q	90	95	100	105	110
pQ	76·5	85·5	100	120·7	148·5
pD	78·2	86·4	100	119·6	145·8

When these figures are plotted in a graph, they are consistent with curves similar to OS and OD in Fig. 14.

The OD-curve of Fig. 14, then, is merely a translation into money terms of a 'real' aggregate demand function which is not itself affected by the fact that prices change when the level of real income alters. However, variations in the price-level may very well exert an influence of their own on the volume of 'real' demand, and to the extent that they do so, they will cause the shape of the OD-curve to be different from that shown in Fig. 14.

This possibility arises from the fact that price-changes may bring about alterations in the distribution of income. It will be remembered that when the aggregate supply curve was first introduced, it was assumed that money-wages were constant at all levels of output and employment. As long as this is the case, changes in prices will bring about changes in *real* wages in the opposite direction. When the volume of output increases, and prices rise because of the consequent fall in the MPL, workers will find that the purchasing-power of their money-wages is reduced, so that they now have lower real income than before. This does not mean that the *total* earnings of labour have necessarily fallen in real terms, since the lower real wage per man-hour may be more than offset by the fact that more man-hours are being employed to produce the increased volume of output. What *is* likely, however, is that the total of real wages will now bear a smaller *proportion* to total real income, because of diminishing returns to labour.[1] If wage-earners have a higher marginal propensity to consume than profit-recipients, the reduction in their share of total income will now cause consumption to fall below the level which it would otherwise have attained; and this 'redistribution effect' on

---

[1] Total real wages are the real wage per man-hour multiplied by the number of man-hours employed, i.e. NW; their share in total real income is NW/Q. Since N/Q is the inverse of the *average* product of labour (APL), and W equals the MPL at any point on the aggregate supply curve, the 'wage-share' can also be written MPL/APL. As output rises, the MPL falls; the 'wage-share' will therefore be reduced if the APL does not fall as fast as the MPL. Marginal quantities fall less fast than their corresponding average quantities only when the latter are falling at a decreasing rate (for example, when a firm's average production cost is approaching its minimum). In the case of labour productivity, it seems unlikely that this would be the case, so the 'wage-share' may be presumed to diminish as output and employment increase.

consumption will become stronger and stronger as the price-level climbs with further increases in output. The 'real' aggregate demand function of Fig. 10 will be shifting bodily downwards as real income increases; when it is transformed into the OD-curve of Fig. 14 by multiplying 'real' demand by the price-level appropriate to each volume of output, it will no longer have the curvature shown in the diagram. At the very least, the convexity of the right-hand section of the curve will be diminished—that is, its slope will now increase less rapidly as it climbs towards the right. A strong 'redistribution effect' may actually flatten it into a straight line, or even reverse its curvature so that it resembles the OD-curves of Fig. 15 below. But since there is no *a priori* reason why the effect should either be strong or weak, it is not possible to assign a characteristic shape to the curve; those shown in Fig. 15 have been drawn as they appear solely for reasons of visual clarity.

It is worth noting that the 'redistribution effect' just considered will operate equally well when, instead of prices rising with money-wages constant, it is prices which remain constant while money-wages fall; it is not necessary that prices should rise in absolute money terms, but only that they should rise *relatively* to money-wages so that the value of p/w increases. A change in 'absolute' prices (i.e. in p alone) may affect aggregate real demand in a number of other ways, which have already been noted in previous chapters;[1] but the strength of these influences is uncertain, and in any case they cut in both directions, some causing real demand to fall when prices rise, others causing it to increase, so that their combined effect will not necessarily change the shape of the aggregate demand curve in one way rather than another. Changes in p can also have certain monetary consequences which may affect real demand: for example, the financing of real investment will require larger amounts of money when prices rise; if firms' efforts to obtain it drive up the cost of borrowing, some of them may decide to curtail or postpone capital projects, and investment will then be reduced in real terms. For the present, however, these financial effects will be left out of account until money has been brought into the analysis—as it will be in the next chapter.

(c) Variations in prices and money-wages

The intersection of the aggregate supply and demand curves indicates both the equilibrium level of physical output and (given

---

[1] See Chapter Four, pp. 111–3 for effects on consumption, and Chapter Seven, pp. 178–9 for effects on investment.

the constant money-wage w) the equilibrium level of prices. If an autonomous change in 'real' demand now occurs, this will shift the aggregate demand curve so that it intersects the aggregate supply curve at a new equilibrium position. Thus, in Fig. 15 below, an increase in real investment will raise the aggregate demand curve

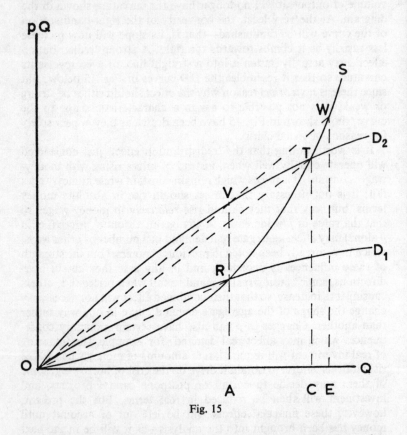

Fig. 15

from OD_1 to OD_2; equilibrium moves from R to T, output rises from OA to OC, and prices increase from the level indicated by the slope of OR to that indicated by the slope of OT. As long as firms continue to offer their output at its supply-price (i.e. w/MPL), their response to the increase in demand will be to attempt to produce more commodities, raising their selling prices only when the expansion of output and employment reduces the marginal product of labour and so makes price-increases necessary to meet the rising value of w/MPL. The transition from the old equilibrium at R to the new one at T will then take the form of an upward movement along the aggregate supply curve OS.

However, firms might well have reacted in a different way. Faced with excess demand equal to VR in money terms, they might have begun by raising prices to the level which buyers seemed willing to pay—namely, the price-level indicated by the slope of OV. This will immediately create an incentive for firms to increase production, since the excess of price over marginal labour-cost w/MPL shows that they will add to their profits if they employ more labour and expand output; but before the expansion can get under way, the situation may be made more complicated by the effects of the price-increase on aggregate demand. If the 'real' relationship between income and demand remains unchanged, the amount of money buyers wish to spend will rise in the same proportion as the price-level, and the excess demand will now be still larger than before in money terms. On the other hand, the price-increase will also have set the 'redistribution effect' to work, because with money-wages constant, real wages will have fallen; at the original level of output OA, both total real wages and the 'wage-share' in income will be reduced in proportion to the rise in prices, causing a fall in real consumption to the extent that the wage-earners' MPC exceeds that of profit-recipients.[1] Conceivably, the two effects might exactly offset one another, if the 'redistribution effect' happened to be just strong enough to eliminate the excess demand and no more; but there is no necessary reason why it should be, and if it is not, aggregate demand will now be higher than VA in money terms, and firms may increase prices further. But even if they do not do so, the price-level given by the slope of OV is an inducement to expand output well beyond the new equilibrium level OC; if they now increase it to the point at which $p = w/MPL$—i.e. W, where OV meets the aggregate supply curve OS—they will have created an excess of supply over demand, at a level of output OE which is considerably larger than the equilibrium level OC; and they will be obliged to reduce prices and production again. Eventually, by a sequence of over-shootings and over-corrections, output and the price-level will reach the new equilibrium

---

[1] Suppose total income is 100, wages 60, and profits (assumed for simplicity to be the only other form of income) 40. Prices rise 10%; income is for the moment unchanged in real terms, but rises to 110 in money terms; wages remain 60, and profits rise to 50. If the wage-earners' MPC is 0·8 and the profit-recipients' MPC is 0·2, consumption will now be 58 in money terms and 52·7 at the original price-level. Previously, before prices rose, consumption was 56: thus, it has fallen in real terms by more than five percentage points because of the fall in the 'wage-share' from 60% to 54·5% of income.

H

position at T, but the path of convergence will have been much less smooth than the movement along OS which occurred when firms kept prices continuously at the w/MPL level.

For the new equilibrium at T to be attainable, it is of course necessary that the output OC should not be greater than the quantity of goods and services that the economy is able to produce at full employment. If the latter had already been reached at the original level of output OA, no convergence towards T would have been possible. In such a situation, efforts to increase total production would be unavailing, and firms will be much more likely to raise their selling prices in response to the pressure of excess demand; and this, as has already been seen, will shift the aggregate demand curve upwards except in so far as its movement is restrained by the 'redistribution effect'. At this point, however, the aggregate supply curve OS is also likely to shift, because the original assumption that money-wages are constant will now be breaking down. To the extent that firms try to increase output to meet increased real demand, their attempts to employ more labour for the purpose will create an excess of demand over supply in the labour market, and this will cause the money-wage w to rise. Alternatively, if firms' initial reaction to the rise in real demand is to raise prices rather than output, the consequent fall in real wages may cause the supply of labour to fall[1] below the level needed to sustain the current level of output, so that money-wages must now be increased to restore real wages to their original level; also, trades unions can be expected to react to the rise in prices by insisting on compensating increases in money-wages to maintain their members' living standards. Since the OS-curve shows the money-value (pQ) of each level of output (Q) when it is multiplied by its supply-price w/MPL, the rise in w will now increase the value of pQ associated with each level of Q; the OS-curve will therefore move vertically upwards in proportion to the increase in w, and will continue to do so as long as w goes on rising.

With money-wages and prices rising at the same rate, there will be no reduction in real wages and therefore no 'redistribution effect' to restrain the upward movement of the aggregate demand curve. *Both* curves will now be shifting upwards simultaneously, as shown in Fig. 16 on p. 227. Initially, the aggregate supply curve is OS_1. An autonomous increase in real demand has just shifted the aggregate demand curve up to OD_1; this intersects OS_1 at R—but this equilibrium cannot be attained, because it is not possible for output to expand beyond the full-employment level OF. For the moment, then,

---

[1] Provided that the labour supply-curve slopes upwards from left to right, as in Fig. 3 on p. 81 above.

the money-value of aggregate demand is LF, while that of aggregate supply is MF, so that there is an 'inflationary gap' of excess demand equal to LM. Both prices and money-wages now rise in response to this situation, with the result that the aggregate demand curve shifts to OD_2 and the aggregate supply curve to OS_2. Once again, their intersection shows that equilibrium is unattainable, since W lies to the right of the full-employment output OF; the 'inflationary gap'

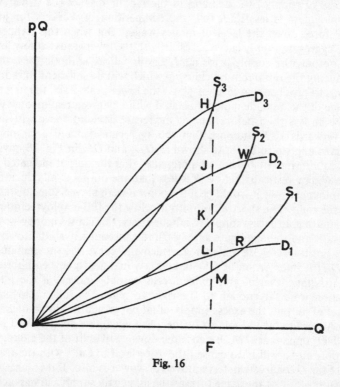

Fig. 16

therefore persists and is now equal to JK. This will bring about further increases in prices and money-wages, causing the aggregate supply and demand curves to move still further upwards: the process will continue indefinitely, unless for some reason the aggregate demand curve should fail to keep pace with the movement of the aggregate supply curve. If, when the latter has reached the position OS_3, the former has risen only as far as OD_3, an equilibrium will at last be attainable at H; here the inflationary gap will have been eliminated and the upward movement of the two curves will now cease.

A similar sequence, but with the curves shifting downwards instead of upwards, can be expected to occur when the initial position is *below* the full-employment level of output—provided that money-wages are free to fall as well as to rise. Up to this point, it has been assumed that money-wages were 'inflexible' downwards, being prevented from falling by the existence of strong trades unions. If this assumption is now abandoned, it follows that whenever there is an excess of supply over demand in the labour market (i.e. whenever employment is less than full) the competition of workers for jobs will force down the level of money-wages. But when this happens, the aggregate supply curve necessarily shifts downwards: at any level of output, the supply-price w/MPL will fall as w diminishes, thus reducing the minimum revenue pQ which will be sufficient to induce firms to produce that level of Q. At the lower price-level, the money-value of the 'real' demand associated with any given real income will now be less than before: so the aggregate demand curve will shift downwards also. Suppose that the aggregate demand and supply curves happen to be those shown as OD_2 and OS_2 in Fig. 18, giving an equilibrium of W; but suppose, also, that the output indicated on the Q-axis vertically below W is less than the output available at full employment—as it would be if the point F were moved some distance to the right. The shortfall of output below the full-employment level means that an excess supply of labour exists; this causes money-wages to fall, and the aggregate supply curve consequently shifts down to the position OS_1. If the aggregate demand curve were to remain at OD_2, the intersection of OS_1 and OD_2 would give a new equilibrium at a higher level of employment and output—indeed, if the intersection were far enough to the right to reach the full-employment level of output, the excess supply of labour would be eliminated and money-wages would fall no further. But aggregate demand will not, in fact, remain at OD_2, because the downward shift of the aggregate supply curve will have caused the price-level to fall,[1] with the result that the OD-curve will have moved downwards also. If it reaches the OD_1 position at the same time as the aggregate supply curve reaches OS_1, their new intersection at R will still be at a less than full-employment level of output; the excess supply of labour will persist, money-wages and prices will continue to fall, and the downward

---

[1] When the two curves intersect at W, prices will equal the slope of the straight line OW. (This has not been drawn in the diagram, but it is hoped that the reader will easily imagine it from similar price-lines in preceding diagrams.) Even if aggregate demand were to remain OD_2, any intersection with OS_1 to the right of W will give a lower price-level—so prices must necessarily fall as soon as the aggregate supply curve moves down.

movement of the OD and OS curves will go on. For the movement to stop, it is necessary that the OD-curve should fall less fast than the OS-curve, so that their intersection gradually moves to the right: when they at last intersect above the full-employment level of output, there will no longer be an excess supply of labour, money-wages and prices will cease to fall, and the two curves will move no further downwards.

The general conclusion of this analysis is that if money-wages and prices are free to rise or fall to any necessary extent (i.e. 'flexible' both upwards and downwards), a full equilibrium will be reached only when both of two conditions are satisfied. First, the aggregate demand for commodities must equal their aggregate supply, in the sense that the volume of output and the price-level must be those indicated by an intersection of the OD and OS curves; and second, the demand and supply of labour must be balanced—that is, the intersection of OD and OS must occur at the full-employment level of output. If money-wages are 'inflexible downwards', so that they do not fall when there is an excess supply of labour, the second condition is no longer necessary for equilibrium at less than full-employment levels of output: with w constant, the intersections R and T in Fig. 15 are perfectly stable equilibrium positions, even though full employment does not obtain in either case.

However, to specify the conditions of equilibrium is not to imply that they will be fulfilled. To say that, with money-wages and prices flexible, equilibrium exists only when aggregate demand and supply are equal at full-employment output, is not to say that the economy will necessarily find its way to such an equilibrium—it means only that it will not find an equilibrium anywhere else. In the particular situations discussed in connection with Fig. 16, it appears that once the OD and OS curves are shifting upwards or downwards together, their movement will be halted (i.e. equilibrium will be reached) only if OD lags behind OS so as to shift their intersection to correspond with the full-employment level of output. This means that when prices are falling, real demand must increase relatively to real income until it is sufficient to absorb the whole of the output produced at full employment; when prices are rising, real demand must fall until full-employment output is enough to satisfy it. Failing this, the curves will continue to move, and prices will go on rising or falling. The outcome will then depend on the speed with which the movement is taking place. If all adjustments (e.g. the revision of expenditure-plans in money terms, firms' decisions to alter their selling prices, and so on) are made almost instantaneously, the curves will move very quickly indeed, and the price-level will collapse towards zero or

zoom towards infinity, depending on the direction of the movement;
the economy will break down unless the government steps in with
measures to restore price-stability. A slow rate of adjustment, on the
other hand, will change the movement of the price-level into a
relatively gentle upward or downward trend, which may not have
time to proceed very far before being reversed by an autonomous
change in real demand or by some other external influence: it is
possible, in fact, to imagine an economy never attaining short-period
equilibrium at all, yet not experiencing great fluctuations in prices
and output either. In such an economy, it would not be disastrous
if the movement of the OD and OS curves was not accompanied
by any tendency for them to intersect at the level of full-employment
output.

Nevertheless, such a tendency might exist. It could result from the
operation of the 'Pigou effect' described on pp. 112–13 above. As
prices fall, the purchasing-power of money-balances continuously
increases; their owners, feeling themselves more affluent, increase
their real consumption relatively to their real incomes; eventually,
this will raise total real demand to equality with full-employment
output, so that there is no longer any excess supply of labour to
push down money-wages and keep the OD and OS curves falling.
When prices are rising, the effect is reversed: the falling real consumption of the holders of money-balances will eventually reduce
real demand to the level required for full-employment equilibrium,
thus eliminating the excess demand for commodities which has been
pushing the OD and OS curves upwards. But it has been suggested
that the Pigou effect is likely to be weak, and that it may be offset by
expectational influences working in the opposite direction: in an
economy where the adjustment process goes forward rapidly, prices
may have to rise or fall a long way before the Pigou effect becomes
strong enough to halt their movement.

If the economy is no longer assumed to be closed, the 'foreign
sector' can be brought in as a stabilizing influence: as prices rise,
reductions in exports and increases in imports will diminish total
real demand, while the reverse effects will expand real demand when
prices are falling. The inclusion of government in the model will have
similar consequences: as money-incomes rise in line with the price-
level, the proportion available for private expenditure will be reduced
by progressive income-taxation, while government spending programmes which are fixed in money terms will represent decreasing
real expenditure as the price-level rises.

One possible source of stabilizing effects, however, still remains to
be considered—namely, the monetary system. When prices are in-

creasing, larger and larger quantities of money are needed to transact all the economy's sales and purchases; when prices are falling, money requirements are correspondingly reduced. In order to consider the implications of this, and to see what other influences may be exerted from the monetary side, it is now necessary to examine in detail the role of money in the economy.

CHAPTER ELEVEN

Money (I)

(a) Money, debt and liquidity

The essential characteristic of money is its general acceptability in exchange for other things. The contents of a weekly wage-packet cannot be eaten or worn, or used in any other way directly to satisfy wants: yet there is no doubt that the wage-earner who gets it prefers to be paid in money instead of being given a part of the physical output he has helped to produce. He is prepared to take payment in this form because he knows that shopkeepers will accept the money from him in return for the goods he buys; and they, in turn, do so because they are confident it will be accepted by the people from whom *they* buy. It is this mutual confidence which enables banknotes and coins of negligible intrinsic worth to be used as a medium of exchange.

By the test of general acceptability, however, notes and coin are far from being the most important form of money. The major part of the United Kingdom's stock of money consists of 'bank deposits', which in mid-1975 amounted to £34,166 millions as against only £6,204 millions of paper currency and £429 millions of coin.[1] There are many small transactions, such as the purchase of a newspaper or bus ticket, for which payment by means of a bank deposit would obviously be unsuitable; but the dealings of business firms with one another, and many payments between firms, governments and individuals, are much more conveniently and safely carried out by the handing over of cheques than by the exchange of notes and coin. Cheques are merely the means of transferring deposits from one owner to another: for example, when firm A pays firm B for a consignment of materials, it will normally do so by sending a cheque,

[1] Figures from *Financial Statistics* (H.M.S.O.), Aug. 1976, Tables 6.4 and 6.6. The figure for bank deposits is that of the whole 'banking sector'. It includes both 'current' and 'deposit' accounts: the former are withdrawable on demand and transferable by cheque, while the latter are not; the latter, however, bear interest, while the former do not. Out of the £6,633 millions of notes and coin, more than £1,100 millions were held by banks as part of their reserves, so that only something over £5,500 millions were in circulation with the general public.

as a result of which A's deposit at the bank is reduced and B's correspondingly increased. It is because such transfers are regarded by the recipients as complete and final settlement, that bank deposits must be classified as money.

Deposits are the obligations of banks to their customers. Against these liabilities, the banks hold assets, such as government bonds and the obligations of business firms to which they have made loans; if they are to remain in business, the interest they earn on these assets, plus the 'bank charges' they collect from their customers, must be enough to cover their operating costs, to meet the interest payable on deposit accounts, and to make a profit for their proprietors. However, each bank must also hold sufficient reserves of 'cash' (consisting not only of notes and coin but also of deposits with the Bank of England) to allow it to meet the claims of depositors wishing to make withdrawals, or of other banks whose customers have deposited cheques drawn on it; as an additional precaution, they maintain certain 'liquid assets', such as Treasury Bills, which can quickly be turned into cash should the need arise. Under rules introduced by the Bank of England in 1971, they are obliged to keep 'reserve assets' (which include their deposits at the Bank, their Treasury Bill holdings, and various kinds of short-term loans[1]) whose total amount must not be less than $12\frac{1}{2}\%$ of their own out-standing deposits.[2] By its own buying and selling operations, the Bank of England can contract or expand the quantity of such assets available to the banks; if this falls below the $12\frac{1}{2}\%$ level, the banks must contract their deposits, e.g. by lending less, until the correct ratio is restored; if it rises above $12\frac{1}{2}\%$, loans and deposits can be expanded. In this way, the Bank can influence the total amount of deposits. The degree of control it can exercise will be qualified by the existence of other pressures (for example, the changing demand of the public for notes and coin, which from time to time drains away or replenishes banks' cash), and by the Bank's own pursuit of objectives other than the control of bank deposits (for example, the maintenance of stable prices in the markets for government securities), but it is reasonable to assume that the Bank could, in principle, control the system in such a way as to set the total quantity of money at whatever level might be thought desirable.

Because bank deposits and currency are generally acceptable as

---

[1] The banks' holdings of notes and coin, however, are not counted as 'reserve assets' for this purpose. For details, see the *Bank of England Quarterly Bulletin*, June and September 1971.

[2] More strictly, 'eligible liabilities', i.e. those allowed by the Bank for the purpose of calculating the $12\frac{1}{2}\%$ ratio.

means of exchange, they have a particular convenience as *assets*: anyone who retains a holding of them possesses a command over goods and services which he can exercise at any time in the future. In the traditional phrase, money acts as a 'store of value'. However, value can be 'stored' in the form of *any* durable asset: the distinctive feature of money in this respect is its *liquidity*. If the owner of a house should wish to exchange it for something else, he must first sell it for money; he may find, at the time when he tries to sell, that buyers are few and prices low; the disadvantage of such an asset is obvious—its holder cannot be sure of realizing its full value quickly at any time in the future. Money is free of this risk: as an asset, it is perfectly liquid and in that respect superior to other 'stores of value'.

But it would be misleading to draw a very sharp distinction between the liquidity of money and the non-liquidity of other assets. Among the latter, considerable differences in degree of liquidity exist. Building society deposits, for example, are so liquid that they are often called 'near-money' or 'quasi-money': though they cannot be withdrawn until a certain period has elapsed, the period is usually a fairly short one,[1] and at the end of it the owners of such deposits are certain to receive the amounts originally deposited, so that there is no risk of loss. By contrast, the owner of ordinary shares in a company can exchange them for money with no delay at all—he need only telephone his broker, who will sell them for him on the Stock Exchange: in this respect, such assets are very liquid. But the price obtained for the shares may be considerably less than the price at which the owner originally bought them; he can never be sure that a quick sale will not involve a capital loss, and this makes his assets less liquid than (say) short-term government bonds. At the extreme of illiquidity come physical assets such as land and buildings, which may take quite a time to find buyers, and may fail altogether to find them at prices which would cause no loss to the sellers. It may happen, of course, that at the moment of sale the price of a particular asset of this type is actually higher than that at which the owner first bought it, so that he reaps a capital gain: the essential point, however, is that he cannot know in advance whether he will make a gain or a loss if he should have to sell the asset at any particular time in the future.

Thus, assets can be ranged in order of liquidity, with currency and bank deposits at the top end of the scale, certain physical assets at the bottom, and the remainder at various points in between. Very near the top come certain forms of 'near-money', such as savings

[1] In the case of small withdrawals, the societies normally waive the requirement of notice and pay cash on demand.

bank deposits and the shares of building societies, which are close competitors with money in its role as a liquid asset. The institutions which supply them have a strong family resemblance to the commercial banks, inasmuch as they hold 'paper' assets—securities and the obligations of individual borrowers to whom they have made loans—the revenue from which provides them with profits after meeting their operating costs and paying interest on their own liabilities. Like the commercial banks, they aim to maximize profit, subject to the requirement that they must always be able to meet their obligations to their creditors; consequently, many factors which influence the behaviour of the banks—for example, changes in interest rates—can be expected to have similar effects on that of the 'non-bank financial intermediaries' (or NBFIs, as these institutions may be called for short). They are not, however, subject to the same conventional reserve requirements as the banks, so that on occasions when the banks themselves are restrained from expanding deposits by the need to maintain their reserves, the NBFIs may still be able to increase the supply of their own liabilities, with the result that liquid assets as a whole will increase even though the quantity of money is being held constant.

For the time being, these complications will be by-passed by assuming that currency and bank deposits are the only liquid assets as well as the only means of exchange in the economy, and that their supply is effectively controlled by the monetary authorities (i.e. the Bank of England). As long as this supply is exactly sufficient to satisfy the demand for it, the behaviour of the monetary side of the economy will be compatible with the equilibrium of aggregate supply and demand described in the previous chapter. However, an excess or shortfall of the demand for money against the supply of it is likely to upset any previously existing equilibrium in the rest of the economy, while disturbances in the markets for commodities and labour will themselves upset the balance on the monetary side. What, then, determines the demand for money? To answer this question, it will be convenient to distinguish between the demand for it as a means of payment and the demand for it as a liquid asset: this is, of course, a highly artificial distinction, extremely difficult if not impossible to apply in practice, but it is adopted here merely as an expository device.

(b) *The transactions demand for money*

Until the inter-war period, economists paid relatively little attention to the asset-demand for money, on the ground that rational individuals would hold only the amounts of it they needed for making current payments. Since money does not yield interest, an individual who found himself with more than he needed for payments purposes would use the surplus to acquire income-yielding assets such as bonds, shares or physical property; he might even increase his consumption rather than continue to hold a 'barren' asset. Consequently, it was argued, the effect of an increase in the supply of money would normally be to raise the level of prices, since the additional money would be financing an increase in the demand for goods and services; conversely, a reduction in the money supply would cause people's holdings of it to fall below the level needed for payments, and their efforts to restore their money-balances by selling other things would force the price-level down. This view, emphasizing money's means-of-payment function to the exclusion of its liquid-asset role, was formalized as the 'Quantity Theory of Money'.[1]

This theory may be stated in terms of Irving Fisher's[2] 'equation of exchange' or 'quantity equation' $MV = PT$. Here, M is the existing quantity of money, and V its rate of turnover per unit, or 'velocity of circulation'; T is the number of transactions occurring within a given period, and P is the average amount of money exchanged at each transaction, i.e. an average of prices.[3] So defined, MV and PT are two ways of describing the same thing: each is a measure of the turnover of money in the economy, so that the equation necessarily holds good under all circumstances—it is an *identity*. Thus, the quantity equation does not itself prove anything: it is not a theory in the sense of a testable hypothesis which could be either true or false. The Quantity *Theory* is the proposition that when M changes, the principal effect will be on P rather than V or T. In its most extreme form, the theory holds that V and T will not normally alter at all when M changes, so that P will change in the same proportion

[1] What now follows in the text is a simple version of the theory as it seems to have been understood by the majority of economists up to the nineteen-twenties. Some writers amended and developed it in various ways, but no attempt is made here to take account of their individual contributions. It is also necessary to distinguish between the very simple theory described above, and the 'Modern Quantity Theory' for which the University of Chicago is well known: in the hands of Professor Milton Friedman and others, it is a much more sophisticated formulation—though it does arrive at many of the same conclusions as the older 'quantity theorists'. See 'The Quantity Theory of Money—A Restatement', Professor Friedman's introductory essay in *Studies in the Quantity Theory of Money* (1956) which he also edited.

[2] Irving Fisher, *The Purchasing Power of Money* (1911), Chap. VIII.

[3] Note that P is not an *index* of prices. An index would give the proportionate change in prices compared with some 'base year': it would not be appropriate here, since M and T are both 'absolute' magnitudes.

as M; doubling the quantity of money, for example, will double the general price-level.

But P is not the price-level in the ordinary sense: it is the average amount of money exchanged *per transaction*, and since transactions include the payment of wages and dealings in bonds and shares as well as the purchase of commodities, P is very far from being merely an average of retail or wholesale prices. This makes the Fisher version of the Quantity Theory ambiguous, unless a special assumption is made concerning the behaviour of non-commodity prices; if a rise in M were to produce an increase in bond prices and nothing else, it would be true that P had risen, but this would not be what is usually meant by 'a rise in the price-level'. In this respect, the Fisher equation is less clear than the 'Cambridge'[1] version, which instead of *all* transactions includes only those 'final' purchases which are counted in National Expenditure; instead of PT, the Cambridge equation has pQ, where Q is the physical quantity of 'final' commodities (consumer goods, investment goods and so on) and p is an average of their prices. By definition, p excludes the prices of securities and of 'intermediate' goods and services; it is, therefore, a reasonable indication of the price-level as the term is usually understood.

The substitution of pQ for PT means that the Cambridge equation cannot include Fisher's 'transactions velocity' V; instead, it introduces 'income-velocity'—the rate of turnover of money, not in *all* transactions, but only in the purchase of 'final' commodities. With V' as the symbol for this, the equation becomes $MV' = pQ$, or $MV' = Y$, since National Expenditure pQ is identical with National Income Y. Usually, the equation is written $M = kY$, where k is $1/V'$, i.e. the inverse of income-velocity: if money turns over four times a year, each unit must 'rest' for a quarter of that time. This is more than a mere manipulation of the velocity concept: when money is 'at rest', it must be in the hands of someone who wishes to hold it instead of spending it immediately: k, then, is the average fraction of income over which people desire to keep command in money form, and kY measures the community's demand for money. Thus, the equation $M = kY$ brings together the supply of money (M) and the demand for it (kY) in an equilibrium condition. If M should increase, equilibrium can be restored by changes in k or Y; but if k is fixed, and physical output is not affected by the change in M, income can

[1] So called because it originated at Cambridge, was taught there for many years, and appears in the writings of the great Cambridge economists: e.g. Marshall, *Money, Credit and Commerce* (1923) pp. 44 *et seq.*; Pigou, 'The Value of Money', *Quarterly Journal of Economics*, 1917; Keynes, *A Tract on Monetary Reform* (1923), Chap. III.

rise only through an increase in the price-level—i.e. since $Y = pQ$, a rise in Y occurs through a rise in p. Thus, changes in the quantity of money will bring about equal proportionate changes in the price-level.

The vital assumption here is not that k and Q cannot change at all, but that they do not do so merely because of changes in M. Obviously, increasing population and productivity are likely to increase Q as time goes by, whatever is happening to money and prices. In the short run, however, it is possible for output to be stimulated by a rise in M if this occurs in a situation of less than full employment. If $M = kY$ to begin with, balances are already high enough to meet holding requirements, so the additional M will be spent. But additional spending in these circumstances will have the effect of drawing unemployed resources into activity, raising output rather than the price-level; only when full employment is reached will the effects of further spending show themselves wholly in price-increases. As an explanation of the general price-level, under which changes in p are attributable solely to changes in M, the Quantity Theory cannot hold good except in conditions of full employment—if, indeed, it holds good even then.

The 'Cambridge version' is more useful, however, if it is regarded not as a theory of the general price-level but as a theory of the demand for money. The equation $M = k(pQ)$ can then be taken to mean simply that the desired quantity of money is a function of the level of money-income. Whether the latter increases because of a rise in Q or because of a rise in p, the effect is the same: the demand for money will rise by k times the amount of the increase in pQ. If k is constant, the relationship between money-income and the desired quantity of money will hold good at every level of output and employment, so that this approach is not subject to the limitation noted at the end of the last paragraph. But *can* k be assumed constant? It certainly cannot, if there exists an asset-demand for money which is determined by influences other than money-income: the desired quantity of money could then rise or fall independently of any change in pQ, and this would necessarily alter the value of k whenever it happened. For the time being, this possibility will be ruled out by assuming that no one wishes to hold money as an asset, and that the demand for it arises only in connection with the need to make current payments: even then, however, the assumption of a constant k is open to an important qualification, as will be shown presently.

The need to hold money for payments purposes ('transactions balances') arises from the fact that the receipts and expenditures of individuals and firms (and indeed all other economic entities) are never perfectly synchronized. For example, a man who is paid a salary at the end of each month will have to keep a certain part of it in hand to cover next month's day-by-day expenditures; as the month goes by, the balance he started with will become smaller and smaller until it disappears and is replaced out of the next salary cheque. If the man spends the same amount each day, his *average* balance will be equal to half his total monthly expenditure. If he were paid his salary by the week instead of by the month, his average 'transactions balance' would be reduced to an amount equal to half his *weekly* expenditure—it would be only a quarter of the average balance he would have required when he was being paid monthly. Even if his salary cannot be paid more frequently than once a month, he could still reduce his average balance by arranging to buy as much as possible on credit during the month, settling his accounts at the end of it when he receives his salary. In either case, he will have improved the synchronization of his receipts and payments by bringing them closer together, with the result that he can manage with a smaller average holding of money.

It will often happen, of course, that an improvement in the synchronization of one person's (or firm's) transactions can be achieved only at the cost of worsening someone else's. When a business allows its customers to buy on credit, the reduction in the customers' transactions balances may be offset by the firm's need to hold a larger balance than would be necessary if all its sales were for cash.[1] The transactions requirements of the community as a whole are therefore likely to be a good deal less compressible than those of any single individual or firm. Given the relative timing of all receipts and payments, and the way they 'interlock' between the various entities that make up the economy—that is, given the 'payments habits' of the community—the total transactions balances required will depend on the level of money income. If prices rise, more money will be needed to buy and sell the same physical quantity of goods and services; if there is no change in 'payments habits', the level of transactions balances will rise in proportion to the increase in prices. If the volume of real output goes up, with equal increases in real incomes and expenditure, the fact that larger quantities of goods and services are now being bought and sold means that a proportionate

[1] It may also work the other way, depending on the timing of the firm's own expenditures. If it pays for its supplies at the end of each month, it will be accumulating a balance in the course of the month if cash sales bring in fairly regular daily receipts: the average balance will be larger than if it could 'clear' receipts against expenditures on the same day at the month's end.

increase in transactions balances will be required.[1] In the assumed absence of an asset-demand for money, the proportion between desired transactions balances and money-income is the k of the Cambridge equation: it seems, then, as though it ought to be quite reasonable to regard k as a constant.

This conclusion, however, rests on the assumption that 'payments habits' are fixed—i.e. that individuals, business firms and other 'transactors' either cannot or do not wish to change the existing degree of synchronization between their receipts and expenditures. But most of them do, in fact, have some control over the timing of their transactions: individuals can choose between running up bills and paying cash for everything at the time of purchase; business firms can postpone their payments by taking up 'trade credit'; by careful planning, transactors may be able to reduce their balances quite considerably. How far they will try to do so depends on a number of things. Holding on to a sum of money involves a sacrifice of interest: the holder either forfeits the interest he could have earned by lending his money to somebody else, or, if he has himself borrowed the money he is holding, he must pay interest on it; so the higher the rate of interest, the greater the cost of maintaining transactions balances and the greater the incentive to keep them as low as possible. On the other hand, it will also *cost* something to economize on them: for example, if a firm delays settlement of suppliers' accounts until they can be met from expected sales revenue, it will lose whatever discount the suppliers give for prompt payment, and this loss must be counted against the saving of interest from the reduction in the firm's transactions balance. Minimizing transactions requirements will involve some effort in arranging the most economical timing of receipts and expenditures; it may also involve other inconveniences, such as that incurred by a consumer who finds himself obliged to buy from shops which give credit, when he would have preferred to make cash purchases elsewhere if his transactions balance had been big enough to allow it. If the interest rate to be paid or forgone on transactions balances is high, it will be worth incurring these costs in order to keep balances low; but if interest rates fall, the convenience of running higher balances will now cost less, and a general increase in them can be expected.

Transactors can hardly ever be sure in advance of the precise

---

[1] It may also happen that changes in the distribution of income (e.g. in favour of people who have more opportunities to buy on credit) and in the commodity-composition of output (in favour of goods whose producers are more willing to sell on credit) may alter the need for transactions balances when money-income varies. To keep the analysis simple, these possibilities are ignored here.

numbers and amounts of the payments they will have to make in the future, and many of them will also be uncertain about their expected receipts over a given period. So in addition to a basic amount which is thought to be sufficient to finance all 'normal' transactions (i.e. those which can be foreseen with a fair degree of certainty), an individual or firm will find it advisable to hold a 'precautionary balance'[1] to provide against possible emergencies. The greater this is, the greater the assurance that its holder will not be caught without sufficient funds to meet some urgent and unexpected need for cash. However, precautionary balances are subject to diminishing returns in terms of the convenience they afford, since the larger they are, the more remote the contingencies to be provided against by further increases in them: it is a good idea to have some extra cash in hand in case one's car breaks down on a long journey, but few people would think it worth while to provide against the possibility of having to take a transatlantic air flight at a moment's notice. The desired amount of precautionary balances will be that whose 'marginal convenience' is just equal to its marginal interest-cost. If interest-rates rise, it will become too expensive to insure against some of the less likely contingencies, and so the demand for precautionary balances will fall; conversely, when interest-rates fall, larger balances will be desired. Demand will, of course, also vary with the level of money-income, just as in the case of 'basic' transactions balances: if prices rise, the amounts of money which may have to be spent in sudden emergencies will be correspondingly increased, while a rise in the volume of output will create greater possibilities of such emergencies occurring.[2]

[1] This term has become conventional since Keynes first used it in the *General Theory* (p. 195). But it may be questioned whether it is really very useful to distinguish between transactions and precautionary balances. The latter could be described as the part of transactions balances intended to insure the holders against uncertainty; but since *all* future transactions are to some extent uncertain, the two kinds of balances shade imperceptibly into one another. It should also be noted that holding money is not the only way of providing against emergencies: even in a sudden crisis, there may still be time to arrange a bank loan or a mortgage, or to sell a non-monetary asset of some kind; a 'precautionary' *money* balance is needed only to cover situations in which cash payment must be made on the spot.

[2] The reasons for holding transactions and precautionary balances are similar to those for holding stocks of input materials and finished products in a manufacturing business. Just as a business firm must decide what amount of stocks to hold in the light of the level of its output and the costs of maintaining the stock, so must transactors decide what balances they need in relation to their financial turnover and the costs involved. See W. J. Baumol, 'The Transactions Demand for Cash: An Inventory Theoretic Approach', *Quarterly Journal of Economics*,

The demand for money for transactions and precautionary purposes (which from now on will be lumped together and called simply
'transactions demand') thus depends on (a) the volume of output (or
real income, which is identical with it), (b) the general price-level, and
(c) the level of interest-rates; it can be expected to rise and fall in
direct proportion to (a) and (b), and inversely with (c). In terms of
the Cambridge equation, k will be a constant only so long as interest-
rates do not change; when they do, transactors' views will change

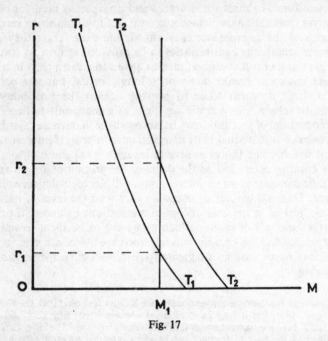

Fig. 17

concerning the fraction of money-income over which it is desirable
to keep command in money form, because the cost of doing so will
have altered.[1] A curve showing the relationship between transactions
demand and interest-rates will have the general shape of $T_1 T_1$ in
Fig. 17 above: when prices rise and/or the volume of output increases
(that is, when money-income goes up for one reason or another) the

1952; also Miles Fleming, 'The Timing of Payments and the Demand for Money',
Economica, May 1964.
[1] Also, since $k = 1/V'$, the income-velocity of money will vary according to
the level of interest-rates; but while k varies inversely, V' will vary directly with
interest.

curve will be shifted to the right, say to position T_2T_2; a further rise
in money-income will shift it still more to the right, while a fall will
move it to the left—in fact, there will be a family of TT-curves, each
one corresponding to a different level of money-income. If the supply
of money available for transactions purposes is fixed at M_1, the
intersection of the various TT-curves with the vertical line above M_1
will show the interest-rates at which the demand and supply of money
are in equilibrium at each level of money-income: thus, when the
demand for transactions balances is that shown by T_1T_1, interest
must be r_1 to equate demand and supply, while at a higher level of
money-income the demand curve will have moved to T_2T_2 and the
equilibrium interest-rate will be r_2.

This way of putting things stresses the role of interest-rates in
balancing transactions demand against the available supply of money.
It would be easy to change the emphasis in favour of the price-level
by drawing a curve such as OT_1 in Fig. 18, which shows the different
amounts of money needed for transactions purposes at the price-
levels shown on the vertical axis (P), given the volume of output and
the interest-rate. Because transactions demand is assumed to vary

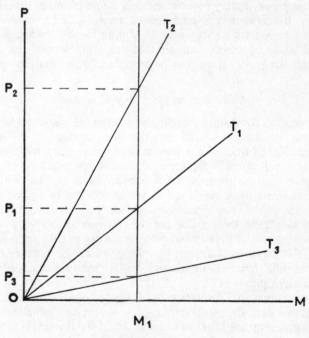

Fig. 18

proportionately with the price-level, OT_1 is a straight line through the origin, sloping upwards from left to right; given the supply of money M_1, demand and supply will be in equilibrium when the price-level is at P_1. If the rate of interest were to rise, the OT-curve would shift to a steeper slope such as OT_2, showing that transactors are demanding lower balances than before at each price-level; to maintain equilibrium, prices must now rise to P_2. An increase in output will cause larger balances to be needed at each price-level, so that the OT-curve will become less steep, as at OT_3, and the equilibrium price-level will fall to P_3. A similar construction can be used to show how transactions demand varies with the volume of output when the price-level and the interest-rate are fixed. When the vertical axis of Fig. 18 measures output (Q) instead of prices, transactions requirements will rise proportionately with Q, giving a demand curve similar to OT_2 (or OT_1 or OT_3, depending on its slope); its intersection with the line above M_1 will indicate the level of Q at which equilibrium exists.

All these relationships have, of course, been put forward on the assumption that transactions demand (in the broad sense which includes precautionary requirements) is the *only* kind of demand for money. It is now time to relax this assumption, and to consider the possibility that transactors may be willing to hold balances which exceed their payments requirements—in other words, the 'asset-demand' for money must now be brought into the analysis.

(c) The demand for money as an asset

Money has the distinctive feature of being the only asset which is perfectly liquid; but it also has the disadvantage of yielding no income. If the owner of a money balance exchanges it for bonds, he will receive a return in the form of interest; the purchase of shares will give him the prospect of dividends, while the acquisition of physical assets to be employed in production can bring him a flow of profits. In the case of transactions balances, it was seen that it is worth sacrificing these yields for the convenience of being able to make payments at times when receipts are not coming in to finance them. But why should anyone be willing to sacrifice income in order to hold 'idle' balances in addition to the 'active' ones needed for transactions purposes?

The reason is that the ownership of illiquid assets involves the risk of loss as well as the prospect of gain, so that it may sometimes seem worth giving up the latter in order to avoid the former. If money is lent out at interest, so that the asset held by the creditor is now someone else's promise to pay, there is the chance that the debtor may default on his obligation; if the money is used to buy shares in a company, it may happen that no dividends are distributed, or even that the company goes out of business with consequent loss to the shareholders; if physical assets are bought for use in production, it may turn out that there is little demand for the resulting output, so that no profits are made; moreover, not all assets are capable of being sold again when the owner regrets having acquired them and wants to get his money back. Even if all these risks are avoided by the purchase of an asset free of default risk, yielding a return which is fixed and certain, and easily re-saleable in a well-organized market, there still remains the possibility that a subsequent fall in its price may cause the owner to incur a capital loss.

Examples of assets with the characteristics just mentioned are the long-term bonds of the government and of large companies. The holder of a £100 bond bearing interest at the fixed rate of 4% is certain to receive £4 a year as long as he holds it. However, the £100 is merely a 'nominal value';[1] the price at which such bonds are currently changing hands in the market may be either higher or lower, according to the continuously changing pressures of demand and supply. Thus, if a man buys one for £90, and the market price then falls to £70, he will have sustained a loss roughly equivalent to five years' interest. The rate of yield when he bought the bond was £4÷90, i.e. 4·4%; now, at a price of £70, it is £4÷£70 or 5·7%; if he had waited for the price to fall before buying it, he would have had a higher return on his money. If, then, a potential bond-buyer thinks there is a strong possibility of a fall in price, and therefore of a rise in the rate of yield, he will prefer to hold on to his money for the time being. It should be noted that it is not the prospective price-fall in itself, but his lack of certainty about it, which makes him do this; if he knew in advance exactly when the price would fall, he could buy the bond now for £90, sell it just before it drops to £70, and then buy it back afterwards. But since, in the nature of things, he cannot be sure just when and by how much the price will go down, he will refrain from buying for the moment; the £90 which he has decided not to spend on the bond will stay in his hands as a '*speculative balance*' over and above any amount which he is holding for transactions purposes.

[1] See above, p. 114. The 'nominal' value is often—though by no means always—the price at which the bond was first issued by the original borrower (i.e. the government or a company). It is usually (but again, not always) equal to the redemption price, i.e. the number of pounds which will be paid to the holder of the bond when the repayment date (the 'maturity') is reached.

In deciding whether or not the price of the bond is likely to fall, the potential buyer will have compared the current price with what he considers to be its normal level in the light of past experience. If the price happens to be much higher than it has ever been in the past, he is likely to feel that it cannot possibly go higher still; since the odds are all on the side of a fall in the near future, he would be sure to incur a capital loss if he were to buy now, so he will hold on to his 'speculative balance' for the time being. At the other extreme, when the bond price is unprecedentedly low and the chances of a further fall seem negligible, he will exchange his whole speculative balance for bonds in order to obtain the capital gain which is in prospect. If the current price happens to be somewhere in between these upper and lower limits, he will have to weigh the chances of a future rise against those of a fall, and divide his 'portfolio' (i.e. his total assets, however composed) between money and bonds according to his estimate of the probabilities. In general, it can be said that the higher the current bond price is, the greater is the likelihood of a future fall and the smaller the number of bonds he will hold; while the lower the price, the greater the chances of a subsequent rise and the larger the proportion of bonds in his total portfolio.

In practice, of course, holding a money balance is by no means the only alternative to holding bonds: if an individual wishes to reduce the number of bonds in his portfolio, he can do it by substituting some non-money liquid asset for them, for example by acquiring building society shares which carry no risk of capital loss but at the same time—unlike money—yield an income. For the time being, however, it will greatly simplify the analysis if it is assumed that the only available asset other than money is a certain type of irredeemable fixed-interest bond. This implies that there are no other 'paper' assets in existence, and that physical assets, such as the machinery operated by business firms, are never offered for re-sale: their owners are assumed to acquire them as soon as they are produced, with the intention of retaining them as long as they last. On this basis, the only rate of interest which is relevant here will be the yield on bonds, which is inversely related to their market price; thus, a high bond price implies a low rate of interest, and a low price a high rate.[1] New borrowing will take the form of the issue of new bonds exactly

---

[1] This relationship can be expressed as $r = iN/P$, where r is the rate of yield, i is the 'nominal' interest rate on the bond (the 'coupon rate', as it is often called), N is the nominal value of the bond and P is its market price. Thus, a £100 bond bearing a nominal 4% will yield 3·3% when the market price is £120, 5% when the price is £80, and so on. If the 'coupon rate' were 1% (i.e. 0·01) on a £100 bond, so that $iN = 1$, the rate of yield r would be the reciprocal of the market price P.

like those already in existence,[1] but it is assumed that the number of bonds is already very large, so that the new ones likely to be issued during any short period will not be enough to increase the existing total by more than a negligibly small proportion. This means that new bonds must be sold at the price already ruling in the market for 'old' bonds; the rate of yield—that is, the market rate of interest—will not be affected by decisions to borrow, but will be determined by the preferences of the community as between the two types of assets, i.e. bonds and money, which are available to them.

If these preferences are the same as those of the individual bond-buyer described a little earlier, the proportions in which the community wishes to hold bonds and money will depend on the market price of bonds: the higher this is, the smaller the number of bonds and the larger the money-balances everyone will wish to hold, while the lower the bond price, the greater the desire to hold bonds and the smaller the demand for money. Since the price of bonds is inversely related to the interest-rate, this means that the demand for speculative balances will be greatest when the interest-rate is low, and will decline as the rate rises; the relationship will be as shown by the LL-curve of Fig. 19 overleaf, sloping downwards from left to right. Like the typical demand curve for an ordinary commodity, LL shows the quantity demanded increasing as the price falls, except that in this case the 'quantity' refers to speculative balances and the 'price' is the interest forgone by holding them.

The position and shape of LL depend on the attitudes of the various individuals and organizations whose separate demands are aggregated in it. Some of them—the 'pure speculators' as they may be called—will be interested only in the prospects of capital gains and losses, because they have very definite expectations about future interest-rates. Anyone who is convinced that a certain bond price is 'normal', and that temporary deviations from it will quickly be corrected, will not wish to hold any bonds at all when the interest-rate is even fractionally below the level corresponding to the 'normal' bond price, since he would (he believes) be certain to sustain a capital loss if he did so. On the other hand, when the interest-rate is above

---

[1] If the bonds were issued by the government, this would imply that only the government could borrow; business firms could then acquire additional capital only by ploughing back undistributed profits. A less restrictive alternative is to suppose that any firm can borrow, but is obliged by law to do so by issuing irredeemable fixed-interest bonds of the same nominal value and coupon rate as those of the bonds already in existence; this, combined with some sort of legal insurance provision to eliminate the risk of default on interest payments, would ensure that all bonds are homogeneous even though they do not all emanate from the same borrower.

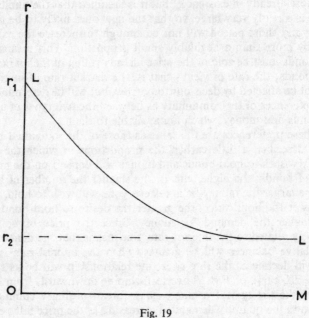

Fig. 19

'normal' (i.e. when the bond price is below its 'normal' level) he will
be sure of a capital gain if he converts his whole portfolio into bonds,
and he will then hold no speculative balance at all. If everyone else
takes exactly the same view, the LL-curve will be a horizontal straight
line lying infinitesimally below the level of the 'normal' interest-rate.
However, other speculators may not agree with him as to which rate
is normal: those who think it is lower will be holding bonds when
he is holding money, while those who think it is higher will still be
prepared to retain their speculative balances when he himself has
exchanged the whole of his for bonds. This will give the LL-curve a
downward slope, starting at the level of interest (r_1 in Fig. 19) which
is high enough to make everyone hold bonds, and reaching horizontal
at some lower level (r_2) at which no one wishes to hold anything but
money. The extent and steepness of the downward-sloping section
will depend on the diversity of opinion among the 'pure speculators',
and the degree of diversity may, like the opinions themselves, change
in the course of time and thereby alter the shape and position of the
LL-curve.[1]

[1] Keynes attached a good deal of importance to this diversity of opinion: see
the *General Theory*, p. 172.

The term 'pure speculator' may, perhaps, suggest the smart operator of popular myth, constantly playing the market in the hope of a killing; but the aim of the 'speculator' may very well be the more modest one of avoiding loss—as he switches from money into bonds and back again, he may be less concerned to secure capital gains than to prevent the total value of his portfolio from being reduced. However, whether they are motivated by hope or by fear, 'pure speculators' have the common characteristic of holding firm views about the future behaviour of the interest-rate. Other people, by contrast, may feel much less sure of the prospects: instead of a single interest-rate, they may regard *any* rate as 'normal' as long as it lies between certain upper and lower limits; within this range they will be undecided as to whether the rate is more likely to fall or to rise. Because their expectations are so uncertain, they will hold both money and bonds simultaneously, in proportions which will depend partly on their willingness to take risks and partly on the yield to be obtained from bond-holdings.

This can be seen by considering the case of an individual whose expectations are 'neutral', in the sense that he thinks the chances of a fall in the interest-rate are just the same as those of a rise: for example, if the rate happens to be 4% at present, he may regard a change to 5% as neither more nor less likely than a change to 3·3%. In terms of the market price of a £100 bond paying a nominal 4%, this means that the probability of a rise to £120 is exactly equal, in his view, to the probability of a fall to £80. The chances are not affected by the number of bonds he buys—with a holding of ten bonds he stands to gain or lose £200, with a hundred bonds, £2,000, and so on; whatever the size of his holding, the risk of loss is always balanced by an equal chance of gain. As a proportion of his total assets, his possible gains and losses depend on the way he distributes his resources between bonds and money. Suppose his total portfolio is worth £10,000. If he retains £9,000 in cash and buys ten £100 bonds with the remainder, a fall of £20 in the bond price will cause the total value of his assets to rise or fall by 2%; if he holds a hundred bonds and no cash, the possible gain and loss are each 20% of his portfolio; on a half-and-half distribution he could lose or gain 10%. His problem, then, is to decide how much of his portfolio he is prepared to risk. The answer will depend on the relative values he puts on the (equally probable) prospects of gain and loss, and on the way those values change as his 'stake' increases; the greater it is, the more the risk of loss is likely to weigh with him in comparison with the chance of gain. Depending on how cautious or adventurous[1] he happens to

[1] But not on how optimistic or pessimistic he is, since he has already been

be, there must be some level of bond-holding beyond which he will feel that the unpleasantness of losing another pound would more than outweigh the satisfaction of gaining one, and this is the level he would choose if the only inducement to hold bonds were the chance of capital gains.

However, bonds offer the additional attraction of yielding interest: against the risk of losing £20 on each bond he holds, the individual must set not only the chance of gaining £20 but also the certainty of a £4 interest receipt per annum—and this will induce him to hold more bonds than he would otherwise have done. Just how many more he will hold depends on a number of things. If he thinks the chances of the bond price changing either way are fairly low, the fact that interest is certain will give it a good deal of weight relatively to the risk of loss; if he thinks that the price, though sure to change, is unlikely to do so by more than the amount of the interest-yield, this too will encourage him to hold bonds, because the risk of loss will be almost completely offset by the prospect of interest, leaving him with a net chance of gain. On the other hand, if he is thinking in terms of probable price-changes only during the next week or month, the amount of interest accruing will probably not be enough to make much difference—4% per annum is only 0·33% per month and 0·077% per week. Within this 'context of expectations', his bond-holding will be determined by the current level of the interest-rate: the higher it is, the greater the compensation it provides for the risk of loss, and the greater the inducement to hold bonds instead of money. The individual's asset-demand for money will therefore be a decreasing function of the interest-rate, of the kind represented by the LL-curve of Fig. 19. It may be that there is no level of interest high enough to induce him to give up holding money altogether, in which case his LL-curve will not meet the vertical axis at r_1, but will become vertical somewhere to the right of it; at the other extreme, there will be some low level of interest (r_2) at which the compensation for risk-taking is so inadequate that he holds all his assets in the form of money, and his LL-curve becomes horizontal.

Those whose asset-demand for money is determined in this way can be called 'risk-averters'[1] to distinguish them from the 'pure

---

assumed to regard the probabilities of loss and gain as equal. He is in the position of a racegoer who has decided that a certain horse has a fifty-fifty chance of winning, and must now make up his mind whether to bet 50p, £5, or £500 on it—or whether not to place a bet at all.

[1] The concept of 'risk-aversion' is especially associated with the name of Professor J. Tobin: see his 'Liquidity Preference as Behaviour towards Risk', *Review of Economic Studies*, Feb. 1958.

speculators' considered earlier. Most people, however, are likely to combine the characteristics of both groups: for example, a man who thinks there is an 80% chance of the interest-rate falling will be a 'speculator' to the extent that he buys bonds in the expectation of a price increase, and a 'risk-averter' to the extent that he retains a holding of money to offset the 20% chance of a price reduction. The higher or lower the level of interest, the less likely it becomes that anyone will keep an open mind as to whether it will subsequently rise or fall; risk-averters will become speculators, and will hold port-folios consisting exclusively of either money or bonds according to whether the current interest-rate is very low or very high. At inter-mediate rates, increasing uncertainty will convert speculators into risk-averters, and their portfolios will now contain a mixture of bonds and money. Since both speculation and risk-aversion separately give rise to asset-demands for money which vary inversely with interest, a combination of the two will do the same, giving a demand curve with the downward-sloping characteristics of Fig. 19's *LL*.

The stability of the combined curve will, of course, depend on how volatile or otherwise its constituent elements happen to be. It seems reasonable to suppose that the risk-aversion element will be the less changeable of the two: people's willingness to face a given risk of loss depends on how cautious or adventurous they are by nature, and though these psychological characteristics may change over time, it is unlikely that they would alter drastically overnight. The greater the risk-aversion content of the combined asset-demand for money, then, the less the likelihood of sudden shifts in the *LL*-curve. The speculation element, by contrast, could change quickly and sharply if expectations about future interest-rates were suddenly revised. For this part of the demand for money to be completely stable, every speculator must be convinced that a certain 'normal' interest-rate will continue to rule in the future: moreover, any departure of the current rate from this level must take him by surprise, and he must expect it to move back to normal fairly quickly rather than move still further away from it. The necessity for this last condition can be seen by considering the case of a speculator who believes 4% to be the normal rate, but interprets a change to 4½% as the beginning of a 'swing' which may go as high as 6% before returning to normal. At the 4½% level, the market price of a £100 bond with a 4% 'coupon rate' is £89; if he were to exchange his money-holding for bonds at this price, he would gain £11 per bond when the normal 4% level was regained. But since he believes the interest-rate will go higher still, he will prefer to wait until the 6% limit is reached: he will then be able to buy at £67, gaining £33 per bond when interest returns to 4% and the bond price is once again £100. If he had initially been holding bonds, his expectation of a rise to 6% will have induced him to sell at the beginning of the movement, with the intention of buying back when the price reached £67. Similarly, a *fall* in the current rate might cause him to expect a further fall, inducing him to buy bonds in order to sell them again when the rate reaches rock-bottom. If all other speculators react in this way to changes in the current interest-rate, the demand curve for speculative money balances will shift upwards whenever the current rate rises, and downwards when it falls; when the rate reaches either of the limits beyond which no further divergence from normal is expected, the curve will immediately return to its original position. Since speculators may also change their views from time to time regarding the 'normal' level of the interest-rate and the upper and lower limits within which it can vary, it would be surprising if their demand curve were to retain a given position for any length of time;[1] the larger the speculative element in the combined asset-demand for money, therefore, the greater the instability it is likely to impart to the overall *LL*-curve.

So far, it has been implicitly assumed that bonds can be exchanged for money, and money for bonds, without expense. But if the ownership of bonds is fairly widespread, there will have to be some sort of market for them in which intermediaries such as brokers bring buyers and sellers together and charge fees or commissions for so doing. If they make a standard charge of x pence on each bond handled, this will reduce the effectiveness of any given interest-rate in compensating risk-averters for the possibility of capital loss, so that the demand for bonds will be less (and that for money greater) than it would have been in the absence of dealing expenses. The importance of this factor will depend on the length of time for which buyers expect to hold the bonds they acquire: if they are sure they will have no need to sell the bonds for at least two years, the dealer's charge will be relatively small when set against the interest accruing over such a long period; but where a buyer thinks he may need to sell

---

[1] It is conceivable that it might be in constant movement between the upper and lower limits, if speculators have no particular views about the existence of a long-term 'normal' rate but merely expect future rates to be anywhere between (say) 3% and 7%. Within these extremes, they will wish to hold money whenever the rate is rising, and bonds when it is falling, irrespective of the absolute level of the interest-rate at any given moment; their demands will cause the movement of the rate to continue until it reaches one of the limits, at which the cessation of movement will cause the demand to be reversed (i.e. so that instead of wishing to hold money, speculators demand bonds when the upper limit is reached) and begin a fresh movement back to the opposite extreme. In this case, the demand curve for speculative balances would be continually rising and falling.

again within a month or two, his prospective interest-earnings over that time may be more than wiped out by the dealing expense, and he will therefore continue to hold money. Also, dealers are unlikely to charge precisely x pence on each bond regardless of the number involved in any given transaction, since their operating costs will be much the same whether it is five, fifty or even 500 bonds which are being bought and sold; if they therefore make a higher charge per bond in the case of small transactions, the owners of small money-balances will be discouraged from buying bonds even at high interest-rates, and their holdings will swell the asset-demand for money beyond what it would otherwise have been. In general, the higher the scale of dealers' charges, and the greater the differential in favour of large transactions, the more the LL-curve will be pushed upwards and to the right.

When the transactions demand for money was examined earlier, it was seen that payments requirements vary directly with the level of money-income: the higher the general price-level and the greater the volume of output, the larger the money-balances needed to effect the economy's sales and purchases. In the case of the *asset* demand, on the other hand, the connection with money income is less obvious and more complex. It might, indeed, seem that on the assumptions so far made there ought to be no connection at all. Suppose (for example) the price-level were to increase: it is true that the real value of money-balances will fall proportionately—but so, too, will the real value of bonds whose yield is fixed in money terms, so that as long as asset-holders are assumed to be choosing only between money and bonds there is no reason why they should alter their holdings of them; the rise in prices will not cause the demand for money to change, except in so far as it may have modified speculators' views about future interest-rates. However, the very fact that the price-level is rising will now make it impossible to leave physical assets out of consideration. It was originally assumed that these were acquired solely for use in some productive activity, with no thought of the possibility of re-sale; on this basis, even a dwelling-house would be bought only with a view to the owner living in it himself or obtaining income by renting it out; he would not regard it as a marketable asset to be held for a limited period as an alternative to money and bonds. As long as everyone believes that the prices and yields of houses, machines and all other physical assets will remain unchanged in the future, there can be no such speculation with regard to them as there is in the case of bonds, and their existence will not affect the choice between bonds and money; even if the range of assets is broadened to include shares (as representing indirect ownership of companies' physical assets), they can be treated as merely another species of bonds. But when the general price-level rises, physical assets and shares will retain their real value while that of money and bonds is falling; if the price-trend is expected to continue, there will be a 'substitution effect' by which the demand for physical assets and shares increases at the expense of the demand for *both* bonds *and* money. In this way, rising prices may be expected to cause the asset-demand for money to fall.

This, however, will be the consequence not of the increase in prices itself but of the general expectation that they will *continue* to rise. Once they have been stabilised at a new, higher level, and everyone is persuaded that no further increases are to be expected, the 'substitution effect' will no longer operate and the asset-demand for money will revive. In fact, it is now likely to be larger than it was before. The rise in the price-level will have increased the money values of all physical assets and equities; if there has been no change in the total quantity of money, existing balances will now form a smaller proportion than before of the nominal value of all assets taken together. However, the original proportion can be supposed to have been the result of deliberate choice on the part of wealth-owners: given the cost of holding money (in terms of yields forgone on alternative assets), they chose to hold $x\%$ of their total wealth in the form of money rather than commit all their resources to holdings of less liquid assets. If they now attempt to restore their money balances to the original $x\%$ of total assets, their asset-demand for money will have risen in proportion to the increase in the general price-level. The same considerations apply when total assets increase in real terms through additions to the volume of physical capital: if wealth-owners do not wish to find their overall holdings becoming steadily less liquid, they will try to increase their money balances more or less in proportion[1] to the growth of their total assets. The accumulation of real assets is, of course, a relatively slow process for the economy as a whole, and is closely connected with the long-run

---

[1] The aggregate proportion may very well change to some extent, since the growth of total assets may be accompanied by changes in the *distribution* of wealth: for example, a tendency for physical assets to be more heavily concentrated in the hands of large firms would reduce the overall money/total assets proportion if such firms habitually maintain lower money balances (relatively to their total assets) than smaller ones. Among individuals, too, the distribution of wealth might change in favour of people whose risk aversion was less than average, and who therefore desired smaller money/total assets ratios—this, too, would pull down the average proportion. A change in the price-level will also redistribute wealth away from money-holders to the owners of 'real' assets, with the possible consequence of a change in the desired money/total assets ratio.

growth of real income—as physical capital increases, it yields greater real output, out of which more can be invested in further additions to the capital stock; but short-run variations in real income will cause little change in the total of real assets, so that they will produce a negligible 'wealth effect' on the asset-demand for money. As long as the analysis is confined to the 'short period', then, changes in money income will raise or lower the asset-demand for money only to the extent that they involve increases or reductions in the general price-level.[1]

These effects can be illustrated diagrammatically in terms of Fig. 19 on p. 248 above. The LL-curve there shown has been drawn on the assumption of a given level of money-income and a given stock of real assets. When money-income rises because of an increase in the price-level, LL will be shifted out to the right, indicating that the asset-demand for money at any given interest-rate will be greater, the higher the general level of prices. If the vertical axis were used to measure prices instead of the interest-rate, a diagram similar to Fig. 18 would result, except that the OT-curves would be replaced by OL-curves showing the asset-demand for money instead of the transactions-demand. At a given interest-rate and volume of output, OL_1 would show the asset-demand varying proportionately with the price-level: like OT_1, it would be a straight line starting at the origin O. A higher rate of interest would cause the curve to slope more steeply (as would be shown by a curve OL_2 in the same place as OT_2), while a lower rate would require a more gently-sloping curve (OL_3, corresponding to OT_3). On the other hand, if the volume of output rather than the price-level were to be measured on the vertical axis, a curve showing the asset-demand for money at different levels of real income (given the interest-rate and the general level of prices) would not resemble OT_1—it would be a vertical line similar to that shown above M_1, indicating that changes in real income would make no difference to asset-demand in the short run. The position of the line will depend on the interest-rate and the price-level: the higher the interest-rate, the closer it will be to the vertical axis, while the higher the price-level, the further away it will lie to the right. It must be emphasized that the expectational effects of price-changes are ignored in these constructions: for example, Fig. 19's LL-curve represents the asset-demand for money which exists when prices are at a given level p_1 and are expected to remain there; if, instead of p_1, the price-level were higher at p_2, and if everyone expected it to remain there, the curve would lie some distance to the

[1] See J. Tobin, *op. cit.*, and D. Patinkin, *Money, Interest and Prices* (2nd edition, 1965), pp. 278-9.

right; but the different positions of LL would show alternative possibilities existing at the same moment of time, not successive stages in a process of price-change.

(d) Monetary equilibrium and the level of output

Now that the transactions and asset demands for money have been examined in detail, they can be put together into a single 'demand for money' (or in Keynes' term, 'liquidity-preference'[1]) function in readiness for confrontation with supply. Algebraically, the transactions-demand (with precautionary demand included in it) can be written

$$M_1 = L_1(pQ,r)$$

where L_1 is the functional relationship between money-income pQ, the interest-rate r, and the demand for transactions-balances M_1. Similarly, the asset-demand can be written

$$M_2 = L_2(p,r,A)$$

where A represents total real assets and is a constant in the short run. Adding the two together gives

$$M = M_1 + M_2 = L_1(pQ,r) + L_2(p,r,A) = L(p,Q,r,A)$$

as the overall demand for money. For equilibrium, demand must be equal to supply. It was suggested earlier that the supply of money can be treated as a constant determined by the monetary authorities; when this is denoted $\bar{M}$, the condition of monetary equilibrium may be written

$$\bar{M} = L_1(pQ,r) + L_2(p,r,A) = L(p,Q,r,A)$$

This means that a given money-supply, $\bar{M}$, will satisfy demand only if

---

[1] See the *General Theory*, pp. 166–74 and Ch. 15. Keynes' 'incentives to liquidity', namely the transactions, precautionary and speculative 'motives', correspond to the subdivisions of the demand for money made in the present text. He regarded the first two as depending on the level of money income (in symbols, $M_1 = L_1(Y)$) and the third as depending on the interest-rate ($M_2 = L_2(r)$), so that the liquidity-preference function as a whole was

$$M = M_1 + M_2 = L_1(Y) + L_2(r).$$

He thus excluded the interest-rate as an influence on transactions and precautionary demand (M_1), and prices as an influence on speculative demand (M_2). Moreover, the latter is the asset-demand only of the 'pure speculators' described above: that of 'risk-averters' does not appear. In diagrammatic terms, $M_1 = L_1(Y)$ gives a vertical line parallel to the r-axis in Fig. 17, while $M_2 = L_2(r)$ is the same as LL in Fig. 19.

prices, output, the interest-rate and real assets are at appropriate levels in relation to one another. If all four variables were completely free to change, a great many combinations of their possible values would be consistent with equilibrium. But it has already been assumed that A is constant in the short run; also, the number of possible combinations of the remaining three variables is limited by the existence of other relationships between them—for example, by the fact that the level of Q depends partly on that of r through the latter's influence on investment. If monetary equilibrium is to co-exist with a balance of the aggregate demand and supply of commodities, it is necessary that p, Q and r should be such that they satisfy not one but several sets of equilibrium conditions. To show this, it will be convenient to begin by making the simplifying assumption (which will be relaxed later) that not only A but also p is constant, so that only Q and r are capable of variation: it will then be seen that, although many different pairs of values of Q and r would be consistent with monetary equilibrium, only one pair will be capable of giving a balance of aggregate demand and supply of commodities as well.[1]

In Fig. 20 overleaf, the DD-curves show how the *total* demand for money varies with the interest-rate at different levels of income. For example, $D_1 D$ is the sum of the transactions and asset demands which exist when income is Y_1, or $\bar{p}Q_1$ (where $\bar{p}$ is the price-level which has been assumed constant). When output increases from Q_1 to Q_2, income rises from Y_1 (or $\bar{p}Q_1$) to Y_2 (or $\bar{p}Q_2$); because a larger volume of goods and services is now being bought and sold, trans-actions-demand will be greater at all levels of interest, and the curve which represents it ($T_1 T_1$ in Fig. 17) will be pushed to the right (i.e. to $T_2 T_2$); when this is added to the asset-demand (which remains unchanged in the position of Fig. 19's LL-curve, since short-run changes in output have no effect on it), the combined curve will show a rightward movement to the position $D_2 D$. A further rise in output to Q_3, making income Y_3 (i.e. $\bar{p}Q_3$), will push the curve still further to the right to the position $D_3 D$. The higher the level of output, the further the demand curve will lie to the right.

It will be noticed that all the curves converge to the horizontal at a minimum level of interest r_0. This may be the rate which, in the opinion of 'pure speculators', is the lowest to which interest can ever

[1] The analysis which follows is based on J. R. Hicks, 'Mr Keynes and the Classics', *Econometrica*, 1937 (reprinted in his *Critical Essays in Monetary Theory* (1967) and in *Readings in the Theory of Income Distribution*, American Economic Association (1950)). See also his *The Trade Cycle* (1950), Chap. XI, and 'The Classics Again' in *Critical Essays*.

I

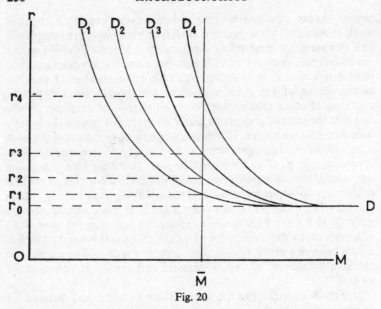

Fig. 20

fall: since the only possible change from r_0 is a future rise in the rate, bond-holding would entail the certainty of capital loss—so speculators will now have zero demand for bonds and an infinitely elastic demand for money. Alternatively, if there are no speculators with firm views of this kind, r_0 may be the rate at which interest is no longer sufficient to compensate 'risk-averters' for the danger of capital loss, so that they will not wish to hold any bonds at all and will be prepared to hold indefinitely large amounts of money. Alternatively again, if risk-aversion happens to be very weak (that is, if there are plenty of people willing to take the chance of loss even with only a very slight offset in the shape of interest), the minimum rate will depend on the level of dealers' charges. The lower the interest rate, the longer the period over which interest receipts are wiped out by the initial dealing expense: when this is so long that no one is prepared to hold bonds for the time needed to begin to obtain a net yield, the minimum rate will have been reached. Whatever the reason for the existence of such a minimum at r_0, it means that the whole of any increase in the stock of money will now be willingly added to the balances everyone is content to hold; it will be absorbed into the '*liquidity trap*' (to use Sir Dennis Robertson's term for the elastic part of the demand-for-money curve).

At very high interest-rates, the curves become vertical: here, the asset-demand for money has disappeared altogether, while transactions (including precautionary) demand has been pared down to the absolute minimum required to effect purchases and sales at the given level of income. The greater the volume of output, the larger this minimum requirement will be; hence, the vertical section of D_2D lies to the right of that of D_1D, that of D_3D to the right of that of D_2D, and so on.

If the supply of money is as indicated by the vertical line at $\bar{M}$—which implies that supply is inelastic with respect to the interest-rate—the intersections between the various demand curves and the $\bar{M}$-line will show the levels of interest needed to give monetary equilibrium at each level of income. Thus, if income happens to be Y_1 (or $\bar{p}Q_1$) so that the relevant demand curve for money is D_1D, supply and demand will be equal when the interest-rate is r_1; when income is Y_2 (or $\bar{p}Q_2$), the relevant demand curve is D_2D, and the equilibrium interest-rate is r_2; at income Y_3 (or $\bar{p}Q_3$), the rate will be r_3—and so on. The larger the value of Y (which in this case means the greater the volume of output, Q, since the price-level $\bar{p}$ is constant throughout), the higher the level of r at which the demand and supply of money are balanced.

This relationship can be shown more directly than appears in Fig. 20 above. In the next diagram, Fig. 21 overleaf, the vertical axis measures the interest-rate as before, but the horizontal scale shows levels of income instead of quantities of money: the curve LM_1 connects all the pairs of values of Y and r (Y_1 and r_1, Y_2 and r_2, and so on) which in Fig. 20 were found to be associated with one another when the demand and supply of money were in equilibrium. It can be seen that LM_1 is horizontal at its left-hand extreme, where very low levels of income are involved; here, the transactions-demand is very small, so that the quantity of money M_1 is capable of satisfying a large asset-demand as well: indeed, to induce wealth-owners to hold the amount of money available for this purpose, the interest-rate must be at its minimum level r_0. On the far right, LM_1 becomes vertical at a high level of income: this is where M_1 is only just sufficient to meet minimum transactions requirements, and the rate of interest has risen to the level needed to extinguish asset-demand altogether. Between these extremes, the curve steadily increases in slope as the level of income rises. Thus, LM_1 shows, for each income-level, the interest-rate at which monetary equilibrium exists when the supply of money is fixed at M_1. If the latter were to be increased to M_2, the equilibrium value of r would be lower at each level of Y, except where the minimum interest-rate r_0 has already been reached; the corresponding LM-curve will now lie to the right of LM_1 in the

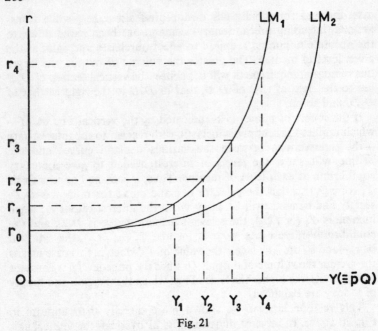

Fig. 21

position indicated by the LM_2-curve in the diagram. Further increases in the quantity of money will shift the curve still further to the right, while reductions will shift it to the left; the LM_1 and LM_2 curves shown in Fig. 21 are merely two members of a numerous family of possible LM-curves, each drawn on the assumption of a different quantity of money.

The LM_1-curve is a pictorial representation of the equilibrium condition $M_1 = L(\bar{p}Q, r)$, which is the same as that given earlier except that the money supply is specified as M_1 and the price-level is constant at $\bar{p}$. If Q were also given a fixed value, it would determine r in the sense of indicating which level of interest is compatible with monetary equilibrium; alternatively, if r were fixed, it would determine Q; but since both of them are free to vary, the equation and its corresponding LM_1-curve merely show which *pairs* of values (such as Q_1, r_1) satisfy the equilibrium condition. To decide which of these pairs is also compatible with equilibrium between the aggregate demand and supply of commodities, it is now necessary to recall the relationship which Q and r bear to one another through the saving-investment relationship.

It was shown in an earlier chapter[1] that when aggregate demand

[1] See pp. 60-2 above.

and supply are in equilibrium, saving must equal investment when both terms are taken in the *ex ante* sense; in symbols, the condition for equilibrium in the market for commodities can be written $I = S$. If the demand for investment is assumed to be elastic with respect to the current interest-rate, while all other investment-determining forces (such as the availability of finance, as distinct from its interest-cost) are constant, the level of I will depend on r; that is, $I = I(r)$, where the $I(\ldots)$ on the right-hand side of the equation represents the functional relationship between the other two terms. Saving, on the other hand, is more likely to depend on current real income than on the interest-rate: if the consumption function is taken to be $C = C(\bar{p}Q)$ (implying that influences other than real income are either absent or constant), then the fact that saving equals income minus consumption means that it, too, is a function of real income— in symbols, $S = S(\bar{p}Q)$. The $I = S$ condition can therefore be rewritten

$$I(r) = S(\bar{p}Q)$$

meaning that the aggregate demand and supply of commodities will be in equilibrium only when the values of r and Q are such as to satisfy the equation ($\bar{p}$, of course, remaining constant throughout). For a given r it shows the equilibrium value of Q, and for a given Q it shows that of r; but (just as with the condition of monetary equilibrium discussed earlier) the fact that both Q and r are variables means that the equation can do no more than indicate which *pairs* of values of Q and r are compatible with an equilibrium of aggregate demand and supply.

This is shown diagrammatically in Fig. 22 overleaf. The top half is identical with Fig. 11 on p. 154 above; the *MEI*-curve shows the various amounts of investment-demand (measured on the upper side of the horizontal axis) which will be forthcoming at the interest-rates indicated on the vertical scale, on the assumption that firms push investment to the point where the expected marginal rate of return is equal to the interest-cost of financing it: thus, r_1 calls forth investment of I_1, r_2 calls forth investment I_2, and so on. The lower half of the diagram shows the relationship between real income (measured downwards from the origin O on the vertical scale) and saving (measured along the under-side of the horizontal axis); this part is similar to Fig. 12 on p. 165 above, except that it has been turned through 90 degrees and contains only a 'saving function' OS which shows how the amount of desired saving varies with the level of income.[1] When real income happens to be $\bar{p}Q_1$, saving is S_1; when

[1] In the diagram, OS has been drawn as a straight line through the origin,

it is $\bar{p}Q_2$, saving is S_2—and so on for other possible values of $\bar{p}Q$. The two halves of the diagram are linked by the equilibrium condition $I = S$. Thus, aggregate demand equals aggregate supply when $I_1 = S_1$—that is, when interest is r_1 and real income is $\bar{p}Q_1$; similarly, $I_2 = S_2$ requires that the interest rate is r_2 and real income is $\bar{p}Q_2$; every other point along the horizontal axis will represent a saving-

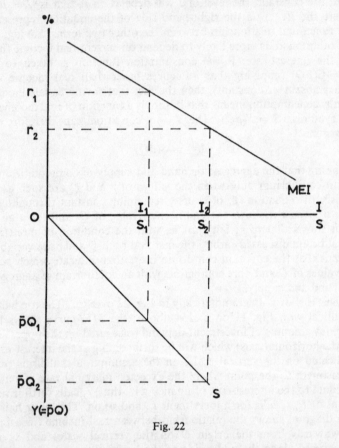

Fig. 22

investment equilibrium for which the appropriate values of r and $\bar{p}Q$ are given by the *MEI* and *OS* curves respectively. It is not difficult

which implies that the community wishes to save the same proportion of income however large or small the latter happens to be. However, it is not necessary to the analysis that this should be so: the same conclusions would follow if *OS* were drawn so as to cut the vertical axis below *O*, or if it were curvilinear.

to see that the lower the level of r, the higher will be that of $\bar{p}Q$; the greater the demand for investment, the larger the real income needed to generate an equal amount of saving.

When this relationship is shown directly in Fig. 23 below, it takes the form of the downward-sloping curve *IS*. Since Fig. 23 has the same axes as the earlier Fig. 21, it can also include *LM*-curves; suppose, then, that the quantity of money happens to be M_1, so that

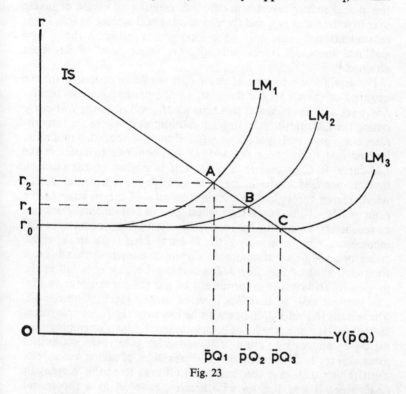

Fig. 23

the various pairs of interest-rates and real income levels consistent with monetary equilibrium are those indicated along LM_1. (The curves LM_2 and LM_3 should be ignored for the moment.) Where *IS* and LM_1 intersect at A, the interest-rate is r_2 and real income is $\bar{p}Q_1$: at this point, there is *both* an equilibrium of the demand and supply of commodities (i.e. $I = S$, or $I(r) = S(\bar{p}Q)$) *and* an equilibrium of the demand and supply of money (i.e. $M_1 = L(\bar{p}Q,r)$). As long as the supply of money continues to be M_1, there is no other point at which the two equilibrium conditions can be satisfied simultaneously. If, for example, interest were r_1 and real income were $\bar{p}Q_2$, saving-investment equilibrium would exist, since B is a point on IS; but the level of interest needed for monetary equilibrium at $\bar{p}Q_2$ would be that indicated by the point on LM_1 vertically above B, and this would obviously be a good deal higher than r_1. At B, then, there would be an excess of demand for money over the supply of it, with the result that the interest-rate would be driven upwards; this would reduce investment-demand, creating an excess of saving over investment at $\bar{p}Q_2$ and thereby causing real income to fall. These movements will cease only when interest has settled at the r_2 level and real income has reached $\bar{p}Q_1$, i.e. when point A has been attained.[1]

For equilibrium to exist at point B, it would be necessary for the quantity of money to rise from M_1 to M_2, causing LM_2 to replace LM_1; yet another increase, this time to M_3, will push the LM-curve out to the LM_3 position, giving equilibrium at C where the interest-rate is r_0 and real income is $\bar{p}Q_3$. But now that the minimum interest-rate r_0 has been reached, IS will continue to intersect the LM-curve at C no matter how far LM is pushed to the right by further increases in the quantity of money; the horizontal stretch which passes through C is common to all LM-curves lying to the right of LM_3. Thus, $\bar{p}Q_3$ is the highest level of real income which can be reached by expanding the money-supply. Further increases in real income can now occur only if the IS-curve itself shifts to the right, either because of an autonomous rise in investment-demand (i.e. a rightward shift of Fig. 22's MEI-curve) or because of a fall in the propensity to save (i.e. a movement of the OS-curve closer to Fig. 22's vertical axis, so that less is saved at any given income-level). This means that, if $\bar{p}Q_3$ happens to be less than the full-employment level of real income, it will not be possible to eliminate unemployment merely by adopting an appropriate monetary policy; the authorities must also try to manipulate the 'real' variables of saving and investment. This situation is conventionally referred to as the 'Keynesian case', since it was Keynes who first suggested it as a theoretical possibility.[2]

Leaving aside the 'Keynesian case', it is conceivable that monetary

[1] The adjustment process is likely to involve a good deal of 'overshooting', as the reader will discover if he traces out the sequence in diagrams 20 and 22; moreover, it may be complicated by time-lags which prevent equilibrium being reached and set up oscillations instead. See J. R. Hicks, *The Trade Cycle*, Chap. XI.

[2] See the *General Theory*, pp. 201–2. He added that 'whilst this limiting case might become practically important in the future, I know of no example of it hitherto' (p. 207).

policy may be ineffective for another reason. In Fig. 23 the IS-curve has been drawn with a fairly gentle slope, so that it cuts LM_1, LM_2 and LM_3 at successively higher levels of real income. But now suppose Fig. 22's MEI-curve slopes very steeply, implying that investment-demand is inelastic with respect to the interest-rate; and that the OS-curve has a more gentle slope, meaning that the Marginal Propensity to save is high so that only a small increase in income is needed to provide the extra saving to balance a substantial rise in investment.[1] These conditions will cause the IS-curve to slope very steeply, and shifts in the LM-curve will then change the equilibrium level of real income very little. In the extreme case in which the IS-curve is completely vertical (so that point B is directly below A, and C directly below B), real income cannot change at all from the level indicated by the position of the IS-curve, however far LM might be pushed to the right by changes in the quantity of money. Just as in the 'Keynesian case', the only way of raising the level of $\bar{p}Q$ (if it happens to be below the full-employment level) will be to act on the determinants of saving and investment.

It may be, however, that the IS-curve is actually more elastic than the slopes of Fig. 22's MEI and OS curves seem to imply. As well as responding to changes in the interest-rate, investment-demand may also be influenced to some extent by the level of real income,[2] rising as income increases and falling when it diminishes. The investment function will then be $I = I(r, \bar{p}Q)$ instead of the $I = I(r)$ assumed earlier; in Fig. 22, an increase in real income will shift the MEI-curve bodily to the right. As long as the curve is not completely vertical, a fall in the interest-rate will therefore have more far-reaching effects than those already described. When the initial increase in investment has brought about a rise in real income via the OS-curve, the very fact that income has risen will cause a further investment-increase through a rightward movement of the MEI-curve; this will produce a further income-rise, inducing another shift of MEI—and so on; the eventual change in $\bar{p}Q$ in response to the original fall in r will consequently be greater than it would have been if MEI had stayed put, and the IS-curve of Fig. 23 will reflect this by sloping less steeply than it would otherwise have done.[3]

Another possibility arises if saving varies with the rate of interest

[1] In other words, the Multiplier $(1/MPS)$ will have a low value. To the extent that a fall in r causes a rise in investment, the consequent rise in income will be smaller, the higher the MPS.

[2] This possibility was considered on pp. 164–6 in Chap. VII above.

[3] This is an example of the working of the 'compound' Multiplier described on p. 133 above.

as well as with real income. The higher the rate of return on bonds, the greater the incentive to save in order to buy them: it may be doubted whether it has very much effect on saving behaviour in practice, but to the extent that it does, the saving function must be amended to read $S = S(r,\bar{p}Q)$ instead of merely $S = S(\bar{p}Q)$ as before. A reduction in interest will therefore not only generate additional investment-demand but will also cause Fig. 22's OS-curve to move closer to the vertical $\bar{p}Q$-axis, indicating that the desire to save has diminished at all levels of real income. The ensuing rise in real income will consequently be greater than if OS had retained its original position, and the slope of Fig. 23's IS-curve will be gentler than it would have been if savings depended only on $\bar{p}Q$. If, in addition, investment-demand responds to changes in real income in the way described in the previous paragraph, the IS-curve may be much more elastic with respect to the interest-rate than the slopes of the original MEI and OS curves would by themselves have suggested. The power of monetary policy to raise the level of real income and employment will then be correspondingly greater, as long as the economy is not pushed into the position described in the 'Keynesian case'.

It must be remembered, however, that the analysis has so far proceeded on the simplifying assumption that the price-level remains constant throughout—so it would be unwise to begin drawing firm conclusions at this stage regarding policy. All that can be said at present is that the intersection of IS and LM_1 in Fig. 23 shows the interest-rate and income-level at which two equilibrium conditions are simultaneously fulfilled: first, that the supply of money equals the demand for it—in symbols, $M_1 = L(\bar{p}Q,r)$; and second, that the aggregate demand for commodities equals aggregate supply, i.e. $S(\bar{p}Q) = I(r)$, or $S(\bar{p}Q,r) = I(r,\bar{p}Q)$ if the modifications suggested in the last two paragraphs are introduced. As long as the price-level is constant, no other conditions are necessary for a complete equilibrium of the economy. The assumption of constant prices implies (as explained at the end of Chapter Four) that labour's marginal product is the same at all levels of employment and that money-wages are inflexible; if unemployment exists because $\bar{p}Q_1$ is less than the full-employment level of output, this will not have the effect of pushing down money-wages, and nothing will happen to disturb the equilibrium situation given by the intersection of IS and LM_1. When these extreme assumptions regarding the labour market are abandoned, so that the price-level is free to change, further equilibrium conditions must be specified—as will appear in the next chapter.

CHAPTER TWELVE

Money (II)

(a) Interest, output and the price-level

The condition of monetary equilibrium was originally expressed as

$$\bar{M} = L_1(pQ,r)+L_2(p,r) = L(p,Q,r)$$

where $\bar{M}$ represents a fixed supply of money.[1] A rise in the price-level p will cause the demand for money to increase: to restore equilibrium, it will be necessary for r to rise, or for Q to fall, or both. Alternatively, the increases in prices can be regarded as reducing the real value of the money supply. If the equation is divided through by p, giving

$$\frac{\bar{M}}{p} = L_1(Q,r)+L_2(r) = L(Q,r)$$

the effect is to express both supply and demand in real terms. Instead of a given number of pounds (or 'nominal' money) the money-supply is now a given volume of purchasing-power (or 'real' money); a rise in p reduces the quantity of goods and services over which $\bar{M}$ gives command, and thereby diminishes the quantity of 'real' money $\bar{M}/p$. On the demand side, $L_1(Q,r)$ and $L_2(r)$ are the amounts of purchasing-power needed to satisfy transactions and asset-holding requirements. If the supply of nominal money happens to be M_1 and the price-level is p_1, the equilibrium condition will be satisfied by any of the pairs of values of Q and r indicated by the curve marked $L(M_1/p_1)$ in the top right-hand quadrant (I) of Fig. 24 overleaf.[2]

This part of Fig. 24 is very similar to Fig. 23 above, with the difference that its horizontal axis is marked Q instead of $\bar{p}Q$: that

---

[1] Here, the symbol for assets (A) has been left out, on the ground that the analysis is at present concerned only with the short period.

[2] The diagram and the ensuing discussion are based on W. L. Smith, 'A Graphical Exposition of the Complete Keynesian System', *Southern Economic Journal*, Oct. 1956, and on M. Blaug, *Economic Theory in Retrospect* (1962), p. 579.

is, it measures volumes of physical output instead of the money-values found by multiplying output by a constant price-level $\bar{p}$.[1] In Fig. 24, the position of the $L(M/p)$-curve depends on the price-level as well as on the quantity of nominal money—thus, a rise in prices

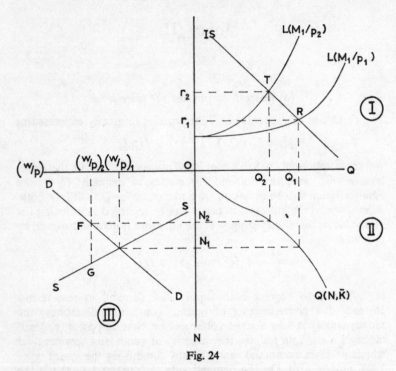

Fig. 24

from p_1 to p_2 will cause $L(M_1/p_1)$ to shift to the left to the position $L(M_1/p_2)$, even though the stock of nominal money is unchanged at M_1. A *fall* in the price-level, on the other hand, will shift the $L(M/p)$-curve to the right. A change in M will have the same effect as in Fig.

---

[1] This raises the obvious difficulty that a heterogeneous collection of goods and services cannot be summed in quantity terms. There would, of course, be no problem if only one commodity were produced—but this would be a highly unrealistic assumption to make about the output of a whole economy. Accordingly, it is necessary to regard each value of Q as representing a set of quantities of the various commodities the economy produces; when Q rises by (say) 5%, this implies that the output of each individual commodity has risen by exactly 5% as well. To avoid index-number problems, it is also necessary to assume that the pattern of relative prices remains the same at all levels of output, whatever happens to the general price-level.

23, an increase pushing the curve to the right and a decrease pushing it to the left; it is quite possible, therefore, that simultaneous changes in *both* M and p could exactly offset one another and leave the $L(M/p)$-curve in precisely the same position as before.

The *IS*-curve has much the same significance as it did earlier: it shows all the pairs of values of Q and r (rather than $\bar{p}Q$ and r as in Fig. 23) at which saving-investment equilibrium can be achieved. As long as the demand for investment and the willingness to save are independent of the price-level, the *IS*-curve will not be affected (that is, it will not change its position or shape) when a rise in p reduces the supply of 'real' money and thereby causes the monetary-equilibrium curve to shift from $L(M_1/p_1)$ to $L(M_1/p_2)$. The latter will now intersect *IS* at T instead of R, indicating that a lower volume of physical output (Q_2 instead of Q_1) and a higher interest-rate (r_2 instead of r_1) are needed if monetary equilibrium is to co-exist with an equilibrium of saving and investment. Had p fallen instead of rising, the $L(M/p)$-curve would have shifted to the right, intersecting the *IS*-curve at a higher level of Q and a lower value of r. In fact, *every* level of p will give a different $L(M/p)$-curve and thus necessitate a different combination of values of Q and r in order to satisfy the equilibrium conditions—except in the extreme case (analogous to the 'Keynesian case' described in the last chapter) when the $L(M/p)$-curve has shifted so far to the right that *IS* intersects it along its horizontal section.

What this part of Fig. 24 does *not* show is why prices should be at one level rather than another. Given p_1 and the nominal money-supply M_1, output will be Q_1 and interest r_1; given p_2, they will be respectively Q_2 and r_2; but why should either p_1 or p_2 prevail? To answer this question it is necessary to consider the other parts of the diagram. The lower left-hand quadrant (III) represents the labour market: it is exactly the same as Fig. 3 in Chapter Four, except that it has been turned round and rotated through 90° to the left; man-hours (N) are now measured downwards from the origin on the vertical axis, while real wages (w/p) are measured leftwards from the origin along the horizontal scale. The *DD*-curve, which shows the marginal product of labour at each possible level of employment, is derived from the production function $Q(N,\bar{K})$ shown in the lower right-hand quadrant (II); this is Chapter Four's Fig. 1 turned through 90°. The supply of labour is shown by the *SS*-curve, whose inter-section with the *DD*-curve shows that full employment exists when N_1 man-hours are being worked and real wages are $(w/p)_1$.

If the labour market is perfectly competitive (i.e. if there are no trades unions, minimum wage laws, or other limitations on the adjustment of money-wages), any imbalance between demand and supply will cause w to fall or rise until real wages are $(w/p)_1$ and employment is N_1. The $Q(N,\bar{K})$ curve of Quadrant II shows that output will then be Q_1. For savings-investment equilibrium at this volume of output, interest must be r_1; for monetary equilibrium at Q_1 and r_1, prices must be p_1 as long as the quantity of nominal money is M_1. With prices at p_1, money-wages will also be determined: though many pairs of values of w and p would be consistent with the ratio $(w/p)_1$, there is only one value of w—which will be denoted w_1—capable of giving this ratio when the price-level is p_1.

When money-wages are w_1, prices p_1, employment and output N_1 and Q_1, and the interest-rate r_1, a complete equilibrium exists in the economy as a whole. The equilibrium conditions in any single part of it depend on those prevailing in every other part. Suppose, for example, that the price-level happens to be p_2 instead of p_1. With a nominal money-supply of M_1, the monetary-equilibrium curve will now be $L(M_1/p_2)$, which intersects the IS-curve at T. Here, investment balances saving, and the demand for money equals the supply; output is Q_2, and interest is r_2. As far as the forces at work in Quadrant I are concerned, equilibrium exists. But an output of Q_2 calls for employment of only N_2 man-hours; if real wages are $(w/p)_2$, they will be equal to labour's marginal product at this level of labour input, and firms will be content to supply the output Q_2; but the demand for labour will fall short of supply by FG, and if money-wages are flexible downwards, the pressure of this excess supply will cause them to fall. As long as the price-level remains p_2, the fall in w will mean a reduction in real wages (w/p), and firms will now increase output up to the point where the marginal product of labour equals the real wage; aggregate supply will exceed the aggregate demand indicated by the Q_2 below point T in Quadrant I. This will cause prices to fall below the p_2 level, thereby increasing the quantity of 'real' money, pushing the monetary-equilibrium curve to the right, reducing the interest-rate and increasing the volume of output needed to satisfy aggregate demand. The fall in prices will tend to offset the effects on (w/p) of the decline in money-wages, necessitating further reductions in w; but both p and w will continue to fall until the real wage $(w/p)_1$ has been reached—at which point an overall equilibrium will obtain, with aggregate demand and supply balanced at Q_1 and the demand and supply of labour balanced at N_1.

A complete equilibrium, then, requires that all of the following conditions shall be simultaneously fulfilled:

(a) saving must equal investment. Since $I = I(r)$ and $S = S(Q)$, the condition '$I = S$' means that

$$I(r) = S(Q).$$

If investment is also influenced by Q and saving by r, the equation becomes

$$I(r,Q) = S(Q,r) \qquad . \qquad . \qquad . \qquad (1)$$

(b) the supply of money must equal the demand for it; when both are expressed in real terms, this means that

$$\frac{\bar{M}}{p} = L_1(Q,r) + L_2(r) = L(Q,r) \qquad . \qquad . \qquad (2)$$

where $\bar{M}$ is a fixed quantity of nominal money.

(c) the demand and supply of labour must balance. Supply is a function of the real wage, i.e.

$$N = N\left(\frac{w}{p}\right) \qquad . \qquad . \qquad . \qquad . \qquad (3)$$

Demand is derived from the aggregate demand for commodities through the production function

$$Q = Q(N,\bar{K}) \qquad . \qquad . \qquad . \qquad . \qquad (4)$$

but it also depends on the real wage, since the level of employment most profitable to firms is found where labour's marginal product equals the real wage, i.e. where

$$\frac{dQ}{dN} = \frac{w}{p} \qquad . \qquad . \qquad . \qquad . \qquad (5)$$

—the marginal product of labour, dQ/dN, being derived from the production function defined in (4).

Given the various functional relationships—namely, the investment and savings functions in (1), the 'liquidity' functions in (2), the labour-supply function in (3) and the production function in (4)—and given, too, the supply of nominal money as fixed by the monetary authorities, there will be a single set of values of r, Q, p, w and N (the 'unknowns' of the system) which will satisfy the whole set of equations simultaneously. When these values obtain, the economy will be in full equilibrium.

Under the conditions set out above, it appears that the economy can reach equilibrium only at full employment, and that the forces of supply and demand will, in fact, ensure that such an equilibrium is attained.[1] But this is not to say that the best way of achieving full employment is merely to leave p and w to vary to whatever extent is needed to give Q_1 and N_1. Such changes are likely to take time, and may entail awkward readjustments of the pattern of relative prices and wages; falling prices, too, tend to reduce business optimism and thereby diminish investment-demand. Instead of waiting for prices to fall from p_2 to p_1, the monetary authority could expand the supply of nominal money, so as to push the monetary–equilibrium curve to the right; an increase from M_1 to M_2, giving $L(M_2/p_2)$ in place of the $L(M_1/p_1)$ shown in Fig. 24, would move aggregate demand from Q_2 to Q_1 just as effectively as a fall in prices would have done. Money-wages must still fall to the level at which real wages are $(w/p)_1$, but with prices unchanged at p_2 the reduction in w will be less than would have been needed if prices had simultaneously fallen to p_1. It would, indeed, be possible even to avoid reducing money-wages, if the monetary authority is willing to expand the nominal money-supply beyond M_2: initially, this would push the monetary–equilibrium curve so far to the right as to intersect the IS-curve beyond the level of full-employment output Q_1, with the result that prices would begin to rise; with w unchanged, this would automatically reduce real wages towards the $(w/p)_1$ level, while it would also cause the quantity of real money to fall until equilibrium was attained with a new monetary–equilibrium curve $L(M_3/p_3)$ taking the place of $L(M_1/p_1)$ and intersecting the IS-curve at R.

A policy of this kind might be called for where it was known that trades unions would effectively resist any reduction in money-wages, but would take no action (because of money illusion) if rising prices caused *real* wages to fall. (In this case, the labour-supply function given in (3) above will no longer be sufficient to describe market behaviour: in addition to $N = N(w/p)$, an extra condition

$$w \geqslant w_0 \qquad . \qquad . \qquad . \qquad . \qquad (3a)$$

will be needed to indicate that money-wages will remain at the minimum level w_0 except when market conditions call for higher values of w—when the original function (3) will once more apply.) The rise of prices to p_3 will then be merely a once-for-all adjustment in order to reduce real wages to $(w/p)_1$ (equal to w_0/p_3); no further

---

[1] Provided, however, that there are no time-lags long enough to prevent the adjustment process being completed before the parameters of the system (e.g. the stock of capital) have altered, or before some exogenous change has produced a fresh disequilibrium; and that the adjustment is not itself complicated by expectational factors—for example, by the possibility that buyers, thinking that price-reductions will continue, respond to a fall in p by cutting expenditure.

change will be needed when full-employment equilibrium has been reached. If, however, the original situation had come about because unions had forced a rise in money-wages with the express purpose of keeping real wages at $(w/p)_2$, every subsequent increase in p will give rise to a claim for a compensating increase in w, and a 'wage-price spiral' will develop. (Here, instead of condition (3a) above, a new formulation

$$w/p \geqslant (w/p)_0 \qquad \cdots \qquad \cdots \qquad (3b)$$

is needed to indicate that *real* wages will not be allowed to fall below a minimum level.) Under these circumstances, if the monetary authority were to stabilize the quantity of nominal money in order to halt the increase in prices, the real wage would remain at $(w/p)_2$, unemployment equal to FG would persist, the interest-rate would be r_2, and output and employment would be Q_2 and N_2 respectively. The prevailing unemployment would be prevented from forcing a reduction in money-wages, and the economy would now settle into a position of 'under-employment equilibrium'.[1]

This is not, however, the only possible situation in which the economy might be unable to reach full-employment equilibrium. Even if wages and prices were completely flexible, it might happen that the IS-curve was inelastic to the rate of interest, and lay wholly to the left of Q_1 in Fig. 24's Quadrant I; or that, no matter how much the quantity of nominal money was increased, the intersection of the IS-curve with the $L(M/p)$-curve would still lie to the left of Q_1 along the horizontal section of $L(M/p)$—the 'liquidity trap'—corresponding to the minimum interest-rate r_0. These, of course, are the two possibilities already discussed in the last chapter[2] in connection with Fig. 23. Either of them will give rise to a downward 'wage-price spiral'. As unemployment causes money-wages to fall, real wages will be pushed down and firms will be induced to increase supply—but because aggregate demand cannot increase, the excess supply will merely force the price-level down; real wages will rise again, only to be further reduced when the pressure of unemployment causes another reduction in money-wages. In these conditions, downward inflexibility of money-wages could be positively advantageous: the economy would still suffer from unemployment, of course, but it would at least avoid continuous price-deflation.

---

[1] The diagrammatic equivalent of condition (3b) above is the suppression of the part of SS to the right of G in Fig. 24's Quadrant III, and its replacement by the vertical broken line between G and the (w/p)-axis. This assumes that trade unions are strong enough to insist on *prompt* increases in w whenever p rises.

[2] See pp. 264–5 above.

Against this, it might be argued that if prices only fall far enough, the 'Pigou effect' is certain sooner or later to shift the *IS*-curve sufficiently to the right to intersect $L(M/p)$ above the full-employment level of output Q_1. As the real value of cash balances grows, their owners will feel more and more disposed to increase the proportion of income they spend on consumption; the *OS*-curve of Fig. 22 will move gradually closer to the vertical axis, so that each level of r will be associated with a higher real income, and Fig. 24's *IS*-curve will consequently shift to the right. If the price-level were prevented from falling by the downward inflexibility of wages, the Pigou effect would be unable to work, and the economy would be left with chronic unemployment; so any policy measures which break down the rigidity of money-wages are, after all, to be welcomed.

However, prices may have to fall a long way before the Pigou effect becomes strong enough to eliminate unemployment, and in the meantime certain other effects will be at work in the opposite direction. If everyone assumes that price-reductions are going to continue, the prospective rise in the real value of cash-holdings may induce people to try to increase their present holdings by saving more—so Fig. 22's *OS*-curve will swing further away from the vertical axis, and Fig. 24's *IS*-curve will shift to the left; aggregate demand will fall, and output and employment will be reduced. Business firms contemplating investment projects will expect future yields to decline in money terms because of the downward trend of prices, and this will depress their estimates of the rate of return on the capital-assets they could buy at present prices;[1] the *MEI*-curve will move to the left, Fig. 24's *IS*-curve will be shifted leftwards, and output and employment will fall. The eventual outcome will depend on whether the Pigou effect, which will be getting stronger and stronger as the price-level falls, at last becomes so strong that it more than offsets the expectational effects just described: if it does, aggregate demand will expand to the full-employment level and money-wages and prices will have no further reason to fall. However, the very fact that prices have been stabilized is likely to cause expectations to be revised. If no one any longer thinks that prices will fall in the future,

---

[1] In terms of the *MEI* formula

$$P = \frac{A_1}{1+r} + \frac{A_2}{(1+r)^2} + \frac{A_3}{(1+r)^3} + \ldots + \frac{A_n}{(1+r)^n}$$

given on p. 151 above, this means that the As will all be reduced in money terms in proportion to their distance ahead in the future; but since P is expressed at current prices, the equation can be satisfied only by a lower value of r (where r is the *MEI*) than would have emerged if prices were expected to remain unchanged.

investment-demand will revive, the proportion of income saved will fall even further than the level to which the Pigou effect has brought it, and aggregate demand will expand *beyond* the full-employment level; this will cause prices and money-wages to rise again, setting the expectational and Pigou effects into reverse, and continuing until the reduction in the stock of real money moves the $L(M/p)$-curve far enough to the left to intersect the IS-curve at the full-employment level of Q. Thus, if wage-flexibility does not lead to continuous deflation, it may nevertheless give rise to considerable instability of the price-level.

Additional complications may be introduced by the 'redistribution effect' described in Chapter Ten.[1] If the share of wages in total income falls when real wages are reduced, the proportion of income saved will increase if the MPC of wage-earners exceeds that of profit-recipients, and the IS-curve will shift to the left. Accordingly, the fall in real wages from $(w/p)_2$ to $(w/p)_1$, which was seen to be necessary to bring about full employment, will involve a greater reduction in money-wages and prices than would otherwise have been needed. The price-level must not only fall from p_2 to p_1—that is, enough to make the monetary-equilibrium curve cut the original IS-curve at R; it must fall still further, so as to push the $L(M/p)$-curve far enough to the right to compensate for the fact that IS has been shifted to the left by the redistribution effect. Provided that it is still possible for the IS and $L(M/p)$ curves to intersect above Q_1, full-employment equilibrium will still be reached, though at a rate of interest lower than the r_1 which would have prevailed if IS had not been displaced; but if the shift of IS has carried it so far to the left that it cuts $L(M/p)$ at a point to the left of Q_1 even at the minimum interest-rate r_0, it will be only through the Pigou effect—if at all—that full-employment equilibrium is reached.

In this last situation, as in earlier ones, the essential reason for the economy's difficulties in reaching full employment lay in the inadequacy of investment-demand relatively to the desire to save; because of this, the IS-curve was positioned so far to the left that neither price-reductions nor the expansion of the supply of nominal money were able to make the $L(M/p)$-curve cut it above Q_1. The implication for government policy is obvious: it should take action to shift IS to the right. If public goods-and-services expenditures are regarded as 'collective consumption'[2] (C_g) financed by the taxation of factor incomes (T_y), saving may be re-defined as

$$S = Y - C_p - C_g = Y(1-c) + cT_y - C_g$$

---

[1] See pp. 222–3 above.   [2] See p. 59 above.

where C_p is private consumption (equal to $c(Y-T_y)$), and c is the MPC; if $(1-c)$ is replaced by s (the Marginal Propensity to Save), the expression becomes

$$S = sY+(1-s)T_y-C_g$$

so that saving now consists of an 'induced' element, sY, and an 'autonomous' one, $(1-s)T_y-C_g$, which will, of course, be zero if the amount of 'collective consumption' C_g is exactly equal to the reduction in private consumption $(1-s)T_y$ brought about by taxation. By increasing C_g, or reducing T_y, or by a mixture of both,[1] the government could reduce the autonomous element, thereby pushing Fig. 22's OS-curve vertically downwards and linking each level of r with a higher level of real income; the IS-curve of Fig. 24 would then shift to the right. This is, of course, merely another way of expressing the possibilities of budgetary policy already outlined in Chapter Nine. However, the analysis of the present chapter will have shown that there is one case in which budgetary policy of this kind might turn out to be inappropriate and ineffective—namely, that in which trade unions' policy is to maintain a minimum *real* wage higher than the level consistent with full employment. Just as the expansion of the supply of nominal money would then bring about a wage-price spiral, so also would the rightward shift of the IS-curve merely create an excess of aggregate demand over supply, which would tend to force the price-level upwards while failing to secure full employment.

(b) Liquid assets, financial intermediaries, and monetary policy

In Fig. 24 above, a number of separate equilibrium conditions were brought together into a 'system' in which the supply and demand of commodities, labour, and money are mutually inter-dependent: a change in any one of the variables is likely to affect each of the others. However, the model is still highly simplified. Its most obvious limitation, perhaps, is that it is *static*: it shows the balance of forces in the economy at a given moment of time, without regard to what has happened in the past or what is to come. If the system were to move forward through time, it would be necessary

---

[1] A further possibility would be to introduce, or increase, 'income transfers' such as social security benefits. The definition of saving would then become

$$S = sY+(1-s)(Ty-Tr)-C_g$$

where Tr represents such transfers; an increase in Tr has the same effect as a reduction in Ty, subject to the qualifications noted on pp. 210–11 above.

to allow for the fact that investment will be gradually increasing the stock of capital, so that the production function of Quadrant II will be moved steadily upwards and to the right; any given level of employment will yield a larger and larger output of goods and services. The movement will be quickened by technical progress— i.e. by improvements in production methods, in the design of capital equipment and in the degree and diffusion of labour skills. Population-growth will cause a gradual downward shift of the labour-supply curve in Quadrant III, while any change in the slope of the production function will cause the *MPL*-curve to move; between them, these changes will alter the equilibrium of the labour market. These effects will be examined in a later chapter.

The second limitation of the analysis centring on Fig. 24 is the result of the assumption (made on p. 246 above) that the only kind of 'paper' asset available as an alternative to money is a single type of irredeemable fixed-interest bond. In reality, of course, there are many different kinds of non-money paper assets. There are, for example, building-society deposits; bonds redeemable within a number of years, as well as irredeemable ones; bills of exchange; company shares; and many others.

In the model specified earlier the bonds were illiquid, since owning them entailed the risk of capital loss; the only way to avoid this risk was to hold money, so that 'liquidity-preference' could be taken to be synonymous with the demand for money. But where there is a wide range of assets to choose from, the illiquidity of one type can be avoided by holding a more liquid one—which need not, however, be the most liquid of all. A wealth-holder can obtain a given degree of liquidity in his portfolio of assets by making an appropriate selection from *all* the available kinds of assets—£x of money, *plus* £y worth of short-term bonds, *plus* £z worth of shares, and so on. If he should come to desire a higher degree of liquidity, he can get it by selling some of his bonds and acquiring (say) building-society deposits in their place, without altering his holding of money at all. Though money is still the only means of effecting transactions, it is far from being the only means of satisfying 'liquidity-preference'.

One way of allowing for this would be to change the meaning assigned to the *LL*-curve in Fig. 19. Instead of representing the asset-demand for money, it could be made to represent the demand for *all* liquid assets. Instead of measuring money, the horizontal scale would have to be regarded as measuring quantities of liquid assets, and the interest-rate measured on the vertical scale would be an average of the yields on illiquid assets (e.g. long-term bonds), the interest on near-money itself being ignored. The *LL*-curve would then imply that the 'long rate' (as the interest on illiquid long-term assets may be called for brevity) depends on the quantity of liquid assets available—and the latter may, of course, change without the quantity of money itself changing. An increase in the supply of Treasury Bills, for example, will mean that there are more liquid assets in existence than the community wishes to hold at the hitherto prevailing 'long rate'; to restore equilibrium, the long rate must fall until the growing fear of future capital loss causes the demand for liquid assets to rise to equality with the supply of them.

From the original interpretation of Fig. 19 (that is, with LL representing the asset-demand for money only) it appeared that control of the money-supply gave the authorities the power to set the interest-rate at any desired level above the minimum r_0; with this power, they could determine real income and the price-level, subject to various limitations regarding the interest-elasticity of investment, the state of the labour market and the flexibility of money-wages and prices. Now, however, it seems that control of the money-supply may not be enough. A reduction in the quantity of money, intended to raise the long-term interest rate, could be offset by an increase in the quantity of other liquid assets, while a fall in the latter could raise the long rate even when the money-supply is being increased. The authorities have to think in terms of influencing the supply of liquid assets in general, as well as of controlling the supply of money in particular. In this, they are helped by the fact that some of the most important non-money liquid assets are government obligations—chiefly three-month Treasury Bills. By replacing Treasury Bills with long-term bonds (that is, by the procedure known as 'funding', which lengthens the average maturity of the National Debt) the authorities can reduce the outstanding volume of liquid assets, while by the reverse procedure they can increase it; 'debt management', i.e. action to change the composition of the public debt as distinct from its total amount, is thus a vital aspect of monetary policy.

However, merely to change the meaning attached to Fig. 19's LL-curve, in the way suggested above, is not a very satisfactory way of handling the 'liquidity-preference' of an economy where there are many types of paper assets other than money. It implies that a hard-and-fast line separates assets which are 'liquid' from those which are not, though the least liquid of the former may actually differ very little from the most liquid of the latter; and it furnishes only one interest-rate, which is an average of those of the arbitrarily selected 'illiquid assets'. In fact, there will exist a *system* of interest-rates, which will be in equilibrium when the quantity demanded of each type of asset is exactly equal to the quantity in existence. Rates will vary according to the relative liquidity of the assets: where two of them differ only in degree of liquidity, higher interest will be needed to persuade the owners of the less liquid one to go on holding it instead of exchanging it for the other. When the quantity of a particular asset rises, the initial effect will be to reduce its price and raise its rate of yield; this will attract an inflow of demand at the expense of other assets, whose prices will fall in consequence, while that of the first is made to rise part of the way back toward its original level; the eventual outcome will be a realignment of the whole interest-rate structure. How widespread these repercussions will be depends on the readiness of wealth-holders to switch from one asset to another, and on certain institutional factors (such as the fact that some assets, such as Treasury Bills, are in high denominations—the smallest is £5,000—so that individuals do not normally hold them; or the commercial banks' need to maintain their reserve ratios, which reduces their ability to exchange short for long-term assets in response to favourable long-term interest-rates). For many assets, there probably exists a solid core of holdings which their owners will not relinquish even when alternatives become a good deal more attractive, and this will limit the overspill of demand from one asset-market to another.

In such realignments of interest-rates, those on illiquid assets change less than those on the more liquid ones. For an irredeemable bond yielding £4 per annum, a fall in the market rate of interest from 4% to 3% means a rise in price from £100 to £133; an increase in interest from 4% to 5% will reduce the market price from £100 to £80. By contrast, a bond which is redeemable in one year's time[1] will rise in price from £100 to just under £101 when market interest falls from 4% to 3%, while an increase in the interest-rate from 4% to 5%

---

[1] The relationship of bond prices and yields is given approximately by the formula

$$r = \frac{iN + \dfrac{N-P}{n}}{P}$$

where r is the yield (i.e. the 'market rate' of interest), i is the 'nominal' interest-rate, N is the nominal value of the bond, P is the market price, and n is the number of years from now to the redemption date. The $(N-P)/n$ term in the formula is a rough measure of the annual capital gain or loss which results from buying a bond at less or more than its nominal value, when the latter is the amount for which it will be redeemed at maturity. The smaller the value of n, the larger the value of $(N-P)/n$ and the greater its importance relatively to the 'flat yield' iN/p. In the case of an irredeemable bond, n equals infinity so that the $(N-P)/n$ term vanishes; the formula then reduces to that given in footnote 1 on p. 246 above.

will cause the price to fall from £100 to only £99. For the 'short' bond, interest-changes have to be very great to alter its capital value very much, whereas the market value of 'long' bonds can swing widely in response to quite small movements in interest. What the market regards as the highest and lowest possible long-term bond prices will thus mark out a fairly narrow band of interest-rates— say 2½% to 8%. If the long-term rate were 8% (implying a price of £50 for the irredeemable bond just mentioned) a subsequent rise in price might seem so certain that many holders of short bonds would try to switch into 'longs', and the diversion of demand from the short bond market would send the prices of 'shorts' down; but the latter need only reach £96 for the rate on one-year bonds to become 8·3%, at which it would be higher than the long rate—though the more liquid asset would normally be expected to yield a lower rate of interest than the less liquid one. At the other extreme, a high price of 'longs' would switch demand *into* the short bond market, forcing the price of short bonds up; but a price of £103, for a one-year bond yielding £4 per annum, would mean that the interest-rate was below 1%. Thus, given the state of expectations about the normal level of long-term rates, the interest-rate structure will be tethered between fairly narrow limits at its illiquid end, while rates at the liquid end will show wider variations.

It follows that when the authorities wish to pull up long-term interest rates they must be ready to let short rates rise a long way— indeed, the Bank of England must give a lead by raising its own Bank Rate drastically. But high short rates have certain disadvantages: they raise the interest-cost of the government's own short-term borrowing, which is substantial; and to the extent that short-term obligations are owned by foreign residents, the flow of current payments to the rest of the world is increased. These considerations may weaken the authorities' resolution, and may induce them to turn to direct controls of various kinds—directives to the banks to reduce lending, controls on hire-purchase terms, or the introduction of some new device such as the Special Deposits scheme of 1958. On the other hand, if they can create the conviction that the 'normal' level of long-term rates will be higher in the future than it has been in the past, the less will be the displacement of short-term rates which results from the inter-market movements described above.

The authorities' task may be made easier by another factor. Once long-term interest-rates begin to rise, the market prices of long-term bonds and other illiquid assets will be falling; if their owners sell them now, they will sustain capital losses. The only way to avoid loss is to retain the assets until interest-rates fall again and bond prices recover; in the meantime, the owners are 'locked in' to their asset-holdings. Thus, business firms will be unwilling to finance new investment by the sale of bonds; individuals, too, are likely to postpone expenditures which they would have to finance by the sale of securities. The most important 'lock-in' effect may, however, be that on financial intermediaries such as banks, which will find that the liquidity of their balance-sheet position has been reduced, as a result of which they will be less willing to lend. This will cause a reduction in the availability of credit as a result of the rise in interest-rates; even if higher rates do not themselves discourage borrowers, the reduced willingness of lenders to lend will frustrate the demand for loans.

This aspect of monetary policy was emphasized by the Radcliffe Committee, which considered that 'monetary action works upon total demand by altering the liquidity position of financial institutions and of firms and people desiring to spend on real resources',[1] and that to alter the 'liquidity position' the authorities 'have to regard the structure of interest rates rather than the supply of money as the centre-piece of the monetary mechanism'.[2] In terms of the earlier argument of this chapter, this is equivalent to saying that though the *IS*-curve of Fig. 24 may be vertical because investment-demand is inelastic to the interest-rate, investment-demand may nevertheless be reduced by the failure of firms to obtain finance.

But business firms and individuals do not usually hold large enough quantities of financial assets for this 'lock-in' effect to work on them very strongly; and the financial intermediaries which may be affected by the 'Radcliffe effect'[3] can only be those which are already established and in possession of long-term bonds whose capital value can be reduced. If an excess of demand over supply of credit were to persist at high interest-rates, there would be an incentive for *new* lending institutions to enter the field. By offering high borrowing-rates, they would attract idle money-balances which they could proceed to lend at still higher rates to borrowers who had been unable to obtain credit through the usual channels, and to the extent that they were successful in doing this, they would be thwarting the monetary authorities' purpose of making credit scarcer as well as dearer. Admittedly, such institutions are unlikely to be created over-night in response to a temporary increase in the level of interest-rates;

[1] Cmnd. 827, p. 135.   [2] *Ibid.*, p. 183.

[3] Also called (in the United States) the 'Roosa effect', after Robert V. Roosa who first described it in his 'Interest Rates and the Central Bank', in *Money, Trade and Economic Growth; Essays in Honor of J. H. Williams* (1951). For criticisms in the U.S. context, see W. L. Smith, 'On the Effectiveness of Monetary Policy', *American Economic Review*, Sept. 1956.

but in so far as there is already a tendency for non-bank financial intermediaries to grow faster than the commercial banks through which monetary policy works, the former will frequently be in a position to reduce the effectiveness of monetary control.[1]

When fiscal policy was under consideration in Chapter Nine, it was noted[2] that changes in taxation and expenditure take time to affect the working of the economy, and that measures which would be perfectly appropriate in the absence of lags may actually turn out to be de-stabilizing. The same can be said of monetary policy. The authorities are continuously reviewing and analysing the situation of the economy, but there will inevitably be some kind of interval between the emergence of a need for policy-changes and their recognition of that need. A further lag will ensue between the authorities' 'pulling the levers' (e.g. undertaking open market operations and changing Bank Rate) and the consequential changes in commercial bank deposits and interest rates; while the economy's response to these changes, for example through the modification of investment plans in the light of increased interest-rates and reduced availability of credit, will take still more time. Meanwhile, many other things may be happening: expectations about future interest-rates and prices may be changing, investment-intentions may be revised for reasons unconnected with the higher cost of finance, and so on; the greater the lapse of time involved, the more complicated and unforeseeable will be the outcome of the initial policy-measures. Some economists, indeed, consider that because the overall lag is likely to be very long, attempts to control the economy by monetary measures could be dangerously de-stabilizing, and should therefore not be undertaken.[3] This view is at the opposite extreme from the

[1] The argument that the expansion of NFBIs has impaired the effectiveness of traditional monetary control has been particularly associated with the names of J. G. Gurley and E. S. Shaw; see their 'Financial Aspects of Economic Development', *American Economic Review*, Sept. 1955.

[2] See above, p. 212.

[3] The best-known proponent of this view is Professor Milton Friedman: see, for example, his 'The Lag in Effect of Monetary Policy', *Journal of Political Economy*, Oct. 1961. He argues (in the context of the U.S. economy) that the lag may be as long as eighteen months, so that when current policy measures finally come to exert their effect on the economy they will have the character of random disturbances; his conclusion is that the monetary authorities should not be allowed to operate a 'discretionary' policy (i.e. a policy of trying to manage the economy by the frequent adjustment of monetary variables in the light of their own judgement of the exigencies) but should be instructed merely to maintain a prescribed rate of growth of the money-supply, the rate being chosen to match the long-run growth-rate of the economy. For a criticism of Friedman's argument, see J. H. Kareken and R. M. Solow, 'Lags in Monetary Policy', in *Stabilization Policies*, ed. E. Cary Brown, for the Commission on Money and Credit (1963).

more traditional conception of monetary policy, which paid little attention to lags and assumed that the weapons at the authorities' disposal would produce an almost instantaneous effect on the level of activity; but while it is right to reject this over-sanguine view, the majority of economists would probably agree that time-lags are not so long as to make the weapons too dangerous to use. The existence of lags does, however, mean that great skill is required in the exercise of monetary policy.

The arguments put forward in this chapter suggest that there is a good deal of scope for the use of monetary policy in controlling the economy, but that it would be unwise to expect too much of it. Control of the supply of money, debt management, and the application of direct controls over lending, may be highly efficacious in some situations but relatively useless in others, depending on the interest-elasticity of investment, the policies of employers and unions in determining prices and wages, the state of opinion as to 'normal' interest-rates, expectations of further increases in the general price-level, and the rate at which output is growing. With a favourable conjunction of all these factors, monetary policy will be effective in checking excessive demand or in preventing unemployment; the occasions when *all* of the necessary conditions are satisfied are likely to be few, but so also will be the occasions when *none* of them are; since the usual situation is likely to be between these extremes, monetary measures will at most times exert a relatively mild influence.

This may seem a disappointing—perhaps even alarming—conclusion when it is put beside that reached at the end of Chapter Nine, namely that fiscal measures may sometimes be unable to control the economy. If neither monetary nor fiscal weapons can be surely relied on, it is possible that in certain situations the authorities will be unable to manage the economy at all: it will be like a disobedient dog which has slipped its leash and refuses to answer the whistle. But it is perhaps salutory to recognize that governments may occasionally be powerless, and to reflect that this may be part of the price of certain freedoms which the community thinks valuable; and since, in any case, the 'conjuncture' of the economy is constantly changing, the authorities may need only to wait a little for control to become possible again.

Kareken and Solow provide alternative estimates of the relevant lags in the United States, showing how they are distributed over time; for example, they find that a little less than half of the overall response of investment-demand to interest-changes can be expected to occur within three months, another quarter of the response within the next three months, another sixth within the next half-year, and so on.

CHAPTER THIRTEEN

Inflation

(a) Definition and measurement

When the conditions of a full-employment equilibrium were presented in the last chapter, much attention was given to the possibility that the economy might under-fulfil them, with the result that output would fall short of the full-employment level, while prices and money-wages, if 'flexible downwards', would fall. But this is not the kind of disequilibrium which has been typical of the years since World War II: in most countries, the problems facing fiscal and monetary policy-makers have not been large-scale 'demand-deficiency' unemployment and falling money-values, but—on the contrary—a continuous and seemingly irresistible upward movement of prices. In Britain, the rate of increase was not especially fast in the 1950s and 1960s, but accelerated noticeably in the mid-seventies. Retail prices rose at an average rate of 3% a year between 1953 and 1962 and 3·3% between 1963 and 1968, but the pace then quickened from 5·4% in 1969 to 16% in 1974 and 24·2% in 1975; prices more than doubled between 1968 and 1975.[1]

In the decade between 1965 and 1975, therefore, Britain passed from a condition of 'creeping' inflation (which can be said to exist when prices are rising at annual rates of 6% or less) to one of 'trotting' inflation (when the rate of increase is between 15% and 30%). Both types can be distinguished from 'galloping' (or 'hyper') inflation, which exists when prices are rising at annual rates of 50%, 100% or even more. It is often assumed that creeping inflation must eventually accelerate through the 'trotting' stage until it is 'galloping' at ever faster rates, with the process culminating in the collapse of the

[1] For comparisons with other countries, see the table of consumer price index numbers in the United Nations *Monthly Bulletin of Statistics*. Britain's price-level is shown as having risen by 84·4% between 1970 and 1975. By contrast, prices in Germany rose only 34·7% over the same period; in the USA they rose 38·6%, in France 52·8% and in Japan 72·4%. Though all countries experienced inflation during the 1970–5 period, Britain's was noticeably faster than that of other major countries. The most rapid inflation in these years was in Chile, where prices rose 27,652%; Argentina, with 1,102%, came second.

currency and the disruption of economic life; but although this has
certainly happened in some cases (the most spectacular being those
of Germany in 1923, Hungary in 1947 and China in 1949), there are
enough counter-examples of strong but non-accelerating inflations
(such as those of Brazil, Argentina and certain other Latin American
countries in the 'fifties and 'sixties) to show that acceleration and
collapse are by no means inevitable.[1]

The word 'inflation' has so far been used in its everyday sense of
'rising prices', but it should be noted that this is by no means the
only meaning which has been given it in the past. To old-fashioned
Quantity Theorists, for instance, it was synonymous with an increase
in the quantity of money: on the extreme assumptions of fixed velocity and transactions, such an increase would necessarily raise the
price-level, but the latter would be the *effect* of inflation, not the
thing itself. A similar distinction has often been made by Keynesian
writers, who have defined inflation as an excess of aggregate demand
over supply in conditions of full employment: in a closed economy
with low levels of stocks and no institutional barriers to price-
increases, this will certainly cause prices to rise—but it is the excess
demand which is the inflation, the increase in prices being merely
the symptom which indicates its existence. However, excess demand
need not lead to increases in the price-level: in an open economy it
could be met by expanding imports, so that as long as it was possible
to finance a balance-of-trade deficit the price-level would remain
unchanged. Also, as will be argued later, a sustained upward movement of prices could be brought about by causes other than excess
demand at full employment, and it would surely be anomalous to
refuse to call it inflation on the ground that no excess demand was
present. For these reasons, it is desirable to have a definition which
refers directly to the phenomenon to be explained—i.e. the rise in
prices—rather than to any of its possible causes; so in what follows,
the word 'inflation' will, much as in everyday speech, be used to
mean no more than a continuing increase in the general price-level.

This is not to say that *every* rise in prices is to be regarded as inflationary. A current increase might be merely one of a series of slight
up-and-down movements round a constant level, or it might accom-
pany a short-run expansion of output as the level of capacity utilization is increased;[2] yet again, it might be a once-for-all adjustment

---

[1] In Brazil, for example, prices increased at the following annual rates during
the nineteen-fifties: in 1952, 25%; in 1953, 20%; in 1954, 19%; in 1955, 20%;
in 1956, 21·7%; in 1957, 19·2%; in 1958, 14·9%.

[2] In Fig. 15 above (p. 224) an increase in aggregate demand from OD_1 to OD_2
caused the intersection with the aggregate supply curve to move from R to T,

to some change in the economy's external situation—for example, it may have become necessary to switch to a new source of imports whose prices are higher than those of the country whose supplies are no longer available. In each of these cases, the rise in prices will lack the chronic, self-sustaining character of inflation, though it might, of course, be difficult in practice to be sure that it was merely a short-run adjustment and not the beginning of an inflationary trend. A very different situation would be one in which inflationary price-increases are prevented (for the time being, anyway) by government controls; this would be 'suppressed' inflation, as distinct from the 'open' inflation which would have existed in the absence of government intervention. Here, too, the definition of inflation in terms of rising prices will no longer be satisfactory. But these are exceptional cases: in all others, the normal usage will be perfectly applicable.

To determine the rate at which inflation is proceeding, it is necessary to decide which of the available index-numbers of prices is the most appropriate indicator. Should it be the index of consumer prices, or that of wholesale prices? Should it be an 'implicit GNP deflator' which includes the prices of all 'final' commodities entering GNP? The trouble is that each index may give a different measure of the rate of inflation; there may even be times when one of them rises while others show no change, so that the diagnosis of inflation would depend on which index was being used as the criterion. Moreover, even if all the various index-numbers are moving exactly in step with one another, it is possible for them to overstate the rate of price-increase because of bias due to their construction: for example, when a cheap new commodity replaces an old one in consumers' expenditure, an index of consumer prices may nevertheless continue to include that of the old commodity at its 'base year' weight, while excluding that of the new one because it was not available in the base year; and if the old commodity has gone up in price because it is now bought in quantities too small to justify large-scale production, the index will show a rise in the general price-level which is out of line with the real state of affairs. There may consequently be some doubt at times, not only about the speed with which inflation is going forward, but even as to whether it is occurring at all. However, when *all* price-indices are continuing to rise month by month and year by year at annual rates of 4% or more, it will be beyond

---

so that the price level rose from p_1 (the slope of OR) to p_2 (the slope of OT). Given constant money-wages and appropriate changes in the money supply, this price-increase would merely reflect the transition from one short-run equilibrium situation to another; once prices reached p_2 there would be no reason for them to rise further.

dispute that inflation is under way; and the faster it goes, the less noticeable will be the discrepancies between the different indices and the less important will be the effect of bias.[1]

The fact that price-movements are measured in terms of percentage changes per month, quarter or year underlines a most important characteristic of inflation, namely that it is a process which unfolds itself over *time*. For people who have to live in an inflationary economy, it makes a great deal of difference whether the price-level is rising at 5%, 15%, or 50% per annum: a pensioner, for example, will suffer hardship if the real value of his income is falling at 5% a year, but it will be tolerable compared with his suffering if the rate is 50%. Under mild inflation, economic behaviour will not be very different from what it would have been with a constant price-level; but when prices are rising fast, much effort will be diverted to finding ways of avoiding loss and if possible profiting from the situation, with the result that resources are likely to be allocated less efficiently than they would otherwise have been—for example, through attempts to accumulate stocks (as an alternative to holding cash) well above the level which would have been aimed at under normal circumstances. The analysis must therefore explain not only what caused the inflationary process to get under way in the first place, but also why it is going forward at (say) 10% a year rather than 5% or 25%; it must take account of the time-lags which occur in it, and allow for the effects of concomitant changes such as the expansion of productive capacity through investment and technological improvements; in other words, it must be dynamic. However, the static analysis centring on Fig. 24 (p. 268 in the last chapter) will be relevant and useful in showing the various ways in which the inflationary process can be set in motion to begin with.

(b) 'Demand' inflation

The first of these has already been briefly described in Chapter Ten (pp. 226–7), and even more briefly in Chapter Three (pp. 55–7 above). An autonomous increase in aggregate demand will at first cause physical output to rise, if it was below full-employment level initially; given fixed money-wages and diminishing returns to labour, some increase in prices will occur as output expands; if, when the latter reaches its full-employment limit, aggregate demand is still excessive, an 'inflationary gap' will exist and the price-level will continue to

---

[1] On the question of the definition and measurement of inflation—and indeed on all other aspects of it—see M. Bronfenbrenner and F. D. Holtzman, 'A Survey of Inflation Theory', *American Economic Review*, Sept. 1963, pp. 593–661; and H. G. Johnson, *Essays in Monetary Economics* (1967), Chap. III.

rise. Some offset to the excess demand may be provided by increasing imports, but it may be supposed that the government will sooner or later take action to limit this; and although excess demand in one sector may be met for the time being by drawing on stocks and switching supplies from other sectors (for example, by diverting goods to the home market which had been intended for export), this will merely generalize the excess demand by diffusing it among all branches of the economy. By causing a proportionate increase in the money-value of full-employment output, the rise in prices will automatically generate an equivalent expansion in the total of money-incomes; far from choking off demand, it will provide the community with the means to spend more—though much will depend, of course, on the way in which the additional money-income is allocated between the different groups of income-recipients. As the newly generated money-income is spent, it will cause prices to rise yet again, generating still more money-income—and so on. The process resembles the working of the Multiplier described in Chapter Six, except that where the latter was concerned with the expansion of output in real terms, the inflationary process increases the value of output only in money terms. Given the shape usually attributed to the short-run consumption function, the 'real' Multiplier is *convergent*, in the sense that the successive increases in aggregate real demand become smaller and smaller until they are negligible and a new equilibrium is attained; under inflation, on the other hand, aggregate demand could be increasing in money terms as fast or even faster than the money-value of output—so that the analogy with the 'real' Multiplier breaks down. None the less, it prompts the question: may the inflationary process be similarly convergent, even though it may be so for different reasons?

The analysis of section (a) in the last chapter (pp. 267 ff.) suggests that the answer is 'yes'—provided that the quantity of 'nominal' money is not allowed to increase. This can be shown with the aid of Fig. 25 below, which is the same kind of three-quadrant diagram as Fig. 24 on p. 268 above. To begin with, full-employment equilibrium exists, with output at Q_1, employment at N_1, and interest, prices, money-wages and the money-supply at r_1, p_1, w_1, and M_1 respectively. This situation is now upset by an autonomous increase in aggregate demand, which shifts the *IS*-curve to the right[1] to a new

---

[1] If the initial change was an autonomous rise in consumer's demand, this will have reduced the propensity to save. In Fig. 22 (p. 262 above) it will have shifted the curve *OS* closer to the vertical income axis. If the original increase was in investment demand, it will have pushed the *MEI* curve further to the right. Either of these effects will in turn cause the *IS* curve to shift to the right.

position IS_2; this intersects the original monetary-equilibrium curve, $L(M_1/p_1)$, above point Q_2 on the output-axis, so that aggregate demand could be satisfied only by a level of output higher than the Q_1 available at full employment. This excess demand in the market

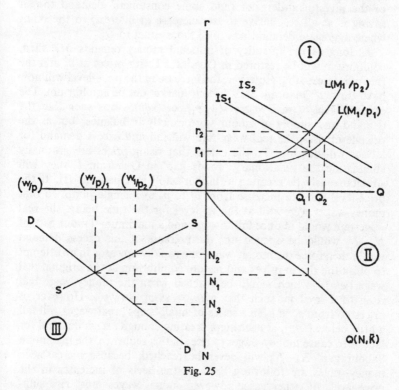

Fig. 25

for goods and services (the 'inflationary gap') will cause the general price-level to rise, thus reducing the purchasing-power of the original stock of nominal money (M_1) and causing the $L(M/p)$-curve to shift to the left. When prices have risen as far as p_2, the monetary-equilibrium curve will have moved to the new position $L(M_1/p_2)$, intersecting the IS_2-curve vertically above Q_1; at this point, aggregate demand will once again be equal to the output forthcoming at full employment, the 'gap' will have been eliminated, and prices will rise no further—the inflationary process will have 'converged' on a new equilibrium. What happened was this: as the price-level rose, the demand for money for transactions purposes increased, leaving less of the existing quantity M_1 available to satisfy asset-demand;

K

the interest-rate increased in order to eliminate enough of the asset-demand (and also of the transactions-demand, since this too is interest-elastic) to bring the total demand for money back into balance with the supply; the rise in the interest-rate choked off some of the investment-demand (and some consumers' demand too, if saving is at all responsive to the increase in interest) to the point where aggregate demand was once more equal to Q_1.

As long as the quantity of nominal money remains M_1, then, equilibrium will be restored in Quadrant I with prices at p_2 and the rate of interest at r_2. However, the increase in the price-level will now have thrown Quadrant III's labour market out of equilibrium. The original level of real wages—(w_1/p_1), or $(w/p)_1$—was such that the demand and supply of labour were exactly in balance; but as the price-level rises, the real wage-rate will fall and excess demand for labour will develop. To the extent that rising prices are gradually eliminating the inflationary 'goods gap' in Quadrant I, they will simultaneously be creating a 'labour gap'[3] in Quadrant III. If the price-level were to increase from p_1 to p_2 in a single jump, so that money-wages were still at the w_1 level for the time being, the real wage-rate would at once fall to w_1/p_2 and a maximum 'labour gap' of $N_3 - N_2$ would be opened up; the pressure of this excess demand would then force the money wage-rate rapidly upwards in an attempt to offset the rise in prices and restore equilibrium at the original real wage $(w/p)_1$—which would be reached when the money wage had risen to a level w_2 such that $w_2/p_2 = w_1/p_1 = (w/p)_1$. However, if prices go from p_1 to p_2 in a series of small 'steps', real wages will fall a little below $(w/p)_1$ at each step, creating enough excess demand for labour to cause money-wages to rise; in this sequence, the maximum 'labour gap' $N_3 - N_2$ will never be reached, because increases in money-wages are following hard on the heels of increases in the price-level. In either case, however, money-wages must rise sufficiently to restore the level of real wages at which labour-market equilibrium is achieved.

An appreciable lag of money-wages behind prices will mean that the real wage-rate is constantly below $(w/p)_1$ as long as the price-level is rising. If the labour-supply curve has the slope of SS in Quadrant

[1] These terms are similar to those introduced by Bent Hansen in his *A Study in the Theory of Inflation* (1951). He, however, speaks of a 'factor gap' rather than a 'labour gap': the latter term is preferred in the present text because labour is the only factor of production whose supply and demand are specified. In so far as the difficulty of obtaining extra labour may lead firms to demand more capital equipment, this will shift Fig. 25's *IS* curve further to the right; the 'capital gap' will give rise to a new 'goods gap'. See also R. Turvey and H. Brems, 'The Factor and Goods Markets', *Economica*, Feb. 1951, pp. 57–68.

III, the number of man-hours for which the labour force is willing to work will be reduced below N_1, and the volume of output will consequently fall below Q_1: this will widen the 'goods gap' of Quadrant I and put additional upward pressure on the price-level. On the other hand, the wage-lag will also mean that labour's share of total income is reduced; if wage-earners have a higher MPC than other income-recipients, aggregate real saving will be increased[1] and the IS-curve will be shifted leftwards from its original position IS_2, causing the 'goods gap' to narrow and to some extent offsetting (perhaps even more than offsetting) the widening which resulted from the fall in the labour-supply. Both effects will, of course, disappear when equilibrium has at last been regained in the labour and goods market.

If the level on which prices eventually converge is a good deal higher than that from which they started, and if it takes some time for the new equilibrium level to be reached, the process of getting there is likely to be complicated by expectational effects. Having been accustomed to price-stability at the p_1 level, individuals and firms may at first assume that the rise in prices will soon be reversed, or at any rate that it will not be followed by further increases; but when the upward movement does, in fact, continue, they will come to count on an upward trend in the future, and this will alter their behaviour in a number of ways.

One effect will be to reduce the demand for money in real terms (i.e. for M/p). The expectation of future reductions in its purchasing-power will create an incentive to economize on the holding of money-balances: if prices rise 5% a year, £100 will be worth only £95·24 (i.e. £100 × 100/105) in terms of what it will buy at the year's end, and the holder will have incurred a real cost of £4·76, in addition to the yield forgone by retaining the money instead of exchanging it for a remunerative asset. It is true that the expected return on fixed-interest loans will also be reduced in real terms by the prospective price-increase: if the current interest-rate happens to be 5%, the £5 receivable on a £100 loan will be just enough to offset the reduction in the real value of both principal and interest if prices rise 5%, so that the 'real' interest-rate will be zero and the holding-cost of the £100 will be no more than the fall in its purchasing power. But when prices are rising, shares and physical assets provide a more attractive alternative to money-holding than do fixed-interest loans (as noted earlier on pp. 253–4), and when the real yields obtainable from such assets are added to the expected fall in the purchasing-power of money, it is evident that the cost of retaining money-balances will

[1] This is the 'redistribution effect' described in Chapter Ten, pp. 222–3 above.

appear to be higher than before—with the result that the demand for them will be reduced. Thus, the current fall in the quantity of 'real' money which is occurring as a result of *actual* price-increases, and which is causing Fig. 25's $L(M/p)$-curve to shift to the left, will be matched to some extent by a reduction in demand due to the expectation of *future* price-increases—so that the leftward movement of the $L(M/p)$-curve will be less than it would otherwise have been. To bring about a new equilibrium in Quadrant I, the *actual* price-level will therefore have to rise further than it would have needed to do in the absence of these expectations.

However, while a given rate of increase in actual prices will be causing the quantity of 'real' money (M/p) to fall continuously over time, the demand for it will go on falling only if the *expected* rate of increase is itself continually increasing. A given rise in the expected rate (say from zero to 5%) will cause a once-for-all reduction in the amount of 'real' money everyone wishes to hold. When firms and individuals have adjusted their balances to the level they think desirable in view of the increased real cost of holding them, there is no reason why they should wish to reduce them any further; they will seek to do so only if they come to expect that prices are going to rise still faster than they had earlier supposed—say by 8% instead of 5%. For the demand for 'real' money to go on falling, then, the rate of expected price-increases must itself be continually increasing. Moreover, demand will not continue to fall in exact proportion to the rise in the rate of expected price-increases. As the increasing real cost of retaining balances causes them to be reduced, the inconvenience of further reductions in them will become greater and greater; as long as money continues to be used at all, there will be some minimum real quantity below which demand cannot fall, since a complete synchronization of receipts and payments can never, in the nature of things, be achieved throughout the whole economy. Thus, the fall in the supply of 'real' money must eventually overtake the fall in demand, with the result that the price-level will at last be stabilized—though at a higher level than would have been reached if price-expectations had remained passive (in the sense that the price-level attained at each stage was expected to remain in force indefinitely). When this position is achieved, and the actual price-level at last ceases to rise, there will be a downward revision of expectations which will now cause the demand for 'real' money to increase; the $L(M/p)$-curve will be shifted to the left, the interest-rate will rise above the level consistent with full-employment equilibrium, and the economy will move into a recession unless the monetary authorities (having up to this point refrained from increasing the quantity of nominal money) now provide whatever increase is needed in the nominal money-supply to satisfy the revived demand for it.

Expectational effects on the *IS*-curve, through changes in investment-demand and in the willingness to save, have already been briefly indicated in Chapter Twelve (on p. 274–5 above)—though the analysis there was concerned not with rising but with falling prices. If business firms believe that prices are going to rise continuously in the foreseeable future, they will expect the stream of prospective net returns from current investment to increase steadily in money terms compared with what it would have been if prices were to remain unchanged. If, in their view, the selling-prices of their products will be going up at the same rate as the prices of their inputs (including the money-wages they will be paying their labour), and if both input and output prices are expected to keep step with the general price-level as it rises, then the prospective *rate* of return on current investment (i.e. the *MEI*) will increase in money terms by exactly enough to offset the expected upward movement of prices, so that it will be unchanged in real terms. However, the expected price-increases will reduce the real cost of financing investment-projects through fixed-interest loans: if the current interest-rate happens to be (say) 6%, and if prices are thought likely to rise continuously at 4% per annum, the cost of borrowing will be (on the firms' reckoning) only 2% in real terms, so that projects which would not have been considered on the assumption of constant future prices will now appear worth undertaking. This will cause Fig. 25's *IS*-curve to shift to the right of the IS_2 position to which the initial increase in aggregate demand had originally moved it, with the result that prices will have to rise further than would otherwise have been necessary in order to make the $L(M/p)$-curve intersect the *IS*-curve above Q_1 in Quadrant I and thereby restore a non-inflationary full-employment equilibrium.

From the point of view of investing business-firms, the prospective rise in prices means that they can look forward to a continuous fall in the real value of the interest payments they will be making; but from the point of view of lenders (if they have price-expectations similar to those of the firms) it means a fall in the real value of their future *receipts*. It follows that, in so far as interest-rates influence saving, the expectation of rising prices will cause a reduction in the propensity to save, and this will reinforce the movement of the *IS*-curve to the right. But making loans at fixed interest is not the only way of employing savings; there are others, such as the purchase of company shares or real property, which yield returns whose money-value rises along with the price-level, and to the extent that savers are able to take advantage of these possibilities they may very well go on saving as high a proportion of income as before—perhaps even increasing it, if they believe that rising prices will enhance the real yield on these assets, for example by bringing them large capital gains as share prices go up. The acquisition of such 'inflation-proof' assets may not, however, be possible for people with low incomes; they may not be purchasable in small quantities, dealing expenses may be high on modest transactions in them, and they may carry risks which cannot be offset by diversification when portfolios are small.[1] Instead of venturing into the share or real estate markets, therefore, the lower income groups are likely to 'hedge' against inflation by accelerating their purchases of consumer durables; this will increase their consumption relatively to income and represent a fall in the propensity to save.[2] If they can count on future increases in their money-incomes (for example, because their money-wages are subject to escalation, or because past experience has made them expect that their wages will rise), it will even pay them to get into debt for this purpose, if finance companies are still prepared to give instalment credit—since the future repayments will fall steadily as a proportion of their incomes.

Thus, the expectation that prices will go on rising will cause the *IS*-curve to lie further to the right than it would have done if expectations had been 'passive', and it will make the 'goods gap' wider than it would otherwise have been. It should be noted that a given rate of expected price-increase will be associated with a given *position* of the *IS*-curve; for the curve to go on moving further and further to the right, it would be necessary for the rate of expected price-increase to be continuously increasing, causing the 'real' interest-rate to go on falling so as to induce more and more investment-demand and less and less saving. In this respect, the response of the *IS*-curve to price-expectations resembles that already observed with regard to the real demand

[1] Even when the average yield on shares of all kinds is rising in line with the price level, there will be some whose yields lag behind and others which race ahead. With ample funds, a buyer can hold a large enough selection to ensure that his overall return is about average; but if he could not afford more than a small holding of the shares of a single company, which through bad luck or management failed to make a profit, he would be worse off than if he had lent at fixed interest.

[2] If it is thought preferable to regard as consumption only the part of the durables' value which is used up during the current year, the remainder will still count as saving (see pp. 18 and 106 above); but it will simultaneously count as investment in 'consumers' capital'—as, indeed, it does in the case of the purchase of a house. Either way, it has the effect of helping to push the *IS* curve further to the right.

for money as it affects the $L(M/p)$-curve. Thus, if prices are rising at a steady 5% per annum, and if everyone expects this rate of increase to be maintained in the future, the position of the IS-curve will be fixed, and the real demand for money will be of a given size relatively to real income and the nominal interest-rate; the only continuing change, in these circumstances, will be the steady fall in the real money-supply M/p brought about by the *actual* rise in the price-level, and this will eventually bring the inflation to an end—always provided, of course, that the quantity of nominal money is not allowed to increase.

If, then, inflation can be made to 'converge' by holding the nominal money-supply constant, what is to prevent the monetary authorities from doing just that? Indeed, why should they not prevent inflation developing in the first place, by actually *reducing* the quantity of nominal money? If, when the initial increase in aggregate demand takes place, they were to reduce M_1 to a lower level M_0 such that $M_0/p_1 = M_1/p_2$, the monetary-equilibrium curve would immediately move to a new position coinciding with the $L(M_1/p_2)$-curve shown in Fig. 25; aggregate demand would balance aggregate supply at the level of output Q_1, there would be no 'goods gap', the labour market would remain in equilibrium at the N_1 level of employment, and the price-level would continue unchanged at p_1. Why not, then, leave it to the monetary authorities to prevent inflation, or at any rate to check it once it has begun?

Unfortunately, such a policy would be much more difficult to apply in practice than it appears to be in the simplified model of Fig. 25, and it could easily be incompatible with the maintenance of full employment. Suppose the authorities were to adopt the simple rule of reducing the nominal money-supply whenever prices begin to rise, and continuing to do so until price-stability is regained; and suppose that the labour market is not the 'competitive' one of Fig. 25's Quadrant III, but (more realistically) one in which trade unions are strong enough to enforce a minimum level of money-wages. An autonomous increase in aggregate demand, occurring when output happens to be below the full-employment level Q_1, will not only cause output to expand but will also cause prices to begin rising well before Q_1 is reached.[4] If the authorities react by immedi-

---

[1] Provided, of course, that there are diminishing returns to labour, as implied by the shape of Quadrant II's production function $Q(N,\bar{K})$. With money-wages fixed, the existence of diminishing returns means that the 'aggregate supply curve' introduced in Chapter Ten will have the upward-curving shape of the curve in Fig. 13, so that higher levels of output are associated with higher price levels: see pp. 216–8 above.

ately reducing the nominal money-supply, with the result that the interest-rate rises sufficiently to choke back aggregate demand to its original level, prices and output will both remain the same as before;[1] price-stability will have been maintained at the cost of preventing any reduction in unemployment. On the other hand, a policy of permitting prices to rise as long as employment is less than full, and reducing the nominal money-supply only when excess demand at Q_1 is forcing up the price-level in an unambiguously inflationary manner, would require the authorities to know precisely what level of employment *is* 'full'—and this, as has already been argued in Chapter Four,[2] may be very difficult where there is a large amount of frictional unemployment due to current changes in the structure of the economy. Moreover, the authorities' task is one which continues endlessly through time: as the stock of capital grows and technology gradually improves, the full-employment level of output will be increasing and the real demand for money associated with it at any given interest-rate will be growing; external disturbances, changes in payments habits and variations in the pattern of relative prices will also be altering the amount of nominal money needed to satisfy the demand for it at any given price-level; the authorities will not only be making constant adjustments from day to day and week to week, but will also have to consider the rate of growth in the money-supply likely to be needed over the next twelve months or more. For these purposes, no simple rule can be laid down: the authorities must run a continuing analysis of the situation as it develops, and alter the nominal money-supply whenever and to whatever extent they think proper in the circumstances. This will raise all the problems of timing noted in Chapter Twelve (on pp. 282–3 above) as well as involving the possibility of errors of judgement, with the result that monetary restriction may either be so severe as to 'overkill' the inflation and cause recession, or else be too late so that the price-level goes on rising after all.

However, these difficulties are not peculiar to monetary policy as such: if, instead of relying on the action of the monetary authorities, the government tried to check inflation by means of budgetary policy (which would exert its effects via the *IS*-curve instead of the $L(M/p)$-curve), it too would be faced with the problem of time-lags and might over- or under-estimate the amount of pressure required. What *is* special about monetary policy is that reductions in the nominal

---

[1] That is, by reducing M the authorities will have caused the $L(M/p)$ curve to shift to the left so that it exactly offsets the original rightward shift of the *IS* curve, which it will now intersect at a point vertically above the original level of Q.

[2] See pp. 89–93 above.

money-supply will cause the interest-rate to rise. If the original movement from IS_1 to IS_2 in Fig. 25 had been precisely offset by a rise in the monetary-equilibrium curve from $L(M_1/p_1)$ to $L(M_0/p_1)$ (which coincides with the $L(M_1/p_2)$-curve shown in the diagram, since $M_0/p_1 = M_1/p_2$ by assumption), the price-level and the volume of output would have remained unchanged at p_1 and Q_1 respectively, but the interest-rate would have risen from r_1 to r_2; if further rightward movements of the IS-curve were similarly offset by leftward shifts in the $L(M/p)$-curve, r would climb still higher. But increases in the interest-rate create a problem with regard to the government's borrowing requirements. If the budget is currently in balance, with revenue exactly sufficient to finance expenditure, the total public debt will be neither increasing nor diminishing: the 'net borrowing requirement' will be zero. However, unless the outstanding debt was originally financed entirely by the sale of irredeemable bonds, some part of it will be coming due for repayment at any given time, and the government will need to sell new securities in order to redeem the maturing old ones; thus, there will still be a 'gross borrowing requirement' even when no net borrowing is taking place. The amount of this gross requirement depends on (a) the average length of the outstanding debt—if it consists mainly of long-term bonds, the proportion maturing in any week or month will be small, while if it is made up wholly of three-month Treasury Bills it must be re-financed in its entirety four times a year; (b) on the way in which past borrowing has been done, since this may cause a bunching-up of maturities at a given time; and (c) on the total amount of debt in existence. If a large proportion of the debt happens to fall due for re-financing just after the interest-rate has been forced up by the monetary authorities' efforts to prevent inflation, the government will find that the interest-cost of the public debt has sharply increased; the longer the period for which interest stays high, the greater the proportion of the debt which will have to be renewed on unfavourable terms. If re-financing is done by the issue of long-term bonds, the higher interest-cost will persist until they reach maturity many years later; on the other hand, the replacement of maturing bonds by short-term borrowing, in the hope that this can later be re-financed by long-term bond issues when the interest-rate has fallen again, will have the effect of reducing the average length of the total debt[1] and increasing the gross borrowing requirement in the future. The prices of existing government bonds will fall, with the likelihood that speculation on further falls will drive

[1] This is the reverse of the 'funding' described on p. 278 above. When long-term bonds are replaced by Treasury Bills or other short-term obligations, the government may be said to be 'un-funding' its debt.

them lower still; the public credit will be eroded, and the government may begin to fear that it will soon be unable to raise fresh loans on any terms at all. If it could run a budget surplus large enough to permit all maturing debt to be redeemed out of current revenue, the need for new borrowing would be eliminated and the problem would be solved; but it is difficult to increase rates of taxation quickly, and it may be impossible to reduce expenditure sufficiently to yield a big enough surplus, since the latter would have to be very large indeed if the total debt is high in proportion to revenue and the average length of the debt fairly short.[1] If this solution is ruled out, and the government is unwilling to see bond prices falling below some minimum level, it will have to instruct the monetary authorities to intervene in the market and absorb any excess supply of bonds which would otherwise have pushed the price below the designated 'support level'. But this means that the authorities will now be compelled to abandon their earlier policy of restricting the nominal money-supply, and actually reverse it by creating new money through the purchase of bonds.[2]

Preventing the price of bonds falling is equivalent to preventing the interest-rate rising. Suppose the aim is to keep interest at the r_1 level in Fig. 25, in spite of the fact that the IS-curve has just moved from IS_1 to IS_2. It was seen earlier (p. 289) that the excess demand will generate a rise in prices which will carry the $L(M/p)$-curve from $L(M_1/p_1)$ to $L(M_1/p_2)$, and cause interest to rise to r_2, as long as the nominal money-supply remains M_1. To maintain the interest-rate at r_1, the authorities must *increase* the money-supply so as to push

[1] The surplus will be sufficient to redeem all maturing debt if $sR = kD$, where R is tax revenue, s is the proportion of it not required to meet current expenditure, D is total debt, and k is the fraction of D maturing in the period over which R is measured. Dividing both sides by R gives

$$s = k\frac{D}{R}.$$

If the ratio of debt to annual expenditure, D/R, is 4, and if the average maturity is four years so that $k = 0.25$, new borrowing can be avoided only if $s = 1$, i.e. if government spending is stopped altogether and all tax revenue is used to retire debt. Britain's D/R was roughly 2 in mid-1971, while k was about 0.2, so that s would have had to be 0.4 to satisfy the equation: it need hardly be said that a budget surplus equal to two-fifths of current revenue is not a practical possibility. Still, if even a small surplus can be achieved, it will ease the situation in another way: a cut in public spending (or a rise in taxes which cuts private spending) will reduce aggregate demand, shifting the IS curve to the left; this will lower the interest rate again, even if only by a little.

[2] The authorities' purchases are 'open market operations' of the expansionary kind; they increase the commercial banks' reserves and thereby enable the banks to increase their own deposits, so that the total money supply is increased.

the $L(M/p)$-curve to the right of $L(M_1/p_1)$ until it intersects IS_2 at the level of r_1. This will make it impossible to close the 'inflationary gap', which in fact will now be larger than the original Q_1Q_2; prices will rise, and go on rising; the authorities will be obliged to continue increasing the money-supply indefinitely (or until the IS-curve moves back to the left, either autonomously or under the pressure of fiscal measures) in order to offset the rising trend of prices and keep the $L(M/p)$-curve in the desired position. Interest-rate stability will then be achieved at the cost of continuing inflation.

The government may, of course, take the view that it is more important to prevent inflation than to stabilize the interest-rate, and allow the monetary authorities to contract the money-supply while itself grappling as best it can with the problem of debt re-financing described above. Unfortunately, this is not the only problem it will have to face. Government securities are important assets in the portfolios of banks and other financial institutions, so that a substantial fall in their market values will put a severe strain on the monetary system. There will be widespread discontent among individual bondholders whose assets fall in value, and among home-buyers faced with higher mortgage rates: this will be politically embarrassing to a government which depends on their votes. To the extent that higher interest-rates discourage investment more than other elements of aggregate demand, the economy's growth rate will be reduced because of the slower rate of expansion of the capital stock: if public opinion sets a higher value on growth than on price-stability, this too may inhibit the government's anti-inflationary policy. Foreign countries, forced to raise their own interest-rates to check outflows of capital funds attracted by higher yields in the home country, will protest that they are being pushed into recession and will urge the government to relax the pressure on interest-rates. Though these additional difficulties need not cause the policy of monetary restriction to be abandoned altogether, they may very well cause it to be applied less rigorously, and the $L(M/p)$-curve will not be allowed to move far enough to the left to carry the interest-rate to the r_2 level; the 'inflationary gap' will be reduced but not wholly eliminated, and the price-level will therefore increase. If the rate at which prices rise depends on the size of the 'gap',[1] the inflation will proceed more slowly that it would have done if interest had been prevented from

---

[1] This is an assumption which is 'external' to the static model presented in Fig. 25. The latter merely indicates the condition of short-run equilibrium and the changes which can be expected if these conditions are not fulfilled; it does not show whether the changes will occur quickly or slowly, because it has no time-dimension.

rising above r_1 at all; but as long as the government is not willing to allow the latter to go all the way to r_2, the nominal money-supply will have to be continually increased to offset the tendency of rising prices to shift the $L(M/p)$-curve to the left, and the inflation will not be brought to a halt by monetary restriction.

In these circumstances, the only possibility of convergence will be through a leftward movement of the IS-curve—that is, through a fall in the real demand for goods and services. Various reasons why this should happen have already been briefly indicated in earlier chapters.[1] If there is a persistent tendency for money-wages to lag behind prices, real consumption will be reduced by the 'redistribution effect' if wage-earners happen to have a higher MPC than other groups; however, unless the lag is continually lengthening (so that real wages w/p fall steadily lower) this will merely push the IS-curve a certain distance to the left at the moment when the inflation begins, and cause no further shift thereafter—it will be a 'once-for-all' effect, which could indeed be reversed if the lag were to shorten, in which case the IS-curve would move back to the right. The Pigou effect, by contrast, will be pushing the curve further and further to the left as long as prices go on rising, since the real value of cash assets will then be continuously falling; however, unless the influence of asset-holdings on consumers' behaviour is strong, the push will not be very forceful. Another continuing reduction in real consumption will be brought about by the effect of rising prices on certain money-incomes (such as pensions, interest-payments on bonds, and certain salaries and professional fees) which are fixed by law, contract and custom for long periods. They will be adjusted from time to time, for example by new legislation to increase social security payments, but the consequent revival of their recipients' real consumption will be only temporary, falling away again as prices continue to climb. However, when inflation has gone on long enough to make everyone expect it to continue in the future, fixed-income recipients will try to get them adjusted more and more frequently, for instance by the 'tying' of social security benefits to an appropriate price-index so that they increase automatically when prices rise; the more successful they are in this, the less will their real consumption be reduced, and the smaller, therefore, will be the leftward movement of the IS-curve. If other countries' prices remain unchanged, the inflation will make exports dearer and dearer in foreign markets, while imports will become relatively cheaper in the home market, as long as the exchange-rate is kept unaltered; given appropriate price-elasticities

[1] See above, pp. 111–3 and 178–9.

of demand,[1] the volume of imports demanded will rise and that of exports will fall, thereby diminishing aggregate demand in the home market and shifting the IS-curve to the left. But the concomitant balance-of-payments deficit, which will be continually increasing as inflation proceeds, will sooner or later cause the exchange-rate to fall, reviving the demand for exports and reducing that for imports—with the result that the IS-curve will move to the right again.

When all these considerations are taken together, it seems that the original rightward shift of the IS-curve to IS_2 will be followed by a movement back towards the left during the early stages of the inflation; then, as prices continue to rise—as they will, if the second movement has not completely cancelled out the first—the curve will begin to drift back towards the right; at some point, everyone will begin to expect prices to go on rising in the future, and this (for the various reasons given earlier) will cause an additional rightward shift, carrying the curve to the right of the IS_2 position. If the government tries to push it back by reducing its own demand for goods and services, and/or by raising taxes (and cutting transfers) so as to diminish the private sector's demand, its task will be easier the more quickly it acts; the further the inflation has got into its stride, the larger the budget surplus (measured in real terms) which will be needed to eliminate the inflationary gap. But it was argued in Chapter Nine[2] that public expenditure is hard to contract without major policy changes, that it will be difficu't to increase taxes if they are already at high rates, and that it will take time to do either; so the government may find that whatever surplus it can arrange immediately will not shift the IS-curve far enough to the left to halt the inflation, while during the time it takes to budget for a larger one, the curve will have moved further to the right, making it necessary to increase the surplus yet again. When (and if[3]) the latter eventually becomes large enough to halt the inflation, prices will have risen to a level appreciably higher than that from which they started.

Even if the government makes no deliberate effort to shift the IS-curve by means of budgetary policy, the effects of inflation on its real expenditure and revenue may nevertheless cause the curve to move. As prices rise, spending programmes drawn up in money terms will become inadequate to achieve their objectives; if they are

---

[1] See pp. 191 above.

[2] See p. 211–3 above.

[3] It may be that even the largest attainable surplus is not enough to wipe out the inflationary gap—or even that a surplus is not possible at all. In wartime, for example, no government is likely to reduce military spending merely to avoid inflation.

not suitably adjusted, the amount of government expenditure must fall in real terms, thereby causing the *IS*-curve to shift to the left. Normally, however, governments are expected to provide a given physical volume of services (such as defence, police, and diplomatic representation), increasing their money outlays appropriately when rising prices make such provision more costly; real expenditure will then remain unchanged and the *IS*-curve will be unaffected. On the other hand, revenue will be increasing in real terms if the tax system is progressive. When prices and money-incomes rise simultaneously in the same proportion, real income remains unchanged; but the increased money-incomes will now be subject to higher rates of tax, so that a smaller proportion of real income will be left in the hands of the taxpayers, causing them to reduce their real consumption. Provided the government does not increase its own real expenditure, this will shift the *IS*-curve to the left.[1] The effect will be less, the longer the time-lag between the receipt of income and the payment of tax on it, since the intervening rise in prices will have reduced the real value of the tax by the time it comes to be paid; even so, prices would have to be rising faster and faster, accelerating at the same rate as the average rate of taxation was increasing, to prevent tax-payments taking a larger proportion of real income.[2] If, in addition, the government is slow to adjust pensions and other transfer incomes to offset the effects of price-increases, the real consumption of the recipients will fall, and this too will assist the leftward move-

---

[1] The taxpayers will, of course, be saving less than before in real terms, as well as consuming less; the increase in saving which shifts *IS* to the left will be that done by the government—that is, the budget surplus due to the rise in revenue in excess of expenditure.

[2] With a one-period lag, the proportion of current income paid in tax in period 2 will be $t_1 Y_1 / Y_2$, where t_1 is the average rate of tax applicable in period 1; similarly, the proportion in period 3 will be $t_2 Y_2 / Y_3$, where t_2 is higher than t_1 because higher money incomes have moved all taxpayers further up a progressive tax scale. If money incomes have risen in exactly the same proportion as the price level, $Y_1 / Y_2 = p_1 / p_2$ and $Y_2 / Y_3 = p_2 / p_3$, and the condition for tax payments to be a constant fraction of income can be written

$$t_1 \frac{p_1}{p_2} = t_2 \frac{p_2}{p_3},$$

which can be rearranged as

$$\frac{t_2}{t_1} = \frac{p_3}{p_2} \bigg/ \frac{p_2}{p_1}$$

—so that if t_2 were 12% and t_1 10%, the rise in prices between periods 2 and 3 will have to be 20% greater than that between periods 1 and 2 if the proportion of total income taken in tax is not to increase. It follows that if prices are rising at a constant rate, a progressive tax system *must* reduce taxpayers' disposable real incomes in spite of the existence of the lag.

ment of the *IS*-curve. The larger the part the government plays in the economy—i.e. the greater the proportion of public to private goods-and-services spending, the bigger the share of transfers in the total of private incomes, and the higher the general level (as distinct from the progression) of taxes—the more strongly these effects will operate, and the more the system of public finance will act as an 'automatic stabilizer' which will reduce inflationary pressure even when the government takes no special measures to that end; while if the latter does adopt a positive budgetary policy, the effects just mentioned will make its task easier.

(c) 'Cost-push' and 'demand-shift'

At the beginning of Section (*b*) it was assumed that inflation was started by an autonomous increase in aggregate demand, occurring at a time when output was already at its full-employment level: the excess demand 'pulled' the price-level of goods and services upwards, and though the level of money-wages was also made to rise, this was a consequence and not a cause of the inflationary pressure. In the 'cost-push' theory of inflation, by contrast, the causal sequence is reversed: the initial impulse is given by an autonomous rise in money-wages or other input prices, in response to which the prices of 'final' goods and services are raised so as to cover the increase in costs; the rise in prices, however, will have caused real wages to fall back to their previous level, and the forces which brought about the original rise in money-wages will now cause them to increase yet again, with the result that prices will be raised once more—and so on. At each stage, it is the rise in costs which pushes up prices: it is not necessary for there to be any excess demand for goods and services —indeed, the process could go forward even if aggregate demand happened to be somewhat below the level needed for full-employment output.

A basic assumption of the 'cost-push' theory is that there are strong trades unions which insist on compensating increases in money-wages whenever the price level rises, so as to prevent any reduction in real wages: the labour market consequently has a 'floor' of the kind described earlier in Chapter Four (p. 95 above). From time to time, when the unions feel strong enough, they will try to increase the real wage by claiming money-wage adjustments in excess of those needed merely to offset rising prices, and when they succeed, this will give the initial 'push' which sets the wage-price spiral in motion. Alternatively, an autonomous rise in the cost of imported inputs might provide the push; as long as the unions respond to the consequent increase in output prices by forcing a rise in money-wages, a cost-inflationary spiral will ensue. It is also assumed that business enterprises fix the selling prices of their products by calculating 'direct' costs per unit of output (i.e. wages and materials) and adding a conventional percentage 'mark-up' to cover overheads and provide a margin of profit. Where prices are 'cost-determined' (or 'administered') in this way, an increase in money-wages will automatically be followed by compensatory price-increases, which will reduce the level of real wages again and lead to further wage-claims. The timing of the process will, of course, vary from one industry to another, depending on differences in the strength and leadership of unions, on the amount of resistance which employers put up against wage-claims, and on the rapidity with which firms raise their products' prices when higher wages have increased their production costs; and it will be complicated by unions' attempts to maintain 'differentials' between their own members' earnings and those in other occupations, as (for example) when locomotive engineers demand higher wages on the ground that a recent rise in porters' pay has narrowed the gap between them. If there is an appreciable lag in the adjustment of selling-prices when money-wages have risen, real wages will be increased for the time being at the expense of profits, and this may stimulate aggregate demand through the 'redistribution effect'—with the result that some demand inflation will be injected into the original 'cost-push' sequence if the economy is already in the vicinity of full employment.

In the case of demand-inflation, it was seen earlier that it must eventually be halted if the supply of nominal money is not allowed to increase; the same thing is true of cost-inflation. Suppose the economy is initially in the equilibrium situation given in Fig. 25 by the intersection of IS_1 and $L(M_1/p_1)$, with output and employment at Q_1 and N_1 respectively; but with the difference that the supply-curve of labour is no longer the SS of Quadrant III but the vertical broken line below $(w/p)_1$ as far as its intersection with DD—this is the 'wage floor' established by the unions. If the latter now try to raise the floor by insisting on increases in money-wages, this will tend to move the supply-curve to the left; but if business firms immediately raise their selling-prices when higher money-wages increase their production costs, the labour supply-curve will be held back in its original position and real wages will remain $(w/p)_1$. However, the rise in prices and money-wages means that more and more money will be needed for transactions purposes; if the nominal money supply is not increased, less of it will be available to satisfy asset-demand, and the rate of interest will be forced up; in Quadrant

I, the $L(M/p)$-curve will move to the left as the real quantity of money falls, and will now cut IS_1 to the left of Q_1 so that aggregate demand is no longer sufficient to absorb the whole of full-employment output. As demand falls, firms will be more cautious about raising prices, and will begin to cut output instead; with employment somewhat reduced, the marginal productivity of labour will have risen, and firms will be willing to pay higher real wages than before; further increases in money-wages will no longer be offset by price rises, and the vertical wage-floor will at last move to the left, intersecting the DD curve at a level of employment less than N_1. When real wages have reached the level aimed at by the unions, no further wage-claims will be presented, and prices will cease to rise. The cost-inflation will have converged on a new equilibrium.

This outcome, however, will be possible only if the government and monetary authorities are prepared to allow the interest-rate to rise, and the level of employment to fall, to whatever extent is necessary to halt the inflation. If they are unwilling, for any of the reasons put forward in the previous section, to let the interest-rate go above a certain level, it will be necessary to increase the quantity of nominal money whenever rising prices threaten to push the $L(M/p)$-curve too far to the left; while if the government is politically committed to maintaining full employment, the money supply must be expanded to prevent price increases pushing $L(M/p)$ away from its original intersection with IS_1. As long as aggregate demand is prevented from falling, firms need have no hesitation about raising their prices whenever increases in money-wages push up production costs, nor need the unions moderate their wage-claims for fear of creating unemployment among their members; thus, the wage-price spiral will continue indefinitely—or rather, it will not be prevented from doing so by any obstacle on the monetary side of the economy. If, in these circumstances, the inflation should converge after all, it will be because progressive taxation is reducing real consumption through its effect on disposable incomes, or because government expenditure is declining in real terms, or because fixed-income recipients' real demand is falling, or because of the Pigou effect—that is, for the various reasons which have already been noted as likely to operate under demand-inflation. Expectational effects, too, will be generated in the same way as they were seen to be earlier; if they are so strong as to outweigh the forces making for convergence and so cause a net increase in aggregate demand, they will inject an element of 'demand-pull' into the cost-inflation already under way.

The fact that money-wages are being raised through collective bargaining between trades unions and employers is not in itself evidence that inflation is of the 'cost-push' type: given the institutional structure of the labour market, the negotiating procedure will be the same whether wage-claims are prompted by rises in the cost of living, or by unions feeling that labour shortage has improved their bargaining power, or by a determination on their part to increase real wages. Similarly, the fact that business firms are raising prices only in response to increases in wage-costs is not an infallible indicator of cost-inflation: the rise in money-wages may have been due to their own attempts to take on more labour in order to expand output to meet an autonomous increase in demand,[1] as an alternative to raising their prices in the first instance. Even if prices and wages are spiralling upwards against a background of excess capacity and unemployment, it is still not safe to assume that no 'demand-pull' is present. Recent changes in the composition of demand may have created a good deal of frictional unemployment, so that the full-employment level of output (at which the number of people seeking jobs is equal to the number of vacancies)[2] is actually less than the current level of aggregate demand, low though that may appear to be.

Thus, a process which seems at first sight to be one of cost-inflation may in reality be due to the pressure of excess demand, or at any rate may combine both demand-pull and cost-push elements. The problem is to determine the comparative strength of the two. In his well-known study of the relationship between unemployment and money-wage changes in Britain during the last hundred years,[3] A. W. Phillips found that wage-rates rose rapidly when unemployment was low, fell when it was high, and remained unchanged when about $5\frac{1}{2}\%$ of the labour force were out of work; plotting in a diagram the points relating wage changes to unemployment in the various years, he found that the best 'fit' was given by the curve shown as AA in Figure 26 opposite. The shape of AA suggests that when unemployment was below $5\frac{1}{2}\%$ the number of vacancies exceeded

[1] In a perfectly competitive labour market, firms' efforts to outbid one another for labour will push up money-wages directly; but where they belong to employers' organizations which negotiate collectively with unions, individual firms will be inhibited from offering higher wage-rates, and the increase will come about through unions realizing that the demand for labour has risen and that employers are now likely to offer less resistance to a wage-claim. If, pending the negotiation of new standard rates, firms try to attract more labour by offering 'bonuses' and other above-standard inducements which are not counted as part of the wage-rate proper, there will be a tendency for earnings to rise faster than wage-rates. This 'wage-drift', as it is called, is usually regarded as a symptom of demand-inflation.

[2] See the definition given above on p. 86.

[3] A. W. Phillips, 'The Relationship between Unemployment and the Rate of Change of Money Wage Rates in the United Kingdom, 1861–1957', *Economica*, Nov. 1958, pp. 283–99.

the numbers seeking work, i.e. that there was an excess of demand for labour over the supply of it, and that this excess demand caused wage-rates to climb; while a level of unemployment greater than $5\frac{1}{2}\%$ meant excess supply of labour, which caused wages to fall. If it is assumed that the demand for labour was a reflection of the aggregate demand for goods and services, and that money-wage changes caused the general price-level to alter (though not to the same extent,

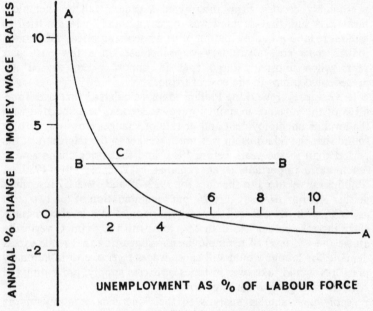

Fig. 26

because of year-to-year increases in labour productivity which in themselves reduce wage-costs per unit of output), the shape of AA— the 'Phillips curve'—is consistent with the hypothesis that price increases, when they occurred, were mainly caused by the pressure of excess aggregate demand. Had money-wages risen only in response to unions' efforts to maintain or increase real wages regardless of the supply-and-demand balance in the labour market, there would have been a scatter of points indicating money-wage changes in the different years, with the height of each point depending only on the magnitude of recent price changes and the unions' success in obtaining equivalent (or more than equivalent) money-wage adjustments; a line showing the *average* annual change in money-wages would then have been horizontal like Figure 26's *BB*, implying that wage and price increases were not determined by demand and supply pressures in the labour and goods markets—which would, of course, be consistent with the hypothesis of pure cost-inflation. The shape of *AA* thus suggests that the 'demand-pull' element was stronger than 'cost-push' during the period covered by the figures. Phillips also found that *changes* in the level of unemployment, as well as the absolute level, affected the rate at which money-wages rose or fell— presumably because firms interpreted a general fall in unemployment as a sign that demand was increasing, and therefore tried to hire more labour in anticipation of it; while rising prices did, in fact, induce *some* cost-inflationary wage-increases in a few particular years when unusually large rises in import prices caused unprecedented jumps in the cost of living.

R. G. Lipsey, reworking Phillips' data, calculated[1] that over four-fifths of the variance in money wage-rates could be associated with the level of unemployment and its rate of change. However, he also found that the relationship was much weaker in the later part of the period than in the years before 1913, and that price changes were much more important as an explanatory variable after 1920. A 'Phillips curve' fitted to the data for 1923–39 and 1948–57 resembles neither *AA* nor *BB* in Figure 26, but a combination of the two such as *ACB*, with the *CB* section nearly horizontal at a level of money-wage increase rather less than 1%, and with the point *C* vertically above the 4% level of unemployment—suggesting that while excess demand for labour would still cause wages to rise, cost-inflationary pressures would take over in times of excess supply, preventing the latter from forcing wage rates down.[2]

Applying a similar analysis to the American economy in the 1900–58 period, R. J. Bhattia found[3] much less evidence of a Phillips-type relationship: the effect of cost-of-living changes on changes in earnings appeared to be greater than that of the level of unemployment in the period as a whole, while in the post-1948 years it was 'not possible to determine whether changes in prices are the causal variable, or whether prices rise because the unions are able to extract large wage concessions independently of price changes'.

[1] R. G. Lipsey, 'The Relation between Unemployment and the Rate of Change of Money Wage Rates in the United Kingdom, 1862–1957: A further Analysis', *Economica*, Feb. 1960.

[2] It should be emphasized that the evidence here is 'suggestive' rather than conclusive: see Lipsey's own caution on the point, *op. cit.*, p. 31.

[3] R. J. Bhattia, 'Unemployment and the Rate of Change of Money Earnings in the United States, 1900–1958', *Economica*, Aug. 1961, pp. 286–96.

Other studies[1] have found some connection between changes in money-wages and the level of profits in the United States since the war, but it is not clear whether this ought to be attributed to demand-pull or to cost-push pressures. If it resulted from business firms autonomously increasing their profit margins, it would be the latter: 'mark-up inflation', or 'profit-push', is simply another possible species of cost-inflation. If, on the other hand, profits rose because excess demand was forcing up prices ahead of money-wages, the observed relationship would be consistent with a diagnosis of demand-inflation. Another relationship, this time clearly indicative of cost-push, is that found by A. G. Hines between increases in money-wages and rises in the percentage of the labour force belonging to unions, the latter variable being taken to indicate the growth of the unions' 'pushfulness' in wage negotiations.[2] Over the period 1921-61, he showed that a 1 % growth in unionization was associated with a 1·6 % rise in money wage-rates, as against the 0·7 % rate of wage-increases associated with a 1 % rise in prices;[3] the level of unemployment, on the other hand, did not appear to be an important influence on money-wages, and Hines felt justified in concluding that 'contrary to the prevailing view, trade unions do affect the rate of change of wages *independently* of the demand for labour'.

All these considerations suggest that, whatever may have been the case before 1914 or even 1939, the possibility of cost-inflation is a real one in present-day conditions; and this, as will be seen presently, is of some importance from the point of view of public policy. Meanwhile, it is necessary to take note of one more theory of inflation, namely the 'intersectoral demand shift' hypothesis of C. L. Schultze.[4] This was put forward as an attempt to explain the price-increases of 1955-7 in the United States, in view of the fact that neither demand-pull nor cost-push appeared to be operating at that time. Schultze argued that if prices and money-wages are assumed to be rigid downwards but flexible upwards, a change in the *pattern* of demand will cause prices

[1] E.g. a further one by Bhattia, 'Profits and the Rate of Change in Money Earnings in the United States, 1935-1959', *Economica*, Aug. 1962, pp. 255-62.

[2] A. G. Hines, 'Trade Unions and Wage Inflation in the United Kingdom, 1893-1961', *Review of Economic Studies*, Oct. 1964, pp. 221-52.

[3] It must be remembered, however, that a 1 % rise in prices can come about much more easily than a 1 % increase in unionization. Between 1921 and 1961 the proportion of the labour force belonging to unions varied between 11 % and 44 %, remaining roughly stable around the 40 % level during the 1950s. The retail price index, on the other hand, rose approximately threefold during the period, increasing by about 30 % in the 1950s alone.

[4] Charles L. Schultze, 'Recent Inflation in the United States', Study Paper No. 1 for Joint Economic Committee, *Study of Employment, Growth and Price Levels* (Washington: Government Printing Office, 1959).

to rise in those sectors of the economy where demand has risen, but will not cause them to fall in the sectors where demand has been reduced, with the result that the average of all prices will necessarily rise even though *aggregate* demand has neither risen nor fallen. As the demand-gaining sectors attempt to increase output, they will bid up money-wages and the prices of the material inputs they use; to the extent that labour and materials cannot simply be re-allocated to them from the demand-losing industries (i.e., if these factors of production are neither homogeneous nor perfectly mobile) this will cause the general level of money-wages and other input prices to rise; the disturbance of wage differentials between industries and occupations will also cause some upward readjustment of money-wages in sectors which have not themselves gained demand. In some of the demand-losing sectors, prices may actually be raised: with diminished sales and output, overhead costs per unit of output may have risen sufficiently to cause firms to feel that an increase in mark-up is needed to cover them.

On the other hand, there are sectors in which the assumption of downward price-rigidity is not valid, and if they happen to be the demand losers, they will register a fall in prices which could offset the rises in the demand-gaining sectors, leaving the general price-level unchanged. Moreover, when demand shifts back to a sector which had lost it earlier and which still has unemployed labour and excess capacity, it will be possible for it to re-expand output to meet the revived demand without raising prices; conceivably, demand-shift to an excess capacity sector, from one whose prices are flexible downwards, could cause prices to fall in the latter without rising in the former—thus causing the general price level to move *downwards* in a 'demand-shift *deflation*'. Much will depend, too, on the amount and the speed of the change in the composition of demand. If the demand for each sector's output is either rising at the same pace as its productive capacity is growing through investment and techno-logical progress, or else falling at a rate which just matches the run-down of its capacity through depreciation and the 'wastage' of its labour force, all prices could remain unchanged. The mere fact that the pattern of demand is changing is not in itself sufficient to cause inflation, and Schultze's claim that it must be regarded as a continu-ing source of upward pressure on the general price-level does not, therefore, seem well founded; but it is certainly possible to agree that there will be times when the large-scale introduction of new commodities, or sudden changes in preferences or in the distribution of incomes, will produce a sufficiently large dislocation of the demand pattern to start the price-level rising in the way he describes.

Like demand-pull and cost-push, 'demand-shift' inflation will eventually bring itself to an end if the quantity of nominal money is not increased. Rising prices will reduce the real quantity of money, increase the rate of interest, and cause aggregate demand to fall: when not a single sector remains in which demand exceeds supply— or alternatively, when excess supply in some sectors has become so great as to break through the downward rigidity of prices, so that price-reductions now offset such price-increases as still occur in demand-gaining sectors—then the general price-level will at last have been stabilized, though at the cost of considerable unemployment in the 'excess supply' sectors.

(d) The pace of inflation

So far, attention has been focused mainly on the possible *causes* of inflation. But, as noted earlier on p. 287, it is particularly important to account for the *speed* at which inflation goes forward, whatever may have been the impulse which originally started it off; for this purpose, a dynamic analysis is needed. The reader may already have noticed that the 'Phillips curve' introduced in the last section does, in fact, embody a dynamic hypothesis: it asserts not only that money-wages rise in response to excess demand in the labour market, but also that they rise at an *annual* rate which depends on the amount of excess demand relative to the full-employment labour supply. A similar hypothesis with respect to the market for goods and services would make the annual rate of increase in the price level ($\dot{p}$) a function of the proportion by which aggregate demand (D) exceeds supply (S): in symbols,

$$\dot{p} = f\left(\frac{D-S}{S}\right)$$

—so that if $(D-S)/S$ happens to be 2%, $\dot{p}$ will be (say) 4%, while a 5% value of $(D-S)/S$ will give a $\dot{p}$ of (say) 10%, and so on. The essential point is that the movement of the price-level is expressed as a rate of increase over *time*. In the case of a convergent demand-inflation, the proportion by which prices must rise to restore equilibrium will depend on the size of the initial 'goods gap'—in symbols,

$$\frac{\Delta p}{p} = \phi\left(\frac{D-S}{S}\right).$$

However, the left-hand side has no time dimension: unlike $\dot{p}$, which is a rate of increase *per year*, the price-rise $\Delta p/p$ could be accomplished in a few hours or days, or be stretched out over many months or even years, without ceasing to satisfy the equation. To explain why the price-level should rise at a particular rate over *time*, it is necessary to examine the various lags which operate in the economy, and to allow for concomitant changes—such as the expansion of productive capacity through investment and technical improvements—which will be taking place as time elapses.

First of all, there will be a *price-adjustment lag* in the markets for goods and services: this is the length of time between the emergence of excess demand, and/or increases in production costs, and the consequential rise in prices. When a 'goods gap' suddenly opens up, there will be some delay, even if only a very short one, before firms become aware that the pressure of demand has risen and decide on their response to it. In some markets, the latter will be merely a passive acceptance of the increased prices offered by buyers who are trying to outbid one another for limited supplies, and the price-adjustment lag will then depend on the rate at which buyers escalate their bids. Where it is the sellers who take the initiative in setting prices (that is, where firms are 'price makers' rather than 'price takers'), some of them may be held back for a time by the fear of losing sales to competitors if the latter should refrain from increasing their own prices; others may wait to see whether the expansion of demand will be maintained or turn out to be merely a temporary fluctuation, and raise prices only when they are sure it is the former; in certain cases, the increase in prices may itself involve certain costs, such as those of printing and issuing new price-lists, which may cause firms to postpone price-increases for a time. Thus, even where prices are 'demand determined' in the sense that they respond directly to the emergence of excess demand, their increase will be subject to a time-lag varying from market to market.

In sectors where prices are 'cost determined' (or 'administered'), firms fix their selling-prices by the conventional procedure of adding a given mark-up to their direct costs of production: here, the existence of excess demand will not *directly* affect prices, though it may do so indirectly if firms' efforts to increase output cause their costs to rise as a result of pressure on supplies of inputs. Except in the case of 'final' products, any given sector's output is also an input from the point of view of other sectors, so that a rise in the price of any 'intermediate' commodity will set up a chain reaction of price-increases elsewhere; with a price-adjustment lag at each stage, the repercussions of an initial price-increase in the market for a basic commodity could take a long time to work themselves out. For the economy as a whole, the ultimate direct costs, after the cancelling-out of intersectoral transactions, are those of labour and imported inputs: if all prices were cost determined, the rate of increase of the general price-level ($\dot{p}$) would depend on (i) the rate at which money-wages are rising ($\dot{w}$), (ii) the rate ($\dot{x}$) at which productivity, in the sense of output per unit of labour, is increasing, (iii) the rate of increase in import prices ($\dot{m}$); and (iv) the time-lags between changes in wage- and import-costs and the consequent changes in prices. Over a period of time, increases in output per unit of labour will reduce the effect of rising money-wages on wage-cost per unit of output; if there is an overall one-period lag, the relationship can be written

$$\dot{p}_t = a(\dot{w}-\dot{x})_{t-1}+(1-a)\dot{m}_{t-1}$$

where a is the share of wage-costs in total direct cost. Thus, if money-wages were to rise 6% and productivity 3% in a given period, if import prices were unchanged, and if wage-costs were two-thirds of the total (i.e. $a = 2/3$), the price level would rise 2% in the following period. There is, of course, no reason why the time-lags should necessarily be the same for all the variables: for example, firms may know that import prices fluctuate rapidly, and may therefore refrain from adjusting their selling prices until they are sure a given rise in import costs will not soon be reversed, whereas an increase in money-wages, coming at the end of a period of negotiations with trades unions, is likely to be reflected in higher prices almost immediately because firms have had notice of it and know that it will remain in force for some time.[1]

Increases in money-wages are themselves subject to a *wage-adjustment lag*. When excess demand in product markets causes firms to try to expand output, their efforts to hire more workers will create excess demand in the labour market if employment is near full to begin with: with excess demand (D) measured as the excess of job vacancies (V) over unemployment (U) in proportion to the level of employment (N), a one-period lag between the emergence of the excess demand and the adjustment of money-wages will mean that

$$\dot{w}_t = f(D_{t-1}) = f\left(\frac{V-U}{N}\right)_{t-1}.$$

Phillips found that the lag was negligible over most of the period he studied, but in the years 1948–57 he obtained the best 'fit' for his

---

[1] L. A. Dicks-Mireaux found that during the years 1946–59 the lag between wage increases and price adjustments was three months or less, and was about half that between changes in import prices and changes in the domestic price level. See his 'The Interrelationship between Cost and Price Changes, 1946–59: A Study of Inflation in Post-War Britain', *Oxford Economic Papers*, Oct. 1961.

relationship by assuming a wage-adjustment lag of seven months; L. A. Dicks-Mireaux, on the other hand, found a shorter lag—something less than six months, with an average length of three.[1] Where money-wages are being pushed up not by the pressure of excess demand but by unions' efforts to offset increases in the cost of living, their rate of increase will depend partly on the rate at which prices are rising and partly on the unions' success in obtaining their demands, but the processes of collective bargaining will take time; thus $\dot{w}_t = a\dot{p}_{t-1}$ where negotiations impose a one-period time-lag and a measures the extent to which wage claims succeed (complete success being indicated by $a = 1$). If unions are strong and 'aggressive' enough to obtain wage-increases over and above those needed to make good the effects of cost-of-living increases, so that money-wages would be rising even if $p_{t-1} = 0$, the equation would become

$$\dot{w}_t = \dot{p}_{t-1} + \beta_{t-1}$$

where β represents this additional 'push', and a has been omitted since it must be equal to one if β is positive. The term β may itself be dependent on other variables, such as increasing unionization (as suggested by Hines), or increases in profits and productivity where these are made the basis for unions' wage claims.

The various lagged relationships described in the last few paragraphs can be combined in a number of ways to show the development of an inflation through time. For example, a one-period price-adjustment lag, in a closed economy where prices are cost-determined, will mean that $\dot{p}_t = \dot{w}_{t-1} - \dot{x}_{t-1}$; if there is a wage-adjustment lag of one period, and wage-increases are due solely to union pressure which is more than offsetting past price-rises, $\dot{w}_{t-1} = \dot{p}_{t-2} + \beta_{t-2}$ as in the last paragraph; combining the two equations gives

$$\dot{p}_t = \dot{p}_{t-2} + \beta_{t-2} - \dot{x}_{t-1}$$

—which means that the current period's rate of price-increase will be equal to that registered two periods previously, plus an additional percentage if unions were successful in raising real wages in the last period, but minus a percentage due to last period's increase in labour productivity. If prices had been stable in $t-2$, so that $\dot{p}_{t-2}$ was zero, but if unions were at that time putting forward wage-claims which

---

[1] Dicks-Mireaux, *op. cit.*, p. 275; Phillips, *op. cit.*, p. 297. It should be noted that their results are not quite comparable, since Phillips' $\dot{w}$ is the annual change in an index of wage-rates, while that of Dicks-Mireaux is the annual change in total wage and salary payments divided by the number of employees—i.e. an index of earnings which implicitly includes a 'wage-drift' element absent from Phillips' measure.

were greater than could be met by increasing productivity in $t-1$, the result would be a pure cost-inflation beginning in period t; and if, from $t-1$ onwards, each period's β is exactly equal to the $\dot{x}$ of the succeeding one, prices will now rise every second period by the same proportion as in t, i.e. by $\beta_{t-2} - \dot{x}_{t-1}$.

This highly simplified model is, of course, only one of many possible ones which could be set up by combining excess-demand and cost-determination assumptions in different ways and by varying the length and pattern of the time-lags. More detailed and realistic models would have to include additional variables, for example by disaggregating demand into its component elements so as to allow for differences between consumers' behaviour and that of government expenditure, and by bringing in the supply of money; with each new variable, another time-lag would be added to the model. The possibilities raised by lags in the collection of taxes, and in appropriating additional funds for government expenditure, have already been noted;[1] on the monetary side, too, there will be lags in the adjustment of supply and demand in financial markets, and in the response of aggregate demand to higher interest rates.[2] Instead of the simple one-period lags assumed so far, a more complicated pattern may exist: for example, the price-adjustment lag may be distributed over several periods because of differences in the speed of response of the various industries to excess demand and rising costs, so that (say) food prices rise immediately, clothing prices one period later, durables' prices in the one after that, and so on. The lags themselves are likely to vary with the proportionate amount of demand-pull or cost-push: where firms would hesitate to raise prices immediately on the strength of a 1% increase in costs or a fairly small excess of demand over capacity, they will lose no time in putting them up when costs have risen 10% or when they are swamped with orders they cannot fill. A particularly important lag—yet one which is extremely difficult, if not impossible, to measure—is that between changes in the current rate of price-increase and changes in the rate of expected *future* price-increase; it may be that once people have revised their expectations regarding future price changes, the very fact of their having already done so will dispose them to adjust expectations more quickly in future, so that the lag

[1] See p. 302 above. An interesting theoretical model in which, after an initial inflationary shock, prices continue to rise indefinitely solely because of a one-period lag in tax collection, is presented by Julio H. G. Olivera in 'Money, Prices and Fiscal Lags: A Note on the Dynamics of Inflation', *Quarterly Review*, Banca Nazionale del Lavoro, Sept. 1967, pp. 258–67.

[2] See above, pp. 282–3.

will shorten and cause inflationary pressure to rise in the way described on pp. 292–5 above.

Obviously, the possible combinations of lags are so numerous that an enormous variety of dynamic models of inflation could be constructed. The essential point, however, is that the existence of lags ensures that prices will rise at some given rate over time, instead of shooting up instantaneously either to some new equilibrium level (in the case of a convergent inflation) or to infinity; and with the lapse of time, investment will be gradually augmenting the economy's capital stock, technical progress will be increasing its productivity, and the growth of the labour force will be expanding potential total output. Where prices are being pulled up by excess demand, the continuing increase in supply will eventually remove the source of inflationary pressure unless aggregate demand is itself growing at the same rate or faster; in the case of cost-inflation, it has been seen that rising productivity offsets the effect of money-wage increases on labour costs; while 'demand-shift' inflation will be mitigated to the extent that the growth of resources makes it possible for demand-gaining sectors to expand otherwise than by attracting factors of production from demand-losing ones by the offer of higher remuneration. Thus, an important strand of official policy against inflation, supplementing the fiscal and monetary measures described earlier, is to encourage the growth of output and productivity, for example by tax provisions favouring investment at the expense of consumption, and by helping the movement of resources into markets where demand is growing and away from those where it is declining.[1]

(e) Incomes policy

The anti-inflationary policies which have so far been considered were concerned wholly with eliminating or offsetting excess demand: either fiscal policy would shift Fig. 25's *IS* curve back towards the left, or monetary policy would do the same to the *L(M/p)* curve; whichever method was chosen, the object was to cause the two curves to intersect vertically above the full-employment level of output, instead of intersecting to the right of it as they were initially made to do by the autonomous increase in demand which started the inflation. However, these measures will no longer be appropriate when prices are rising in response to 'cost-push', which (as was argued above on pp. 303–4) can cause inflation to occur without

[1] This side of government policy has been called 'supply management', as distinct from the 'demand management' which seeks to manipulate consumption, investment, etc.

there being any excess of aggregate demand over supply, and to continue indefinitely as long as the authorities are prepared to expand the quantity of nominal money sufficiently to prevent rising prices shifting the $L(M/p)$ curve to the left. If the government were to stabilize the price level by refusing to allow the money supply to be increased any further, or by reducing its own expenditure and/or raising taxes, the result would be the creation of unemployment, and if the amount of unemployment needed to stop the inflation turns out to be a large percentage of the labour force, the remedy will be thought worse than the disease.

In these circumstances, the government may attempt to check inflation in another way—namely, by an *'incomes policy'*, the object of which is to keep the prices of factors of production (which are incomes to their owners, and costs to their hirers) from rising at rates which are too fast to be compatible with price stability. If, for example, prices are rising only because wage-costs are increasing, and higher money-wages are being asked and given only because prices are going up, an incomes policy would try to halt the spiral by directly restraining price-increases and by preventing money-wages from rising faster than productivity and so raising wage-costs. Thus, the 1965 White Paper on *Prices and Incomes Policy*[1] proposed (*a*) that wage and salary increases should not exceed a 'norm' (then given as 3–3½%) corresponding to the expected annual growth of output per head, and (*b*) that prices should be kept unchanged wherever possible, rising only in the case of enterprises whose output per employee increased less than the norm, and actually being reduced where above-normal productivity growth occurred. A National Board for Prices and Incomes was set up to review wage and price increases; the 1966 Prices and Incomes Act made the Board a statutory body, and gave the government certain powers to enforce its recommendations. In 1966 the norm for wage-increases was reduced to zero under the 'prices and incomes standstill' adopted in July of that year, and when the figure of 3½% reappeared in 1968 it was as a 'ceiling' rather than a 'norm'.[2] Provisions were made for the restraint of dividends and other forms of non-wage income; great stress was laid on positive measures to raise output per head, with 'an exception to the ceiling for agreements which genuinely raise productivity and increase efficiency sufficiently to justify a pay increase above 3½%'; the appropriate bodies—the T.U.C. on the side of labour, and the C.B.I. on the side of management—were consulted and as far as possible

---

[1] Cmnd. 2639.

[2] See the 1968 White Paper, *Productivity, Prices and Incomes Policy* (Cmnd. 3590).

associated with the policy as it developed; and the Prices and Incomes Board was very active, reporting on remuneration and prices
in a large number of industries and occupations.

It is hard to say just how successful this policy was in the years
after 1965. Complete success can certainly not be claimed, since the
price-level continued to increase; on the other hand, it did so at a
diminishing rate—by 3·9% in 1966 and 2·9% in 1967, as compared
with 4·6% in 1965 and an annual average of 3·5% in 1961–4; after
1967 the pattern was disturbed by the effects of devaluation, making
judgement even more difficult. Certainly, the results were not such
as to convince everyone of the effectiveness of a statutory incomes
policy, and its use was repudiated by the Conservative government
which succeeded the Labour one of 1964–70.[1] Yet by the autumn of
1972, views had changed sufficiently for another attempt to be made.
An initial prices and incomes 'freeze' was followed by an eight-month
'phase two' in which wages could not be raised by more than 4%
plus £1 a week; a more complex 'phase three', beginning in late
1973, was challenged by a miners' strike and abandoned when the
government changed again in February 1974. The incoming Labour
administration, like its Conservative predecessor, had renounced
statutory incomes policy—yet by the summer of 1975 it too felt
obliged to adopt strict guidelines for a 'Social Contract' which,
though nominally voluntary, was in effect compulsory. It seems that
governments, regardless of party, found it impossible to do without
incomes policies for very long.

Yet even the most skilfully administered incomes policy is liable to
break down in face of the conflicts of interest that arise once inflation
is under way. The difficulty is that although labour as a whole gains
nothing in real terms if money-wage increases are countered by equal
proportionate increases in prices, matters do not present themselves
in this way to any *single* group of workers. Suppose industry X
produces commodities which make up 5% of the GNP, and that
wages are half its total production costs. A 10% increase in its
workers' money wages will raise X's prices by 5%, and put up the
general price level by only 5% of that, i.e. by 0·25%; provided no
other industry's workers obtain wage increases leading to rises in
the prices of *their* products, the workers in industry X will enjoy an
increase of 9·75% in *real* wages at the expense of a 0·25% reduction
in everyone else's. Some of the gain will be at the expense of profits
if firms in X are slow to raise their selling-prices; there will also be

[1] See R. G. Lipsey and J. M. Parkin, 'Incomes Policy: A Re-appraisal',
Economica, May 1970.

some transfer of real income from the recipients of social security benefits and other fixed incomes. It is only when prices are fully adjusted, when social security benefits have been revised, and above all when trades unions in other industries have obtained offsetting increases in money wages financed by raising *their* products' prices, that real wages in X will be back at their original level; and by that time X's union may have submitted demands for a fresh increase in money wages. Thus, there is a distinct advantage in being the first in the field with wage claims, and as this becomes more widely appreciated a competitive scramble is likely to develop; to end it, it is necessary to obtain general agreement not only on the division of the National Income between wages, profits and other forms of income, but also on the division of the wage-share itself between workers in different industries and occupations. This, however, implies some kind of inter-union agreement regarding the pattern of relative wages, in addition to the more traditional processes of collective bargaining between unions and employers regarding absolute wages; or alternatively, an acceptance on everyone's part of the pattern of relative wages as it happens to be at the moment when the incomes policy is first introduced. If appropriate norms could be adopted at a time when relative wages are considered generally satisfactory, they would have a fair chance of halting cost inflation— at any rate for a time, since the growth of the economy would eventually make a different relative wage-pattern necessary in view of the changing composition of output and its implications for labour requirements. But it is precisely when the previously existing wage-pattern has been upset in the inflationary process, that the necessity for an incomes policy will be most felt; if new restraints are then introduced, unions which have so far been lagging in the race to claim higher money-wages will feel that their position of temporary inferiority in the wage structure is now being made permanent, and their resentment may be enough to make the policy unworkable.

However, this is not to say that nothing can be hoped for from an incomes policy. It certainly means that it must be applied with political skill as well as economic expertise, but considering that the alternatives may be either to let the inflation proceed unhindered or to check it by monetary and fiscal policies which produce severe unemployment, it would be unwise to dismiss it as unworthy of further trial.

CHAPTER FOURTEEN

The Trade Cycle

(a) The problem

In the last few chapters, various methods have been described by means of which the authorities may attempt to maintain full employment and avoid inflation. Each of them was seen to have its difficulties and weaknesses. How important those weaknesses are, depends on the nature and size of the disturbances the economy is likely to encounter. Some of them may be of a far-reaching, long-term character: for example, the invention of a cheap synthetic substitute for a raw material of which a country has previously been the sole supplier may depress its economy for decades. A more frequent type of disturbance, however, is the periodical rise and fall in the level of activity and employment which has come to be known as the trade cycle, and which has been experienced by all industrial countries since the nineteenth century. While governments may have the greatest difficulty in overcoming the effects of major structural changes in the economy, they should be able at least to mitigate cyclical fluctuations by means of suitable monetary and fiscal policies.

This would, indeed, be a simple matter if fluctuations occurred in truly cyclical fashion, so that they were as foreseeable as the ebb and flow of the tides. A perfectly regular cycle would carry the economy from 'peak' to 'trough' and back again with uniform *frequency* and *amplitude*: that is, the time taken to move from one peak level of output to the next would always be the same, and the level of output and employment would always vary in the same proportion between the upper and lower turning-points. But such cycles have never occurred. Even if the economy would, left to itself, have generated them, their regular sequence would have been upset by external happenings such as wars and political changes; sudden advances in technical knowledge, discoveries of oil and gold, spontaneous changes in consumers' preferences, good and bad harvests—any of these and countless other possibilities may alter the underlying pattern. A single country, moreover, will be influenced by fluctuations in others, since these will affect its trade with the rest of the world. Not surprisingly, then, the historical record shows considerable variations in the frequency and amplitude of cyclical movements—for example, Britain experienced cycles between 1870 and 1914 whose peak-to-peak duration varied from seven to ten years, while in the United States during the same period there were eleven cycles, of which the longest took eight years and the shortest three.[1] To complicate matters still further, there have been marked differences between individual industries with respect both to the timing and severity of cycles: for example, the output of the capital goods industries has always varied much more than that of others, while house-building has pursued a rhythm of its own, with cycles of 20-25 years proceeding independently of the fluctuations taking place in the economy as a whole. Finally, the behaviour of indices other than output and employment, such as share prices, stocks, and the general price-level, has often been at odds with the pattern of fluctuations in output and employment.

It is hardly to be expected, then, that anything like a perfectly uniform and symmetrical cyclical movement is to be discerned in the historical record. None the less, past fluctuations have not been so irregular as to make the use of the word 'cycle' entirely inappropriate. Some of the apparent irregularity, indeed, can be attributed to the fact that not one but several cycles seem to have been operating concurrently. J. A. Schumpeter distinguished three: the short *Kitchin* cycle of approximately forty months' duration, the longer *Juglar* averaging nine and a half years' length, and the very long *Kondratieff* *wave* taking more than fifty years to run its course.[2] To these may be added the *Kuznets* cycle, or 'secular swing', of 16-22 years,[3] which has been described as 'so pronounced that it dwarfs the 7- to 11-year cycle into relative insignificance'.[4] With cycles of different lengths superimposed on one another, it is not surprising that the shorter ones should have been somewhat distorted in frequency and ampli-

[1] For details, see R. C. O. Matthews, *The Trade Cycle* (1959), pp. 205–26, and the references there given.

[2] J. A. Schumpeter, *Business Cycles* (1939) pp. 169 ff. The names given to the various cycles are those of the economists who first suggested them. Kitchin and Kondratieff wrote in the early 1920s, but Juglar's work was published as early as 1862.

[3] Cf. S. Kuznets, *National Product Since 1869* (1946); the suggestion that it should be called the 'Kuznets cycle' was first made by P. J. O'Leary and W. A. Lewis, 'Secular Swings in Production and Trade, 1870–1913', *The Manchester School*, May 1955.

[4] O'Leary and Lewis, *op. cit.*, p. 113.

L

tude: for example, the effect of the Kuznets cycle has been to make successive Juglars mild and severe by turns. The rhythm, then, is complex: but it has been sufficiently regular to suggest that past fluctuations may have been due to certain recurring causes which it should be possible to identify and perhaps to control. The attempt to find them has brought forth a large number of theories, some attributing cycles to wholly *exogenous* causes (i.e. arising from outside the economy) such as periodical variations in climatic conditions affecting crop yields,[1] others asserting them to be generated *endogenously* through the inner nature and motion of the economic system itself. An extreme example of the former group is the theory that cycles are entirely the result of random 'shocks' which, in a completely irregular and uncoordinated fashion, disturb the economy's component parts; it has been shown that the application of such shocks, to models so constructed that no endogenous fluctuations are possible, is capable of generating fairly regular cycles which closely resemble those actually recorded in the past.[2] If a *stochastic* hypothesis of this sort is correct, it would be pointless to look for a single causal factor recurring at regular intervals, since each fluctuation must have been the result of a unique set of circumstances; the fact that cycles run similar courses need not (on this view) be taken to imply similarity of causation.

However, the ability of stochastic models to produce lifelike cycles does not rule out the possibility that past fluctuations may, in fact, have been generated endogenously. If there are good reasons for supposing the existence of certain functional relationships within the economy (such as that between personal incomes and consumers' demand) whose interaction seems likely to give rise to systematic fluctuations, no cycle theory can be acceptable which does not take account of them—if only in a negative sense, by showing that their influence is negligible compared with that of outside disturbances.

[1] This was the essence of the celebrated 'sun-spot theory' advanced by Jevons in 1875. The periodicity of sun-spots caused an equivalent periodicity in weather and thus in harvests; the resulting fluctuations in agricultural prices, through their effects on the industrial sector, brought about variations in output as a whole.

[2] Cf. Irma Adelman, 'Business Cycles—Endogenous or Stochastic?' *Economic Journal*, December 1960. Mrs. Adelman set up a 'naïve model' in which consumption, investment, etc., were assumed to grow at steady rates over time and to be independent of one another, so that in the absence of external influences the system would have traced a straight-line growth-path without fluctuations; when 'erratic shocks' were applied to the variables, in the form of random departures from their trend values, the effect was to generate systematic cycles. See also G. H. Fisher, 'Some Comments on Stochastic Macroeconomic Models', *American Economic Review*, September 1952.

The particular interaction on which several 'endogenous' theories[1] have been based is that between the Multiplier and the Accelerator, which will now be considered in detail.

(b) The Multiplier–Accelerator interaction

In the dynamic Multiplier sequence worked out in Chapter Six (p. 135 above) it was shown that, given a one-period consumption lag, an autonomous rise in demand will give rise to a succession of income-changes in subsequent periods; these changes become smaller and smaller as a new equilibrium is approached. In Chapter Seven (p. 169 above) it was shown that, on certain assumptions, changes in income will induce investment-demand through the Accelerator (v). Thus, each stage of the original Multiplier process will give rise to fresh investment-demand, which will set another Multiplier going; this, in its turn, will give rise to additional investment-demand, which will set up fresh multiplier-effects—and so on. By this interaction, income will be made to rise by more than it would have done if the Multiplier had been acting alone. It might appear that the combined effects of the Multiplier and Accelerator must cause income to rise continuously, and this will indeed be the case if the Accelerator is unlagged[2] in the form $I_t = v(Y_t - Y_{t-1})$. The introduction of a one-period lag, however, creates the possibility of a cyclical movement, as the following analysis will show.

Assuming no government, no foreign trade and no output lag, income in period t will be $Y_t = C_t + I_t$. Consumers' demand depends on last period's income, but has an autonomous element: that is,

---

[1] Cf. J. R. Hicks, *A Contribution to the Theory of the Trade Cycle* (1950); R. M. Goodwin, 'A Model of Cyclical Growth', in *The Business Cycle in the Post-War World* (ed. Lundberg, 1955); M. Kalecki, *Theory of Economic Dynamics* (1954), Part 5; and N. Kaldor, 'A Model of the Trade Cycle', *Economic Journal*, September 1940.

[2] With $C_t = cY_{t-1}$ and $I_t = v(Y_t - Y_{t-1})$,

$$Y_t = cY_{t-1} + v(Y_t - Y_{t-1})$$

which can be rearranged to give

$$\frac{Y_t}{Y_{t-1}} = \frac{v-c}{v-1}$$

which means that the income of any period must exceed that of the previous period by a fixed proportion, as long as c is less than $1\cdot0$; c.g. if $v = 2$ and $c = 0\cdot5$, Y_t will be 50% greater than Y_{t-1}, Y_{t+1} will be 50% greater than Y_t, and so on. If the consumption function were unlagged, so that $C_t = cY_t$, the proportion Y_t/Y_{t-1} would be equal to $v/(v-s)$ (where s is written in place of $1-c$); with $v = 2$ and $c = 0\cdot5$, Y_t would be one-third larger than Y_{t-1}, Y_{t+1} one-third larger than Y_t, and so on indefinitely.

$C_t = a + c Y_{t-1}$. The one-period lag in the Accelerator means that $I_t = v(Y_{t-1} - Y_{t-2})$; when aggregate demand changes, firms try to adjust their capacity to it in the following period. There is no autonomous investment, so the equilibrium condition can be written

$$Y_t = a + c Y_{t-1} + v(Y_{t-1} - Y_{t-2}).$$

If there has been no change in income during previous periods, so that Y_{t-1} and Y_{t-2} are both equal to (say) 100, there will be no investment in period t, and Y_t will be equal to consumption expenditure; if a equals 20 and c equals 0·8, it can be seen that Y_t will be 100— exactly the same as the income of the two preceding periods. As long as no autonomous investment occurs and the value of a remains unchanged, income will continue to be 100 in the future. But now suppose there is an upward shift in the Consumption Function so that the value of a rises permanently from 20 to 30: this will make Y_t equal to 110 instead of 100. When the next period is reached, consumption will be $30 + 0·8(110)$, i.e. 118; the Multiplier has been set in motion, and if left to itself would cause income to converge on a new equilibrium value of 150. But it will not be left to itself, since the rise in income in period t will have induced some investment through the Accelerator; if v equals 1·2, investment in period $t+1$ will be $1·2(110\text{-}100)$, i.e. 12; when added to the consumption-demand of 118, this makes Y_{t+1} equal to 130. Similarly, income in the next period will be

$$Y_{t+2} = 30 + 0·8(130) + 1·2(130\text{-}110) = 158$$

—so that it has already been carried above the value towards which the Multiplier alone would have moved it. When the value of income is calculated for succeeding periods, it is found that Y_{t+3} is 190, Y_{t+4} is 220·4, Y_{t+5} is 242·8, and Y_{t+6} is 251·12. It can be seen that, although income is still rising in period $t+6$, the *rate* of increase has declined considerably; and the next period's income actually falls *below* the level reached in $t+6$, since

$$Y_{t+7} = 30 + 0·8(251·12) + 1·2(251·12 - 242·8) = 240·88.$$

From this point onwards, income continues to fall, because the Accelerator has now been thrown into reverse: successive reductions in the level of income induce *dis*investment, which has the effect of making income shrink still further. Thus, investment in $t+8$ is equal to $1·2(240·88\text{-}251·12)$, i.e. $-12·288$, and Y_{t+8} is consequently 210·416. By the time period $t+10$ is reached, income has returned approximately to its original level; but it is still falling, so that it is subsequently carried to still lower levels until the rate of fall at last slackens, another turning-point is reached,[1] and it begins to rise once again.

The effect of introducing the lagged Accelerator, therefore, is to change the original multiplier-sequence into a cycle. At first, income rises faster than it would have done if the Multiplier alone had been at work: 'accelerator-induced' investment-demand is added to the consumption-demand induced by successive increases in income. But there is now no question of a gradual convergence towards a new equilibrium income-level at which the system can settle down once the adjustment-process is completed. The essence of the Acceleration Principle, it will be recalled, is that once investment has risen in response to an initial increase in income, no further rise is called for if income goes on growing by successive amounts equal to its original increase, while a subsequent diminution in the rate of income-growth will cause the amount of investment actually to fall. Thus, unless the values of v and c are so high as to cause income to grow at a progressively increasing rate, investment cannot go on rising as fast as it did in the early stages of the sequence. But since investment-demand is itself one of the determinants of income, a slackening of the rate of growth of investment will cause a decline in the rate of growth of income, which in turn will cause the *amount* of investment to fall;[2] this will still further diminish the rate at which income is growing, until at last it stops rising altogether. At this peak level of income, however, investment will still be positive: because of the lag in the Accelerator, investment-demand is still being generated by the rise in income which occurred in the period just before the peak was reached. This makes it inevitable that income must fall again as soon as the peak has been reached: the fact that, at the peak itself, income has ceased to rise means that investment-demand will fall to zero immediately afterwards, so that aggregate demand is reduced below what it was at the peak. Since income is now falling, the capital stock built up earlier is larger than is required to produce current output, and firms will attempt to reduce their capacity by disinvestment, i.e. by not replacing equipment as it wears out; the faster the rate at which income falls, the greater the disinvestment. The same considerations now apply as when income was rising, except that everything is

---

[1] If the numerical calculation had been continued to this stage, it would have been seen that there is something very odd about this part of the cycle. To avoid undue complication, the point is ignored for the moment; but it will be taken up again on p. 329 below.

[2] In the numerical example already given, investment reaches a peak of 38·4 in period $t+4$; in the following three periods, it is successively 36·48, 26·88 and 9·984, after which it becomes negative, with a value of $-12·288$ in $t+8$. Thus, the level of investment begins to fall two periods before the decline of income starts.

moving in the opposite direction, with income falling and investment negative instead of positive. Eventually, the decline of income will slow up and halt, disinvestment will cease, and that very fact will cause aggregate demand, and therefore income, to revive again; the system will rise once more into the positive phase of another cycle.

In this sequence, the values of v and c are of great importance. If they are high, income will rise continuously at an ever-increasing rate, and there will be no downturn and therefore no cycle; thus, if

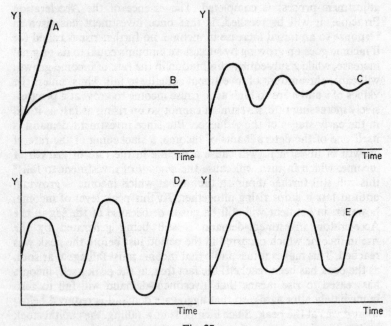

Fig. 27

the value of v is changed from $1 \cdot 2$ to 3 in the numerical example given earlier (all other values remaining the same), income will reach a value slightly above 10,000 in period $t+6$ instead of the 251 which was attained with $v = 1 \cdot 2$, and it will still be increasing: its path will be similar to curve A in Fig. 27 above. At the opposite extreme, low values of v will also fail to generate a cycle: income will merely converge to the new equilibrium level which would have been achieved by the operation of the Multiplier alone, and will stay there: the Accelerator will cause income to grow faster during the initial stages of the expansion process, but it will not be strong enough to alter the eventual outcome. Such a convergence would occur if, for example, the Accelerator were 0·25 instead of 1·2 in the sequence worked out above, and it is exemplified by curve B in Fig. 27. For cycles to occur, then, it is necessary that the values of v and c should lie between certain upper and lower extremes: provided they do so, income will oscillate about a central value equal to the equilibrium income which would eventually have been reached by the Multiplier had v been zero.

Three distinct types of cycle may be generated, according to the values of v and c. If v is small relatively to c (which itself is assumed to be less than 1·0) the oscillations will be 'damped'—that is, they will become weaker and weaker and eventually die away altogether, leaving income constant at its central value: curve C in Fig. 27 illustrates this kind of fluctuation. High values of v, on the other hand, give rise to 'anti-damped' cycles which, in the manner of curve D, become stronger as time passes, with the vertical distance between turning-points increasing at every revolution. The third type of cycle is the perfectly regular one exemplified by curve E, which once started continues indefinitely at a constant amplitude and is neither 'damped' nor 'anti-damped'. It can be shown[1] that the present model will generate E-type cycles only when v is exactly equal to 1·0, and, since this is only one among many possible values of v, the chances that such a stringent condition will be fulfilled for any length of time must be considered very small. A rough comparison of the 1967 figure of GNP with the estimates of the capital stock given on p. 70 (footnote 1) above, suggests than when v is calculated on an annual basis[2] its value is about 3·0; if this were assumed in the present

[1] See J. R. Hicks, *The Trade Cycle* (1950), pp. 69–72 and Mathematical Appendix, pp. 184–6. P. A. Samuelson, in 'Interactions Between the Multiplier Analysis and the Principle of Acceleration' (*Review of Economic Statistics*, May 1939) used a model in which consumption is lagged one period and investment is induced by the current change in consumption, so that

$$Y_t = 1 + cY_{t-1} + vc(Y_{t-1} - Y_{t-2})$$

—the '1' being a dollar of government spending which acts as a multiplicand. He found that the condition for E-type cycles was $c = 1/v$. In the model given in the text, v does the work of vc in Samuelson's; replacing his vc by v turns the equation into $v = 1$. See also R. G. D. Allen, *Mathematical Economics* (2nd edition, 1959), Chapter 7.

[2] This would assume that the 'investment period' defined on p. 170 above is one year in length. In fact, it is difficult to estimate the true investment period for the whole economy; for some industries it will be short, and for others long, so that an aggregation problem would exist even if each individual industry's investment period were known (which it is not). If new evidence were to show that six months was more realistic than a year, it would be necessary to think of the multiplier–accelerator interaction as running in terms of half-year periods with a v of 6·0.

model, the cycle would be either the anti-damped D-type or the 'explosive' A-type.

Meanwhile, it must be emphasized that the Multiplier–Accelerator interaction illustrated above is by no means the only possible one. It would no doubt be more realistic to suppose that the consumption-lag is shorter than the investment-lag—say, three months as against one year. Both lags might be distributed over several periods, so that investment, for example, would depend on the changes in income which had occurred during the past two or three years instead of a single one. The values of v and c might very well change in the course of the cycle, perhaps for exogenous reasons, or perhaps in response to the cyclical movement itself: for example, the onset of a depression, causing a sudden worsening of expectations, would no doubt increase firms' desire to disinvest and thereby cause v to increase during the down-turn. If an output-lag (hitherto excluded by assumption) is brought into the model, this will complicate things still further. Finally, there is the possibility, not so far considered, that autonomous investment may occur in addition to the investment induced through the Accelerator. If, in the sequence traced earlier, the rise in autonomous demand in period t had been for investment-goods instead of for consumption, the satisfaction of this demand (which, in the absence of an output-lag, may be assumed to have taken place within period t itself) would have raised productive capacity as well as setting off a multiplier-process. The output-capital ratio is the inverse of the Accelerator v (i.e. $1/1 \cdot 2$), so autonomous investment of 10 units will raise output by $8 \cdot 3$, that is, by roughly the amount of additional production needed to satisfy the multiplier-induced increase in consumers' demand in $t+1$; alternatively, it will meet a good part of the demand for investment-goods induced in $t+1$ through the Accelerator.[1] If autonomous investment now remains at 10, it will therefore have the effect of partially damping-down the cycle, as well as ensuring that fluctuations take place about a rising trend instead of the constant income-level which has so far been assumed.

[1] The argument here assumes that capital installed in period t becomes productive in $t+1$: that is, that the periods t, $t+1$, etc., are so chosen as to be equal in length to the 'investment period', which is taken to be uniform throughout the economy. This may, of course, be untrue in particular cases: the autonomous investment of a given period may be part of a long-range project (such as the building of a Channel Tunnel) which will take many years to complete and which can produce nothing until it is finished. In the meantime, its contribution to productive capacity will be nil, and its current effects will be precisely similar to those of the autonomous increase in consumption assumed in the original sequence.

The original Multiplier–Accelerator interaction can thus be modified in various ways so as to achieve greater realism, albeit at the cost of increased complexity. Its chief offence against realism, however, may be thought to require modifications of a kind not so far suggested. It has already been noted that the simple model is very unlikely to generate E-cycles (because this would require v to be precisely $1\cdot0$) and will most probably (since v is judged to be typically greater than $1\cdot0$) produce either anti-damped D-type or explosive A-type movements. Yet the historical record shows that actual fluctuations have not continually increased in amplitude in the manner of a D-cycle, nor has there been an 'explosion'. If the economy really has a tendency to generate such movements, they must somehow have been prevented from developing their full effect. An obvious limit to upward movements is the economy's productive capacity at full employment; if there is a downward limit also, the amplitude of fluctuations will be less than the value of v would by itself have caused it to be.

(c) Floors, ceilings and shocks

The possibility of such a lower limit is easily seen by considering the 'downswing' phase of the cycle in the numerical example given earlier. When income reached its peak, the fact that it had ceased to grow caused investment to fall; this reduced income in the following period, the fall in income induced disinvestment, income fell further —and so on. If the arithmetical calculations of pp. 323-4 are continued, it will be found that income reaches -15 in period $t+12$, with investment at the very low figure of -75 (both figures having been rounded to the nearest whole number). In the next period, consumption is at its minimum[1] level of 30, investment is -64, and income is therefore -34; this, it turns out, is the 'trough' of the cycle, since income recovers to a positive value of $7\cdot6$ in $t+14$ and to 86 in $t+15$, after which it goes on rising towards a new peak. That both income and investment should become negative during the downswing is, of course, highly unrealistic, but it is not impossible as long as both are defined as net of depreciation. Negative net investment implies that all or part of current depreciation is not being made good, so that the capital stock is shrinking as more and more units reach the end of their productive lives without being

---

[1] It is assumed that a, the autonomous element in consumption, is a minimum level (here equal to 30) below which consumers will not reduce their expenditure; the consumption function $C_t = a + cY_{t-1}$ is not valid for negative values of Y_{t-1}. Without this condition, consumption would itself become negative in $t+14$, which would be nonsensical.

replaced: but disinvestment can hardly exceed the amount of depreciation, since that would mean that capital was being destroyed before it had ceased to be productive. If the disinvestment *desired* in any period is greater than current depreciation, the excess will have to be carried forward and added to the desired disinvestment of the following period. In the numerical example, the capital stock has an average value of 180, i.e. v times the 'central value' of income (150) about which the cycle rotates; if the average 'life' of capital is ten periods, depreciation in any single period will average 18·0, so that the large amounts of disinvestment called for in $t+12$ and $t+13$ could not have been realized.[1]

The fact that disinvestment cannot exceed depreciation means that income cannot fall below a minimum value, or 'floor', equal to autonomous consumption minus current depreciation—in symbols, $Y_{min} = a - D$, where D is depreciation.[2] If a exceeds D, the 'floor' value of income will be positive, and the economy will be prevented from plunging into the depths into which the numerical example originally carried it in periods $t+12$ and $t+13$. When income has been at its minimum level for two consecutive periods, the fact that it is no longer falling means that no further disinvestment will be required—apart, of course, from the backlog already accumulated in the past. When the backlog has been worked off, the term '$-D$' will disappear from the income-determining equation, and income will once more rise, setting the Accelerator in motion and starting the upswing of a fresh cycle. However, the new cycle will not be the next phase of the original one. Even if the value of v is such that it would generate anti-damped cycles in the absence of constraints, the fact that income has been stationary for several periods at its 'floor' value means that the cycle must start again at the beginning.[3] Instead of a succession of

---

[1] The figure of 18·0 is merely an average over the whole cycle: it takes no account of possible 'echo-effects' (see above, p. 170). If all equipment is assumed to fall due for replacement precisely ten periods after installation, depreciation will depend on the amount of gross investment ten periods earlier: e.g. depreciation in $t+14$ will be 38·4 (the net investment of $t+4$) plus the depreciation made good in $t+4$ which is now again due for replacement. On this basis, the amount of depreciation will vary from period to period, and will greatly complicate the working of the numerical example; however, except in the very special case in which the life of capital is equal to exactly half the duration of a complete E-cycle, it will not change the fact that some desired disinvestment will fail to be achieved during the downswing—which is the essential point in the text above.

[2] Since Y is *net* income, gross income is $Y+D$; and gross income cannot be less than minimum consumption a. The value of D will, of course, be smaller, the longer the average 'life' of capital-assets.

[3] At the point where recovery begins, the situation will be the same as it was in period t, except that the multiplicand is now D instead of the original increase in a.

fluctuations of increasing amplitude, there will be an endless repetition of the first revolution of a D-cycle; in this way, the occurrence of fairly regular fluctuations could be consistent with a high value of v.

The 'floor' which has just been described is a very low one. Autonomous investment, due to technological innovations and long-range planning, may be a substantial amount in each period, and may indeed be increasing through all the phases of the cycle in response to a long-term growth trend in the economy. If population is growing, this is likely to increase the amount of minimum consumption a from period to period. These factors will not only raise the height of the floor, so that income reaches its minimum value while net investment is still positive; they may also give it an upward tilt, so that recovery begins earlier than it would otherwise have done. Each time the economy rises from the floor to begin a new revolution of the cycle, it will do so from a higher level of income than on the previous occasion. Instead of revolving around a stationary central value, as it was assumed to do in the numerical example, the cycle will now be moving around a rising trend of income.

Just as the downswing of the cycle may be stopped by a 'floor', so may the upswing be halted by coming into contact with a 'ceiling'. The ultimate limit to the rise of real income is the economy's productive capacity at full employment: if this happens to lie below the maximum level of income which the cycle would have reached had it been free to run its course, investment-demand will be in excess of saving when the system runs up against the ceiling, and a backlog of demand will have to be carried forward to the next period; meanwhile, the cessation of income-growth will reduce the amount of accelerator-induced investment to zero, so that as soon as the backlog of investment-demand has been satisfied income will fall again and the downswing phase of a new cycle will have begun. The sequence is, it appears, much the same as that which occurred when the downswing encountered the 'floor', except that the algebraic signs are all reversed: instead of the desire to *dis*invest, it is now the desire to invest which is frustrated.

It may be objected, however, that the analysis fails to allow for the effects of the inflationary pressures which will be set up when the economy draws close to the full-employment ceiling.[1] As the growing shortage of labour forces wages up, a wage-price spiral is likely to develop and inflation may become chronic. Instead of being reduced

---

[1] It should be remembered that the income-determining equation is in real terms. Thus if Y_t and Y_{t+1} are both equal to full-employment real income, real investment demand in $t+2$, i.e. $v(Y_{t+1} - Y_t)$, will be zero even though the money value of Y_{t+1} exceeds that of Y_t because of rising prices.

to zero, the amount of induced investment-demand may actually increase: the shortage of labour and the rise of wages give firms an incentive to substitute capital for labour in production; conscious that there is excess demand for their products, and wishing to expand production to meet it, firms will try to invest more than before; and capital-goods may be sought as a hedge against inflation if prices are expected to go on rising. Thus, the excess of investment-demand over saving may actually increase, so that it is no longer a question of merely working off a backlog. But the historical record does not show regular bursts of strong price-inflation; price-changes certainly occurred during past cycles, but not in such a way as to suggest that upswings normally gave rise to inflationary gaps at full-employment income. The 'ceiling hypothesis' must therefore be regarded as doubtful.

It may also be unnecessary. If downswings are stopped by a floor in the way described earlier, each cycle starts afresh from the beginning: instead of following the D-curve along its full length, the system will merely repeat part of the first revolution over and over again. If the upper turning-point of the first revolution happens to lie below the ceiling, each upswing will come to an end of its own accord before full employment has been reached. If there were no floor, of course, the cycle would be able to proceed unhindered to its second, third and subsequent revolutions, and this would eventually bring it up against the ceiling; when, in due course, income fell below the ceiling and the cycle was resumed, it would begin again at the downswing phase of the first revolution, and a series of apparently regular fluctuations would then follow in spite of the 'anti-damped' value of v. Thus, it is not necessary that the cycle should encounter *both* the floor and the ceiling.[1] Either of them will be sufficient on its own to prevent the cycle getting beyond the first revolution; consequently, if the role assigned to one of them should appear to be unrealistic, it may be discarded as long as the other is retained. Nor need the choice be irrevocable: it is conceivable that the cycle might proceed for quite a long time as a series of fairly even 'bounces' along the floor, and then be propelled towards the ceiling by an unusually rapid growth of autonomous demand; on reaching the ceiling, it would bounce back, but it would reach a lower turning-point which was now well above the floor, at which the accelerator would go into reverse and cause

---

[1] There is, however, one case in which both floor and ceiling would be required: this is where the value of v is so high as to cause an 'explosion' in the manner of curve A in Fig. 27. The ceiling will then break the rise of income, which in due course will 'explode' downwards until checked by the floor; the next movement will be an upward explosion which proceeds until checked by the ceiling—and so on.

income to rise again for another collision with the ceiling; subsequent fluctuations would then be a series of bounces off the ceiling.[1] However, as long as the value of v in the simple multiplier–accelerator interaction is too high to be consistent with regular E-type fluctuations, either a floor or a ceiling must be brought into the model: it is not possible to dispense with both of them.

Nevertheless, it is extremely difficult to argue from empirical evidence that either the floor or the ceiling has ever actually played the part assigned to it in the model. Reasons have already been given for doubting whether the ceiling was ever reached in the course of the nineteenth century, and it was certainly not touched in the inter-war period. It would be equally certain that the floor was never reached either, if the criterion were assumed to be the occurrence of negative net investment, since net investment seems to have been positive even in the worst depression years.[2] But it was suggested earlier that accelerator-induced disinvestment is likely to be offset by some amount of autonomous investment; the difficulty is to distinguish one category from the other, and to decide whether a given year's net investment was positive only because autonomous investment-demand was present, or because the cycle had come to its lower turning-point before reaching the floor. It is therefore possible to argue that past fluctuations should not be interpreted as anti-damped cycles whose movement was interrupted by collisions with the floor and/or the ceiling, but that—on the contrary—they may actually have been C-type damped cycles which were continually strengthened by exogenous 'shocks' of one kind or another.

This need not involve unrealistic assumptions about the value of v. Though the condition for damped fluctuations in the simple model is that v should be less than $1 \cdot 0$ (a value which was earlier dismissed as unreasonably low), it is possible to raise this 'critical value' by altering the model in various ways: for example, distributing the consumption-lag over several past periods will allow damped cycles to occur with v greater than $1 \cdot 0$.[3] Another possibility is that the price of capital-goods (relatively to other commodities) may vary directly with the amount of investment-demand, and that this changes the

[1] Thus, it would not be inconsistent to regard pre-1939 cycles as 'floor-based' fluctuations, while considering the milder fluctuations of the post-1945 period to have been a series of 'bounces off the ceiling'—the ceiling itself, of course, being upward-sloping because of the long-run growth trend.

[2] The severe depression of the early 1930s is the sole exception to this.

[3] For example, if the income-determining equation were changed to $Y_t = c_1 Y_{t-1} + c_2 Y_{t-2} + v(Y_{t-1} - Y_{t-2})$, where $c_1 + c_2 = c$, the condition for damped cycles would be $v = 1 + c_2$, so that if c_2 were $0 \cdot 5$ the 'critical value' would be $1 \cdot 5$. See R. G. D. Allen, op. cit., Chap. 7.

value of v in the following period: for example, when investment is high during the upswing of the cycle, the consequent rise in capital-goods' relative prices would make firms seek less capital-intensive methods of production; the variation in v would then have a damping effect, even though its average value over the whole cycle happened to be quite high.[1] Suitably modified, then, the model could be made to give damped oscillations which, if permitted to run their course without disturbance, would allow the system to settle down to an even tenor; the appearance of regular fluctuations would be due to the occurrence of erratic shocks which set fresh cycles going, or which reinforce existing ones so that they are prevented from dying away. A model of this sort[2] might be claimed to accord better with the observed course of events than do 'anti-damped' models, since the cycles it generates are necessarily somewhat irregular and therefore lifelike, and it makes provision from the outset for the 'external happenings' which are constantly affecting the economy; on the other hand, since it allows the internal functional relationships to play a part in producing cycles (in other words, since it contains an endogenous as well as a stochastic element) it is not open to the objection raised earlier against the *purely* stochastic hypothesis, viz. that it explains too little.

It cannot yet be claimed that any single theory of cycles commands universal assent, though there has undoubtedly been a marked narrowing of the area of disagreement in recent decades: for example, very few economists now accept a purely monetary explanation, though such a theory was strongly held as late as the nineteen-thirties.[3] On one important point, however, it may be said that there is now fairly general agreement, namely that fluctuations are to be regarded as a part of the process of long-term economic growth. Such a view was put forward as early as 1912 by J. A. Schumpeter,[4] who argued that fluctuations were an integral part of long-run develop-ment, in the sense that they were both a consequence and a cause of it. Since then, and especially within the last twenty years, the theory of long-run growth has received increasing attention; and it will be considered at length in the next chapter.

[1] The investment-function $I_t = v(Y_{t-1} - Y_{t-2})$ would then become $I_t = v_1 Y_{t-1} - v_2 Y_{t-2}$, where $v_1 < v_2$ if $Y_{t-1} > Y_{t-2}$ and $v_1 < v_2$ if $Y_{t-1} < Y_{t-2}$. The term $v_2 Y_{t-2}$ would represent actual capital existing at the beginning of period t, while $v_1 Y_{t-1}$ would represent desired capital.

[2] This type of theory is particularly associated with the name of Ragnar Frisch: see his 'Propagation Problems and Impulse Problems in Dynamic Economics' in *Economic Essays in Honour of Gustav Cassel* (1933).

[3] Notably by R. G. Hawtrey and F. A. von Hayek.

[4] In his *Theory of Economic Development*, first published as *Theorie der Wirt-schaftlichen Entwicklung* in 1912.

CHAPTER FIFTEEN

The Theory of Growth

(a) Investment and the growth of income

As one year follows another, output may remain the same or even fall, but in the long run it can be expected to follow an upward trend. This presumption accords with historical experience: Britain, for example, produced in 1975 more than twice the goods and services that she did in 1929, and more than eight times what she produced in 1864; in the rest of the world, some countries have grown faster, others more slowly, but the universal tendency has been for output to expand considerably from decade to decade. One obvious reason for this is the growth of population, which in Britain has risen by a half, and in the world has more than doubled, since the turn of the century.[1] Even if the stock of capital and methods of production had remained unchanged, a steady increase in the number of workers would have caused output to grow, though at a lower rate than that of the labour force itself because of diminishing returns.[2] But capital has, in fact, increased substantially. In most economies, investment is normally greater than the amount required to make good capital consumption, so that each year's flow of output includes the means of increasing the flow in the following year; in Britain, the stock of capital in manufacturing alone rose by 39% between 1965 and 1975.[3] Methods of production, too, have been continually improving, though it is impossible to say at what rate: many technological advances have to be 'embodied' in new equipment, so that their effects on output cannot be unambiguously separated from those of the investment which 'carries' them. The dissemination of technical knowlege, educational expansion, public health improvements which enhance

[1] For a useful collection of figures showing the growth of output and population in various countries since 1899, see A. Maizels, *Industrial Growth and World Trade* (1963), Appendix E. For British figures since 1900, see *The British Economy: Key Statistics, 1900–70* (London and Cambridge Economic Service, 1972).

[2] See pp. 71–3 above. In Fig. 1 on p. 72, a steady increase in employment beyond ON_2 brings progressively smaller additions to output.

[3] See *National Income and Expenditure, 1965–75*, Table 12.12.

workers' longevity and vigour, and other kinds of 'investment in human resources', have also helped to bring about a long-run growth in output. All these growth-inducing factors—population increase, technological progress, and investment in both material capital and human resources—may be expected to continue operating in the future; accordingly, the working of the economy should be examined in a context of secular expansion of resources and output. Some of the questions which have to be answered are: what determines the rate of growth in a given economy? Is the growth of output likely to exceed that of population, so that income per head and living standards rise in the long run? Under what conditions will the growth rate accelerate, decelerate or stay constant over the years? Is growth inherently stable or unstable? As productive capacity increases, will it all be utilized, or will an increasing proportion of labour and capital be unemployed? Alternatively, is growth likely to be inflationary?

The theory of income-determination presented in earlier chapters does not attempt to provide direct answers to questions of this sort, because of its short-run character. Diagrams like Fig. 10 (p. 130) and Fig. 12 (p. 165) are drawn on the assumption that population, the stock of capital and the techniques of production are all fixed for the time being; even though net investment is currently adding to the stock of capital, the time-perspective is too short for this to make any appreciable difference to the situation—investment is merely one element of aggregate demand, and changes in it are of interest only because of their effects on the equilibrium of the economy. But when the analysis is no longer confined to the short run, it is necessary to allow for the fact that investment adds to productive capacity, and that if the additional capital is all brought into use there will be a consequential rise in income and output: in symbols, $\Delta Y = \sigma I$, where σ is a measure of the productivity of capital[1] (and, it will be noticed, the inverse of v, the 'capital-output ratio' defined on p. 169 above). The question then arises, will aggregate demand increase sufficiently to absorb the whole of the additional output? The rise in income generated by the latter will certainly induce an increase in consumption, provided the MPC is greater than zero; but unless the MPC is equal to $1 \cdot 0$, this will take up only a part of the additional production, leaving a remainder ($s\Delta Y$, where s is the Marginal Propensity to save) which will have to be absorbed by an increase in investment if

---

[1] More precisely, σ is the *marginal* productivity of capital; it may not be the same as *average* productivity, i.e. that of the capital stock as a whole (symbolized as Y/K). However, it is a convenient simplification to assume that marginal and average productivities are equal, so that $\Delta Y/I = Y/K$.

it is to be absorbed at all. The likelihood of such an increase occurring depends on the extent to which the demand for investment responds to the rise of income; for the moment, it is sufficient to note that the condition for continuing growth without the development of excess capacity is that there must be an increase in investment-demand, ΔI, equal to $s\Delta Y$. Since $\Delta Y = \sigma I$, this condition may be re-stated as $\Delta I = s\sigma I$, or

$$\frac{\Delta I}{I} = s\sigma.$$

Thus, if s is 0.1 (i.e. if one-tenth of income is saved), and if σ is 0.5 (i.e. £1 worth of output requires £2 worth of capital to produce it),

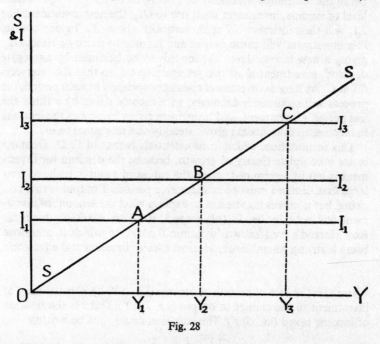

Fig. 28

it will be necessary for investment-demand to grow at the rate of 0.05, or 5% per annum, if the economy's productive capacity is to continue to be fully used. If the s in $\Delta I = s\Delta Y$ is a constant (in other words, if the community always saves a fixed proportion of income, whatever the amount of the latter may be), the proportionate increase in investment $\Delta I/I$ will be the same as the proportionate growth of income $\Delta Y/Y$; the term $s\sigma$ will then define the rate of growth of income as well as that of investment.

This is illustrated in Fig. 28, which is similar to Fig. 12 on page 165 above: income is measured on the horizontal axis, and saving and net investment on the vertical: all quantities are in real terms. The savings function SS is a straight line starting at the origin: its slope is equal to both the MPS and the APS, and it is assumed to remain unchanged for a considerable period of time. The initial level of investment-demand is shown by I_1I_1, which intersects SS at A to give an equilibrium income of Y_1; here, it is assumed, full employment exists. As soon as the new capital equipment represented by investment OI_1 comes into service, income will rise to Y_2—the proportion between the rise in income $(Y_2 - Y_1)$ and investment OI_1 being the 'output-capital ratio' σ. For Y_2 to be the new equilibrium level of income, investment must rise to OI_2; the new investment-line I_2I_2 will then intersect SS at B, vertically above Y_2. In due course, this investment will cause output and income to rise by σ times OI_2, giving a new income-level Y_3; for this to be balanced by aggregate demand, investment must rise yet again to OI_3 so that I_3I_3 intersects SS at C. As long as investment rises appropriately in each period, the process will continue indefinitely, with income rising by σ times the last period's investment, and investment rising by s times the increase in income, so that income grows steadily at a rate equal to $s\sigma$.

This formulation, which in its essentials is that of E. D. Domar,[1] is not a complete theory of growth, because the demand for investment is left undetermined: given the values of s and σ, it shows how large that demand must be in successive periods if output is to go on rising, but it makes no attempt to explain what the amount of investment will actually be. In this respect, it differs markedly from Sir Roy Harrod's well-known 'dynamic theory', to which it otherwise bears a strong resemblance. Harrod uses a 'fundamental equation'[2]

$$GC = s$$

where G is the rate of growth of income (i.e. $\Delta Y/Y$), C is the ratio of investment to the change in output (i.e. $I/\Delta Y$), and s is the fraction of income saved (i.e. S/Y). The equation could thus be written

$$\frac{\Delta Y}{Y} \cdot \frac{I}{\Delta Y} = \frac{S}{Y}$$

which, when the Y's and ΔY's are cancelled out, reduces to the familiar ex post identity of saving and investment. If I and S are taken in the ex ante sense, however, the equation defines an equilibrium

[1] Evsey D. Domar, *Essays in the Theory of Economic Growth* (1957), p. 91.
[2] R. F. Harrod, *Towards a Dynamic Economics* (1948), p. 77 et seq.; see also his 'Second Essay in Dynamic Theory', *Economic Journal*, June 1960.

condition in which $\Delta Y/Y$ is what Harrod calls the 'warranted rate of growth', denoted G_w to distinguish it from the actual growth rate G. In static equilibrium, producers are satisfied with the level of current output if they are neither accumulating unwanted stock nor conscious of excess demand for their products; similarly, growth will be proceeding at an equilibrium (or 'warranted') rate if producers find that the increase in output they have planned[1] is exactly balanced by a concomitant increase in aggregate demand. They will then be, in Harrod's words, 'content with what they are doing' and 'in a state of mind in which they are prepared to carry on a similar advance' in the future. If growth is to proceed at this 'warranted' rate, saving must continue to be matched by *ex ante* investment, the amount of which is assumed to depend on the current increase in income and output. In symbols, $I = C_r\Delta Y$, where C_r is a 'coefficient of capital requirements' showing the amount of new capital[2] needed to produce an additional unit of output; at a given rate of interest,[3] and with technical progress which is 'neutral' in the sense that it does not change the capital-intensity of production as times goes by,[4] C_r will be constant; it is, in effect, the capital-output ratio v of the Acceleration Principle as defined on page 169 above. If an equilibrium of *ex ante* saving and investment existed to start with, it will be preserved, as output increases, if $C_r\Delta Y = sY$. This condition can be rearranged to read $\Delta Y/Y = s/C_r$; the value of $\Delta Y/Y$ which satisfies the equation is the 'warranted' rate of growth G_w, and the 'fundamental equation' can accordingly be rewritten

$$G_wC_r = s.$$

If the economy continues to grow at this rate, it will be following an 'equilibrium path'.

[1] It is not, of course, necessary that each individual firm should find that its planned output is equal to demand; the condition described above applies to planned output as a whole, and could be consistent with surpluses and shortages in particular industries.

[2] In his definition of capital, Harrod emphasizes that he is including all stocks and work-in-progress, as well as fixed capital. 'Required' investment, therefore, consists not only of new machinery, buildings, etc., but of additions to stocks in proportion to the increase in output. At a later stage of his argument, Harrod puts some weight on this point (*Towards a Dynamic Economics*, p. 90). His fixed investment is, of course, net of depreciation.

[3] Changes in the cost of financing new investment may alter firms' views as to the most remunerative proportions in which to combine capital goods with other productive factors, thus changing the value of C_r. The same considerations apply to changes in real wages.

[4] Harrod's usage of 'neutral' differs from that of other writers, especially Sir John Hicks; see F. H. Hahn and R. C. O. Matthews, 'The Theory of Economic Growth: A Survey', *Economic Journal*, December 1964.

A graphical illustration of the theory is given in Fig. 29, whose axes measure income horizontally and saving and investment vertically.[1] The savings function OS is the same as in Fig. 28; its slope is the s of the 'fundamental equation'. The straight line AI represents Harrod's investment function $I = C_r \Delta Y$, which may also be written $I_t = C_r(Y_t - Y_{t-1})$: investment is zero if current income is the same as that of the previous period (i.e. if $Y_t = Y_{t-1}$), so AI cuts the income-axis at a point A representing last period's income; the

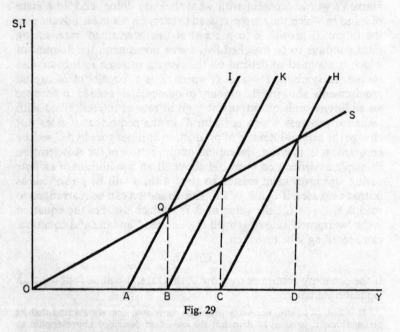

Fig. 29

slope of AI is equal to C_r, and is steeper than 45° on the assumption that $C_r > 1$. Saving-investment equilibrium exists when income is OB; this exceeds the previous period's income by AB, so that the warranted rate of growth (defined as $(Y_t - Y_{t-1})/Y_t$) is equal to AB/OB. When the next period $(t+1)$ is reached, OB will have become the preceding period's income, and the investment-function will have shifted to BK; if the value of C_r has not changed, BK will be parallel to AI. The intersection of BK with OS now gives equilibrium income of OC, so that the warranted rate of growth in period

[1] For a diagrammatic treatment in terms of growth rates rather than absolute levels of income, see C. S. Soper, 'Jorgenson on Stability in the Sense of Harrod', *Economica*, November 1964.

$t+1$ equals BC/OC. Similarly, $t+2$'s investment function will be CH, giving equilibrium income of OD and a warranted growth-rate of CD/OD. By the properties of similar triangles, it can be seen that CD/OD, BC/OC, and AB/OB are all equal to one another; thus, warranted growth proceeds at a constant proportionate rate as long as the values of s and C_r remain unchanged. As time goes by, the investment-function will shift further and further to the right, so that income will continue to increase at the warranted rate provided saving-investment equilibrium is maintained from period to period.

Since investment-demand here depends on the growth of income, Harrod's model appears to be an example of the multiplier-accelerator interaction described in the previous chapter—but with the special feature that the accelerator is unlagged. The implied assumption is that firms compare the existing state of demand for their products (of which they are assumed to have precise knowledge) with that of the previous period, and *simultaneously* carry out whatever investment is needed to bring their capital up to current requirements. This, it may be argued, is not very realistic: firms take time to become aware of the state of their markets, and by the time they make the appropriate investment-decisions the next period will already have arrived; even if such decisions *are* made simultaneously with the growth of demand, time is needed to give effect to them, so that the investment actually being carried out at a given moment will not be related to current changes in demand. The insertion of a lag into Harrod's investment-function, however, changes the model almost out of recognition. If, instead of $C_r(Y_t - Y_{t-1})$, I_t is made equal to $C_r(Y_{t-1} - Y_{t-2})$, it immediately becomes autonomous of current income, since both Y_{t-1} and Y_{t-2} have become unchangeable historical facts once period t has been reached. Instead of AI in Fig. 29, period t's investment-function will be a horizontal straight line, whose distance above the income-axis depends on the amount of income-growth which occurred in the previous period. If both saving and investment are lagged one period, the model is identical with the multiplier-accelerator interaction presented on pages 323–4 above, in which income did not grow but merely fluctuated about a constant level;[1] the inclusion of lags, with the object of increasing the realism of the Harrod model, may therefore disqualify it altogether as a theory of growth.[2]

Autonomous investment does not appear in the 'fundamental

[1] It will be remembered, however, that given a sufficiently large value of v (in Harrod's terminology, C_r) the model will produce an uninterrupted rise in income; in this case, the system continues to be a 'growth model' even when lagged.
[2] See J. R. Hicks, 'Mr Harrod's Dynamic Theory,' *Economica*, May 1949.

equation', but Harrod is prepared to bring it in, if necessary, as an additional variable k: the equation then becomes

$$G_wC_r = s - k$$

where k is the proportion between autonomous investment and current income.[1] Since C_r and s are assumed constant, the presence of k has the seemingly paradoxical effect of reducing the warranted rate of growth G_w. In Fig. 29, the introduction of autonomous investment-demand will shift AI vertically upwards, and since it slopes more steeply than OS (i.e., because C_r exceeds s) it will now intersect the latter to the *left* of Q; the equilibrium output of period t will be reduced below OB, and the warranted rate of growth will be less than AB/OB; it may, indeed, fall to zero or even become negative if the amount of autonomous investment happens to be sufficiently large. This brings out the fact that the role of growth in Harrod's model is to induce sufficient investment to offset current saving; the appearance of an additional offset, in the shape of autonomous investment, means that less *induced* investment is required for the purpose, so that the growth-rate must fall if equilibrium is to be maintained.

Another consequence of the fact that C_r exceeds s is that the short-run equilibrium positions shown in Fig. 29 are *unstable*. A slight divergence from Q, for example, will produce a tendency towards further divergence: if output in period t should turn out to be slightly greater than OB because firms have overestimated the demand for their products, the demand for investment will exceed saving, and firms will be under pressure to expand output still more; conversely, a slight shortfall of production *below* OB will create a surplus of saving over investment-demand, which will tend to depress output to still lower levels; and the further output moves from equilibrium, the greater the pressure forcing it still further away. Such a movement will mean that the excess of current income over last period's income is no longer equal to AB, so that the actual growth-rate now differs from the warranted rate AB/OB. A change in the value of C_r or s will have similar consequences: an increase in s, for example, will

---

[1] *Towards a Dynamic Economics*, p. 79. Harrod argues that 'in the long run k must disappear, for in the long run all capital outlay is justified by the use to which it is put', though 'it may be very important to separate it out in the short period'. When k is thus specified, the alternative expression for the 'fundamental equation', as given on p. 338 above, now becomes

$$\frac{\Delta Y}{Y} \cdot \frac{I_t}{\Delta Y} = \frac{S}{Y} + \frac{I_a}{Y}$$

where I_t is induced and I_a is autonomous investment. This simplifies to $S = I_t + I_a$—a slightly more elaborate version of the saving-investment equilibrium condition.

cause OS to slope more steeply, and therefore to cut AI at a point above and to the right of Q; the equilibrium level of income will now be higher than before, but because the initial effect of the movement of OS is to create an excess of saving over investment at the existing income-level OB, income will tend to fall instead of rising towards its new equilibrium value. In this case, the fact that the equilibrium level of income has increased means that the warranted growth-rate has risen—yet the very increase in G_w will have set up pressures causing the *actual* growth-rate G to fall below its original value.

Harrod's own demonstration of this instability begins by comparing the *ex post* and *ex ante* versions of the 'fundamental equation'. Since GC and G_wC_r are both equal to s, they are equal to one another;[1] consequently, any difference between G and G_w entails an equal but opposite difference between C and C_r. Thus, if G exceeds G_w, C_r exceeds C, which means that the amount of investment required to produce the current increase of output is greater than the amount actually being done; firms will be demanding more equipment and materials than are currently available, and the effort to supply them will cause output to rise faster than before; but this will make the excess of G over G_w still greater, so that the actual growth-rate, far from returning to equality with the warranted rate, will run away from it. In the same way, an initial shortfall of G *below* G_w will cause C to exceed C_r, with the result that G will be reduced still further. This is the argument of the preceding paragraph put into Harrodian terms. The symbols C_r and C represent $I/\Delta Y$ in the *ex ante* and *ex post* senses respectively; *ex post* investment is identical with saving, so C could equally well be written $S/\Delta Y$; a difference between C_r and C, therefore, is a difference between investment-demand and saving.[2] Similarly, since G is defined as the actual value of $(Y_t - Y_{t-1})/Y_t$, and G_w as the value which would be consistent with saving-investment equilibrium, a difference between G and G_w means that Y_t happens not to be at its equilibrium value.[3] To say

---

[1] This, it may be noted, implies the assumption that *ex ante* saving always equals *ex post* saving. The s of $GC = s$ is merely the proportion of income *actually* saved, while that of $G_wC_r = s$ is the proportion which income-recipients *wish* to save. The two could very well be different, for example when shortages frustrate consumers' buying-plans.

[2] $C_r \neq C$ implies $I/\Delta Y \neq S/\Delta Y$; multiplying both sides by ΔY gives $I \neq S$. It is assumed (as has already been noted) that saving plans are always realized, i.e. that *ex post* equals *ex ante* saving.

[3] Since the value of Y_{t-1} is fixed (being a matter of past history by the time period t is reached), Y_t is the only term which can vary in the expression $(Y_t - Y_{t-1})/Y_t$; consequently, G and G_w, if different in value, imply different values of Y_t.

that $C_r > C$ when $G > G_w$ is thus the same thing as saying that invest-ment-demand exceeds saving when income is above equilibrium level. The instability of the warranted growth-rate is the instability of saving-investment equilibrium, at a given moment of time, when the slope of the investment function exceeds that of the saving function.

With equilibrium thus unstable, the consequences of a departure from it depend on the rapidity with which the level of production can be changed in response to such a disturbance. If the reaction is instantaneous, output will immediately fall to zero or rise to the limit of productive capacity, according to the direction of the displace-ment. With a one-period lag, on the other hand, output will remain unchanged for the time being; an excess of investment-demand over saving will be carried forward as unsatisfied demand, while a deficiency of investment will cause an accumulation of unsold goods to be carried over; when the next period is reached, and firms take fresh production decisions, they will presumably try to work off the backlog of demand (or the accumulation of stocks, as the case may be) by making output higher (or lower) that it would otherwise have been; income will once again differ from its equilibrium value, and a fresh backlog of demand (or accumulation of stocks) will have to be carried forward, creating similar situations in the next and sub-sequent periods. Since Harrod does not include any lags in his model (and indeed seems to rule them out by insisting that its instability 'has nothing to do with the effect of lags'[1]), it might be supposed that he is assuming the first of these possibilities, i.e. an immediate run-away of output to one extreme or the other; but when he speaks of 'centrifugal forces . . . causing the system to depart further and further from the required *line of advance*',[2] he seems to be thinking of the more gradual divergence that would occur if an output-lag were present, with output tracing a path which, over a succession of time-periods, deviates more and more from the course it would have taken if warranted growth had continued. Given appropriate values of s and C_r as well as a one-period output-lag, the system will certainly be unstable in this second sense;[3] Harrod, however, implies that its in-

----

[1,2] *Op. cit.*, p. 86. Italics supplied.

[3] If, in Fig. 29, *AI* slopes much more steeply than *OS*, an excess of output in period t over the equilibrium level *OB* will create an excess of investment-demand over saving larger than itself. With a one-period output-lag, this will be carried forward to $t+1$; if firms try to clear the whole backlog by adding an equivalent amount to $t+1$'s equilibrium output, the difference (D) between actual and equilibrium output will be greater in $t+1$ than in t (in symbols, $D_{t+1} > D_t$). But $t+1$'s equilibrium output (Ye_{t+1}) will itself be larger than that of t, since the investment-function will by now have shifted to the right (and will, in fact, lie

stability over time is unconditional, i.e. that the system will never, under any circumstances, return to the warranted-growth path once it has deviated from it. In view of the ambiguity of his concept of instability, arising from his failure to specify the lags involved, it is not surprising that he has been criticized on this point by a number of writers.[1]

If warranted growth *is* unstable over time, an upward deviation will carry the actual growth-rate progressively farther above it: but there is an ultimate limit to this divergence, namely, the 'natural rate of growth' G_n, which Harrod defines as 'the rate of advance which the increase of population and technical improvements allow'. Actual growth G may exceed G_n for a time, for example when the economy is emerging from a recession and re-employing labour and equipment previously idle, but once full employment has been regained it will be impossible for output to grow faster than G_n. There is no similar limit, however, to the possible value of G_w: a high propensity to save, for example, might well cause the warranted growth-rate to exceed the 'natural' rate—in which case G, even if it is at first equal to G_w, will soon fall away from it because of its inability to exceed G_n for very long; the initial divergence will then increase, pulling G below G_n and dragging the economy into a recession. If, on the other hand, G_w is below G_n, it is no longer inevitable that G must deviate from it, though it may still do so because of some chance disturbance; with G and G_w equal but less than G_n, there will be an increasing gap between actual output and the output which the economy is capable of producing when all its resources are employed. Only if G_w equals G_n will it be possible to combine steady growth with full employment: yet there is no reason to suppose that this equality will be achieved except by accident, since the magnitudes which determine the two growth-rates (s and C_r in the case of G_w, and the rates of population-increase and technical progress in the case of G_n) are all assumed to be determined independently of one another

---

somewhat to the right of BK). If D_{t+1}, as a proportion of $Y_{e_{t+1}}$, is greater than D_t as a proportion of Y_{e_t}, the system will be unstable in the sense Harrod seems to have in mind. This condition will be fulfilled if, for example, $C_r = 4$ and $s = 0.2$, but not if (say) $C_r = 1.5$ and $s = 0.5$.

[1] See, for example, H. Rose ('The Possibility of Warranted Growth', *Economic Journal*, June 1959) and Dale W. Jorgenson ('On Stability in the Sense of Harrod', *Economica*, August 1960). Jorgenson argues as follows: actual growth equals G_w plus the growth of a 'disequilibrium variable', D, which at the outset will have been equal to $\Delta Y(C_r - C)$ and which will have gone on increasing at a rate k; if, however, k is less than G_w, the 'disequilibrium variable' will eventually become negligible relatively to total income, so that the economy will ultimately return to the warranted-growth path instead of moving ever further away from it.

and of the actual rate of growth G. Thus, the prospects before an economy which resembles Harrod's model are unattractive—it will experience either a succession of booms and slumps, or a steady advance accompanied by growing unemployment, with the chances in favour of the first alternative because of the instability of the warranted-growth path.

It is easy to see that there would be no problem of reconciling steady growth with full employment if the 'required' capital-output ratio C_r were a variable:[1] even with s and G_n fixed, the equality of G_w and G_n would be permanently assured if C_r could be relied on to assume whatever value was necessary to satisfy the equation $s/C_r = G_n$. Under certain circumstances, indeed, this might well happen: if an excess supply of labour (i.e. the unemployment associated with $G_w < G_n$) were to force down real wages, while the cost of employing capital (represented by the rate of interest) remained unchanged, labour would be substituted for capital in the productive process, the value of C_r would fall and that of G_w would rise; conversely, a shortage of labour ($G_w > G_n$) would raise real wages, alter the relationship of factor prices, cause capital to be substituted for labour, and thereby increase C_r and reduce G_w. If nevertheless, C_r remains constant, it must be because it is physically impossible to substitute labour for capital and vice versa, or else because the prices of the factors remain unchanged relatively to one another in spite of imbalances of supply and demand—the latter being the explanation put forward by Harrod.[2] In either case, given certain assumptions about the technique of production,[3] both factors will be employed in fixed proportions to the level of output and to one another: the amount of labour required to increase output by one unit will be constant, just as capital requirements are. Once full employment has been attained, therefore, output cannot grow

[1] It may be noted that Harrod allows the possibility of *temporary* variations in C_r, for example when the economy is recovering from a depression and is able to expand output by bringing idle plant back into use instead of investing in newly-produced equipment; in these circumstances, C_r will be below its normal value until full-capacity output is regained.

[2] He concentrates attention on the possibility of changes in the interest-rate rather than in real wages (which are assumed constant) and concludes that interest is not sufficiently flexible, and investment-demand not sufficiently interest-elastic, to bring about the necessary changes in C_r. See *Towards a Dynamic Economics*, p. 96 ff., or better, Harrod's 'Comment' (on an article by H. Pilvin, which see also) in the *Quarterly Journal of Economics*, November 1953, p. 555 ff.

[3] They are (a) that capital and labour are the only factors of production, and (b) that there are 'constant returns to scale'. For the significance of these assumptions, see the discussion of production functions in the next section of this chapter.

any faster than the supply of labour, except to the extent that labour's productivity is being raised by technical progress as time goes by; in the absence of the latter, output *per head* cannot rise, since output and population will be growing at exactly the same rate, and no increase in output will be possible at all if the population is stationary.[1] It is hard to believe that upward trends in *per capita* output are to be attributed entirely to improvements in technology and not at all to increases in the amount of capital per worker—yet this is what is implied by the assumption of fixed factor-proportions. On the other hand, to abandon that assumption as too restrictive is to change the Harrod theory out of recognition, and to take the first step in the so-called 'neo-classical' approach to the problem of growth.

(b) 'Neo-classical' growth theory

Harrod's point of departure was the short-run theory of income-determination, originally developed by Keynes as a means of analysing the causes of mass unemployment in the nineteen-thirties. Just as Keynes stressed the role of aggregate demand in determining output and employment in the short run, so, in his turn, Harrod approached the analysis of growth in terms of the long-run evolution of demand, and (as has been seen) was not optimistic about the possibilities of combining steady growth with full employment over a long period of time. But it can be argued that Keynesian principles, now generally accepted, have provided governments with an armoury of weapons for tackling short-run difficulties, and that it is now legitimate to proceed on the assumption that full employment will somehow or other be assured: output may then be expected to grow at the maximum rate permitted by the increase of productive capacity. The Harrod model could be made to give this result by including in it a government whose taxes and expenditure adjust s in such a way as to keep G_w permanently equal to G_n, or by including a monetary authority which appropriately adjusts both s and C_r; but a simpler approach is merely to relax the assumption of fixed factor-proportions, so that whatever the quantities of capital and labour at the disposal of the economy, they can always be combined in such a way as to ensure that all are employed. This is the starting-point of the 'neo-classical' growth theory associated with the names of R. M. Solow, T. W. Swan and J. E. Meade.[2]

[1] It is assumed for simplicity that population and the supply of labour increase at the same rate. They may, of course, fail to do so: for example, changes in age-grouping may alter the proportion of the population which is of working age.

[2] See R. M. Solow, 'A Contribution to the Theory of Economic Growth',

It is now assumed, therefore, that it is physically possible to substitute factors for one another in the production process, and that such substitution is not in any way inhibited by price-rigidities— in other words, that perfect competition exists. To produce a given

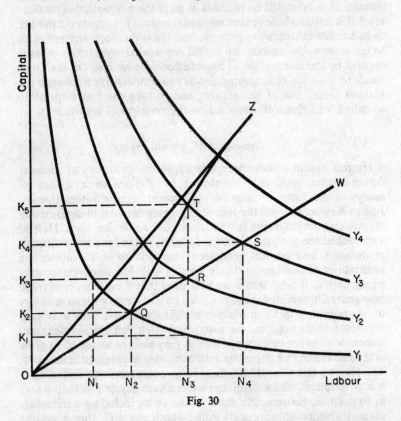

Fig. 30

output, it will then be possible to 'mix' the factors in any number of different proportions. A full statement of the possible 'mixtures' at all levels of output is a *production function*. This is a familiar concept

Quarterly Journal of Economics, February 1956; T. W. Swan, 'Economic Growth and Capital Accumulation', *Economic Record*, 1956; J. E. Meade, *A Neo-Classical Theory of Economic Growth* (2nd edition, 1962). The theory has been called 'neo-classical' because it makes assumptions—perfect competition, full employment, and the payment of factors according to their marginal products—which were customary with the so-called 'neo-classical' economists whose work appeared between (roughly) 1870 and 1920.

in microeconomic analysis, which uses it to explain the individual firm's choice of inputs at a given set of factor prices:[1] in macro-analysis, however, the problem arises that 'output' is not a single homogeneous commodity but a mass of different ones aggregated in terms of their money values, so that a change in the composition of output, or in the relative prices of its constituent commodities, could produce a change in total output even though the quantities of the factors employed remained unaltered. To avoid this difficulty, it will be assumed that the output of the whole economy consists of a single good which is equally suitable for both consumption and investment purposes. It is also assumed that the factors of production are themselves homogeneous; that capital is 'malleable' in the sense that a unit of it can be used in conjunction with any quantity of labour, large or small; that labour and capital are the only factors of production, and that (for the time being, anyway) there is no technical progress. A production function with all these characteristics is shown in Fig. 30, whose axes measure quantities of labour and capital respectively, and whose Y-curves are 'isoquants' each of which refers to a given level of output and shows the various combinations of capital and labour capable of producing it: for example, output Y_1 can be produced by K_3 units of capital and N_1 of labour, or by K_2 and N_2, or by K_1 and N_3, or by any other pair of factor-quantities indicated by the curve. The greater the quantities of both factors employed, the greater the amount of production, so that Y_2 represents a larger output than Y_1, Y_3 a larger one than Y_2, and so on; as growth proceeds and the economy's factor-supplies increase, successively higher Y-curves will be reached, and the points attained on them will form a 'growth-path' leading upwards and to the right. If capital and labour always increase in the same proportion, the growth-path will be a straight line (or 'ray') through the origin, like the line OW passing through points Q, R and S. Given 'constant returns to scale', output will grow in exactly the same proportion as the factors of production, and equal distances along a ray such as OW will represent equal increases in output.[2] The Y-curves of Fig. 30 have been drawn so as to intersect OW (and any other ray through

[1] See, for example, K. E. Boulding, *Economic Analysis* (3rd edition, 1955), Chap. 34, p. 741; W. J. L. Ryan, *Price Theory* (1958), pp. 50–63; R. G. D. Allen, *Mathematical Economics* (2nd edition, 1959), pp. 332 ff.

[2] If 'increasing returns to scale' operate, a given length along QRS will represent a greater rise in output, the further away it is from the origin; the output yielded by equal successive additions to both factors will be increasing. 'Diminishing returns to scale' implies the contrary. In the absence of any *a priori* reason for assuming either increasing or diminishing returns to scale, constant returns is the most reasonable supposition.

the origin) at equal intervals: under constant returns to scale, therefore, a movement from one Y-curve to the next always implies the same amount of change in output.

Now suppose that the economy starts at point Q, producing output Y_1 with K_2 units of capital and N_2 of labour; and that the supply of labour grows at a constant rate n which is exogenously determined. The rate of growth of capital ($\Delta K/K$) is the rate at which the initial stock K is being increased by net investment, which is assumed[1] equal to *ex ante* saving; if the community saves a constant proportion s of income, $\Delta K/K$ will be equal to sY/K, or s/v when the capital-output ratio K/Y is written v. If s/v equals n, capital and labour will be growing at the same rate, so that the growth-path will be OW; along this line, output will be increasing at the same rate as the factors of production because returns to scale are constant, so that

$$\frac{\Delta Y}{Y} = \frac{s}{v} = n.$$

This equation defines a condition of *steady growth*, because as long as the values of s, v and n which satisfy it remain unchanged, output will continue growing indefinitely at the same rate. At first sight, this result seems to be identical with that obtained from the Harrod model when $G_w = G_n$, since G_w equals s/C_r, C_r is equivalent to v, and G_n equals n when there is no technical progress. The difference lies in the fact that C_r is a constant, while v is not. If, in Harrod's model, the value of C_r happens not to satisfy the equation $s/C_r = n$, no pressures arise to bring it into line,[2] and G_w and G_n continue to differ. In the neo-classical model, on the other hand, v will adjust to whatever value is required to satisfy the steady-growth condition given above.

This can be shown by means of the following example. Suppose the economy has hitherto experienced steady growth, and has advanced up OW in Fig. 30 as far as Q; at this point, however, it is assumed that there is a sudden once-for-all increase in the propensity to save. The rise in s means that s/v now exceeds n; a larger proportion of income is being saved and invested, so that the capital stock is growing faster than the supply of labour. Instead of rising from K_2 to K_3

---

[1] This may be regarded as a necessary consequence of the assumptions of perfect competition and continuous full employment. Alternatively, it can be assumed that there is a monetary authority behind the scenes which constantly adjusts interest rates in such a way as to ensure saving-investment equilibrium at full employment: see Meade, *op. cit.*, p. 3.

[2] Where $s/C_r > n$, i.e. $G_w > G_n$, there will of course be a fall in the *actual* growth-rate G, but this does not imply any adjustment of G_w; it merely means that the system is out of equilibrium.

in the next period, capital rises to K_5; the labour-supply, however, rises only to N_3 (as it would have done in any case, since labour's growth-rate is exogenously determined), and the system consequently moves to point T (on Y_3) instead of to R (on Y_2). At T, the capital-intensity of production is greater than it was along the original growth-path OW: had Y_3 been reached at S instead of T, the amounts of capital and labour employed would have been K_4 and N_4 respectively instead of K_5 and N_3, that is to say, less capital and more labour would have been used to produce the same level of output. This means that the capital-output ratio v has risen, so that s/v is now somewhat smaller than it was just after the initial increase in s occurred; capital is growing more slowly, but its rate of growth still exceeds that of labour. As long as s/v continues to be greater than n, the capital-intensity of production will go on increasing, with the result that v will continue to rise until the value of s/v once more equals n and steady growth is resumed at the original rate. However, the growth-path will now be steeper than it was at first: it is drawn in Fig. 30 as OZ, which like OW is a straight line through the origin, but which represents a higher capital-labour ratio than that given by OW. Because the capital stock has increased faster than n for a time, it is now greater than it would have been if the economy had continued to expand along OW; consequently, the resumption of steady growth means that capital is growing by a larger *amount* per period even when its *rate* of growth is identical with that implied by OW. It may seem paradoxical that an increase in s should bring about no permanent increase in the rate of growth of capital—yet this is a necessary consequence of the adjustment of the proportions in which the factors are employed.

In the case which has just been examined, the system was pushed off the original growth-path by an increase in the propensity to save. If s had initially fallen instead of rising, the consequence would have been a reduction in the value of v, to the point where s/v regained equality with n; production would have become less capital-intensive, and the system would have moved on to a new steady-growth path less steep than OW. A fall in n itself, unaccompanied by a change in s, will be accommodated by a *rise* in v; to offset the slower growth of the labour force, production will become more capital-intensive, but because s is unchanged, the growth-rate of capital will fall until it is equal to the reduced value of n. In all cases, the system will react to a disturbance by forcing a change in v sufficient to allow a resumption of steady growth at the rate n.

As long as steady growth continues at a given rate, the fact that $\Delta Y/Y$ equals n means that no change in output per head can occur;

but any of the disturbances described above will raise or lower it to a new level, at which it will remain when steady growth is resumed. An initial rise in s, causing capital to grow faster than labour, also causes output to rise faster than it would otherwise have done: in the example given earlier, the increase of capital from K_2 to K_5 in Fig. 30 allowed the system to reach output Y_3, instead of Y_2 as it would have done had steady growth continued. As long as s/v is greater than n, output will be growing faster than labour, and output per head will be rising; when s/v is at last equal to n again, output per head will have been stabilized at a higher level than before. Conversely, a reduction in the value of s will bring about a fall in output per head. Changes in n have similar effects to those of *opposite* changes in s: thus, output per head will rise when the growth-rate of labour diminishes, and fall when the latter increases.

Nothing has so far been said about the time likely to be needed for the adjustment of the system back to steady growth after a disturbance has occurred. It seems probable that the process will be a lengthy one. Suppose, for example, that s is 0.06, v is 3, and n is 0.02; if all rates of change are annual rates, output will be increasing steadily at 2% per year. Now let s suddenly rise to 0.08: to restore s/v to equality with n, it is necessary that v should be raised from 3 to 4. This implies a substantial increase in the capital stock, which (since $K = vY$) must now rise by an amount equal to a whole year's output. Even after the initial rise in s, however, only 8% of current income is being saved and invested, so that $12\frac{1}{2}$ years would be required to bring capital up to the required level even if output were stationary; and since output will, in fact, be growing at annual rates higher than 2% during the adjustment process, it is easy to see that a very long time will elapse before steady growth is resumed. Indeed, R. Sato has shown that on realistic assumptions regarding the values of the parameters of a neo-classical model, the system may take more than a century to accomplish as much as nine-tenths of the adjustment back to steady growth.[1] It is hardly likely that such a lengthy period will go by without the occurrence of fresh disturbances, so the chances of steady growth ever being attained seem very small: accordingly, it may be said that the behaviour of the system during the adjustment process is of much greater interest than its behaviour

[1] Ryuzo Sato, 'Fiscal Policy in a Neo-Classical Growth Model', *Review of Economic Studies*, February 1963, and 'The Harrod-Domar Model *versus* the Neo-Classical Growth Model', *Economic Journal*, June 1964. Sato's model is more complicated than that discussed in the text above, since it includes technical progress, direct taxation and public investment: but his general conclusions are also valid in the simpler case.

when following a steady-growth path. From this point of view, it is of less consequence that (for example) a rise in s will *eventually* be offset by a rise in v in such a way as to leave the growth-rate unchanged, than that it will cause s/v to exceed n for a considerable time, in the course of which both capital and output will be increasing faster than they would otherwise have done. Though their rates of increase will be gradually falling towards equality with the steady-growth rate, the diminution may be so slow that for quite long periods it will be reasonable to treat them as constants; economic policy will be realistic if it seeks to produce a continual rise in output per head by encouraging a high rate of capital accumulation, even though this will in the long run be offset by the adoption of more capital-intensive methods of production.

There is one way, however, in which output may continue to increase faster than the factor-supplies even when steady growth has been attained, though this possibility has up to now been excluded by assumption: that is, through technical progress. When new and better techniques of production[1] are devised, their effect is to enable the existing quantities of capital and labour to produce more than they were capable of doing previously. This may be illustrated in Fig. 30 in either of two ways. The Y-curves can be shifted inwards towards the origin, so that Y_2 replaces Y_1, Y_3 replaces Y_2, and so on; any pair of quantities of capital and labour will then reach a higher Y-curve than before. Alternatively, the Y-curves may be left as they are and the points K_1, K_2, N_1, N_2, etc., moved further out along their respective axes in proportion to the increase in productivity brought about by technical progress; the effect will then be shown as precisely equivalent to that of an increase in the physical quantities of the factors. Even if the capital stock and the labour supply remain unchanged in physical terms (i.e. if s and n are both zero), continuous technical advance will allow the system to reach successively higher Y-curves, tracing a growth-path similar to that which would be followed if the factor-supplies were themselves increasing. If technical progress raises the productivity of both factors in the same proportion r, output will itself rise at the rate r and the system will move along a steady-growth path such as OW or OZ. Where the physical quantities of the factors are already increasing in such a way as to give steady growth, the addition of technical progress will cause a more rapid

---

[1] It is important to distinguish between 'changes in methods of production' in the sense of changes in the proportions in which the factors are employed (which in Fig. 30 would be represented by a movement along one of the isoquants, e.g. from R to T), and 'technical progress' by which a given combination of factors is enabled to produce more than it did before.

M

advance along the same growth-path, and the steady-growth condition will become

$$\frac{\Delta Y}{Y} = \frac{rK + \Delta K(1+r)}{K} = \frac{rN + \Delta N(1+r)}{N}$$

or

$$\frac{\Delta Y}{Y} = r + \frac{s}{v}(1+r) = r + n(1+r)$$

where, it will be noticed, the influence of the capital-output ratio v diminishes in proportion to the rate of technical progress.

It may, of course, happen that the productivity of one factor increases more quickly than that of the other. Suppose the rate of growth of capital-productivity, a, exceeds that of labour-productivity,[1] b, and that factor-supplies are fixed in physical quantity (i.e. $s = 0$, $n = 0$); if the latter are respectively K_2 and N_2 in Fig. 30 (so that, in the absence of technical progress, output would have been stationary at Y_1), the system will move upwards along a straight line starting at Q and sloping more steeply than OW. Because a is greater than b, the scale of the capital-axis will be increasing faster than that of the labour-axis, and K_2 will be moving outwards more rapidly than N_2; as they move, K_2 and N_2 will trace a growth-path which, not being a ray through the origin, cuts the successive Y-curves at continually increasing intervals, which means that output grows at a rate which is less than a and greater than b, and which gradually diminishes as time goes by. Eventually, the growth-rate of output will approach the value of b, and the path along which output is rising will approximate to one of steady growth.[2] When, in addition, the physical quantities of capital and labour are increasing, the effects just described will be superimposed on those of the growth of the factor-supplies themselves: if the latter would on their own have

[1] In this case, technical progress might be described as 'capital-biased'; this implies 'labour-bias' when b exceeds a, and 'neutrality' when a and b are equal. But this conflicts with the usage already noted (p. 339, n. 4) in connection with the Harrod model, where technical progress was said to be 'neutral' if it did not change the value of C_r: 'Harrod-neutrality' therefore requires that $a = 0$. The definition of neutrality as the condition in which $a = b$ is associated with the name of Hicks (*The Theory of Wages*, 2nd edition, 1963, pp. 121–3). Accordingly, technical progress is said to be 'Hicks-neutral' when the productivity of capital is rising at the same rate as that of labour, so as to leave the *capital-labour* ratio unchanged; and 'Harrod-neutral' when only the productivity of labour is rising and the *capital-output* ratio remains unaltered.

[2] In mathematical language, the growth-path is *asymptotic* to a ray, i.e. the two will meet only at 'infinity': thus, the rate of growth of output will never fall quite far enough to be precisely equal to b.

brought about a steady growth of output, technical progress with a greater than b will push the system off the steady-growth path; on the other hand, a growth-rate of labour in excess of that of capital might conceivably just offset the excess of a over b, leaving the system on a steady-growth path which it could not otherwise have attained. The greater the difference between a and b, the more it will complicate the adjustment process which takes place when the values of s and n change.

So far, technical progress has been assumed to raise the productivity of each unit of capital, old or new, in exactly the same proportion, and to do the same to the entire labour force; like manna from heaven, it descends on the whole of the system's factor-supplies. This is clearly unrealistic. When an advance in the design of machinery makes it possible to produce higher output for the same cost as before, only newly-built machines get the benefit of it; technical progress must be 'embodied' in new investment if it is to exert an effect on the level of output. (Similarly, the productivity of labour may be increased by improvements in the educational system, but only new recruits to the labour force will 'embody' this sort of progress: older workers' abilities will not be affected.) Thus, the rapidity with which the economy reaps the benefits of technical advance depends on the rate of growth of the factor-supplies as well as on the rate of technical progress itself. The steady-growth condition given earlier may be amended to show this by the omission of the terms rK and rN, so that it becomes

$$\frac{\Delta Y}{Y} = \frac{\Delta K(1+r)}{K} = \frac{\Delta N(1+r)}{N},$$

where, if ΔK and ΔN are both zero, output remains stationary whatever the value of r. This formulation, however, ignores the possibility that some part of the capital stock and labour force is being retired and replaced as time goes by; that is, it neglects the question of depreciation. Even if the factor-supplies are not growing in total amount, technical progress may still be embodied in new units which replace those currently being withdrawn. The faster the rate of depreciation, the greater the response of output to technological advance: the steady-growth condition is

$$\frac{\Delta Y}{Y} = \frac{rdK}{K} = \frac{rdN}{N}$$

where d is the proportion of K and N replaced per period of time, and where ΔK and ΔN are assumed to be zero. It is, of course, unlikely that the value of d will be the same for both capital and labour,[1] and a difference in the factors' replacement-rates may be supposed to have consequences similar to those of a difference between their rates of productivity-growth. However, the analysis of these effects runs into difficult problems of aggregation. Instead of the homogeneous, 'malleable' capital stock assumed at the outset, there will now be a collection of assets of various 'vintages', each embodying a different technology and each differing in productivity from the others: whatever device is adopted to aggregate them (e.g. the addition of money values, or the use of some physical measure such as horse-power) is bound to be more or less unsatisfactory; and where physical differences between capital-goods are allowed to come into the reckoning, the original assumption of a one-product economy becomes more artificial than ever.[2] Another difficulty arises concerning the 'malleability' of capital, i.e. its ability to co-operate with any amount of labour, large or small. When the adoption of a newly-devised technique requires that the capital embodying it shall differ in physical characteristics from capital of earlier vintages, it is hard to imagine it still to be malleable; yet without the assumption of malleability, the factor-proportions are no longer variable (i.e. the isoquants of Fig. 30 can no longer be drawn as smooth curves) and the model ceases to conform to neo-classical specifications.

Complications of this sort draw attention to the extreme simplicity of the basic model, in which as many problems as possible have been avoided by making appropriate assumptions: when these are relaxed in an attempt to achieve greater realism, the model becomes much more difficult to handle. It is not feasible, within the limits of a single chapter, to explore all the possibilities which then arise, but it will be useful to note some of the more important modifications which can be made.

The first, and perhaps the most obvious one, is to abandon the assumption that output consists of a single all-purpose commodity. The simplest way of doing this is to divide the economy into two 'sectors', one producing a capital good K and the other a consump-

---

[1] It need not be supposed that labour's d is simply the rate at which school-leavers step into the shoes of elderly workers (in which case it would be about 0·02). Workers can be retrained at any age: those who acquire new skills may be regarded as replacing their old, unskilled selves, so that d will be higher, the greater the amount of 'on-the-job' training.

[2] But not completely untenable. Suppose (as suggested by Meade, *op. cit.*, p. 6) the single product is cows, which may be consumed as meat or used to breed more of them. Improved breeding may make the currently-produced cows more fecund than previous 'models'; technical progress will be embodied in them, yet production will still consist of a single homogeneous commodity.

tion good C; the labour-supply and the capital stock are divided between them, and the K-sector provides new equipment both for itself and for the C-sector; each sector has its own production function. No stocks of C are accumulated, so that investment is equal to the output of the K-sector; given the neo-classical assumption that investment-demand equals saving at full employment, K-output equals sY, where s as usual represents a constant propensity to save. But Y itself is now an aggregate of C and K, and to reduce it to a single measure it is necessary to know the relationship between the prices of the two commodities, p_k and p_c; a change in p_k/p_c can alter Y and sY, thereby causing the output of the K-sector to vary. Under perfect competition, factor-prices are the same in both sectors, and equal the value of the factors' marginal physical products, so that (for example) $\mathrm{MPL}_c p_c$ equals $\mathrm{MPL}_k p_k$, where MPL is the marginal physical product of labour and the subscripts refer to sectors; to find relative prices, i.e. p_k/p_c, it is necessary to evaluate $\mathrm{MPL}_c/\mathrm{MPL}_k$. The uniformity of factor-prices also means that the proportion between the wage-rate (w) and the rate of profit per unit of capital (π) is the same in both sectors, which implies that $\mathrm{MPL}_c/\mathrm{MPK}_c$ equals $\mathrm{MPL}_k/\mathrm{MPK}_k$ (where MPK is the marginal physical product of capital). To satisfy this equation, the capital stock and labour force must be allocated between the sectors in certain proportions;[1] the ratio $\mathrm{MPL}_c/\mathrm{MPL}_k$ gives the commodity-price ratio p_k/p_c, which in turn defines Y; given the value of s, the output of the K-sector will then be determined, while that of the C-sector will be whatever is produced by the labour and capital not in use in the K-sector. If the output of K is such as to increase the total capital stock at the same rate as the labour force, total output will grow steadily as long as the allocation of new factor-supplies is such as to maintain the conditions set out above. Where this is not possible (for example, because the K-sector itself has a very high requirement for additional capital), the ratios w/π and p_k/p_c will change as output grows, thereby altering the valuation of Y; this will cause sY, and therefore the output of K and the rate of increase of the capital stock, to differ from their steady-growth values, and the rate of growth of output will be changed in consequence. The adjustment process is more complicated than that

[1] In either sector, the greater the amount of capital used and the less that of labour, the greater the value of MPL/MPK (on the usual assumption of diminishing marginal rates of substitution). If $\mathrm{MPL}_c/\mathrm{MPK}_c$ is higher than $\mathrm{MPL}_k/\mathrm{MPL}_k$, a transfer of labour from the K-sector to the C-sector, and/or a transfer of capital in the opposite direction, will equalize the two ratios. This would be consistent with a *number* of allocations of the factors; however, when K-output is determined as above, only one of these allocations is possible. The system could be described algebraically by a set of simultaneous equations: see Meade, *op. cit.*, Appendix II.

of the single-good model, but the general presumption is that a stable
steady-growth path exists—that is, there must be a set of values of
all the variables which would permit output to grow at a constant
rate, and the system will return to this steady-growth condition after
a disturbance.[1]

A second way of modifying the original model is to relax the
assumption that saving is a constant proportion of income. An
alternative hypothesis is the *classical saving function*[2], which makes
saving depend on the distribution of income between wages and
profit by assuming that the proportion of profit saved (s_π) is greater
than that of wages (s_w). Total profit equals the capital stock, K,
times the rate of profit π, which itself is equal to MPK;[3] the share of
profits in total income is thus $K.\text{MPK}/Y$. Similarly, the share of
wages is $N.\text{MPL}/Y$, and the overall propensity to save is

$$s = s_\pi \frac{K.\text{MPK}}{Y} + s_w \frac{N.\text{MPL}}{Y}.$$

Given steady growth, K, N and Y will all be increasing at the same
rate, MPK and MPL will remain unchanged,[4] and s will be constant.
If, however, K is growing faster than N, the share of profit will increase
unless MPK falls relatively to MPL sufficiently to restore the balance;
whether it will do so depends on the shape of the production function,[5] but if it does not, the fact that s_π exceeds s_w means that s will
now increase as Y grows. To restore the steady-growth condition
$s/v = n$, the value of v must rise by more than would have been
necessary had s remained constant; the adjustment-process will take
longer, and it will bring the system on to a more capital-intensive

[1] See Hahn and Matthews, *op. cit.*, pp. 820–1.

[2] So named by Hahn and Matthews, *op. cit.*, pp. 793–4, because of its affinity
with the saving-behaviour postulated by Ricardo and other 'classics'.

[3] The assumption of a single homogeneous product is now restored, so that all
quantities except N are measured in the same units and it is unnecessary—indeed,
it would be meaningless—to specify a price in order to indicate the value of a
factor's marginal physical product.

[4] Had N remained unchanged, the growth of K would have meant diminishing
returns to capital, i.e. a falling value of MPK; similarly, N increasing with K
unchanged would have reduced MPL; but since N and K here rise at the same
rate, marginal returns to the factors remain constant in the 'homogeneous'
production function shown in Fig. 30.

[5] In Fig. 30, the slope of an isoquant at a given point is the inverse of MPK/MPL
(for proof, see Boulding, *op. cit.*, p. 748); the steeper the slope, the smaller this
ratio. As the system moves from Q to T, diverging from the steady-growth path
because K is growing faster than N, QT crosses the successive isoquants at points
of increasing slope, so that MPK/MPL is reduced. Whether it falls sufficiently to
offset $\Delta K/\Delta N$ depends on how much more steep the slope of Y_3 is at T than that
of Y_1 is at Q; and this depends on the shape of the isoquants.

growth-path than would otherwise have been reached. There is no doubt, however, that steady growth will eventually be restored, because s cannot rise above some maximum value less than $1\cdot0$, while no similar restriction applies to v. Where the shape of the production function is such[1] that MPK/MPL falls by *more* than is needed to keep the factor-shares constant, the value of s will decline, the adjustment-process will be shorter, and the new growth-path will be *less* capital-intensive than it would have been with s constant. It may be noted that where s_w is zero (e.g. because the wage-rate is at subsistence level), s equals s_π times the profit-share, and the condition $s/v = n$ becomes $s_\pi(P/Y)(Y/K) = n$, where P is total profit and Y/K replaces $1/v$. The left-hand side of this equation reduces to $s_\pi \pi$ (π being the rate of profit P/K), and in the extreme case in which $s_\pi = 1\cdot0$ (e.g. because all profits are earned and retained by companies) the steady-growth condition becomes $\pi = n$—that is, the growth-rate must equal the rate of profit.

The next variation from the basic model concerns n, the rate of growth of the labour-supply, which instead of being exogenously determined might be assumed to depend in some way on the growth of output. An obvious example is Malthus' celebrated population theory, whereby the labour-force expands or contracts in such a way as to maintain the real wage-rate at subsistence level: this would make n depend on the rate of growth of the capital stock, s/v, instead of the other way round. This may be seen by considering a case in which both capital and labour have hitherto been stationary (i.e. $n = 0$ and $s = 0$) with the wage-rate at subsistence level, but in which s now becomes positive so that the capital stock begins to grow. If n were to remain zero, the profit-rate would decline and the wage-rate would rise; but as soon as the latter begins to exceed subsistence level, population will grow, the labour-supply will increase, and the wage-rate and profit-rate will be maintained at their original values. If the production function is of the type shown in Fig. 30, this means that the labour-force will be induced to grow at the same rate as the capital stock (so that $n = s/v$) and that there will be only one possible growth-path, namely that which cuts the successive isoquants at points whose slope (i.e. MPL/MPK) is consistent with a subsistence-wage value of MPL: variations in s will then be offset, not by changes in v as described earlier, but by changes in n. There will, however, be a considerable time-lag involved in such adjustments: when a rise in

[1] That is to say, where the slope of Y_3 at T is very much greater than that of Y_1 at Q, because the isoquants have a very pronounced curvature. In this case, the isoquants may be said to have a low 'elasticity of substitution' (on which see R. G. D. Allen, *Mathematical Analysis for Economists* (1938), pp. 340–3).

real wages causes an increase in the birth-rate, as Malthus assumes, it will be some years before this brings about a corresponding rise in the growth of the labour-force; in the meantime, the system will have behaved as though n were exogeneous—v will have risen, only to fall again when n attains its steady-growth value.

Not only n but also r, the rate of technical progress, was assumed to be given exogenously in the original model: this assumption, too, might be dropped and the model further modified by relating r to one or more of the other variables in the system. For example, a rapid rate of capital-growth may be supposed to stimulate inventiveness by providing opportunities for testing new processes, so that r varies with the value of s/v; and r may itself influence the growth of capital by furnishing new investment-opportunities. If the amount of capital (as distinct from its growth-rate) is large relatively to output, technical knowledge will be greater and more widespread than if production were less capital-intensive, and this will of itself be favourable to the discovery and adoption of new techniques; in this case, r will be greater, the higher the value of v. If the neo-classical full-employment assumption is relaxed so as to allow the possibility of a discrepancy between *ex ante* investment and saving, technical progress may be stimulated by the existence of shortages of capital and labour—and also, of course, discouraged in the face of excess supplies of the factors. Yet another kind of complication arises if technical progress has the effect of altering returns to scale, for example causing them to increase where previously they had been constant. Finally, there is the possibility that the value of r varies over time in some way, because new inventions tend to be 'bunched'—one invention leading to another until all possible applications of a newly-discovered principle are for the time being exhausted.

Other modifications of the basic model include the employment of a third factor of production, such as a fixed quantity of land, which would affect returns to the other factors and make the distribution of income more complicated (and which would, incidentally, make it impossible to depict the production function in a two-dimensional diagram such as Fig. 30); the replacement of Fig. 30's smoothly-curving isoquants by 'kinky'[1] ones so arranged as to offer only a limited number of possible steady-growth paths (the so-called 'linear programming production function'); the dropping of the assumption of perfect competition, so that factors are no longer remunerated at

[1] Such isoquants have the same general shape as those of Fig. 30, but are made up of a number of straight lines coming together at obtuse-angled corners. For an illustrative diagram and discussion, see R. G. D. Allen, *Mathematical Economics* (2nd edition, 1959), p. 338.

rates equal to the value of their marginal physical products; and the introduction of money to serve as a means of exchange when the system has two or more sectors. These modifications, and those noted in the previous paragraphs, may be combined and re-combined in a variety of ways, and by ringing the changes on the choice of assumptions it is possible to construct a very large number of models, of varying degrees of complexity and realism according to the purposes for which they are required. The original neo-classical model, highly simplified though it is, provides a useful point of departure for such further developments.

(c) Growth or stagnation?

By assuming from the outset that full employment is continuously maintained and that factor-proportions are variable, neo-classical theory avoids sharing the pessimism of Harrod and Domar about the long-run prospects of advanced economies. It will be recalled that it was Harrod's assumption of 'fixed proportions' which made it highly unlikely that the natural and warranted growth-rates would coincide for long, so that the economy would suffer a continuous sequence of booms and slumps. Domar thought it improbable that his steady-growth condition $\Delta I/I = s\sigma$ would be continuously satisfied: 'it is difficult enough,' he wrote, 'to keep investment at some reasonably high level year after year, but the requirement that it always be rising is not likely to be met for any considerable length of time.'[1] His doubts recall Keynes's discouraging picture of an economy in which capital has become so abundant that there is no further incentive to invest, yet whose saving-propensity is still positive at full employment: the accumulation of capital will have caused it to 'suffer the fate of Midas', in the sense that severe and chronic unemployment will prevent it enjoying the standard of life which its wealth makes possible.[2] In the depressed conditions of the 1930s such pessimism seemed justified, and it was reinforced by the arguments of the 'secular stagnation thesis' associated with the name of A. H. Hansen.[3]

[1] *Essays in the Theory of Economic Growth*, p. 99. It is fair to add that the article from which these words are taken was actually written in 1947, while the collected *Essays* were not published until 1956. In his foreword to the 1956 volume, Domar modified his earlier pessimism, though without completely renouncing it.

[2] *General Theory*, pp. 217–19.

[3] See A. H. Hansen, 'Economic Progress and Declining Population Growth', *American Economic Review*, March 1939; reprinted in *Readings in Business Cycle Theory* (American Economic Association, 1944).

Hansen drew attention to the current decline in the rate of population-increase in the United States and Europe, and suggested that the rapid economic growth experienced during the century before 1914 had been 'unique in history' because of the unprecedented rise in population and the settling of new territories; he estimated that 'somewhere near one-half' of the investment expenditure of that period was attributable directly or indirectly to these two influences. By the 1930s, however, there were no important areas left for settlement, and population-growth seemed within sight of complete cessation; technical progress was slowing down and assuming an increasingly 'capital-saving' character, and was now of less importance than before as a stimulus to new investment; consequently, in the absence of massive deficit spending by governments, investment-demand would henceforth continue to be inadequate to absorb full-employment saving, and chronic unemployment was to be expected in the future.

As a forecast of what was to happen in the next few decades, the 'stagnation thesis' was a failure. Instead of declining, population-growth accelerated in the 1940s, output rose in most countries at unprecedented rates, and levels of employment were much higher than before the war—which by itself would have been enough to upset any prediction based on pre-war trends. But even had there been no war and no 'population explosion', it is not clear that stagnation must have ensued. The connection between population-growth and investment is not as straightforward as Hansen made it seem: in a country where incomes are very low, a rapid increase of numbers may merely turn its cities into overcrowded slums instead of stimulating new construction, whereas a rich country may still do a good deal of new building even when population is stationary, because its people can afford to improve their standards of accommodation. Similarly, the fact that no empty lands remain to be opened up does not necessarily imply a great reduction in the demand for investment in communications, public utilities, etc.; there are still plenty of 'underdeveloped' countries which, though already well settled, are poorly equipped with capital of this kind. A deceleration of technical progress, with a 'capital-saving' bias, would certainly depress investment-demand relatively to saving if it existed; but it is impossible to say whether this condition held in the thirties, and even if it did, there are reasons for supposing it to have been reversed since then. One of the striking features of the 'fifties and 'sixties has been the rapid growth of expenditure on research and development, both by governments and private enterprise—in Britain, for example, it rose from 1·7% of GNP in 1955 to 2·5% in 1960, and in the

United States from 1·4% to 2·8%;[1] this does not, of course, provide a measure of the rate of technical progress itself, but it certainly suggests a speeding-up rather than a slowing-down; and the examples of post-1940 technological advance which most readily come to mind, for example the application of atomic power and the automation of manufacturing processes, are of an eminently 'capital-using' rather than 'capital-saving' nature.

These considerations suggest that the pessimism of the stagnationists was unjustified, and that there is no inescapable reason why aggregate demand should in the long run fall further and further below the economy's capacity to produce. This is not to say that demand and capacity can always be relied on to grow at exactly the same pace: changes in the rate of technical progress and population-increase, as well as autonomous shifts in the propensity to save, may always upset the balance; but there is no presumption that advanced economies must, in the long run, either suffer increasing unemployment or else run larger and larger budget deficits in the effort to keep employment full. It is true that in the post-1940 period there has been, in most countries, a marked increase in government spending both in absolute terms and as a proportion of GNP, but this has been accompanied by corresponding increases in taxation; there has been no need to use it as a device for offsetting demand-deficiency in the private sector. The growth of public expenditure has, in fact, been an autonomous development, arising not only from the scale of armaments maintained since 1945 but also from the rise in demand for many publicly-provided services, such as the construction of motorways to accommodate the growing car population, and the expansion of educational facilities to train the increasing number of scientists and technologists required in industry. Its upward trend is another reason for supposing that the long-term growth of capacity is likely to be matched by a similar growth of demand.

(d) Growth policy and the management of the economy

If continuing expansion is not to be feared for stagnationist reasons, it might seem that the government ought positively to encourage it; the greater the annual increase in output, the better the living standards the community will be able to enjoy, and the more easily can social tensions be alleviated in so far as they arise from economic causes. To raise the growth-rate, the tax system can

[1] United Nations, *Economic Survey of Europe in 1961, Part 2; Some Factors in Economic Growth During the 1950's* (1964), Chap. V, p. 5.

be used to stimulate technical progress, for example by the favourable treatment of research expenditures and by depreciation allowances which encourage the early replacement of machinery; expenditure on education can improve labour skills and diffuse new technology; fiscal and monetary policies can be applied in such a way as to favour investment rather than consumption, and to redistribute income towards groups with high propensities to save. The higher the growth-rate aimed at, however, the stronger the measures which must be used to achieve it, and the greater the likelihood that the government's growth policy will be incompatible with its other objectives.

Suppose, for example, that it is possible to stimulate investment sufficiently to make output rise 5% a year, but that other elements of demand cannot be reduced by an amount equal to the increase in investment; aggregate demand will then exceed full-employment output, with the result that prices rise at (say) 6% per annum. To prevent prices rising at all, it is assumed that investment would have to be kept down to a level which is sufficient to give only a 1% annual increase in output. In this case, then, the government can aim at rapid growth, or at price-stability, but not both. It could, perhaps, try for an intermediate outcome, such as a 3% growth of output combined with a 2% increase in prices, if the latter is the highest rate thought to be tolerable; as long as it does not allow output to grow at the maximum 5% rate, it will be 'trading off' some potential growth against a lower rate of price-increase. The trade-off could, of course, be more complicated than this; for instance, the fact that money-wage increases are no longer offset to the same extent by rising productivity (as described on p. 313 above) when the growth-rate is reduced, may mean that cost-inflation takes over when demand-inflation is eliminated—so that the growth-rate would have to be neither more nor less than (say) $2\frac{1}{2}$% to minimize the rate at which prices are rising.

Similar trade-offs may be called for between growth and other policy objectives. As output expands, it will induce a greater demand for imports, thereby weakening the balance of payments; on the other hand, rising productivity will be cutting costs and permitting reductions in export prices, which (given a large enough demand-elasticity) will cause overseas earnings to rise; this, plus the possibility that advancing technology may be developing entirely new products for sale abroad, will improve the balance of payments and offset the effect of rising imports. But if the expansion of imports tends to pull ahead of the rise in exports whenever output-growth exceeds (say) 3%, this will impose a further constraint on government policy. If the 5% growth-rate is nevertheless chosen, part of it will have to be 'bought' with a balance-of-payments deficit.

It might seem that no trade-off problem can arise between rapid growth and full employment as aims of policy: the higher the level of employment, the higher the level of output and the greater the margin of resources which should be available for growth-promoting investment. Yet even here the possibility of conflict cannot be ruled out. If high levels of employment are accompanied by redistribution effects in favour of groups with low saving propensities (for example, because trades unions are then very powerful and use their strength to raise money-wages faster than prices), consumption may increase so much in proportion to income that less is left over for investment than would have been available had employment been lower. Again, the faster the growth-rate, the larger may be the proportion of frictional unemployment as new technologies are rapidly introduced and demand-patterns change; if, for social reasons, the community prefers to keep employment as high as possible, it may be prepared to accept a lower growth-rate in order to do so.

Because of the difficulty of reconciling growth policy with its other objectives, the government might decide to abandon it altogether and to concentrate its attention wholly on the short-run aims of avoiding inflation, unemployment and balance-of-payments deficits; the growth-rate would then be determined entirely by private decisions regarding saving and investment, and by such technical progress as will be made independently of government encouragement. There is a good deal to be said for such a course. Full employment, price stability and external balance are relatively simple objectives, and there is not much difficulty in judging the degree of success or failure in attaining them; nor is there any doubt of the unpleasant consequences which ensue from failure, so that they are clearly worthwhile policy aims. Growth is a different matter: there is no obvious way in which the government can be sure that a growth-rate of (say) 5% is the 'correct' objective rather than 4% or 6%, while a failure to achieve the 5% target could hardly be regarded as disastrous if the community already enjoys an ample amount of consumption per head. National pride will no doubt suffer if other countries are seen to be progressing faster, but no positive hardship will arise as long as living standards do not actually decline below their existing level. It is only in countries whose standards are intolerably low that faster growth must be taken as the overriding policy objective; elsewhere, it can be argued that whatever growth would take place without government intervention will be in accordance with the community's preferences as between current consumption and provision for the future, and that the government has no business to force the economy to behave differently.

Even so, it is possible to make out a case for a positive growth policy. It has already been seen that in the absence of technical progress, income per head will rise only if the stock of capital is increasing faster than the labour force is growing, i.e. if $s/v > n$; however, the very fact that capital per worker will then be rising means that there will be diminishing returns to capital, so that the productivity of capital (Y/K) will gradually fall—that is, the value of the capital-output ratio v (or K/Y) will slowly increase; as it does so, the value of s/v will decline until the economy at last converges on a 'steady growth' path along which $s/v = n$, and income per head will then be stabilized at the level reached at the end of the convergence process. If it is to rise further, s must be increased so that s/v once more exceeds n; when the consequent increase in v has again restored s/v to equality with n, yet another rise in s will be needed to bring about a further increase in income per head. If private preferences are such as to give a stationary value of s, income per head cannot in the long run go above the level which obtains along the growth-path determined by that value of s. By taking action to increase s, therefore, the government can ensure that income per head goes on growing.

Provided that short-run stabilization policies succeed in maintaining a non-inflationary full-employment equilibrium throughout (so that full-employment saving is always exactly matched by investment-demand), there is no limit to the level of income per head which can be reached. But income per head is not, after all, the best measure of the community's economic welfare: it is much more important to know how much of it remains available for consumption after the amount of current saving has been deducted. If, in order to raise income per head from 100 to 110, it is necessary to increase the proportion saved from 34% to 40%, there can be no increase in consumption per head, which will remain unchanged at 66; the rise in s will have served no good purpose unless the community for some reason derives satisfaction from the mere possession of a larger capital stock as well as from the consumable goods and services it produces. If this possibility is ruled out, it follows that income per head should not be raised beyond the point where consumption per head is a maximum.

Along any given steady-growth path, consumption per head (c) will be equal to the amount of capital per head (k) times its average productivity (σ), minus the output which must be set aside to equip each new entrant to the labour force with the necessary capital equipment (nk): that is

$$c = \sigma k - nk = k(\sigma - n)$$

where σk is income per head and nk is the saving needed to maintain the existing capital/labour ratio.[1] As long as steady growth is maintained, the capital stock and the labour force will be growing at the same rate, so that k will be constant over time; but the absolute value of k will be larger, the steeper[2] the growth path the economy is following, i.e. the more capital-intensive the method of production. By causing the value of s to increase, the government will be pushing the economy on to successively steeper growth-paths, along each of which the value of k will be greater than it was on the last; the equation shows that increases in k will in themselves have the effect of raising c. But as capital per head grows, diminishing returns will cause the average product of capital (σ) to fall, so that equal successive increases in k will give smaller and smaller increases in c; eventually, a point will be reached at which the influence of the decline in σ begins to outweigh that of the rise in k, so that c will cease to grow and then, given further increases in k, will actually diminish. When the economy is moving along the growth-path on which c is at its maximum value (in other words, when the gap between σk and nk is greatest), it will be following what E. S. Phelps has called 'the Golden Rule of Accumulation.'[3] If private preferences do not happen to give a value of s which is of exactly the right size to put the economy on the 'golden rule' path (and there is no reason to suppose that they will, except by accident), maximum consumption will be reached only if the government takes appropriate action to adjust s to the required level.[4]

---

[1] The equation can be derived from the 'steady growth condition', $s/v = n$, by putting $1 - c$ in place of s, multiplying both sides by v, and rearranging to give $c = 1 - nv$; replacing v by K/Y and multiplying through by Y gives cY (or C) $= Y - nK$. Putting σK in place of Y, and dividing through by the number of workers, N, gives $C/N = \sigma K/N - nK/N$, or $c = \sigma k - nk$ where $c = C/N$ and $k = K/N$ as in the text.

[2] 'Steeper', that is in terms of the slope it would have in Fig. 30 above: see p. 351.

[3] Edmund S. Phelps, 'The Golden Rule of Accumulation: A Fable for Growthmen', *American Economic Review*, Sept. 1961; see also his *Golden Rules of Economic Growth* (1966).

[4] The criterion of 'golden rule' growth is that $\Delta c/\Delta k = 0$, which means that it is no longer possible to increase consumption per head by moving to a steeper growth-path through raising the amount of capital per head. In general, $\Delta c = \Delta k(\mu - n)$, where μ is the marginal productivity of capital; the condition that $\Delta c/\Delta k$ is zero thus implies that $\mu = n$. If factors of production are remunerated with their marginal products, total profit is μK; on any steady-growth

The preceding argument is, of course, subject to many qualifications. Technical progress can easily be fitted in if it is 'Harrod-neutral' (i.e. such that it leaves all capital-output ratios unchanged),[1] since it will then be equivalent to an increase in the rate of growth of the labour force: instead of n (the rate at which labour-supply grows in physical terms) it will now be $n+\tau$, where τ is the rate of increase in labour efficiency due to technical progress, and the problem will be to maximize $\sigma k - k(n+\tau)$ instead of $\sigma k - nk$. Any other kind of technical progress, however, will reduce, prevent or even reverse the decline in σ which would otherwise have resulted from diminishing returns to capital, with the result that $k(\sigma - n)$, and therefore c, may have no maximum value: *every* increase in income per head will then cause consumption per head to increase. Further complications (which will not be explored here) arise if factor-proportions are assumed to be fixed, instead of variable as shown in Fig. 30; if the assumption of constant returns to scale is dropped; if it is no longer supposed that only one commodity is being produced, so that the economy now has two or more sectors; if an additional factor of production is introduced—and so on. The 'golden rule' path then becomes much harder to discern, even if it can still be supposed to exist; none the less, the mere suggestion that there may be such a path is a useful corrective to the uncritical presumption that growth performance is always to be judged by the increase of income rather than consumption per head, and that, however large the capital stock has already become, a further increase can do nothing but good.

However, even though the Golden Rule may indicate the ultimate objective of growth policy, it offers no guidance as to the best way of getting there. It might seem that all the government has to do is to cause the community to save that proportion of income, s^*, which is consistent with 'golden rule' growth; as income and capital per head gradually increase, the economy will converge on the steady-growth path along which consumption per head is maximized. But a community whose income per head is low, and which at present saves a much smaller proportion of it than s^*, would suffer hardship if the amount of consumption per head were suddenly and severely reduced through the immediate raising of s to the s^* level. It has already been seen (on p. 352 above) that the convergence process is likely to be slow, perhaps spanning several generations; the assurance

path, saving is nK, i.e. just enough to equip new workers with the existing amount of capital per head; and since $\mu K = nK$ when $\Delta c/\Delta k = 0$, it can be said that 'golden rule' growth will be characterized by the equality of saving with total profit.

[1] See footnote 1, p. 354 above.

that their grandchildren's consumption will be high may be small comfort to the present generation if they must pass their lives on short commons to make it possible. If the government therefore raises s only a little at first, with the intention of gradually increasing it when the subsequent growth of income per head permits it to do so without causing hardship, it will be reducing the benefits accruing to the next few generations, and diminishing the burden on the present one, as compared with those which would have resulted from s^*; the problem is to choose the value of s which brings about the best possible distribution of burdens and benefits between the generations—that is, one which could not be changed without causing those whose consumption per head was reduced to lose more satisfaction than would be gained by those whose consumption was increased. But this raises enormous difficulties, even in theory: obviously, there is no way of knowing in advance how much satisfaction future generations will derive from increased consumption, even if it is thought to be meaningful to compare degrees of satisfaction enjoyed by different generations; nor is it at all clear how many generations ought to be brought into the reckoning, nor whether the more distant ones' expected gains should be discounted according to their remoteness in time. Even in a highly simplified theoretical model, therefore, it is impossible to fix on a particular value of s as being optimal without making some drastic assumptions, and it is clearly out of the question in the complex economy of real life. All that can be claimed is that if the choice of s is left entirely to the private saving decisions of the present generation, they will naturally tilt the distribution of burdens and benefits in their own favour by undervaluing their successors' expected gains relatively to their own loss of satisfaction through consumption forgone; the government, as the guardian of future generations' interests, should therefore intervene to redress the balance by making them save more than they would otherwise have chosen to do. But even this general presumption is doubtful, since it may turn out that technical progress raises future generations' gains to an extent unforeseen by the present one, so that it can more than offset the latter's undervaluation of them—in which case, the present generation will have imposed a saving burden on itself which, instead of being too light, will prove to have been too heavy.

It follows that measures to increase s, and thereby raise the growth-rate, can be firmly recommended only when the economy seems to settling down on a steady-growth path along which consumption is not maximized. In any other situation, it is conceivable that an over-enthusiastic growth policy might actually diminish economic welfare rather than increase it. It must be remembered, too, that the expansion of the economy can involve certain social costs, such as the destruction of natural amenities through urban sprawl and river pollution, which are not reflected in statistical indicators of growth but which are none the less real; apparent advances in personal consumption per head might be offset to a considerable extent by deterioration in the consumers' environment. In the light of current emphasis on the importance of growth as a policy objective, it is important to bear in mind that it could be too fast as well as too slow.

APPENDIX: KEYNES AND THE CLASSICS

The ideas set forth in this book have been offered to the reader on their own merits, not as the views of a particular school of thought. Twenty-five years ago, they would inevitably have been labelled 'Keynesian', not only because the main lines of analysis derive from Keynes' work, but also because his theories continued to be controversial for some time after *The General Theory of Employment, Interest and Money* appeared in 1936. In that book, he vigorously attacked the teachings of what he called 'the classical school' —the line of economists beginning with Ricardo and descending through J. S. Mill to Marshall and Pigou; he drew the sharpest possible distinction between his own theories and those of the 'classics', and denounced the doctrines of the latter as misleading and disastrous. There ensued a long and often bitter controversy, in which questions of definition and terminology were sometimes debated as hotly as issues of substance, till at length the 'Keynesian Revolution' had run its course and the Keynesian teaching, developed and refined in various ways, was absorbed into the canon of accepted theory. The present-day student may feel that this should now be regarded as a past episode in the history of economic thought, and that the battles of an earlier generation need not be re-fought within the covers of a modern textbook. He will find, however, that references to 'the classics' and 'classical theory' occur quite frequently in the literature of the subject, and the object of this Appendix is to clarify the usage of the terms 'Keynesian' and 'classical' by means of a brief comparison of the theoretical systems to which they refer.

The economists characterized by Keynes as 'the classics' were not, as the label might suggest, the exponents of a single, monolithic system of thought, on every detail of which they were in unanimous accord. Nevertheless, they did agree in emphasizing the importance of the 'theory of value', the purpose of which is to explain the relative prices of commodities in terms of one another; the tradition in which Keynes was brought up visualized the economy as a set of markets, in which the forces of supply and demand together determined output and relative prices. The natural approach to the problem of unemployment, therefore, was to examine the market for labour and the determinants of supply and demand therein. An excess of supply over demand for any commodity implied that its current price was higher than the competitive equilibrium price; if, in the labour market, more people were seeking work than could be employed at the existing wage-rate, it could be presumed that current wages were too high, and that the situation would of itself create pressures to bring them down; if this failed to happen, it was to be attributed to the existence of minimum-wage laws, to the bargaining-power of workers' organizations, or to some other restraint on the forces of competition. The remedy for chronic unemployment, then, was to make wages 'flexible' by removing such restraints. Once competition was allowed to work, the market would move toward equilibrium and full employment would be achieved.

Whatever the input of labour at full employment, it would co-operate with the other factors of production to produce given quantities of goods and services. For the economy to be in *general* equilibrium, demand and supply had to balance in each of the markets to which these goods and

371

services were being furnished; but as long as there were no impediments to the free movement of prices, it could be assumed that each commodity's price would rise or fall sufficiently to bring about such a balance. For any economy in which prices and wages were flexible, it was thought that there must exist some pattern of relative prices (including wages, as the price of labour) which would permit equilibrium to be attained in all markets (including the labour market). This seemed so obvious to the 'classics' that they could find little use for a separate concept of aggregate demand, since it was logically identical with aggregate supply. Under the principle known as *Say's Law*,[1] the very act of production implies an equivalent demand for goods and services, since the aim of each producer must be either to satisfy his own wants directly, or to exchange his output for other commodities. It is true that producers offer their wares in exchange for money in the first instance, but they want the money not as an end in itself but for the sake of what it will buy: money, indeed, is merely a device for avoiding the awkwardness of barter, a 'veil' which conceals the fact that 'what constitutes the means of payment for commodities is simply commodities'.[2] The supply of any particular commodity, then, is *ipso facto* a demand for others, and it follows that the mass of goods and services produced in the whole economy is *both* aggregate supply *and* aggregate demand at the same time. It may happen, of course, that supply exceeds demand in the market for a particular commodity, but this would merely imply a corresponding excess of demand over supply in some other market or markets. It is logically impossible, under Say's Law, for the sum of demands in *all* markets to be greater or less than the sum of supplies, since they are merely two ways of describing the very same thing.[3]

The fact that producers save part of their money receipts, instead of spending them all on commodities, was not admitted as an objection to this principle. Saving (argued the 'classics') requires abstention from immediate personal consumption, but not the accumulation of idle cash: rational individuals, seeking remunerative employment for their savings, either spend them on capital goods for use in enterprises of their own, or lend them at interest to others who, in their turn, use them to buy the means of production. The higher the interest-rate, the more they will save, and the equilibrium rate is that which exactly balances the amount of saving against the amount which entrepreneurs wish to borrow for investment purposes. Since the borrowed funds reappear on the demand side of the market for capital goods, the identity of aggregate demand and supply is maintained— all that has happened is that savers have purchased commodities indirectly instead of directly. Thus, saving does not diminish aggregate demand, but merely determines the proportions in which the latter is allocated between consumption and investment.

[1] Propounded by Jean-Baptiste Say in his *Traité d'Economie Politique* (1803), and adopted by Ricardo, John Stuart Mill and others. There has been much disagreement as to the interpretation of the Law: for quotations, references and further discussion see D. Patinkin, *Money, Interest and Prices* (2nd edition, 1965), Note L, pp. 645–50; and J. A. Schumpeter, *History of Economic Analysis* (1954), pp. 615–25.

[2] J. S. Mill, *Principles of Political Economy*, Bk III, Chap. XIV, sec. 2.

[3] It should be noted that Say's Law is not just another way of stating the accounting identity by which National Product ≡ National Expenditure, though it has sometimes been so interpreted.

So far, it has not been necessary to mention the quantity of money. This reflects the fact that it is not essential to the main part of the classical 'system', in which all prices are *relative*, in the sense of being ratios in which goods and services exchange for one another. Such relationships could hold good at any level of *absolute* money prices: to say that a banana is worth twice as much as an orange makes the same sense whether their money prices are respectively 2p and 1p, or 50p and 25p, or £300 and £150. So far, then, money values are indeterminate, and something else is needed to explain them. Here the 'classics' invoked the Quantity Theory of Money. They assumed that payments-habits are not liable to change in the short run, and that transactions will be at the full-employment level if the labour market is in equilibrium; given constant values of V and T in the celebrated equation $MV = PT$, the level of money prices P depends entirely on the quantity of money M. On the other hand, M and P have no influence on any of the 'real' variables in the system, except through the 'Pigou effect' whereby price-level changes cause the owners of money-assets to feel richer or poorer and consequently to alter their saving behaviour.[1] If the Pigou effect is neglected, on the ground that it was a very late addition to the classical edifice, it can be said that a complete dichotomy existed between the real and the monetary sides of classical economics.

The essence of the classical doctrine, then, was that the economy would of itself move towards a full-employment equilibrium if the forces of competition were allowed to work without restraint; that any departure from that equilibrium would necessarily set up forces pushing the system back to it; and that this held good whether the disposition to save was great or small, and whatever the quantity of money might be. Every one of these propositions was denied by Keynes. He argued that full employment was only one of the possible situations in which the economy might find itself, and that the classics had merely treated a special case which was subsumed in his own *general* theory of output and employment.

Keynes' two great innovations were the consumption function and the liquidity-preference schedule. The first of these made saving depend on income instead of the interest-rate, so that the amount of saving done at the full-employment level of income might exceed planned investment even when interest was fairly low. A further reduction in interest might raise investment to equality with full-employment saving, if the demand for investment happened to be sufficiently elastic with respect to the interest-rate; but the liquidity-preference theory showed that this might require very large increases in the supply of money, and that the rate of interest could not, in any case, fall below a minimum level given by the 'liquidity-trap' (as shown in Fig. 20, p. 258 above). If, when this minimum interest-rate had been reached, the amount of investment-demand was still insufficient to absorb the whole amount of full-employment saving,[2] the level of income would be forced down until saving was reduced to equality with investment. At this point, aggregate demand would be in equilibrium with current output, but there would be an excess of supply over demand in the labour market: if money-wages were flexible, they would fall and bring

---

[1] See above, pp. 112–13.

[2] This extreme situation has been called (cf. p. 264 above) 'the Keynesian case', as opposed to the 'classical case' in which liquidity-preference is inelastic with respect to the interest-rate. See F. Modigliani, 'Liquidity Preference and the Theory of Interest and Money', *Econometrica*, 1944.

down the price-level with them, but this would not restore full employment (in the sense of an equilibrium of demand and supply in the labour market) unless it were to bring about an appropriate rise in investment-demand and/or the propensity to consume; though this might conceivably occur, there was no reason to suppose that it would *necessarily* do so, and the consequence could well be a bottomless deflation without any diminution of the amount of unemployment.[1] However, since money-wages are not, as a matter of observed fact, very 'flexible downwards', their rigidity would prevent such an outcome, and the economy would continue (for the time being, at any rate) in a situation of less than full employment.[2]

By making the level of output and employment depend on aggregate demand, Keynes put Say's Law into reverse: instead of supply creating its own demand, it was now demand which called forth an equivalent supply—which might not be such as to require the employment of the whole labour force in its production. The focus of analytical interest was thus shifted to the determinants of consumption and investment, and particularly to the connections between them and the level of income; the originality of Keynes' approach lay in combining all these elements, both real and monetary, into a single system of interlocking relationships which together determined employment and output. Even those who disagreed with his conclusions were constrained to adopt his methods and to express the classical tradition in terms of systematic models which they would not otherwise have been led to construct;[3] when these were compared with the Keynesian model, it became clear that the choice between them was essentially a matter of empirical assumptions. If the speculative demand for money is not, after all, very important quantitatively, nor very elastic with respect to interest rates; if wages are not, in fact, very 'inflexible downwards'; if saving *does* respond more to changes in interest-rates than in income; and if the economy adjusts quickly to changes in the various parameters—then the classical presumption of a strong tendency to full-employment equilibrium is justified. If, on the other hand, one or more of these assumptions cannot be made, the Keynesian apparatus is needed to show what levels of employment and output will actually be reached in the short run, and the Keynesian policy prescriptions (for example, budget deficits and low interest-rates when aggregate demand is too low to give full employment) become appropriate.

The original 'Keynesian model' of the *General Theory* was unsatisfactory in a number of ways.[4] It was completely static, in the sense of being wholly concerned with equilibrium conditions during the short period in which changes in technology and in the capital stock could be ignored; it con-

[1] See the *General Theory*, pp. 262–9.

[2] Such a situation is often described as 'under-employment equilibrium': but since excess supply persists in the labour market, it is clear that no *general* equilibrium exists, and the term is used in a loose sense to mean that no forces are set up to dislodge the system from the position it has reached.

[3] They were, as Professor Haberler put it, 'forced to think through things which they used to leave in an ambiguous twilight, and to draw from accepted premises conclusions of which they were unaware or which they left discreetly unexpressed' ('The General Theory after Ten Years', in *The New Economics*, ed. S. E. Harris, 1947).

[4] On this, see H. G. Johnson, 'The General Theory after Twenty-five years', *American Economic Review*, May 1961.

tained no lagged relationships, thus excluding both the dynamic multiplier and the accelerator, and it was drawn in terms which made it much more adaptable to the analysis of demand-deficiency situations than those of excess demand and inflation. Keynes did not distinguish clearly enough between *ex post* and *ex ante* magnitudes (so that a sharp controversy raged for some years on the exact meaning of saving and investment), and he offered no empirical evidence for some crucial assumptions, for example those concerning the characteristic shapes of the consumption and liquidity-preference functions. But he did, nevertheless, set out his system in terms of relationships which were capable of being statistically tested, thereby stimulating empirical investigation and giving a great impetus to the growth of econometrics; his emphasis on the importance of expectations and uncertainty about the future gave a strong impulse to the development of dynamic analysis; and his clear distinction between macro- and microanalysis[1] caused many fallacies to be discarded. By providing a base from which later economists were able to go forward—even though their work often caused his own detailed conclusions to be changed—Keynes opened a new and vital chapter in the history of economics.

[1] See the *General Theory*, p. 293.

INDEX